T0312245

Systemic Risk, Crises, and Macroprudential Regulation

Systemic Risk, Crises, and Macroprudential Regulation

Xavier Freixas, Luc Laeven, and José-Luis Peydró

The MIT Press
Cambridge, Massachusetts
London, England

This book was set in Palatino LT Std 10 on 12 pt by Toppan Best-set Premedia Limited.

Library of Congress Cataloging-in-Publication
Freixas, Xavier.
Systemic risk, crises, and macroprudential regulation / Xavier Freixas, Luc Laeven, and José-Luis Peydró.
  pages cm
 Includes bibliographical references and index.
 ISBN 978-0-262-02869-1 (hardcover : alk. paper)
 ISBN 978-0-262-54901-1 (paperback) 1. Monetary policy. 2. Finance–
Government policy. 3. Economic policy.
4. Financial crises. 5. Risk. I. Laeven, Luc. II. Peydró, José-Luis.
III. Title.
 HG230.3.F744 2015
 339.5--dc23

                              2014034226

Contents

Foreword

Macroprudential is the latest buzzword in economics. But it means different things to different people. For some, macroprudential policy is about managing the economic cycle. For others, it is about controlling financial stability stemming from systemic financial institutions. For others, it is simply an empty term. These skeptics hold the view that macroprudential policy has no teeth because the political economy of booms is such that financial regulators will always find it hard to smooth them, as booms bring large benefits (in the form of wealth and employment) while they last. Some go even further and claim that macroprudential policy may bring new risks when misused. Unfortunately, there is much confusion about what constitutes macroprudential policy and little agreement about how to operationalize it, in part because its objective is not clearly defined and in part because there is scarce historical experience about the use of macroprudential tools to gauge their effectiveness and calibration. Moreover the measurement and the theory of financial fragility and systemic risk of the financial system is still in its infancy, and there is little agreement on the scope of financial regulation and the institutional framework for macroprudential policy. What are the strengths and limitations of the current prudential policy framework and how should it change? What are the differences between micro- and macroprudential policy? What is the boundary of financial regulation? Should it cover all institutions that engage in the provision of financial services? What are the limitations of current theories of financial fragility and systemic risk? And how can systemic risk be measured and monitored in real time? What lessons can be drawn from the history of the financial crises, including the most recent one, for the management of credit and asset price bubbles and bursts? How should macroprudential policy interact with macroeconomic policy? Is there any role for monetary policy for combatting systemic risk? Does macroprudential regulation always reduce excessive risk-taking or can it also encourage it?

The purpose of this book is to offer a framework to operationalize macroprudential policy. We will define systemic risk and macroprudential policy, discuss its differences with microprudential policy and its interactions with macroeconomic policies (notably monetary policy), and describe the macroprudential toolkit and experiences around the world with a view to operationalize macroprudential policy to fit to country circumstances (whether emerging economies or advanced economies). We conclude with a list of challenges in the implementation of macroprudential policy and discuss its limitations.

To our knowledge, this is the first and only book on this topic. By design, some topics are covered in more detail than others. This is in large part because our knowledge on these issues is still limited, as this is a new field. In particular, there is disagreement about the optimal policy mix and the measurement of systemic risk. And there is large uncertainty about the unintended consequences of macroprudential policy on systemic risk and the constraints imposed by polical economy forces. But there is much that we can offer, based on a growing body of academic and policy-oriented literature, the history of financial crises, and the limited historical experience with the use of macroprudential policy. Moreover much has happened since the global financial crisis of 2008 to shape a new regulatory framework for deposit-taking financial institutions with a view to build a system of regulations that take a more macro perspective of the financial system with a focus on managing systemic risk rather than the risk of individual financial institutions, and macroprudential authorities have been established in a number of countries with responsibilities in the area of macroprudential policy.

This book has grown out of our desire to offer clarity in an area of much confusion, drawing on our combined knowledge in this area based on academic research, policy and advisory work. Our focus is on the United States and Europe where much of the debate about macroprudential policy has centered, but we will also cover topics relevant to other parts of the world, including the role of macroprudential policy in managing foreign capital flows and the need for global coordination of macroprudential and monetary policies.

But knowledge and sweat and tears from hard work alone cannot create a book. It requires close cooperation and team work, and the joy of working together, which in our case has translated into new friendships. Being physically located in different parts of the world did not help, but Skype and occasional trips offered solutions. A book like this one always takes more time than originally envisaged. This book would not have been possible without the continued support and professional editorial work of Jane Macdonald and Emily Taber at the MIT Press. The diligent editing work by Dana Andrus at the MIT Press and the editorial assistance from Maria Jovanovic and Patricia Loo at the IMF are also gratefully acknowledged.

We would also like to thank Olivier Blanchard, Christian Brownlees, Charles Calomiris, Stijn Claessens, Charles Goodhart, Enrico Perotti, Raghu Rajan, and Fran R. Tous for commenting on earlier drafts of the book. The sometimes long debates with our colleagues and friends have markedly improved the quality of this book. Part of this book has been taught at the Barcelona GSE professional course on Systemic Risk and Prudential Policy that Xavier and José-Luis organized and we thank all the participants (mainly from central banks and supervisory agencies) for all their comments and suggestions. Above all our thanks go to our families who gave us the precious time to work on this book. José-Luis especial thanks go to his wife, Lambra Saínz Vidal, and his parents.

The book was written while Luc Laeven was a staff member of the IMF. This book represents our own views, not those of the IMF or IMF Board.

Barcelona and Washington, DC, November 2014

Glossary

ABCP	Asset-backed commercial paper
ABS	Asset-backed security
AMC	Asset management company
AQR	Asset quality review
BIS	Bank for International Settlements
BoE	Bank of England
BoJ	Bank of Japan
BLS	Bank Lending Survey
CCP	Central counterparty clearinghouse
CD	Certificate of deposit
CDO	Collateralized debt obligation
CDS	Credit default swap
CEO	Chief executive officer
CET1	Common equity tier 1
CFO	Chief financial officer
CGFS	Committee on the Global Financial System
CLS	Continuous linked settlement
CoCo	Contingent convertible capital instrument
CPSS	Committee on Payments and Settlement Systems
CRA	Credit-rating agency
CVA	Credit valuation adjustments
DSGE	Dynamic stochastic general equilibrium
DvP	Delivery versus payment
DTI	Debt to income

EBA	European Banking Authority
EC	European Commission
ECB	European Central Bank
ESRB	European Systemic Risk Board
ESM	European Stability Mechanism
EU	European Union
FDI	Foreign direct investment
FDIC	Federal Deposit Insurance Corporation
FDICIA	Federal Deposit Insurance Corporation Improvement Act
FLS	Funding for Lending Scheme
FPC	Financial Policy Committee
FSA	Financial Services Authority
FSB	Financial Stability Board
FSOC	Financial Stability Oversight Council
GDP	Gross domestic product
GIIPS	Greece, Ireland, Italy, Portugal, and Spain
G-SIFI	Global systemically important financial institution
IMF	International Monetary Fund
IOSCO	International Organization of Securities Commissions
LCR	Liquid coverage ratio
LoLR	Lender of last resort
LTRO	Long-term refinancing operation
LTV	Loan to value
MBS	Mortgage-backed security
MM	Modigliani–Miller
MMMF	Money market mutual fund
NPL	Nonperforming loan
NSFR	Net stable funding ratio
OECD	Organisation for Economic Co-operation and Development
OFR	Office for Financial Research
OLA	Orderly Liquidation Authority
OMT	Outright monetary transactions
OTC	Over the counter

PD   Probability of default

PvP   Payment versus payment

RBS   Royal Bank of Scotland

RMBS   Residential mortgage-backed security

RTGS   Real time gross settlement

SIFI   Systemically important financial institution

SLOS   Senior Loan Officer Survey

SME   Small- and medium-size enterprise

SOX   Sarbanes–Oxley Act

SPV   Special purpose vehicle

SRM   Single resolution mechanism

SSM   Single supervisory mechanism

TARP   Troubled Asset Relief Program

TBTF   Too big to fail

TIPS   Treasury inflation-protected securities

UBS   Union Bank Switzerland

VaR   Value at risk

VAR   Vector autoregressive

VIX   Chicago Board Options Exchange Volatility Index

1   Introduction

The global financial crisis that started in 2007 has reinvigorated a debate on how to regulate banks and other financial institutions to ensure financial stability. Central to this debate has been the recognition that financial regulation has been largely microfocused on the risk of individual financial institutions rather than the financial system as a whole. Capital adequacy levels were set on the implicit assumption that, by creating buffers to absorb unexpected shocks at individual banks, the system as a whole was safer. Yet, by responding to capital regulations with only their own interest in mind, banks can potentially behave in ways that collectively undermine the system as a whole.[1] For example, banks hit by a negative shock may prefer to delever when faced with binding capital constraints, causing a credit crunch and a generalized drop in asset prices, thereby exacerbating the initial negative shock. Negative spillovers can be substantial, as financial institutions have incentives to take correlated exposures in credit and asset price bubbles. To control such systemic risk that may jeopardize financial stability with strong negative real effects for the economy, regulation and supervision would need to become more macroprudential, concerning itself with the stability of the financial system as a whole and its relation with the economy at large.

Calls for a more macroprudential approach to bank regulation can be traced back to the late 1970s on the back of growing concerns associated with the rapid pace of bank lending to developing countries. However, despite numerous financial crises since the 1970s and throughout history, the term macroprudential was little used prior to the recent global financial crisis and its meaning remained somewhat obscure.[2] A Google search of the term "macroprudential" only produces 639 hits prior to 2000, while it generates over 500,000 hits today. Similarly the term "systemic risk" has been relatively new—with only four thousand Google hits prior to 2000 and half a million today—and its meaning has been ambiguous: for example, is systemic risk just the risk of financial instability or does it also reflect risks to the real economy?

The reason for writing this book is straightforward. In our daily interactions with policy makers, central bankers, regulators, and academics, we have noticed a generalized confusion of the meaning of systemic risk and macroprudential regulation. Both terms are frequently used as buzzwords in the realm of policy-making. Systemic risk is often equated to the risk of the day, ranging successively from excessive lending to developing countries in the late 1970s, to concerns over financial innovations in the 1980s, to short-term dollar borrowing by East Asian corporations with revenues in local currency in the 1990s, to the procyclicality of the financial system and the implications of the failure of systemically important institutions in the first decade of the twenty-first century, or to problems in global capital flows in emerging economies in the 2010s. And macroprudential policy is often viewed interchangeably as a particular perspective of existing prudential policy or a new policy area in its own right. In part, this confusion stems from the lack of a framework to analyze the optimal design of prudential policy, but it is also due to differences in opinion and ideology about the need to establish a separate macroprudential framework and the possible complications such a framework could cause for the setting of monetary policy. The purpose of this book is to offer a working definition of systemic risk in the financial system, to explain its causes, consequences, and measurement, and to present an operational framework to guide macroprudential analysis and regulatory policy. We base this analysis on a growing body of academic and policy-oriented literature, including on the lessons from the history of financial crises and on the existing experiences of macroprudential policies around the world.

Indeed policy makers are struggling with numerous questions about the institutional design of monitoring systemic risk and about the design and implementation of macroprudential policy and its interactions with other policies. In particular, there are concerns about conflicts between macroprudential policy and monetary policy, and about the institutional arrangements for macroprudential policy-making. What should be the focus of prudential regulation? Should the macroprudential approach be completely separated from microprudential regulation? Should micro and macroprudential regulation be enforced by the same supervisor or under a different construct? What are the benefits and the limits of both macroprudential and microprudential policy? How should one measure systemic risk in practice? What are the incentives for banks and other intermediaries to take excessive risks that create a buildup of financial imbalances? What are the main negative spillovers within the financial system, and from the financial to the real sector? Do we need structural reforms in banking? What can we learn from previous financial crises for the setting of macroprudential and regulatory policy? How should one operationalize and institutionalize macroprudential policy? Should other public policies such as monetary and competition policy pay attention to systemic risk? What are the limitations of macroprudential policy? This book will answer these and related questions.

While the focus of the book is on macroprudential policy, it is important to point out from the start that the lack of a macroprudential framework to tame systemic risk is not seen as the only "culprit" to the recent global financial crisis. Regulatory failures and political economy constraints in dealing with the buildup of financial imbalances are by many seen as equally if not more important. A discussion of macroprudential policy therefore cannot occur without consideration of political and regulatory motives especially around the times of financial crises. The book therefore discusses also the politics of financial booms and crises and the challenges in building an effective financial regulatory apparatus.

The answer to what the regulatory response to the recent financial crisis should be very much depends on one's view of the origins of the crisis. On the one hand, some (still) view financial crises as a natural consequence of business cycles. As such, the occurrence of financial crises simply has to be accepted although their ex post negative impact on the economy should be minimized. Regulation plays a minor role in this view, namely minimizing only the fallout on the economy. To the extent that regulation could lower the cost of ex post crisis resolution, for example, by facilitating orderly resolution of failed institutions, regulatory reform should be encouraged. But according to this view, regulation is not seen as needed or effective in (ex ante) preventing financial crises or in managing the cycle.

On the other hand, there is the view (to which we subscribe) that financial cycles are distinct from economic cycles, that the buildup of risk is endogenous in the financial system and that financial crises bring about real costs that go beyond those associated with normal economic downturns. Important channels through which financial cycles operate include asset price bubbles, excessive risk-taking, credit booms and crunches, debt overhang and deleveraging, balance sheet channels, fire sales, and market and funding illiquidity. According to this view, the level of risk that was undertaken by the banking system prior to the recent crisis was excessively high and the mostly microprudential-oriented regulation in place was unable to identify the endogenous risks associated with it. Macroprudential regulation then is needed to identify and limit systemic risk over the cycle, including a preventive, ex ante role for the buildup of systemic risk.[3]

Banks indeed have a natural tendency to take on excessive risks: it is a natural consequence of shareholder limited liability combined with the fiduciary duties of bank managers to shareholders and not to the debt holders and other stakeholders of the bank, despite that in most banks equityholders are only a very small fraction of the liabilityholders.[4] This, together with the presence of implicit and explicit government guarantees, renders corporate governance in banks flawed. It leads to badly designed executive compensation that rewards excessive risk-taking such as to induce unregulated corporate governance to promote risk-taking at the expense of debtholders, depositors, and taxpayers but to the benefit of banks' shareholders. As Adam Smith put it, the basic postulate of a market economy is self-interest, even greed, which leads to an efficient allocation. It is not from the benevolence of the butcher, the brewer, or the baker, or in this case the banker, that we expect our loans. However, in this process of failed corporate governance and market disciplining in banks, banks also take excessive risks that pose financial stability concerns and are deemed socially excessive. Following the crisis, bank executives have been criticized for their behavior, which has been described as gambling with taxpayer money, and their executive compensation has been viewed by many as having encouraged short-termism and excessive risk-taking.

However, before concluding that such behavior of banks should be confronted with more and better regulation, one needs to ask the question why banks were not adequately regulated in the first place. A bit of history is in order here. In most countries concerns for financial stability of banks followed the Great Depression. However, the subsequent period of tight regulation ended with the wave of deregulation starting in the 1980s. Since then, a rise in financial fragility has been evidenced by numerous incidences of banking crises (Laeven and Valencia 2012). The excessive risk-taking that preceded the most recent crisis was in fact not suddenly discovered with the current crisis; such credit and leverage booms preceded most of the financial crises throughout history. Nevertheless, particularly severe this time were the bad incentives created by the recent process of financial innovation and deregulation, combined with poor corporate governance, government safety nets, and weak supervision.

Therefore, once we look beyond the popular view of greedy bankers, we can discern that bank regulations were badly designed in the first place. But why? A benign view of regulatory failures is that the regulatory framework was inadequately focused on microprudential risks and that the monitoring of financial system risks had become increasingly complex.

The failure of appropriate risk management during the recent global financial crisis came in various forms and disguises. There was the creation of "fake alpha," whereby managers of financial intermediaries appeared to create excess returns but in fact were taking on hidden tail risks and illiquid investments, which produced a steady positive return (fees) most of the time as compensation for a rare, very negative return. There were credit booms and asset price bubbles producing high profits in the short run with the risk of generating large potential losses in the medium run. It was inevitable that the herding behavior in correlated risks within the financial system would cause most institutions simultaneously to experience losses in bad states of the world, generating systemic risk.[5] Moreover high correlated risks were substantially increased because financial intermediaries financed themselves mainly from other financial intermediaries using short-term debt, thus creating a fragile and dense network of short-term financial connections among institutions around the world in a globalized financial system. Then again, financial innovation in great part contributed to these credit and asset booms, resulting in a lowering of credit standards and an increased interconnectedness with other parts of the financial system. In addition, a drive for home ownership generated a concentration of banks' loan portfolios in mortgages where an asset price bubble was forming, with banks bound to fail simultaneously as soon as the bubble would burst. In such an environment even medium-size banks were expected to be bailed out as otherwise there would be too many to fail simultaneously. Potential bailouts and compensation structures based on relative performance and convex payoffs (stock options) encouraged ex ante collective excessive systemic risk, as potential losses were low relative to (short-term) profits.[6] Expansive monetary policy and the expectation of liquidity assistance by central banks in crises (known as Greenspan put) appear also to have contributed to ex ante excessive risk-taking and the creation of an asset price bubble financed with credit. And there was a kind of "irrational exuberance" in a world of incompetent, overconfident, and/or overoptimistic bank managers and investors with limited memory over past crises, who neglected tail risks and had group behavior biases (Shleifer 2000; Akerlof and Shiller 2009; Kahneman 2011). Deregulation thus enabled larger global financial institutions that were too large, connected, and complex to fail to take excessive ex ante risks and lobby against new regulations. Yet financial regulators failed to identify these risks early on.

Some of the regulatory failures could be linked to shortcomings in the regulatory framework, notably the lack of discernment of macroprudential regulation and systemic risks. Indeed, in the aftermath of the current crisis, the consensus among policy makers and academics has been that regulators did not pay sufficient attention to the financial fragility of the financial system— the correlated risks in the financial system arising from perverse incentives—and the necessity to monitor systemic risk by putting in place a macroprudential regulatory framework.

It has become evident that existing banking regulation, with the safety net it provides to credit institutions, is badly equipped to deal with the channels of contagion that link banks to the market and other institutions, such as securitization, asset-backed commercial paper, repos, and credit default swaps among others, and that bank regulators need to improve their understanding of all financial intermediaries and markets. Moreover the poor design of existing regulatory frameworks is now recognized to be the cause of regulatory distortions that contribute to systemic risk, such as the procyclical implications of traditional capital regulation (there are important exceptions that we will explain in the book as dynamic provisioning in Spain and in some Latin American countries) and the arbitrage of capital regulation by banks in creating special purpose vehicles in the shadow banking sector. Additionally it has become evident that regulators did not have adequate powers or tools at their disposals to intervene early on in failing banks and to efficiently resolve (through assistance or closure) those that fail. For example, at the onset of the 2008 crisis many countries did not have adequate resolution frameworks in place to intervene in large and complex financial institutions, whereas others did not have sufficient and detailed information (data) on the banks and other institutions.

A more disconcerting view is that the regulatory framework failed because of regulatory failures and weak supervision. Indeed doubts have been raised as to the willingness of and incentives for bank regulators to intervene in failing banks, either because of too big to fail considerations, career concerns, or powerful bank lobbies. Some have argued that self-interested regulators responded to industry pressures and lobbying, closing an eye to regulatory arbitrage and the excessive buildup of risks in the financial system during the boom period and failing to respond to signs of distress early on. Indeed, the UK FSA's response to the failure of Northern Rock (which failed after repeated concerns about its liquidity and solvency position) does not exemplify the reaction of a strong, independent supervisor. And when confronted with costly bank failures, many regulators turned to regulatory forbearance. This engenders fundamental questions about the political economy of banking regulation and its design going forward.[7]

While some of these shortcomings in the regulatory framework are addressed by the Basel III regulations and US financial reform under the Dodd–Frank Act, some fundamental questions remain unaddressed as we explain in the book. For example, resolving the too big to fail problem and the implementation and interactions of macroprudential policy with monetary policy remain open questions.

Financial regulatory reform is thus still very much a work in progress. New powers have been given to federal regulators to intervene in large and complex financial institutions (e.g., the European Central Bank (ECB) in the euro area), but these powers have not been tested thus far and questions remain about the willingness of federal regulators to act in the midst of another systemic crisis. The limits of macroprudential regulation thus appear quite visible. Given these limits, it is our view that macroprudential policy should concentrate on preventing the excessive buildup of booms where its effectiveness is likely most potent. This book offers a framework to guide policy makers in this process of financial regulatory reform.

The book proceeds as follows. In short, chapters 2 to 7 give the building blocks of systemic risk, chapters 8 to 10 cover the implications for prudential and monetary policy, and chapter 11 concludes with the challenges the current regulatory reform agenda faces. More specifically, chapter 2 gives a definition of systemic risk, describes the real consequences of systemic risk, and presents a taxonomy and illustration of systemic financial crises throughout history. In the definition and throughout the book, we put a lot of emphasis on the real effects for the economy at large, as systemic risk is not only simply financial instability but a strong impairment of the financial system that causes substantial negative aggregate output and employment effects.

Chapter 3 presents a basic theoretical framework of systemic risk to explain its underlying drivers and to guide regulatory policy, in particular, the rationale for macroprudential regulation (and its difference from microprudential regulation). The basic framework incorporates macroeconomic considerations that are not internalized by individual financial intermediaries, such as the aggregate buildup of financial imbalances. The ex ante macroeconomic and financial drivers of systemic risk, contagion risk, the real macro effects of systemic risk, and the measurement of systemic risk are reviewed in depth in the subsequent chapters 4 to 7.

The basic theoretical framework in chapter 3 offers a general approach for thinking about externalities associated with systemic risk and desirable policy responses to mitigate such externalities. In particular, the framework considers the incentives for financial intermediaries' risk-taking and herding (the moral hazard view), the building of financial imbalances, and the role of competition and financial institutions' corporate governance. The discussion covers the classical view of banking crises (Diamond and Dybvig 1983) and the contagion view, with special emphasis on liquidity risk arising from interconnectivity and the interbank market. Moreover the general equilibrium impact of a banking crisis and its feedback and nonlinear effects are explored, thus covering the relation between financial and real crises. Specific regulatory policies and practical considerations to implement such policies are considered in subsequent chapters. Finally, the chapter offers a list of the essential elements that a model of systemic risk should have to allow public policy analysis through (model) counterfactuals, but as the chapter highlights, the existing theoretical literature—based on either banking (corporate finance) or macroeconomic models with a financial sector—has not yet developed models that incorporate all of these key elements. Therefore empirical analysis of existing prudential measures is crucial to guide new policy reforms in the area of macroprudential policy.

Chapter 4 offers a complete overview of the causes of systemic financial crises. Systemic risk is not an exogenous risk, but is endogenously taken by the financial intermediaries. It summarizes the literature on credit booms, asset price bubbles and other macro buildup of financial imbalances and the endogenous financial fragility stemming from the financial sector (both the traditional and new models). The chapter covers the role of leverage, especially financial intermediary credit, in systemic crises, and also reviews the particular prominence of asset price bubbles in systemic crises, such as real estate bubbles. It draws on recent episodes of financial crises and on historical evidence. Moreover the chapter also offers explanations of systemic risk based either on distorted incentives of financial intermediaries (agency view) or on behavioral finance explanations (preference view), such as psychological biases including overconfidence, group think, and neglecting tail risks. In particular, it discusses how herding behavior by financial intermediaries can translate into correlated risk exposures among financial intermediaries and create systemic risk. Finally, this chapter also discusses the role of regulatory distortions, financial liberalization (including the creation of too large global banks), financial innovation (including securitization), and other structural changes that influence the buildup of macroeconomic financial fragility.

Chapter 5 presents an overview of the literature on financial contagion, with special emphasis on interconnectedness and liquidity risk. Not only direct contagion is analyzed, but also the so-called second-round effects and liquidity dry-ups and hoarding. While the emphasis is on contagion across banks, contagion in other parts of the financial system—such as insurance, hedge funds, money market mutual funds, and over the counter (OTC) markets for credit default swap (CDS) contracts); (international) contagion between financial intermediaries and markets is also reviewed. Moreover negative liquidity spirals with market and funding liquidity risks, cash in the market asset pricing and fire sales are discussed. Finally, the effects of recent trends in financial globalization on cross-border financial contagion are also summarized.

Chapter 6 describes the consequences of systemic risk for the economy at large. Financial crises are followed by strong and persistent negative effects in terms of aggregate output, as the history of financial crises shows. The main motivation of macroprudential policy is that the market failures that give rise to systemic risk imply strong real effects when systemically important financial crises materialize. The chapter draws on the literature on credit booms and busts, documenting how bank capital and liquidity problems may create a credit crunch for nonfinancial borrowers (both households and firms), which in turn reduces aggregate output, employment, and welfare. Other important macrofinancial channels such as debt overhang, deleveraging, crowding-out effects of public debt, zombie-lending, and risk-shifting are discussed in detail. The chapter also reviews the literature on the costs of systemic financial crises and illustrates the real effects of systemic risk by presenting information on the real costs of systemic financial crises in terms of output losses and fiscal costs.

Chapter 7 gives an overview of existing methods to measure systemic risk. The objective of this chapter is to provide guidance on how one should measure systemic risk in practice, including in environments with data limitations such as emerging markets and the non-regulated financial system. We discuss methods to develop real time early warning signals to measure excessive credit and other aggregate financial imbalances. We also provide measures based on balance sheet data and on market data, both to analyze contagion risks and macro imbalances, including network analysis. Finally, we summarize how different measures of financial imbalances that are commonly used in policy and academic circles have performed in many financial crises over the twentieth century.

Chapter 8 presents the "old" regulatory framework relying exclusively on microprudential policy and its relevance for future regulatory policy. It offers the rationale for microprudential policy, describes its limitations in managing systemic risk, and discusses the impact of the new regulation framework issued by the Basel committee and the Financial Stability Board, as well as its implementations in the Dodd–Frank Act and the new European Directives. Finally, it shows that microprudential policy alone is not sufficient to manage systemic risk, and thus there is the need for a new, complementary framework that includes macroprudential policy.

Chapter 9 presents the "new," complementary regulatory and supervisory framework that relies on macroprudential policy to manage systemic risk. It gives an overview of possible macroprudential tools, drawing on the theoretical framework in chapter 3 and on the drivers of systemic risk in chapters 4 to 6 to explain their rationale. It also discusses the trade-offs involved in choosing an optimal policy mix (including the interaction with existing regulation) and the practical considerations when implementing these tools. It then analyzes whether macroprudential policy should be under the same organization as microprudential policy, or given that macroprudential policy also cares about real effects and not only financial stability, it should be under a different organization than microprudential policy. The chapter next presents a critical review of the relevant elements of the new Basel III regulatory framework as well as the latest EU and US financial regulations in dealing with systemic risk. The analysis of macroprudential tools is illustrated with case studies on the effectiveness of existing tools, such as dynamic loan loss provisioning rules in Spain, limits on loan-to-value ratios in Hong Kong, liquidity requirements in Latin America, and speed limits on credit growth in Eastern Europe. Finally, it offers a summary of some evidence of unintended consequences of tightening of macroprudential policy on risk-taking through search for yield strategies.

Chapter 10 analyzes monetary policy and systemic risk, and the interrelation with macroprudential policy. It analyzes the role of monetary policy to reduce ex ante buildup of financial imbalances by leaning against the wind and to combat ex post credit crunches and fire sales in asset prices. It discusses also the importance of short- versus long-term interest rates for financial institutions, notably banks. It explains the risk-taking channel of monetary policy, its relation with the credit channel, and summarizes the empirical evidence around the world on these channels. Moreover the chapter discusses that, as monetary policy affects credit and asset prices (thus influencing systemic risk), coordination between monetary and macroprudential policy is key. It analyzes why macroprudential policy and its objective of financial stability could be in conflict with the price stability objective of monetary policy. These and other issues related to interactions between macroprudential policy and monetary policy, including possible conflicts between policy objectives and institutional arrangements, are taken up in chapter 11.

The book concludes with a summary in chapter 11 of the key aspects of an effective macroprudential regulatory framework, a list of remaining challenges for creating such a framework, and an overview of remaining issues in financial regulatory reform more broadly. The chapter presents key elements that are still missing from an effective macroprudential regulatory framework in most countries, and lists the remaining challenges for financial regulatory policy, including the optimal size and structure of the financial system (as well as a diversity in the financial system among market finance, banks, and other financial intermediaries), a credible mechanism to intervene early on in failing financial intermediaries, a restoration of market discipline at financial intermediaries (including good corporate governance standards in banks, disclosure, and accounting reforms), and better macroprudential supervision with systemwide data for supervisors, improved risk models, and real time measures of systemic risk.

Consideration will also be given to the institutional setup and organization of macroprudential policy including the existing set of tools, the regulatory challenges arising from regulatory arbitrage, the multiplicity of regulatory bodies in the United States, the creation of a banking union in the European Union, the supervision and resolution of cross-border financial institutions, and some international policy spillovers, including the impact of monetary policy of the United States and Europe for emerging countries' asset and credit bubbles through international capital inflows. Domestic macroprudential policy may be distortionary, and some international cooperation on macroprudential policies will be essential.

Concluding remarks offer a list of the main takeaways from the book. They emphasize the preventive role of macroprudential policy, the need to complement such policy with higher capital requirements, strong supervision, credible resolution, and sound macroeconomic policies, and the limits and political economy constraints of macroprudential policy.

2   A Primer on Systemic Risk

This chapter gives a definition of systemic risk, identifies the key elements and consequences of systemic risk, and presents a taxonomy, together with some illustrations of past systemic financial crises. The discussion includes other definitions given in the literature on systemic risk, including definitions that we believe are not adequate. We further differentiate between previous financial crises that were systemic and those that were not systemic.

2.1   A Definition of Systemic Risk

We start with a definition of systemic risk, closely following IMF-FSB (2009) and ECB (2009): "Systemic risk is *the risk of threats to financial stability that impair the functioning of a large part of the financial system with significant adverse effects on the broader economy*" (our emphasis).[1] Such threats to financial stability can arise from impairment of all or large parts of the financial system. The financial system is taken to be banking, other financial intermediaries, and financial markets together with payment and settlement systems. Systemic risk can be triggered by events in any of these parts of the financial system. Systemic risk events can be sudden and unexpected, but the history of financial crises (including the 2008 global crisis) tells us that systemic risk events are mostly built up endogenously over time in the absence of appropriate policy responses. For example, credit booms and subsequent asset price bubbles develop over an extended period of time. Systemic risk is not simply financial instability but an unusual financial shock that causes strong negative shocks to the real economy: aggregate output, employment, and welfare.

A difficulty of identifying and quantifying different channels of systemic risk persists as, in general, empirical tests and measures of

systemic risk cannot make a perfect distinction between (1) the transmission of idiosyncratic shocks through the financial system (contagion) and endogenous shocks caused by excessive risk-taking by a
large part of the financial system (e.g., arising from correlated risks
during real estate bubbles)[2] or (2) rational revisions based on news of
wholesale depositors' and investors' expectations about fundamentals
or pure panics unrelated to fundamentals.[3] Our view, based on the
literature surveyed, is that all these mechanisms play a role to some
degree and that these mechanisms reinforce each other (Iyer and Peydró
2011). However, some mechanisms are quantitatively more important
(e.g., asset price bubbles financed by credit booms). The institutional
framework is key in determining the resilience of a financial system.
This is why a similar shock may trigger systemic risk in one country
and not in another, or some shocks may cause systemic crises depending on the structure of the financial network.[4] In any case, the impairment to the financial sector has to be strong enough to produce strong
spillovers to the real sector and systemic crises to occur.

Economic shocks may become systemic because of the existence of
strong negative externalities associated with disruptions in the financial system. Key to the definition of systemic risk—as should be the
basis for macroprudential regulation—is the role of externalities, first,
within the financial system, and second, from the financial system to
the broader economy.

Financial system externalities normally imply contagion effects
running from one part of the financial system to other parts of the
financial system via the wholesale market, through fire sales in the
process of deleveraging or through the contraction of the pool of aggregate liquidity (i.e., a reduction of funding and market liquidity). In the
special case of highly concentrated financial systems, such as those in
Cyprus, Iceland, Ireland, the Netherlands, and Switzerland, the failure
of a single bank or a market can have systemic consequences. It is the
spreading nature of the shock, namely the contagion effect, that distin-
guishes systemic risk from the idiosyncratic risk of individual financial
institutions. In measuring systemic risk, special attention should therefore be given to interlinkages among financial institutions and the
transmission of shocks from one part of the financial system to the
financial system at large. Importantly, these interlinkages can be
the endogenous decisions of financial institutions to take correlated
risks in specific assets or to borrow short-term from other financial
institutions in the wholesale market due to some bad incentives,

including from public policy (e.g., "too many to fail" bailout policies). Therefore we view systemic risk as an endogenous risk (rather than exogenous), though the immediate cause of a systemic crisis could be an exogenous event.

The impairment of the whole or part of the financial system will produce strong negative spillovers to the real sector and welfare of citizens, such as substantial reductions in aggregate output and employment, in the absence of appropriate policy responses. Whether financial failures are a source of systemic risk therefore depends on the impact of such failures on the rest of the financial system and on the real economy. A financial disruption that does not cause a significant disruption of real economy activity is not a systemic risk event. For instance, the burst of the dot-com bubble in 2000 and 2001 did not generate substantial adverse effects to the financial system because investments were mostly equity financed with limited exposure to the whole financial system. Similarly the 1987 stock market crash, while affecting the wealth of investors, did not result in an impairment of the functioning of the banking system. The literature surveyed shows that not only are credit booms an ex ante strong correlate of financial crisis (an early warning signal), they also produce stronger ex post negative economic effects once the crisis starts. Episodes of deleveraging, credit crunches, and debt overhangs, such as those occurring in the 1930s, the 1997 to 1998, and 2007 to 2014 periods, have substantially stronger negative effects on the real sector than stock market-based crises, such as those in October 1987 or the dot-com bubble in 2000. This emphasis on real effects reflects the view that real activity and employment—not merely financial stability—are the primary concerns of economic policy makers. Episodes of high systemic risk are therefore typically associated with financial instability that causes adverse macroeconomic effects leading to systemic crises in the absence of policy responses.

There are two dimensions to systemic risk. First, there is the time dimension of systemic risk, namely the buildup of systemic risk during credit booms and asset price bubbles, and the ex post negative externalities from the financial to the real sector during busts. Key drivers of such forms of systemic risk are considered to be financial innovation, financial deregulation, financial globalization, competition policy, and monetary policy. For instance, financial innovations that facilitate risk-sharing, and thereby lower idiosyncratic risk, may increase systemic risk by exposing a large part of the financial intermediaries to the same aggregate shock (Allen and Gale 2000a) and by increasing the appetite and capacity of risk-taking. A good example is asset securitization which increases the financial system's exposure to the same aggregate asset shock and which increases systemic risk by increasing the credit supply in the financial system (Shin 2009). Excess liquidity resulting from overly accommodative monetary policy for a prolonged period of time or from financial globalization after a process of financial deregulation may produce similar effects. Expectations of public liquidity in the case of systemic problems (central bank intervention with the so-called Greenspan put) may help the buildup of ex ante excessive risk despite central banks' crucial role in minimizing the ex post negative consequences of systemic crises. Moreover financial intermediaries' willingness to take on excessive risk stem from pervasive incentives rooted in moral hazard problems and/or behavioral reasons. Moral hazard problems arise from banks' shareholders having little capital at stake, pervasive corporate governance standards, and from explicit and implicit government guarantees on bank liabilities (Freixas and Rochet 2008). Behavioral reasons include group thinking in bubbles and overoptimism, which can encourage banks to neglect tail risks that have not occurred in the recent past (Shleifer et al. 2010b; Gennaioli et al. 2012).

The second part is the cross-sectional dimension of systemic risk, namely the contribution to systemic risk from negative externalities associated with spillovers and contagion effects. Such spillovers can come in the form of direct contractual spillovers, or indirect spillovers. Direct spillovers include interconnectedness and domino or network effects (e.g., losses a large and interconnected bank's bankruptcy generate on other financial institutions). Indirect spillovers include information spillovers following bank failures (as in Chen 1997) or after policy actions (as in the refusal to bail out Lehman Brothers) and pecuniary externalities arising from fire sale externalities. They also involve negative liquidity spirals as in Brunnermeier and Pedersen (2008) or from credit crunches as in Bernanke (1983).

Macroprudential regulation has a role vis-à-vis both types of systemic risk. It serves both an ex ante preventative role in limiting the buildup of systemic risk during boom times, thus preventing systemic financial crises, and an ex post crisis management function in reducing the negative externalities associated with spillovers and contagion. If systemic crises are not exogenous events, as we explain in this book, but come from an endogenous buildup of imbalances in the financial sector, then prevention of excessive risk-taking should be a central mission of macroprudential policy, not just ex post resolution and crisis management (Goodhart and Perotti 2013). Aggregate risk arises from collective endogenous choices made by financial intermediaries, and not from an individual bank misstep or external force. A macroprudential policy that solely entails ex post intervention would fail to address the root causes. Even worse, such policies could actually increase ex ante risk-taking (moral hazard), with the result that large losses are shifted onto taxpayers (because ex post support works mainly by transferring resources from risk-averse long-term savers to risk-taking short-term borrowers; see Diamond and Rajan 2012). While an expansive monetary policy may reduce credit crunches ex post it could be the wrong policy overall when it increases moral hazard ex ante (Jiménez et al. 2012, 2014a).

Macroprudential regulation is the right approach to regulate systemic risk because it takes into account both the *whole* financial system and its spillovers with the broader (real) economy. In a sense, it takes the perspective of general equilibrium effects, as opposed to the partial equilibrium framework of microprudential policy. For example, by focusing on the liquidity and capital ratios of individual banks, microprudential policy does not take into consideration the negative externalities of not renewing deposits in the interbank market or of deleveraging through a reduction of the supply of credit to firms and households. While better microprudential policy mostly implies safer financial institutions, and thus a safer financial system as a whole, when such spillovers are sufficiently strong, the financial system as a whole may be worse off, even though the behavior of banks individually may be perfectly rational.

To be sure, many other policies can affect the resilience and stability of the financial system and its ability to service the broader economy. Besides the impact of monetary, fiscal, and competition policies, strong influences may come from tax policies (that favor debt over equity or real estate ownership over renting), financial reporting standards (fair value versus historical accounting), and legal frameworks (on bankruptcy, collateral, debt) (see Caruana 2012). For instance, there is an extensive literature on the impact of banking competition on financial stability, with mixed theoretical and empirical results. Also recent theoretical and empirical literature suggests that prolonged periods of low policy rates affect credit and leverage, encourage financial market participants to take on risks, and may at times fuel asset price bubbles (e.g., Dell'Ariccia et al. 2014; Allen and Rogoff 2011). The idea that the liquidity provided by central banks is important in driving excessive risk-taking is not new, however: "Speculative manias gather speed through expansion of money and credit or perhaps, in some cases, get started because of an initial expansion of money and credit" (Kindleberger 1978, p. 54). Therefore externalities in the interaction of different policies can be positive complementarities when the policies are mutually reinforcing, but also negative spillovers when one policy weakens the effectiveness of another. Hence there is a need for coordination. In chapter 10, we also analyze the interactions between macroprudential and monetary policy, and in chapter 11, the international cooperation in macroprudential and monetary policies.

As it is clear from our definition, market risk, aggregate risk, or systematic risk should not be confused with systemic risk, the risk of the impairment of the financial system with strong negative consequences for the broader economy.

2.2   Real Consequences of Systemic Risk

The adverse real economic effects resulting from systemic risk will affect firms and households insofar as banks and other financial intermediaries cannot fulfill their functions. These functions can be classified in three broad classes: provision of payment services, risk-sharing and management, and credit supply.

Payment system disruptions imply that the transfer of property rights can no longer be done through the banking network, with the consequences that transactions may be delayed or simply may not be fulfilled. This is an extreme consequence of a systemic crisis but its possibility is clearly taken into account in the bailout decisions taken during a systemic event. The disruption of payments may originate in a bank failure with the temporary freezing of demand deposits or in the failure of a correspondent bank in the transaction that makes it impossible to make a payment. Disruption of payment can also occur when there is general uncertainty about whether payment will arrive at destination due to either the payee's or the payer's bank facing serious default risk.

The impairment of banks' risk-sharing and management functions implies that the transmission of property rights becomes impossible or extremely costly. The terms of contracts cannot be fulfilled as the payer is then unable to make the payment. Also a number of valuable services that banks and other financial intermediaries offer might not be available or only with a huge counterparty risk. For example, the use of forward contracts in import and export operations, or the provision of banks' guarantees in some contracts may simply disappear. In extreme systemic events, with retail and wholesale runs, the banking system may not perform its maturity transformation and liquidity provision, with substantial welfare costs as retail depositors cannot do temporal risk-sharing (as in Allen and Gale 2000a) or, if the impairment is on financial markets at large, any (cross-sectional) risk-sharing severely suffers. Moreover wholesale markets are important to manage the liquidity risk of financial intermediaries and this may not work during systemic events. Market and funding illiquidity spirals may cause severe problems (Brunnermeier and Pedersen 2008). All in all, problems in the banking and financial sector have negative welfare effects as risk-sharing, risk management, and maturity transformation are impeded.

Because usually it is possible to manage the payment disruption side of a systemic crisis, and because liquidity and risk problems within the financial system can be managed to some extent by public policy, disruptions in credit flows are the major observed impact on the economic activity. Banks choose to reduce their supply of credit due to lack of either liquidity or capital, thus creating a credit crunch for firms and households (Bernanke and Lown 1992). Large numbers of loans are called in as a result of banks' problems.

Jiménez et al. (2012), using loan applications from Spain, show that worsening economic conditions substantially reduce loan granting, especially from banks with lower capital or liquidity ratios; responding to applications for the same loan, weak banks are less likely to grant the loan. Importantly for systemic risk, they show that firms cannot offset the resulting reduction in the availability of credit by applying to other banks. Even if some banks are liquid and solvent, they will not immediately lend to the clients of the banks with significant capital and liquidity problems as their analysis of credit risk will not be based on the same parameters; in particular, in a crisis it will be difficult for a nonfinancial borrower to obtain credit from a bank other than its usual supplier of credit as this other lender would face a winners' curse problem when granting a loan (the other bank cannot distinguish whether the borrower is rejected from its lending relationship because of bad firm collateral and solvency, or because of credit supply restriction across the board from the incumbent banks as in Dell'Ariccia and

Marques 2006). Bernanke (1983) shows the importance of credit supply restrictions in the Great Depression.

Credit conditions can vary over business cycles (Lown and Morgan 2006), partly in responding to variations in the credit supply and partly to variations in credit demand and firm and household net worth and collateral (Maddaloni and Peydró 2011, 2013). Credit might also stop flowing to firms and households that are highly leveraged as a consequence of the credit and leverage boom in the years previous to the systemic crisis. As we show in chapter 4, using empirical evidence based on a large cross-country analysis, credit and leverage booms are the highest ex ante correlate of major financial crises. Therefore, within a systemic crisis, the nonfinancial sector may itself face debt overhang problems, and be forced to reduce the supply of credit. Or banks may choose to deleverage from firms and households with reduced net worth (Bernanke, Gertler, and Gilchrist 1996). Debt overhang problems (Myers 1977) may be, therefore, one explanation for the reduction of credit in systemic crises, and clearly, when good investment opportunities (projects with positive net present value) cannot be implemented because of high firm leverage, the consequence is reduced economic growth.

Negative real effects would be minimized if equity could be substantially increased. However, some agents like households do not issue equity and equity for firms may be limited because the information asymmetry problems associated with equity are higher than with any other forms of financing, especially with debt, and become even more severe during a financial crisis. Indeed, at the midst of a financial crisis, equity capital is most needed but least available. Additionally in some countries equity markets (including investment from venture capitalists and private equity firms) are not well developed for all types of firms.

Not all risk-taking causes financial crises. Long-term economic growth is impossible without risk-taking (e.g., starting a business, expanding an existing one, or radical or incremental innovation). However, excessive risk-taking does cause financial crises. Yet, although we know that changing appetites for risk are central to economic booms and busts, it is difficult to explain their determinants. Potential determinants include changes in preferences—behavioral motives as in Keynes's "animal spirits" (Akerlof and Shiller 2009) or time-varying risk aversion (Campbell and Cochrane 1999)—and lower financial intermediaries' net worth (Adrian and Shin 2011).[5] Crises reduce the risk appetite of lenders and investors alike (Malmendier and Nagel 2011; Knüpfer et al. 2013), reducing the number of projects that gets financed and the riskiness associated with these projects, thus lowering economic growth (Matsuyama 2007; Aghion 2011).

All in all, the previous factors make the credit in the financial system very procyclical. Credit grows rapidly when the economy is booming, as investors turn more optimistic about the future and lending standards become soft. When economic conditions slow, a flight to quality causes a collapse in credit (Minsky 1982). This procyclicality of the financial system makes it fragile and vulnerable to crises. This is an important point that we develop in chapter 4, where we consider the buildup of systemic risk, both based on bad incentives (moral hazard) and behavioral reasons (preferences).

A key question to analyze for the real consequences of systemic risk is whether credit reductions result from bad economic fundamentals and the ensuing reduction in credit demand or through a reduction of the supply of credit, which then causes lower aggregate output and employment by not financing otherwise profitable investment opportunities in the real sector. Therefore a banking crisis may not necessarily be a systemic crisis, if it just follows an economic crisis and the reduction in credit is demand driven.

A different but related effect concerns the potential compositional effects of credit supply during a banking crisis (which needs not be systemic). A bank may prefer to roll over a bad loan rather than reduce lending, a practice known as "loan evergreening" or "zombie lending." If the borrower is unable to repay and the amount of losses may endanger the bank's already fragile capital position, the bank might have an incentive to engage by lending to a zombie firm for a negative net present value project, with the only benefit being delayed disclosure of the bank's actual losses. Indeed research analyzing the Japanese systemic crisis shows that a banking crisis can have negative real consequences over a long period of time because of zombie lending (Caballero, Hoshi, and Kashyap 2008). Similarly some have argued that in the recent systemic crisis in Europe, the funding provided to banks through the ECB's long-term refinancing operation (LTRO) programs kept weakly capitalized banks alive (Veron and Wolff 2013). Zombie lending may substantially increase the negative effects of banking crises because credit is unlikely to flow to the most productive firms.

Moreover the increase in the ECB's LTRO programs coincided in some peripheral European countries with a large increase in public debt holdings by domestic banks, also favored because of the zero regulatory risk weight on own sovereign debt holdings, potentially crowding out investment, thus further lowering economic growth.

2.3   Financial Crises and Systemic Risk

The economic significance of such interruptions of bank credit and other negative spillovers from the financial to the real sector is witnessed by the large real effects of systemic financial crises, as measured in terms of output losses and fiscal costs to resolve failed financial institutions. Bordo et al. (2001) shows that the worst financial crises are the twin crises whereby countries are hit simultaneously by banking and currency crises. Laeven and Valencia (2008) show that the fiscal costs and output losses following banking crises vary dramatically across countries, and that the mix of policy responses is an important determinant of these outcomes. They find that all too often, intervention is delayed because regulatory capital forbearance and central bank liquidity support are used for too long to deal with insolvent financial institutions in the hope that they will recover, ultimately increasing the stress on the financial system and the real economy. More recently Schularick and Taylor (2012) show that not only the likelihood of financial crises substantially increase with ex ante strong bank credit acceleration, but once the crisis happens, the negative real effects are even stronger.[6]

Given that banking crises are so important for negative aggregate real effects, we analyze in detail the costs of these ones drawing on Laeven and Valencia (2013), who compile the most complete dataset on banking crises around the world from 1970 to 2011, including information on the dating of crises and crisis management policies. The fiscal costs to resolve banking crises have been estimated to average about 7 percent of GDP across 147 banking crises since the 1970s. Cumulative output losses—relative to trend GDP—associated with these crises average a staggering 23 percent of GDP (see table 2.1 and Laeven and Valencia 2013).[7]

There is substantial variation in economic outcomes associated with banking crises, with the costliest banking crises in terms of fiscal outlays associated with bank recapitalizations and other forms of bank restructuring policies amounting to more than 40 percent of GDP in at least

Table 2.1
Banking crises outcomes, 1970 to 2011

Country	Output loss	Increase in debt	Monetary expansion	Fiscal costs	Fiscal costs	Duration	Peak liquidity	Liquidity support	Peak NPLs
	Medians								
	Percent of GDP				Percent of financial system assets	In years	Percent of deposits and foreign liabilities		Percent of total loans
All	23.0	12.1	1.7	6.8	12.7	2.0	20.1	9.6	25.0
Advanced	32.9	21.4	8.3	3.8	2.1	3.0	11.5	5.7	4.0
Emerging	26.0	9.1	1.3	10.0	21.4	2.0	22.3	11.1	30.0

Source: Laeven and Valencia (2013)

seven countries, including most recently Ireland, Iceland, and Cyprus where the crises are still ongoing. These real effects and social costs of banking crises show that the financial and real costs associated with banking crises are closely related, and so offer a key rationale for regulating systemic risk. The real effects of financial (notably banking) crises will be dealt with in more detail in chapter 6.

While the proximate triggers of banking crises may differ, there are many commonalities among systemic banking crises (see Reinhart and Rogoff 2008; Laeven and Valencia 2008), including the main drivers and nature of systemic risk associated with the crisis. For example, about one in three banking crisis episodes since 1970 is preceded by a credit boom (Laeven and Valencia 2012), suggesting that excessive credit growth, with individual banks and bankers not internalizing the costs, imposed on the system as a whole, is a key attribute of systemic risk.[8] The type of credit boom may vary, though, from crisis to crisis, being concentrated in the household sector, in the corporate sector, or in the public sector, and risks may arise from default risk, liquidity risk, interest rate risk, currency mismatches, or maturity mismatches. For example, whereas in the 2007 to 2008 crisis in the United States, the credit boom and bust was concentrated in the household rather than the firm sector; in Spain it was just the opposite with a large credit boom–bust cycle in the corporate sector. In Ireland the credit boom was concentrated in both the household and corporate sector, but very much tied to the financing of residential and commercial real estate. In all these crises, liquidity risk, maturity mismatches, and credit default risk were crucial. Additionally interest rate risk was a key source of risk in the United States and Europe where the financial crisis came after a long period of low interest rates followed by a strong and fast increase in monetary policy rates (e.g., from 1 to 5.25 percent in the case of the United States). In all these countries public debt increased ex post because of the financial and economic crises but was not the primary cause of the recession. In Greece, in contrast, problems in the public sector precipitated the crisis.[9]

In most cases the crisis was associated with large negative shocks to the capital positions of individual banks, culminating in heightened systemic risk associated with negative spillovers for other banks in the country (through either a loss in confidence or pecuniary externalities). In some crises there were even contagion effects to financial systems abroad. In response to such systemic events, governments generally intervene heavily in the financial sector, incurring substantial fiscal costs in the process, while the economy generally experiences a credit reduction and significant output losses.

For instance, in the US savings and loans crisis of the 1980s the interest rate risk associated with reckless lending of fixed rate mortgages by savings and loans institutions led to a sharp increase in nonperforming loans when the Federal Reserve increased interest rates. Since most of the losses were limited to savings and loans institutions, contagion to other parts of the financial system was limited, and so was the impact on economic activity. For these reasons, by our definition, this crisis was *not* systemic.

The Nordic banking crises in Finland, Norway, and Sweden in the early 1990s had their origins in real estate bubbles. The fallout from the crisis in terms of lost output was severe in Finland and Sweden. These two countries resorted to asset management companies to accelerate financial restructuring by taking over nonperforming real estate related assets from banks. Two examples of successful "bad banks" or asset management companies (AMCs) are Securum and Retrieva in Sweden, created in 1992 to manage the problem real estate loans of two major Swedish banks, Nordbanken and Gota Bank—both companies managed to recover substantial amounts of their initial investment by selling off their assets. Factors that contributed to their success include an efficient judicial system that forced insolvent debtors into bankruptcy, the banks' real estate related assets that simplified their restructuring, and the strong governance mechanisms and skilled management teams of the companies. Other countries have found it harder to repeat these results, in part because Sweden could reduce their debt overhang problems with the strong 1990s economic growth in the new technology sectors, but in part also owing to weak legal, regulatory, and political institutions. Often banks' assets are transferred to AMCs at above market value prices, resulting in backdoor bank recapitalization and creating moral hazard problems (Calomiris, Klingebiel, and Laeven 2003).[10]

The East Asian financial crisis of 1997 to 1998 resulted primarily from large private current account deficits and the maintenance of fixed exchange rates, which had encouraged external borrowing in foreign currency, thus leading to excessive exposure to exchange rate risk in both the banking and corporate sectors. The financial crisis erupted when large currency devaluations imposed major losses on banks. At the individual level, banks had appeared safe with only small open positions in foreign currency, but indirectly they had been exposed to growing systemic risk associated with extensive short-term wholesale borrowing in foreign currency by unhedged borrowers, ultimately translating into major credit losses for the banks following the exchange rate depreciations. In fact, a terrible combination for a financial crisis is excessive short-term wholesale debt denominated in foreign currency, because besides the financial fragility stemming from short-term wholesale positions, the holders of debt denominated in foreign currency will experience negative balance sheet effects when currencies depreciate. Moreover central banks that cannot print foreign currency are limited in their ability to support a financial sector and economy with excessive exposure to foreign currency debt when a crisis hits because traditional instruments, such as liquidity injections and monetary policy (inflation), are in domestic currency.

The Japanese banking crisis of the 1990s is unlike many other banking crises in the sense that apart from the collapse of the asset price bubble, there was no sudden crisis but rather a prolonged, steady deterioration in the health of Japan's financial system. This prolonged crisis resulted from a combination of inadequate disclosure of information on the true financial condition of financial institutions, and the slow response to the crisis by the government. Only slowly did the public become aware of the full extent of the problem, as the amount of nonperforming loans was repeatedly adjusted upward. Starting in 1992 it became clear that Japanese banks had a huge amount of nonperforming loans, mainly in construction and real estate following a long boom period in these sectors. In the years that followed, the public authorities announced a number of tax policy changes to make it attractive for banks to deduct loans losses for tax purposes. Rather than directly recapitalizing banks and addressing the bad loan problem using public funds, the Japanese government relied on tax incentives for the recognition of loan losses to solve the bad loan problem.

Almost all banks took advantage of these tax incentives and liberally deducted losses on loans to assist related, troubled borrowers. However, this strategy failed to restore the health of Japan's banking system. Financial institutions seriously lacked incentives to engage in effective corporate restructuring as they were allowed to continue to hide their losses and operate with a weak capital base. The resulting moral hazard implicit in the behavior of banks and bank borrowers was exacerbated by the government's explicit and implicit guarantee on all bank deposits. Additionally the Japanese Keiretsu model in which Japanese banks have close relationships with affiliated firms and Japanese banks own substantial equity positions in those firms, reduced market discipline and incentives to attack the mounting bad debt problem, and encouraged banks to use government subsidization of losses largely as a means to assist related enterprises.

When the Japanese authorities finally resorted to direct recapitalization of banks using public funds, there was no differentiation based on the viability of banks going forward and little monitoring occurred to ensure that banks made proper use of public aid. Virtually every bank of significant size received public assistance, though the amounts involved were relatively small and the government did not require banks to find private sources of capital. The recapitalization program thus provided a boost to bank capital but did less to foster corporate restructuring or to restart bank lending. In the end the crisis was contained but over a prolonged period of time and at huge taxpayer expense (Calomiris, Klingebiel, and Laeven 2003).

Banking crises tend to occur in waves, and within each of these waves there are regional clusters often associated with contagion effects (see Reinhart and Rogoff 2009a). This suggests that systemic risk is not constant over time. Figure 2.1 shows the number of banking crises that

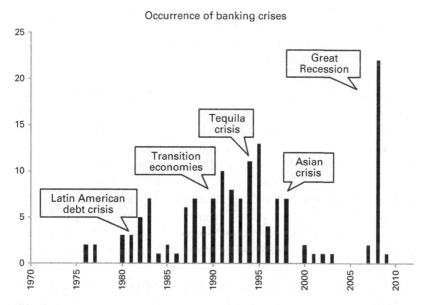

Figure 2.1
Waves of systemic banking crises. Noted is the frequency of the starting dates (years) of systemically important banking crises. Source: Laeven and Valencia (2013).

start in a given year, and notably a marked pick up in crisis activity in the early 1980s. During the 1990s there were four clusters of crises: the Nordic crisis countries of Europe, the transition economies of Europe, Latin America during the Tequila crisis, and East Asia during the Asian financial crisis. The early 2000s were relatively calm but ended with the most recent wave consisting of the largest number of systemic crises since the 1930s.

All these recent crises originated from excessive endogenous risk-taking by the financial system, notably a part (or the entirety) of the banking system. Excessive risk-taking arose in credit exposures, in asset price bubbles, and in short-term wholesale borrowing. Even in the Asian crisis, given the direct international exposures with the financial system abroad, there was an element of contagion through the globalized financial system. All these elements were likewise present in the global systemic crisis that started in 2007 but to a higher degree.

In the US mortgage credit crisis of 2007 and 2008, it was the overextension of mortgage loans to indebted households achieved through securitization, which imposed large losses on banks' holdings of mortgage loans and mortgage-backed securities when house prices stopped rising and monetary rates rose substantially; consequently interest rates on mortgage contracts were reset. Again, at the individual bank level, banks appeared to hold relatively safe diversified mortgages. In fact the relatively small fraction of subprime loans was often held in specialized subsidiaries, but at the aggregate level the systemic risk associated with the excessive leverage through the process of mortgage securitization and the increasing interlinkages between financial institutions (also foreign) had been underestimated and mispriced by the market. In particular, banks had increasingly been using special conduits and structured investment vehicles to fund their mortgage expansion with off-balance-sheet asset-backed securities. This shift in activity away from regulated banks to nonregulated entities had in part been driven by loopholes in bank capital regulation (Acharya et al. 2009). When household defaults started to increase and investors pulled out of these vehicles, banks were forced to take the asset-backed securities onto their own balance sheet (without ex ante capital put aside against these risks), either out of a reputation concern or because they had extended liquidity lines to these vehicles. This created an overhang of asset-backed securities that put downward pressure on the price of these securities and, together with increasing delinquencies and defaults on US mortgages, eroded banks' capital (and market and funding) liquidity. The resulting credit crunch had strong, negative aggregate output and employment effects. However, in the United States there has been an important reduction in household debt over-hang since the crisis through a deleveraging process. One contributing factor to this deleveraging by households is the rise in mortgage defaults, because in the United States a large fraction of mortgage loans are without recourse by the lender. In most other countries, including in Europe, mortgage loans are with full recourse, slowing down the deleveraging process, with negative ramifications for aggregate consumption and employment.

The reliance on asset securitization as a vehicle to spread risks through the system had backfired by endogenously increasing massively the credit supply and leverage in the financial system (Shin 2009) and by creating large cross-exposures among financial institutions. The interaction between falling asset prices and a lack of capital at financial institutions then created a downward spiral in the overall financial system that posed significant risks for the system as a whole through potential spillovers and externalities (also to foreign financial systems). At the individual level, it was rational for banks to sell mortgage assets, hoard on liquidity by pulling out in the wholesale market, and reduce credit supply to increase capital and liquidity ratios, but these individual strategies created negative externalities within the financial and economic system (which were not internalized by individual financial institutions) and were therefore not optimal at the aggregate level, thus creating a systemic crisis.

More recently several euro area economies experienced major boom–bust cycles in real estate (notably Ireland and Spain) that was in large part financed by wholesale funding markets, both through securitization and international banking flows. Once the liquidity in foreign wholesale funding markets dried up, banks were liquidity squeezed, the real estate market boom stopped, the house building driven activity came to a halt, and loan defaults started to arise. There were large liquidity and balance sheet problems for banks, in due course affecting governments. The public sector rescued banks with public recapitalizations, liquidity injections, and explicit guarantees, thus leading to a massive increase in public debt and fiscal contraction, with negative economic effects. Moreover, as banks increased their holdings of public debt, crowding-out effects of private investment caused a credit crunch. The associated concerns about the sustainability of government debt in these and other euro area periphery countries, combined with high private sector indebtedness and local housing busts, created a negative downward spiral by negatively impacting the value of banks' sovereign debt holdings, reinforcing weak sovereign–weak bank linkages. In other European countries with crises, such as Iceland and Cyprus, the size of the banking sector was so large compared to the real economy that large bailouts by the domestic government were impossible. In Iceland, which is not in the European Union, there was a default on foreign bank depositors, and in Cyprus, there was a bail-in of all bank liability holders except for insured retail depositors (with deposits lower than 100,000 euros).

Stress tests conducted by the European Banking Authority (EBA) at the end of 2011 indicated capital shortfalls at EU banks of about €115 billion, though subsequent bottom-up stress tests done in Spain in 2012 indicated that only the Spanish capital shortage could be larger than €50 billion. Yet, with banks becoming increasingly exposed to weak sovereign debt directly through the purchase of domestic government bonds and indirectly through a reduction in the value of government guarantees, the banking system as a whole has become increasingly exposed to systemic risk associated with a sovereign default. The absence of a full-fledged banking union and fiscal union in the euro area (which, if in place, could have facilitated a more rapid recapitalization of weak banks) intensified the weak bank–weak sovereign linkages. The statement by Mario Draghi on July 26, 2012, that the ECB will do "whatever it takes", followed by the announcement by the ECB's Governing Council of the Outright Monetary Transactions (OMT) program on August 2, 2012, allowing the ECB to directly purchase government securities under some conditions, halted the negative spiral, and the decision in 2013 to allow the European Stability Mechanism (ESM) to directly recapitalize banks has been an important step toward using a common pool of resources to recapitalize euro area banks. While so far it has not been made operational, it is limited in scale and scope (it requires the member country to first recapitalize the bank to reach the legally minimum common equity Tier 1 ratio of 4.5 percent before ESM resources can be used, thus placing a large burden on the member country). The absence of a common backstop and common fiscal resources to recapitalize banks partially explains the difference in speed with which the United States and the European Union have been able to resolve their respective financial crises. This absence of a coordinated mechanism for the resolution of banks (that has since been adopted but it not operational yet) has hindered the restructuring of banks in the euro area periphery and dragged down the economic recovery of the euro area as a whole. The US federal government, in contrast, was able to use common fiscal resources to recapitalize banks (e.g., under the TARP program) to jumpstart the financial restructuring and economic recovery. The 2014 Asset Quality Review (AQR) by the ECB indeed indicated capital shortfalls in a number of banking institutions across Europe.

Countries typically resort to a mix of policies to contain and resolve banking crises. The policies can range from macroeconomic stabilization to financial sector restructuring policies and institutional reforms. Macroeconomic stabilization policies include fiscal policy, exchange rate policy, and monetary policy, which in the recent global financial crisis has also included a large component of unconventional monetary policy. Complementing these instruments, restructuring policies range from the recapitalization and reorganization of financial intermediaries (including nationalizations and mergers) to the setting up of asset management companies or bad banks to deal with the recovery of bad assets and generalized debt relief programs to reduce debt overhang problems and to speed up deleverage. The institutional reforms range from reforms in the areas of deposit insurance and bank resolution to structural measures to improve the stability of the financial system. An example of such structural measures is the imposition of activity restrictions on financial intermediaries, namely the Glass–Steagall Act in the United States, which separated commercial banking from investment banking, or more recently the Volcker rule within the 2010 Dodd–Frank Act on limiting proprietary trading for US banks. The related UK Vickers Report proposes to ring-fence retail banking from other parts of the banking firm. Similar proposals have been put forth in the European Union by the European Commission, following the Liikanen Report.[11]

However, despite many commonalities in the origins of crises, existing crisis management strategies have been met with mixed success. Some EU member states have managed to quickly contain systemic risk and its fallout on the real economy, while others have postponed or delayed the resolution of systemic risk, with additional negative consequences for the real economy.

Successful crisis resolutions have been characterized by transparency and resoluteness in terms of resolving insolvent institutions, thus removing uncertainty surrounding the viability of financial institutions. This requires a triage of strong and weak institutions, with full disclosure of bad assets and recognition of losses, followed by the recapitalization of viable institutions and the removal of bad assets and unviable institutions from the system (Honohan and Laeven 2005).

Sweden's experience during its banking crisis in the early 1990s is often hailed as an example of successful crisis resolution. The Swedish government moved swiftly to liquidate failing banks, recapitalize viable institutions, and remove bad assets from the system, avoiding large-scale forbearance and evergreening of assets. As a result Sweden avoided prolonged stagnation that lingering bad assets would have entailed, achieving a quick recovery from the crisis, supported by external demand.

Yet, not all countries achieve Sweden's rate of success. As mentioned, Japan represents the opposite case, with authorities delaying the resolution of insolvent institutions and banks failing to disclose their bad assets (Caballero et al. 2008). Another example is the euro area today, where in part because of the lack of a full-fledged banking union, restructuring of the financial system is progressing at a relatively slow pace. Bank failures in the United States have been much higher than in the euro area where even small (nonsystemic) banks tend to be rescued. And the recapitalization of large banks has also progressed at a much faster pace in the United States than in the euro area, where leverage of several large banks remains high as also reflected in low market-to-book values.

While conventional wisdom would have it that advanced economies with their stronger macroeconomic frameworks and institutional setting would have an edge in crisis resolution, the record during the ongoing global financial crisis thus far supports the opposite: advanced economies have been slow to resolve banking crises, with the average crisis lasting longer than in emerging market economies (table 2.1).

Differences in initial shocks and financial system size surely contribute to these different outcomes. BIS (2011) and Laeven and Valencia (2012) argue that the greater reliance by advanced economies on macroeconomic policies as crisis management tools may delay financial restructuring, with the risk of prolonging the crisis. For example, the central bank provides ample liquidity to weak banks with weak borrowers, who should be denied credit under an efficient resolution procedure, thus generating a weak form of zombie lending.

This is not to say that macroeconomic policies should not be used to support the broader economy during a crisis. Macroeconomic policies should be the first line of defense. They stimulate aggregate demand and sustain asset prices, thus supporting output and employment and, indirectly, a country's financial system. This helps prevent a disorderly deleveraging and gives way for balance sheet repair, buying time to address solvency problems head on and to allow structural reforms in the real sector to gain competitiveness. However, by masking balance sheet problems of financial institutions, they may also reduce incentives for financial restructuring, with the risk of dampening growth and prolonging the crisis. And by providing too much liquidity central banks may plant the seeds for the next asset price and credit bubble (Stein 2013a).

Indeed, crisis responses to date in advanced economies have favored accommodative monetary and fiscal policy, with the increase in public debt and monetary expansion amounting to about 21 and 9 percent of GDP, respectively—compared to about 8 and 1 percent of GDP, respectively, in emerging market economies (see table 2.1). In this context, monetary expansion, measured as the percent increase in reserve money, should not be understood narrowly as conventional monetary policy but also as capturing central bank liquidity support and unconventional measures to the extent that they increase the monetary base.

Advanced economies are generally well placed to resort to macro-economic policies to manage crises without being overly concerned about their impact on the exchange rate, inflation, or public debt. Advanced economies benefit from well-anchored inflation expectations and reserve currencies benefit from flight-to-quality effects during financial crises. Emerging market economies, in contrast, may not have the fiscal space or the access to finance to support accommodative fiscal policy, while excessive monetary expansion can quickly translate into inflation and large decreases in the value of the currency, impairing balance sheets further in the presence of currency mismatches.

Political economy considerations also favor macroeconomic policies over deep financial restructuring policies such as bank recapitalizations. The latter are generally seen by the public as enriching bankers, while accommodative monetary policy, although less targeted to the underlying problem of insufficient bank capital, is more likely to harbor broad-based support: low interest rates will support asset prices for investors and house prices for home owners, and will lower the debt burden for mortgage holders and other debtors.

However, recapitalizations can be done with a strong bail-in from existing bank shareholders and debtholders, and the support of asset prices may favor high income households more than median and low income households. Therefore inequality in a systemic crisis may change not only due to unemployment and other real effects of crises, but also due to public policy. There may be implications for aggregate consumption and recovery from these effects. Indeed some commentators have argued that political economy considerations may imply credit expansions to low income households, and low monetary rates to spur economic activity through bubbles (e.g., Rajan 2010).

Moreover, initially, a country's crisis response will be limited to tools that are readily available and do not require institutional reforms or parliamentary approval. The restructuring of financial institutions will often involve parliamentary approval for government programs to purchase assets or recapitalize banks and the resolution of banks often faces institutional and legal challenges, such as the lack of a resolution framework or the inability to intervene in ailing institutions. For example, many countries did not have the tools in place to resolve complex financial institutions, including nonbanks, prior to the crisis. Macroeconomic policies, and especially monetary policy, will, in spite of all its deficiencies, constitute the alternative first line of defense.

The crisis response during the ongoing global financial crisis, dominated by advanced economies, has indeed relied heavily on monetary and fiscal policy. These countries also used a much broader range of policy measures compared to past crisis episodes, including unconventional monetary policy measures, asset purchases and explicit guarantees, and significant fiscal stimulus packages, in part reflecting the better macroeconomic and institutional setting of the countries involved. These policies were combined with substantial government guarantees on nondeposit bank liabilities and ample liquidity support for banks, often at concessional penalty rates and at reduced collateral requirements. Liquidity support has been particularly large in the United States and the euro area, indicating the significant role played by the eurosystem in managing the crisis. The absence of a common fiscal authority and banking union (at least until November 2014) in the euro area surely also played a role here.

Macroprudential policy thus far has played a limited role in crisis resolution, in part because macroprudential regulatory frameworks were not in place to build up buffers during good times prior to the crisis that can now be tapped into to restore the financial system back to health. An exception is Spain, which successfully introduced dynamic loan loss provisioning rules that forced banks to build up sizable buffers during the boom years that could be tapped in during the ongoing bust.

However, while these policies might have dampened the boom to some extent only and have surely lowered recapitalization needs, they were not substantial enough (as there were only 1 percent of total bank assets) to avoid the use of taxpayer money to recapitalize failed financial institutions. The main effect of this policy nevertheless was positive as it led to an increase in the supply of credit during the crisis (Jiménez et al. 2013).

Additionally some countries, like Brazil and Korea, have had some success in using macroprudential policies and capital controls to limit rapid surges in capital inflows, in an effort to cool off an overheated economy. In these cases macroprudential policies have been used preventively to stave off a looming crisis, thus far with success. However, the test for emerging markets will come in 2014 to 2015 when the US Federal Reserve is expected to tighten its monetary policy.

2.4   Systemic Risk in Financial Institutions and Markets

Systemic risk concerns have traditionally focused on the implications of bank demand deposits for the payments system and supply of credit to the real economy. In practice, this has meant that attention has concentrated on the largest banking organizations. Indeed, since the deregulation that started in the 1980s, the US banking system has become increasingly concentrated, with the largest banking organizations holding an ever increasing share of total assets and deposits. The fraction of assets held by the largest banks, with assets in excess of $10 billion doubled from 41 percent in 1992 to 82 percent in 2011, while the fraction held by the smallest banks, organizations with less than $100 million in assets, decreased from 10 percent in 1992 to only 1 percent in 2011 (figure 2.2). During the same time, the number of commercial banks shrank from 11,463 to 6,290.

However, the advent of deposit insurance, combined with improvements in liquidity management by central banks and the development of prudential supervision and regulation, has significantly reduced the risk of retail deposit runs on insured deposit-taking institutions. Indeed, possibly with the exception of Northern Rock in the United Kingdom where there was no full deposit insurance, widespread retail deposit runs on traditional banks have not occurred in advanced economies since the Great Depression when the United States adopted deposit insurance. As a result discussion of systemic risk has shifted more to issues related to wholesale finance of corporations and banks, and on

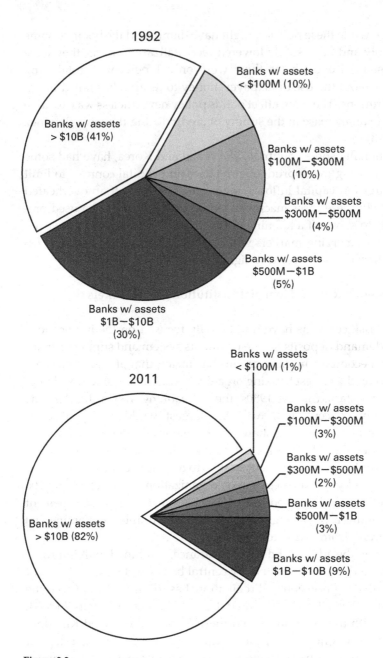

Figure 2.2
Distribution of total assets of US commercial banks, nationwide, by bank size, 1992 and
2011. Source: FDIC Statistics on Banking.

spillovers from wholesale markets to banks. Indeed the recent financial crisis triggered a number of spectacular wholesale runs (e.g., Lehman Brothers and in other financial intermediaries in September 2008), but there were also retail runs (e.g., Northern Rock) that triggered substantial increases in deposit insurance coverage across the world with European countries increasing statutory limits on deposit insurance coverage to 100,000 euros, the United States to 250,000 dollars, and some countries to unlimited amounts (OECD 2010).

Nonetheless the recent crisis has highlighted the growing importance of the wholesale market, including the "shadow banking" system,[12] and the increasing interlinkages between banks and markets (e.g., through asset securitization, asset-backed commercial paper [ABCP], and repurchase agreement [repo] operations), and between different financial systems (e.g., as US money market funds buying European short-term bank debt, German banks buying Spanish asset-backed securities and covered bonds, or European banks financing the US shadow banking system; Shin 2012).

More generally, increasing attention is given to systemic risk arising from nonbank financial institutions, such as large insurance companies and investment banks, as well as from financial markets.[13] Indeed there are renewed calls and proposals to limit the interactions between banks and markets, including restrictions on cross-ownership and proprietary trading by banks (e.g., Volcker rule in the United States, Vickers report in the United Kingdom, and the EC proposals following the Liikanen report in the European Union). Given that threats to financial stability can come not only from banks, our definition of systemic risk spans both other financial intermediaries and markets, and any attempt to measure systemic risk should incorporate interlinkages and spillovers of risk between financial intermediaries and markets.

Moreover, due to increasing internationalization of financial services since deregulation that started in the 1980s, attention has also shifted to the largest multinational financial service providers, including the large European *bancassurance* groups, such as UBS, Deutsche Bank, BNP Paribas, and Royal Bank of Scotland, with significant cross-border exposure and presence in foreign markets, including the United States (figure 2.3). Multinational banks indeed feature prominently among the global list of systemically important financial banking organizations (see table 2.2).

The financial globalization in the 1990s and 2000s, with European banks at the center of the process, affects the synchronization

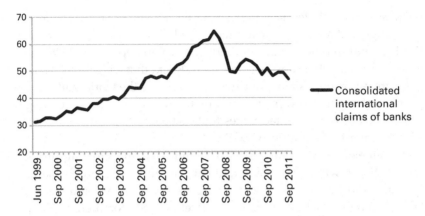

Figure 2.3
Consolidated international claims of BIS reporting banks (expressed as a percentage of world GDP and on immediate borrower basis). Source: BIS International Banking Statistics and IMF's International Financial Statistics.

of business cycles around the world, as shocks are nowadays also transmitted through the globalized financial system (Kalemli-Ozcan, Papaioannou, and Peydró 2013). Indeed Giannetti and Laeven (2012b) show that the internationalization of banking is associated with amplified business cycles.

On the one hand, the empirical evidence on the behavior of multinational banks in their cross-country liquidity management shows that banks might have incentives to repatriate liquidity when in trouble in the home country (Peek and Rosenberg 1997; Cettorelli and Goldberg 2012). For example, using detailed data on syndicated loans, Giannetti and Laeven (2012a) find that banks retreat to their home markets during episodes of banking crises. Similarly Correa, Sapriza, and Zlate (2012) show that European banks faced liquidity drains during the recent crisis if they were exposed to European sovereign distress. The real effects from the transmission of such shocks can be significant: Ongena, Peydró, and van Horen (2013) show that Western European banks created a credit supply reduction in Eastern Europe with the strongest real effects for smaller bank-dependent firms. On the other hand, there is evidence that foreign banks, by relying on internal capital markets, can reduce liquidity and credit restrictions in local economies, as in Italy during the euro area sovereign crisis (see Bonfonfi et al. 2013).

Moreover the largest bank in a country is generally larger than the GDP of the country—this is especially the case in Europe but also in

Table 2.2
List of global systemically important financial institutions, 2011

Name	Country of origin
Bank of America	United States
Bank of China	China
Bank of New York Mellon	United States
Banque Populaire CdE	France
Barclays	United Kingdom
BNP Paribas	France
Citigroup	United States
Commerzbank	Germany
Credit Suisse	Switzerland
Deutsche Bank	Germany
Dexia	Belgium
Goldman Sachs	United States
Group Crédit Agricole	France
HSBC	United Kingdom
ING Bank	Netherlands
JP Morgan Chase	United States
Lloyds Banking Group	United Kingdom
Mitsubishi UFJ FG	Japan
Mizuho FG	Japan
Morgan Stanley	United States
Nordea	Sweden
Royal Bank of Scotland	United Kingdom
Santander	Spain
Société Générale	France
State Street	United States
Sumitomo Mitsui FG	Japan
UBS	Switzerland
Unicredit Group	Italy
Wells Fargo	United States

Source: Financial Stability Board (2011), *Policy Measures to Address Systemically Important Financial Institutions,* November 4, 2011.

other parts of the world. The regulatory framework for banks suffers from the lack of a credible mechanism to intervene early on in failing large banks and the implicit and explicit guarantees of banks, in particular, the too big—or too connected or too complex—to fail problem. As a consequence large banks take excessive risks in the expectation of a government bailout or central bank intervention (Farhi and Tirole 2012a). This moral hazard behavior on the part of systemically important banks endogenously increases the systemic risk to the financial system at large. Of course, smaller banks could take correlated risks (e.g., in asset price bubbles as the recent one in real estate), the government and central bank would then face the too many to fail problem (Acharya and Yorulmazer 2008b), thus leading to ex ante excessive correlated risk-taking by optimal herding behavior in banks. Yet systemically important financial institutions can also fail for idiosyncratic reasons that can cause a systemic crisis.

What sets financial institutions apart from nonfinancial companies is that the threat of bankruptcy is less credible during systemic banking crises, given the strong negative spillovers to the rest of the financial system and the real economy. As a consequence the disciplining device of debt does not function properly in the case of financial institutions. When leverage and bankruptcy enter the picture, the impact of a crisis is likely to be much more severe given the loss absorption capacity of equity over debt. Moreover systemic crises happen after a period of a boom in credit and leverage, thus potentially causing a process of debt overhang, credit crunch, and deleverage once the crisis starts. This partially explains why the recent subprime mortgage crisis in the United States (and likewise the Irish and Spanish crises) had much larger ripple effects on the financial system and the real economy than the dot-com crisis in the early 2000s.

During the subprime crisis, households were holding (mortgage) debt and had to declare personal bankruptcy due to falling house prices and rising unemployment, and banks faced distress as losses on leveraged vehicles with real exposure mounted. This led to fire sales in real estate prices, to more defaults, and to a reduction in aggregate consumption and unemployment (Mian and Sufi 2010, 2011, 2014a). The reduction of leverage following the onset of the crisis came about through a reduction in consumption and investment to pay down debts and a reduction in credit supply by banks that tried to boost capital-to-asset ratios. However, at least in the United States, an important part of the deleraging process also resulted from mortgage defaults because these loans were without full recourse (unlike in most other countries). In contrast, during the dot-com crisis, losses were to a large extent absorbed by investors (households, pension funds, and mutual funds) holding shares. It is excessive debt that leads to bankruptcy, deleveraging, credit crunches, and debt overhangs, causing aggregate economic and financial distress. Mian and Sufi (2010) argue that most of the negative real costs during the crisis in the United States could have been avoided by subsidizing the household (as opposed to the banking) sector, as the large leverage boom in the United States was concentrataed in household debt and these debt overhang problems led to a strong reduction in aggregate consumption and employment.

Given the potentially disastrous real consequences associated with widespread bankruptcies of financial institutions, governments and central banks generally intervene heavily in the financial system to prevent them. Lehman Brothers was a notable exception, and a costly reminder of these consequences. The negative effects of bankruptcies operate through two channels. First, bankruptcy immediately generates the counterparty risk of creditors' claims, posing capital problems to other financial institutions—the so-called first-round effects. Second, bankruptcy immediately reduces the value of capital and assets as they are sold at fire sale prices and appropriated by other holders or managers at liquidation values below going concern values. Moreover the banks directly exposed to the failed institution could trigger further negative effects. All these indirect effects may lead through different contagion channels to a decrease in market and funding liquidity to other financial intermediaries—the so-called second-round effects— which could be more devastating than the first-round effects. Similarly, if the firm enters receivership, asset values are reduced because they stop generating returns.

Insolvency procedures may vary from country to country, an important institutional dimension that will be explored in more detail in chapter 8, with some countries having bank specific bankruptcy procedures, such as the prompt corrective action system in the United States allowing regulators to write down shareholder values to zero, and to possibly impose losses on unsecured debt claims. At the time of the recent crises, regulators in many other countries were not equipped with an equivalent tool and could only resort to general bankruptcy procedures covering both financial and nonfinancial institutions. Since the crisis improvements, many countries have improved their insolvency frameworks for financial institutions, with the United Kingdom adopting a resolution framework for banks in 2009, Spain adopting a resolution framework in 2012, and the European Union adopting a banking union with a European-wide resolution mechanism (in addition to a supervisory framework). Additionally schemes for the implementation of good bank–bad bank structures to facilitate purchase and assumption transactions, as currently in place in the United States, are being proposed around the world.

Banking crises are, in part, a costly affair because regulators find it politically difficult to intervene early on in failing banks. By allowing problems to linger and using a piecemeal approach to crisis management, the ultimate fiscal and economic costs associated with a banking crisis can be significantly higher ex post. The most recent financial crisis has shown that large banks are deemed too big to fail and, when they do fail, too complex to close. The challenge is that large banks are by definition deemed systemically important. The too big to fail problem in banking is not new. For example, US regulators allowed large US banks to grow out of the Latin American debt crisis of the 1980s by temporarily not enforcing regulatory rules, known as regulatory forbearance. However, with banks growing ever larger and more complex from an organizational and product line point of view, the too big to fail problem has become more significant, including because of the enhanced political clout that larger banks have over politicians, with negative ramifications for systemic risk in the financial system. This may lead, as explained previously, to moral hazard problems that could ex ante generate or at least increase excessive bank risk-taking.

2.5   Measuring Systemic Risk

While the definition of systemic risk given above is clear, it is also rather abstract. After all, financial institutions and markets are continuously hit by shocks, originating either in the real sector or in the financial system itself, but only a minority of such cases are systemically important and result in financial crises. Further complicating the matter is that monetary and regulatory authorities traditionally tend to react to the threat of a systemic event—Lehman's bankruptcy being a rare exception in a history of bailouts of large, systemic financial institutions—so that it is seldom the case that we observe a purely systemic event (Goodhart et al. 1995). We rather observe both the illness and its cure. Moreover shocks generally build up endogenously over time.

In order to measure and control systemic risk, it must be made operational. This requires a quantification of the probability that a financial shock may take on systemic proportions. To this end, it is useful to distinguish between direct and indirect transmission effects, as well as between the breadth and depth of the shock. The breadth of a shock can be defined as the fraction of financial institutions and markets simultaneously affected while the depth can be defined as the fraction of institutions or markets subsequently affected by the shock during the transmission phase. Thus a systemic risk event can be viewed as a shock for which the direct and transmission effects are broad and deep enough to severely impair, with high probability, the allocation of resources and risks throughout the financial system, creating important negative spillovers to real economic systems.

The likelihood of a shock becoming systemic as well as the magnitudes of its direct and transmission effects depend on financial institutions' interdependencies. After all, for externalities between financial institutions to exist, institutions must be interdependent in some way. Interdependencies can be either direct or indirect; the size of a financial institution's total interdependencies (the sum of direct plus indirect interdependencies) with other financial institutions and the relative strength of these interdependencies across institutions will be the key determinants of whether a shock to the financial system has the potential to become systemic.

Direct interdependencies arise from inter-firm balance sheet exposures. Examples include exposures arising from short-term interbank loans, or counterparty credit exposures on derivatives and, to a lesser extent, repurchase agreements. Large direct interdependencies can trigger systemic events even in the absence of any indirect effects.

Indirect interdependencies arise from correlated exposures to non-financial sectors and financial markets, such as exposures to the same or similar assets. Examples include asset price bubbles, loan concentrations to the same industry or holdings of government securities, or otherwise highly correlated portfolios. In the presence of such indirect interdependencies it is possible for individual firm risk to move in the opposite direction of overall financial system risk (De Nicolo and Kwast 2002). Indeed, as illustrated by figure 2.4, individual risks of US financial institutions (as measured by the volatility of individual firm stock returns) had been on a downward path prior to the financial crisis in 2008, although interdependencies in the system (as measured by the correlation of stock returns) had been on an upward trend, suggesting that the banking system had become more vulnerable to a systemic shock.[14] This clearly shows that risk in the financial system is not

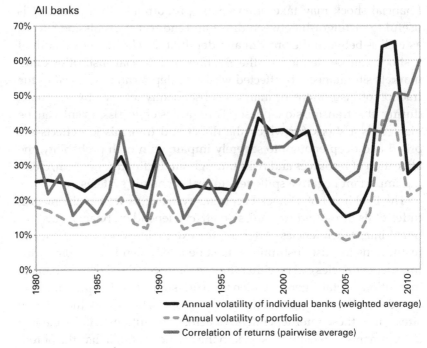

All banks

Annual volatility of individual banks (weighted average)
Annual volatility of portfolio
Correlation of returns (pairwise average)

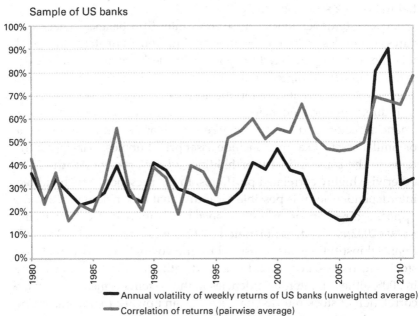

Sample of US banks

Annual volatility of weekly returns of US banks (unweighted average)
Correlation of returns (pairwise average)

Figure 2.4
Volatility and correlation of weekly stock returns, large US financial institutions, 1980 to 2011. Sample of large and complex US financial institutions as defined in Stern and Feldman (2004, p. 39). Sample includes 19 financial institutions: Citigroup, JP Morgan Chase and Co, Bank of America Corp, Wachovia Corp, Wells Fargo and Co, Bank One Corp, MetLife, FleetBoston Financial Corp, US Bancorp, SunTrust Banks, National City Corporation, Bank of New York Company, KeyCorp, State Street Corporation, PNC Financial Services Group, Mellon Financial Corporation, Charles Schwab Corporation, Countrywide Financial Corporation, and Northern Trust Corporation. Source: Datastream and authors' calculations.

simply an aggregation of individual risks but is driven by the collective behavior of financial institutions.

Worse, as we explain in detail in the book, direct and indirect linkages may be the result of endogenous excessive risk-taking by financial institutions that seek correlated risks, and in the process increase their linkages to other financial intermediaries, mainly through short-term debt contracts in the wholesale market and in asset price and credit bubbles (Shin 2009; Diamond and Rajan 2009; Acharya and Yorulmazer 2008b). Models and methods to measure systemic risk and their limitations will be discussed in more detail in chapter 7.

2.6 Conclusions

This chapter has offered a working definition of systemic risk, which we will use throughout the remainder of the book. It has described the key elements of systemic risk, including its time-series and cross-sectional dimensions, and the endogenous nature of systemic risk. We also highlighted the ramifications of systemic risk for financial stability and economic growth, including through an illustration of the real costs associated with previous financial crises. Systemic risk and financial crises that lead to economic recessions or even depressions are two interlinked concepts throughout this book. We next analyzed public policy solutions, including macroeconomic and prudential policies. Finally, we discussed how to make the measurement of systemic risk operational. This will be covered in more detail in subsequent chapters, in particular in chapter 7.

3 Systemic Risk: A Theoretical Framework

This chapter presents a framework for the analysis of systemic risk offering an overall perspective that is helpful both in providing a detailed approach to the analysis of systemic risk and in guiding regulatory policy. Our framework considers the endogenous aggregate (macroeconomic) financial imbalances and the contagion risk dimensions of systemic risk, both of which are not fully internalized by financial intermediaries. The ex ante macrofinancial drivers of systemic risk, contagion risk, and the ex post real macro effects of systemic risk are reviewed in detail in subsequent chapters 4 to 6. Using this framework we analyze both the time and cross-sectional dimensions of systemic risk, and offer a general view that is useful for the study of the externalities and financial fragility associated with systemic risk, the measurement of systemic risk, and desirable public policy responses to mitigate the likelihood and severity of systemic financial crises (which are analyzed more fully in chapters 7 to 11). Unfortunately, there is no unique modeling approach encompassing all the relevant dimensions of systemic risk. Thus we are compelled to present a number of models, each with different strengths and weaknesses. From this collection of modeling approaches and perspectives, we can then take a tentative view of what aspects an ideal model of systemic risk should cover.

Some of the models we will explore emphasize the dynamics, some the general equilibrium dimension, and others the realistic aspects of financial frictions including asymmetric information, endogenous risks, incomplete contracts, and incomplete markets. For our analysis, we are particularly interested in the incentives of financial intermediaries for excessive risk-taking and herding behavior, the endogenous buildup of financial imbalances, the network structure of financial linkages among financial intermediaries, financial relationships, and the role of competition and financial institutions' corporate governance.

There are, in general, two types of models that do not speak to each other. These are extreme opposites: at one pole we have static, partial equilibrium microeconomic models of financial frictions, and at the opposite pole, we have the dynamic, stochastic, general equilibrium models. The static partial equilibrium models typically do not predict the real impact of any shock, since they lack the general equilibrium dimension. Yet they give us sound understanding of the financial frictions and their immediate effects. The macro-based models provide us with a clear perspective on the intertemporal and spillover effects of an exogenous shock to the economy, but finance, in general, and systemic risk, in particular, do not matter much, since financial frictions have a limited role in these models. We could say, in a simplistic, provocative way that static asymmetric information models provide us with the understanding of phenomena we cannot measure, while DSGE models provide us with the measure of phenomena we cannot understand. To be sure, one cannot do public policy analysis without understanding and measuring the specific externalities (market failures) at work. So ideally a third, middle-of-the-road approach would synthesize elements of both approaches. A recent number of attempts at such a model have appeared in the literature (e.g., Diamond and Rajan 2006, 2012; Allen and Gale 2004a), but a truly synthesized approach is thus far still missing.

Therefore, as we compare and assess the merits of the different models as well as their limitations, we will keep to our objective of securing a better understanding of systemic risk (and of systemic financial crises), not of business cycles or of (idiosyncratic) individual agents' incentives. Such a model holds the promise of providing a solid foundation on which to construct a theory of systemic risk and consequently guidance for drafting efficient macroprudential policy.

As a starting point we briefly define the objectives a model of systemic risk should serve. In section 2.2 we turn to the classical static approach to banking crises based on asymmetric information and incomplete contracting. Section 2.3 is devoted to a description of the DSGE models with financial frictions, which allow for a characterization of the general equilibrium effects of a banking crisis and subsequent feedback effects, based on the amplifying relationship between financial and real crises. We do not cover contagion mechanisms, banks' connectivity and the interbank markets, or the recent literature on liquidity risk, as these aspects are discussed in detail in chapter 5. Section 2.4 presents alternative models that afford us some additional insights on systemic risk and are neither static partial equilibrium models based on asymmetric information nor DSGE models. Section 2.5 concludes and provides a synthesis of the traits of such a desirable unified view of systemic risk.

3.1 Modeling Objectives

We start by clarifying the objectives of modeling systemic risk. To do so, we consider a number of features of financial markets and intermediaries that are agreed upon and considered relevant. We begin by reviewing the characteristics of financial intermediation, and in turn the characteristics of systemic risk and crises. This leads us to consider, first, the micro-foundations of financial frictions, then the effects across markets, and, finally, the intertemporal effects, which are the key drivers of systemic risk.

3.1.1 Why Financial Fragility Is Necessary

In the last twenty years a vast literature has firmly established, both across time and across countries, that financial development is a key determinant of economic growth (e.g., see King and Levine 1993; Rajan and Zingales 1998; Beck et al. 2000; Aghion et al. 2010).[1] The efficient allocation of capital to firms and households, either directly or indirectly through intermediated finance, which would allow the funding of efficient investment projects (i.e., those with positive, risk adjusted, net present value) while discarding inefficient ones, is a crucial function the financial system should cope with in any country. In an Arrow–Debreu world, or in a world without capital market imperfections (e.g., complete markets and complete contingent contracts), as postulated by Modigliani–Miller, the financial market reaches the optimal allocation without any help from the regulatory authorities' visible hand (Allen and Gale 2004a).

Nevertheless, once we are confronted with the real world of incomplete financial markets and of information, transaction, and contracting problems for financial markets and intermediaries, these paradigms are only useful as benchmarks. Indeed, as stated by Freixas and Santomero (2004), "financial institutions begin where the conditions for the application of the Modigliani–Miller (1958) theorem ends." Consequently the analysis of banks (and bank risk-taking) makes sense only when the existence of these institutions helps reduce financial market imperfections. Still, the very creation of financial intermediaries may introduce some financial fragility that will require additional regulation to prevent biases and gridlocks in the process of funding efficient investment projects.

Consequently the issue of identifying (and measuring) the key financial frictions that are relevant for the building of systemic risk should be the main objective of systemic risk-modeling.[2] To better see this, we need to consider the role of banks (and other intermediaries) in the economy and why they imply a form of financial fragility. Without attempting at a complete list, we can trace the rationale for banks' existence back to five societal functions:

1. Reduction of transaction costs by building an efficient payment system network and by reducing monitoring costs both in the wholesale (interbank) markets (Rochet and Tirole 1996) and in lending to firms and households (Diamond 1984).

2. Asset transformation, as banks hold long maturity large denominations required by their borrowers while issuing demand deposits (in variable denominations and short maturity) as required by their customers.

3. Liquidity insurance as provided by demand deposits as well as liquidity management. Short-term deposits (and in the extreme case demand deposits) provide liquidity for customers and can also provide incentives for banks to reduce their moral hazard problems (as in Calomiris and Kahn 1991; Diamond and Rajan 2001).

4. Loan monitoring that could either occur ex ante (e.g., the screening of loans by the loan officer), at an interim stage (e.g., the monitoring of the project during the life of the loan), or ex post (e.g., banks being able to specialize and act more efficiently in enforcing repayments by borrowers). As Holmstrom and Tirole (1997), among others, show, bank capital is crucial for bank monitoring and the efficient provision of credit.[3]

5. Risk management, as a well-diversified bank with access to the derivative markets is better equipped to offer protection against risk (e.g., currency depreciation) to its customers.

As a by-product of financial development, the management of risk has become more sophisticated and, as witnessed in the last crisis, the identification of systemic risk and the management of a systemic crisis have become more intricate. Also a fraction of what was traditionally part of banks' business is now being restructured and sold to the market, giving rise to the so-called shadow banking, which includes operations as diverse as securitization, credit default swaps, and investment in or by money market mutual funds, a close substitute for deposits. This process of risk management and risk fragmentation was intended to provide a better assessment of risks by market participants and a better diversification in the financial system as a whole (both bank and nonbank portfolios). Still, the efficiency of this model of risk diversification was conditional on the individual risk assessment being an unbiased estimate of the actual risk which, in fact, depended upon the aggregate risk generated by banks' individual decisions. This was far from being the case during the run-up to the global financial crisis when underestimation of overall systemic and macroeconomic risk led to a bias in risk assessment. Moreover, once risks were being viewed as low due to this diversification of the financial system, financial intermediaries took greater risks via an increase in credit supply with potential negative implications for financial stability as shown by Shin (2009). As we explain in this and the next chapters (see also Rajan 2005), the incentive by the financial intermediaries was not simply to use derivatives and the shadow banking system to do risk management (hedging) but to substantially increase risk, including by moving activity away from "under the radar" of the supervisors (e.g., engaging in regulatory capital arbitrage or engaging in excessive liquidity risk).

These functions lead to financial fragility because items 2 and 3 imply a maturity mismatch that makes banks and other intermediaries financially fragile, with potential funding and market illiquidity implications for the rest of the financial intermediaries and markets; item 1 and the shadow banking system in item 5 imply a network of interbank and wholesale reciprocal (short-term) obligations that triggers contagion and other spillovers in case of a bank's bankruptcy or weak bank fundamentals; item 4 could be disrupted if bank capital is severely reduced thus potentially leading to a credit crunch with substantial negative effects for the economy at large; and item 5 could lead to excessive risk-taking in the aggregate, as each bank only knows the risk it takes and ignores the risks taken by its peers and the negative externalities caused to others in reducing their provision of liquidity and credit in the system, or in taking correlated risks with other financial intermediaries in, for example, lending to a bubble in real estate markets.

Because financial markets and intermediaries (notably the banking system) are fundamentally fragile, it is reasonable to state that some systemic risk is the price to pay for their existence. Yet regulatory authorities were at fault in the recent crisis at three levels: first, they failed to understand the limits of shareholders' corporate governance and market disciplining in the banking sector and some pervasive incentives by banks (e.g., excessive leverage and executive compensation based on short-term profits and share prices); second, they assessed the risks only within the banking industry underestimating the important links with the financial markets for securitization, derivatives and in particular for CDS (naively they thought that these links could in fact enhance financial stability); third, they did not account for the general equilibrium effects of banks' (and other intermediaries') correlated risk taking and hedging decisions (e.g., credit booms in real estate markets financed by short-term wholesale liquidity), something that is now clearly acknowledged with the higher emphasis on macroprudential policy. That is, one part of the financial intermediaries was imperfectly regulated, another important part was not regulated at all, and the interrelations among all financial intermediaries, with respect to the real sector, were basically not taken into account.

3.1.2   Systemic Risk Modeling

In chapter 2 we offered a definition of systemic risk. Such a definition may take slightly different forms but its main characteristics are well defined. Systemic risk is characterized by the financial fragility of financial intermediaries, a general lack of confidence in financial intermediaries and markets, and in extreme cases the impairment of the payment system, all leading to substantial negative real effects. In a systemic crisis the negative real effects can be massive because financial intermediaries can no longer adequately perform their roles in asset transformation and credit and liquidity provision, while their risk management roles can only be fulfilled with severe difficulties.

There are different degrees of systemic risk. In its extreme form, systemic risk would imply a complete gridlock of the banking system with no transactions being made by the banking, wholesale, and payment system. This is seldom the case, as regulatory authorities will intervene before reaching this extreme situation. More often the payment system continues to operate, but banks face huge losses and great difficulties in performing their functions, in attracting funds in wholesale markets and in making loans and also in managing their maturity mismatch.

A systemic crisis will occur when three factors concur. First, the presence of macro fragility makes financial institutions prone to losses in the value of their assets and therefore leads to a reduction in their level of capital. In general, the macro risk is endogenous, stemming from the materialization of ex ante excessive and correlated risks by financial intermediaries via financial bubbles and credit booms. At this moment, which may be due to a relatively small exogenous shock (and this can differ across systemic financial crises), losses start to happen, reducing bank capital and generating losses across the financial system, as the crisis begins.

Second, contagion and other spillovers that trigger the troubles of a bank reinforce those of the others. As interbank and other wholesale markets are crucial for funding liquidity, this wholesale liquidity evaporates as claims are mainly short term. Moreover financial claims come mainly in the form of short-term contracts from other financial institutions because they constitute a cheap source of finance (Diamond and Rajan 2001; Acharya and Yorulmazer 2007; Farhi and Tirole 2012a).[4] Because funding and market illiquidity problems reinforce each other, there is contagion among financial intermediaries and across markets (Brunnermeier and Pedersen 2008). The banking sector and other wholesale markets, reinforced by the strong financial globalization, also determine the financial network and so the stability of financial institutions (Allen and Gale 2000a). In addition the uncertainty surrounding the true exposures and linkages among modern financial institutions—called complexity in Caballero and Simsek (2012)—amplifies banks' perceived counterparty risk in crisis moments, thus generating funding and market illiquidity.

Third, a trigger can take multiple forms but lead to the sudden convergence of investors' expectations in a new equilibrium. This factor in the emergence of a systemic crisis is more difficult to characterize from a theoretical perspective, however there are some theoretical mechanisms. Historically it has taken different forms, the most recent one being the subprime crisis that affected a segment of the US credit market that represents only some 4 percent of the total amount of credit. For example, as in Chen (1997), failure of some financial institutions can lead investors to run on other institutions if they think that banks took correlated risks. This could have implied that losses in the small US subprime market were transmitted to other markets where there was a real estate boom as in the case of the United Kingdom, Ireland, and Spain. It could be also caused by any public signal that leads investors into revising their confidence (private information) in the banking industry as in Vives (2013), which follows Morris and Shin (2004) on how public information coordinates investors with strategic complementarities as in bank runs or currency crises.

As a consequence it is desirable to build a model that takes into account these three elements and the possibility that they concur. Yet a key modeling choice is to be made. Indeed a systemic risk could be seen as a situation of extreme stress within the business cycle or as a point of discontinuity, a singularity, where the usual predictions of business cycle in "normal" times, whether a boom or a bust, do not apply and the functioning of financial markets and institutions follow different patterns. As we will see, some models build on the "continuity" assumption while others consider a switch between "normal" business conditions and systemic events. It is important to understand that each of the three elements reinforce one another—contagion effects are strong when overall fundamentals of financial intermediaries are weaker and, in this situation, coordination problems (panics) increase (Iyer and Peydró 2011)—therefore a discontinuity appears with a strong financial system impairment and negative effects for the economy at large. For example, in models based on coordination problems with global games, weak fundamentals imply stronger runs, and contagion effects; in fact, given the (equilibrium) threshold strategies in these models, there is a threshold on fundamentals such that weaker fundamentals imply a strong discontinuity in financial fragility (see Morris and Shin 1998; Dasgupta 2004).

In the rest of this chapter, we discuss how macrofinancial fragility can trigger systemic crises, and in particular, consider the mechanism through which such fragility can trigger bank runs and banking panics. A more general exposition of the ex ante buildup of macroeconomic financial fragility is discussed in chapter 4, contagion as a trigger of systemic crises in chapter 5, and the real macroeconomic effects in chapter 6. Chapter 7 is devoted to the measurement of the different channels of systemic risk.

3.1.3   Micro-Foundations

The first characteristic we expect from a model, whether of corporate finance, banking, or systemic risk, is that it makes explicit the micro-foundations of the financial frictions. What are the postulates? What is the source of uncertainty (e.g., Knightian uncertainty as compared to risk)?[5] Are there incomplete markets? What is the asymmetric information? Are there problems of adverse selection or moral hazard? What are the incentives of every single agent and how they interact? Are contracts optimally chosen, given the information available? Are contracts and trades optimal given the information limitations and given the general equilibrium effects?

Given some potential market failures and therefore public policy actions, how does public policy affect the incentives of financial market players? All these elements should be taken into account by a theory of systemic risk, but empirical analysis and quantification of each financial friction and the incentives of financial firms and market participants are crucial to build up a (as much as possible) parsimonious model of systemic risk that only encompasses the main elements affecting systemic risk.

3.1.4 Spillover and General Equilibrium Effects

Notice that once we analyze the effect of one market on another, this is a first step toward understanding the interaction between markets, thus departing from the restrictive view of partial equilibrium and setting the foundations for a general equilibrium view. Nevertheless, exploring general equilibrium effects does not represent here a dominating research strategy, as focusing on a subset of markets can offer crucial intuition on how the spillovers operate and how financial and nonfinancial firms as well as households react, a dimension that may be absent in the direct analysis of the comparative statics of general equilibrium. This is crucial for policy-making: on the one hand, without knowing well the externality it is not possible to apply good public policy analysis to correct the market failure; on the other hand, without a quantitative model that incorporates all the general equilibrium effects it is not possible to measure systemic risk and, hence, to do (macroprudential) supervision and regulation. For example, measures that reduce the systemic risk in one market, such as capital surcharges on systemically important banks, can shift risky activities to other parts of the financial system, and while strengthening the stability of the banking system in a strict sense may increase systemic risk for the financial system as whole. The overall effect of such measures can only be analyzed in a model that incorporates general equilibrium effects.

The first type of spillover that comes to mind is the one that exists within the financial sector. Apart from direct financial linkages, how does banks' distress affect the wholesale market, the price of financial assets, the value of collateral through increased haircuts, and the repo operations? Once this is assessed, the feedback of the effects of these markets on financial intermediaries' solvency and liquidity should be considered.

Still, as systemic risk has, by definition, substantial real effects, the same feedback assessment should be performed between financial markets and the markets for goods, services, and labor. So the question here is how the malfunctioning of financial markets can lead to a decrease in GDP and an increase in unemployment. The combination of a decrease of credit supply, credit-rationing, a drop in the value of collateral, with the corresponding decrease in solvent demand for credit, and debt overhang problems in financial and nonfinancial firms and households will lead to a decrease of investment, consumption, and real activity. Again, these negative effects to the real sector will feed back into the financial system (e.g., loan defaults and agents' incentives, willingness and ability to borrow, lend, take excessive risk, and invest).

The spillovers both within the financial sector and to the real sector are different for each financial institution; consequently there is a cross-sectional dimension of systemic risk depending on the risks of financial intermediaries and markets and their spillovers on the financial and economic system.

3.1.5 Dynamic Effects

The second dimension on which it is interesting to expand the basic micro-foundations is across time—the so-called time dimension of systemic risk. Indeed the existence of financial frictions can lead to persistence of exogenous shocks. An exogenous shock can change the value of assets as well as the value of collateral leading to the inability of some agents to access the credit market. As a consequence the economy "fundamentals" may return to its original values, and the shock period will be over but not without diminishing wealth in both firms and households. Borrowers will then face harsher financial conditions in terms of the cost of borrowing (external risk premium) or simply because their credit is rationed. The combination of intertemporal and across market spillovers can occur quite naturally because markets can adjust with a lag creating persistence and amplification. As we explain later, financial intermediaries and markets are not a simple amplification mechanism of exogenous (productivity) shocks; they are instead first-order generators of business cycles and booms/crises due to their endogenous buildup of excessive risks (e.g., with credit supply booms and asset price bubbles) as in Adrian and Shin (2011).

3.2 Asymmetric Information and Incomplete Contracting Approach to Financial Fragility and Systemic Risk

As mentioned before, the role that financial intermediaries play in reducing transaction costs, providing asset transformation, and taking maturity and liquidity risks exposes them to the possibility of a financial crisis. Moreover, as we will explain more fully in chapter 4, pervasive incentives due to some public policy (e.g., deposit insurance or bailouts), excessive banking competition (notably increased by deregulation and globalization), and deficient corporate governance in banking (including massive short-term leverage) can provide incentives for correlated risks that increase excessively systemic risk.[6] In fact the likelihood of a banking crisis depends on the overall macrofinancial conditions, and these can be endogenous, because, for instance, financial intermediaries invest in asset bubbles fueled by credit booms. Of course, macro conditions can change exogenously, as has been the case historically because of wars or bad harvests.

A natural way to view systemic risk is, despite all its limitations, to consider an economy with a unique bank. This representative bank will be subject to the same liquidity risk as the whole banking system, and this allows us to disregard contagion and focus exclusively on the characteristics of the banking system as a whole. Moreover, we will take the risk of the asset side and the composition of the liabilities as given, so risk is not endogenously chosen by the bankers.

The pioneering article by Diamond and Dybvig (1983) constitutes the standard reference in the analysis of bank fragility.[7] A bank is to provide its clients with the ability to consume at an early period or at a late period, simply because initially the clients (consumers) do not know at which stage (early or late) they will have to consume. Still the bank has the possibility to invest in long-run projects that provide high returns. As it is efficient for a bank to provide liquidity through demand deposits, each depositor will choose when to withdraw its deposits. Because the bank is investing a fraction of its assets in a long-run profitable technology, this allows paying a higher return to long-run depositors that wait until later periods to withdraw. The bank might also provide depositors withdrawing at an early stage with a consumption level that is higher than what the technology permits, as it is efficient to provide ex ante insurance to customers facing a liquidity shock—that is, both early and late consumers benefit from the long-term investment. This offers a justification for banks, in general, because of their role in the provision of liquidity insurance, which provides an allocation that is ex ante Pareto superior to that of a market with exchange of real goods between periods.

Diamond and Dybvig (1983) show that this game has two pure strategy equilibria, the efficient equilibrium allocation and the (inefficient) bank run equilibrium. The latter is also an equilibrium because it will be optimal for each depositor to run the bank (if they think other depositors are also running); otherwise, if it does not withdraw its deposit, the bank will not have sufficient assets to repay the deposits in the future. This is the result of a coordination game that fully justifies bank run as an equilibrium strategy. Notice the interesting property that banks can be ex post either solvent or insolvent depending on the equilibrium we are considering—that is to say, the bank can only fail because of illiquidity, since the bank will remain solvent if depositors do not make a massive run on their deposits. If patient depositors wait, the bank will be solvent; if, instead, depositors do not confide in the bank's ability to repay their deposits in future periods they will withdraw, thus causing the bank to liquidate profitable projects at a loss (fire sales). Clearly, this self-fulfilling equilibrium is inefficient: depositors are better off without massively withdrawing their money from the bank.

The difference between insolvency and illiquidity is nonexistent in the Diamond and Dybvig (1983) model. A bank becomes insolvent when it cannot find the liquidity to repay its customers; it will be solvent if the customers do not withdraw their deposits. Consequently, from the Diamond–Dybvig perspective, systemic risk is seen as a coordination issue and, importantly, the probability of bank failure as exogenous and undetermined, which prevents any public policy analysis. Goldstein and Pauzner (2005) endogenize the bank's probability of failure by inserting the previous model into a global games model, where the optimal strategy is to run if the private signal of depositors about the fundamentals of the bank is below a threshold (a low signal indicates both weak bank fundamentals and that other depositors will also have a low signal, with high likelihood, so they too will run). In this case bank fundamentals (bank capital) interact with liquidity. The higher the bank capital buffer, the lower will be the bank's fragility. Therefore prudential policy plays a role in determining bank fragility.

Another interesting global game approach has been explored by Rochet and Vives (2004) who consider that the bank's investors will receive a noisy signal representative of the bank's solvency. Then the decision of each investor to withdraw affects the decisions of other customers to do so. The bank's investors will indeed become excessively cautious because they face a cost if they do not withdraw when all other agents are withdrawing. The implication is that there is an insolvency threshold that is different from the illiquidity threshold. Banks can, in this view, be solvent from a technical point of view (i.e., they would pay off all depositors if the bank would continue) yet illiquid, and therefore the market will lead them to bankruptcy.

A related bank run-based view of systemic risk was developed by Calomiris and Kahn (1991) and subsequently by Diamond and Rajan (2000). In these two cases, banks' agency problems are solved by the existence of demand (or in general, short-term) depositors. Bank managers in both cases are disciplined because they know that the deviation from the optimal strategy will be penalized by a bank run. Here, in contrast to Diamond–Dybvig, runs constitute a form of market discipline and have a role in improving banks' management—that is, disciplining does not come through "voice" from corporate governance (e.g., in shareholders' meeting) or with covenants, but through "exit" in the form of bank runs.[8] Nevertheless, runs imply, as before, an ex post efficiency loss on the economy if market discipline is imposed when the bank is solvent (but illiquid) and are also socially inefficient if they bring a banking crisis with huge social costs.

However, in this type of model, unlike the Diamond–Dybvig (1983) model, limitations to short-term wholesale depositors will imply inefficiencies, such as a high cost of finance for banks, since short-term depositors are crucial to reduce excessive risks in banks and thus are a cheaper source of finance. If contracts were complete, then there could be other ways to discipline banks and bank managers, and shareholders, without imposing such a high cost; however, in the real world, financial contracts are incomplete and, given the frictions with information and contracts (action or state of nature not verifiable in court), second-best options can bring some important costs.

An alternative view of the disciplinary role of bank runs is suggested by Chari and Jagannathan (1988) who consider the profitability in the return of bank assets. Again, managers' disciplining is important. Here managers prefer to continue managing the bank even if liquidation would increase the value of the banks' assets. The implication is that if customers have perfect information on the bank returns, bank failures are efficient because the value of the bank when liquidated is higher than the value of the bank that is kept in operation. Nevertheless, when customers receive imperfect signals they will incur type-1 and type-2 errors, so some bad banks will be left in operation while some good banks are closed down through the bank-run mechanism. Improving transparency (as in Pillar 3 of Basel II) and forcing the liquidation of some banks (as in the new EU directive on bank resolution) would greatly reduce all these inefficiencies.

The previous models explain financial fragility in financial intermediaries such as banks even in the extreme case of exogenous risks and a single (representative) intermediary. We relax these assumptions on the nature of risks in chapter 4 and consider the issue of multiple intermediaries in chapter 5. Importantly, these theoretical models of bank runs are somewhat at odds with the lack of market discipline by depositors because of the pervasiveness of deposit insurance. In our view, in today's world these models are more applicable to banks financed with a lot of short-term, unsecured debt, such as wholesale funds.

3.3   DSGE Approach to Systemic Risk

3.3.1   Appeal of the DSGE Approach

Dynamic stochastic general equilibrium (DSGE) models compute general equilibrium solutions of a complex, multiple-agents, multiple-markets setup. They encompass agents' preferences, firms' technology, and an institutional framework, and as a consequence allow a computing of effects of a shock (e.g., on productivity), its amplification, and its persistence, describing the most likely business cycle dynamics of an economy as well as the welfare implications of alternative policies.

As explained by Caballero (2010), the canonical DSGE model begins with a neoclassical growth model then developed into a stochastic form. The initial models, the so-called real business cycles, have technology shocks, and households optimize in equating their marginal rates of substitution between consumption and leisure to real wages (determined by the marginal product of labor), and in their choices between consumption and saving, where a household's marginal rate of substitution between present and future consumption equals the rate of return (determined by the rate of return that firms receive on invest-ment). Firms optimize the use of labor and capital according to a pro-duction function. The standard approach in macroeconomics is then to add to this canonical model some imperfections. For example, Galí and Gertler (2007) build a related model and then add money, monopolistic competition (and price markups), and nominal price rigidities (the so-called new Keynesian models). Variants of this new Keynesian model have become the workhorse model in research departments of central banks.

One of the benefits of using DSGE models is that policy measures can be introduced and their effects computed. This way it is possible to measure the overall effects, short-term and long-term (contempora-neous and cumulative) impacts as well as the impact on different markets and variables. Because DSGE models provide precise quantita-tive predictions on the impact of policies, on both the equilibrium path and the way policy mitigates an exogenous shock, these models have become a standard means of representing an economy.

When compared to vector autoregressive (VAR) analysis, the benefit of DSGE models is obvious: while unrestricted multivariate such as VAR describes the dynamic relationship between variables without any link to the underlying microeconomic behavior, DSGE is a micro-founded approach that allows a better identification of the chan-nels through which the effects take place. This structural restriction implies less flexibility but greater internal consistency. Of course, VAR having less structure should better match the data. Still, Smets and Wouters (2003) show that the estimated DSGE model is able to compete with more standard, unrestricted time series models in out-of-sample forecasting.

3.3.2 Financial Frictions in DSGE Models

DSGE models offer a very general framework, so theoretically it should be possible to extend these models to take into account realistic finan-cial frictions. When analyzing systemic risk, these types of models have the advantage that they take full account of spillovers taking place through time (dynamic effects) and among different markets (general equilibrium effects).

Despite these important advantages, a general criticism remains: the model has to be calibrated out of "normal" times parameters, so as to allow a unique equilibrium, and moreover there can be no discontinu-ity between normal times and crisis times. Equivalently, this is to say

that the models are limited to the exploration of linear dynamics around
the equilibrium, while in crisis times nonlinearities will be prevalent.
So, when the model is fitted to the data, as detrending, the elimination
of outliers and the selection of appropriately stable periods or the
elimination of structural breaks are common prerequisites. One should
therefore be concerned that systemic risks are outliers that are simply
not considered in the model.

At their initial stage DSGE models assumed that financial markets
were perfect, focusing on the money market and ignoring all the financial dimensions, but with the development of a credit view of monetary policy, according to which the level of credit matters for monetary
policy transmission mechanisms, the impact of the financial sector and
of financial institutions was beginning to be emphasized. As DSGE
models then failed in predicting the 2007 crisis, or in determining the
best policy responses to the shock, they have recently been evolved to
include details of the financial sector and the limits to financial contracting. So the current crisis induced researchers to develop a financial friction side to the DSGE models, and there has been a rapid
growth of such models with more precise analyses of the mechanism
underlying the financial accelerator. However, a key issue that we
analyze below is whether DSGE models can take into account all the
relevant financial frictions and spillovers that a model of systemic risk
should have.

The main shortcoming of current research on DSGE models is the
lack of a consensus on how best to incorporate financial frictions. The
introduction of a realistic set of financial frictions in our DSGE models
would allow us to explore new areas of analysis and better calibrate
the impact of existing policies, including monetary and macroprudential policy. For instance, it would allow to improve our models of the
monetary transmission channel and to explore the impact of financial
shocks, capital regulation, stress tests, and macroprudential policies on
economic activity. Given these challenges to embed financial frictions
in DSGE models, a key question is whether these models can take into
account all the relevant financial frictions and spillovers that a model
of systemic risk should have, such as the endogenous risk-taking
behavior of financial institutions (which we introduce in chapter 4), the
contagion effects in network models (chapter 5), and the real effects of
a crisis arising from credit crunches or debt overhang (chapter 6).

Before we turn to DSGE models of systemic risk, we need to consider
whether the main shocks are arising from the real or in the financial

sector. In the extreme case, real activity causes changes in financial flows, but not the opposite. For example, if investment only responds to changes in real factors such as movements in productivity, nonfinancial borrowers reduce their credit because they need less funds to conduct economic transactions once there is a negative real shock in the economic system. If this were the only linkage between real and financial flows, the explicit modeling of the financial sector would be of limited relevance for understanding movements in real economic activities.

The opposite case is where the initial driving forces of movement in economic activities are still real factors such as drops in productivity shocks, but as investment falls, the credit ability of borrowers deteriorates more than the financing need after the drop in economic activity. Bernanke and Gertler developed the first model to introduce such financial frictions (Bernanke and Gertler 1987, 1989, 1990). They consider a costly state verification framework where banks have to pay a cost to enforce payment. These ex post monitoring costs imply the existence of an external finance premium, as it is more expensive for a firm to borrow from external investors than to use its internal funds. This external finance premium exists and, in equilibrium, varies with the borrowers' conditions. The existence of an external finance premium led to the concept of "financial accelerator" whereby financial frictions amplify business cycles stemming from real shocks.

Bernanke, Gertler, and Gilchrist (1999) expand this framework by observing that in equilibrium the external finance premium should decrease with net worth while leverage depends on the external finance premium, so the supply of external finance increases with the firms' net worth. The subsequent fall in investment can generate a fall in the market value of assets used as collateral and, in the presence of financial frictions, a larger decline in investment compared to the decline one would observe in the absence of financial frictions. Financial frictions (e.g., those arising from differential costs between external and internal finance due to costly state verification, net worth, and collateral) would then amplify the macroeconomic impact of the exogenous changes.

While these models incorporating external finance premiums have provided an interesting and relevant refinement of the business cycle models, it is not clear that the external finance premium represents the main financial friction in an economy, at least from the perspective of systemic risk. Beyond this price dimension of financial frictions, quantities should be taken into account. Indeed the credit view of monetary policy has established how the impact of monetary policy can originate in the supply of credit (Kashyap and Stein 2000, Jiménez et al. 2012, 2014a). Also credit-rationing (Stiglitz and Weiss 1981) or the changes through the cycle of credit standards (Lawn and Morgan 2006; Maddaloni and Peydró 2011) should be taken into account when considering financial frictions in the economy, insofar as these phenomena are empirically relevant.

The alternative to the external financial premium in the initial models of macrofinance is based on the existence of borrowing constraints stemming from agency problems. Borrowing constraints can be justified by enforceability of contracts, or agency problems that require the borrower to have sufficient "skin in the game." They can take the extreme form of 100 percent collateral, as in Kiyotaki and Moore (1997), and/or a sufficient stake in the investment, as in Holmstrom and Tirole (1997), or simply reflect the strength of firms' balance sheets. As the price of collateral is endogenous, borrowing constraints can also affect repo operations if haircuts are determined in equilibrium as in Brunnermeier and Pedersen (2009). The modeling of borrowing constraints will usually take into account an equilibrium price for the asset serving as collateral, as in Kiyotaki and Moore (1997). Nevertheless, it is clear that any market malfunctioning will have an effect on the borrowing constraints, for instance, because market clearing is based on the available liquidity, as in the cash in the market models, or because endogenously the limited ability of the constrained arbitrageurs (Shleifer and Vishny 1997; Brunnermeier and Pedersen 2009) implies a departure of the prices from fundamentals. Notice nevertheless that this effect can be detrimental or beneficial because distortions in prices can compensate for other market imperfections. This is why bubbles can be efficient in some cases if they allow an increase of an inefficiently low level of credit supply (Martin and Ventura 2012).

If the banks' role in an economy is to reduce market imperfections and allocate funds to the most efficient investment projects, their presence should improve the overall performance of the economy. A number of DSGE models thus embed a banking sector where households deposit their savings that are used to lend to firms, thus introducing a connection between household wealth and credit accessibility. Liquidity and solvency problems would then affect the financial intermediaries and become a new source of fluctuations.

Christiano et al. (2003) expand the standard DSGE framework by adding a banking sector with financial frictions. Goodfriend and McCallum (2007) also introduce the explicit role of banks into the DSGE model by departing from the nonmonetary nature of some DSGE models and introducing money and banking into an otherwise standard growth model. This way they are able to explore the relationship between consumption and the demand for bank deposits through the demand for money and to identify a "banking accelerator" and a "banking attenuator" effect.

Not surprisingly, the new DSGE models that have emerged after the 2008 financial crisis assign a more active role to financial intermediaries. For instance, Gertler and Karadi's (2011) model objective is to assess the impact of unconventional monetary policy through the banking sector. In doing so, they introduce financial intermediaries whose lending depends on the strength of the firms' balance sheet, and thus they analyze the role of central bank monetary expansion in offsetting a disruption in the credit supply. As financial intermediaries may be subject to endogenously determined balance sheet constraints, stemming from their agency problems, the model enables a rich analysis of the interaction between financial intermediaries and the real economy. The role of banks in allocating resources to agents with the best projects is also explored by Brunnermeier and Sannikov (2011). The heterogeneity of investors allows them to consider the impact of the distribution of net worth between more and less productive agents and the impact of banks' credit supply on the overall performance of the economy.

As we mentioned earlier, one of the main criticisms of the DSGE models is that they have to be computed in "normal times" rather than in times of crisis that constitute the outliers. The recent model of Brunnermeier and Sannikov constitutes an exception in this regard. Their model studies the full dynamics of the equilibrium and thus explores the "nonlinearities" (or rather discontinuities and regime switching). They obtain a model characterized by an inherent instability. They show that close to the steady state, the financial system is characterized by low volatility while its behavior away from the steady state has some of the characteristics of a systemic event. Additionally the stochastic stationary distribution is bimodal, so once a depressed regime is reached, it will show some degree of persistence. A similar approach characterizing the full equilibrium dynamics is developed by Boissay et al. (2012) who analyze critical nonlinearities, such as the freezing of interbank markets. This allows them to model systemic risk as the consequence of excessive credit supply in a DSGE model. The Brunnermeier and Sannikov and Boissay et al. models are a clear improvement upon the usual approach of DSGE models that has been criticized because it constitutes an exploration of a linear approximation around the steady state in a world of complete markets.

3.3.3   Criticisms of DSGE models

Despite the increasing attention to financial frictions, we believe there are important flaws in the DSGE models to analyze systemic risk and that we should be skeptical of their ability to deliver realistic models of systemic risk in several aspects. These shortcomings can be grouped into six categories:

1.   No endogenous risk-taking by financial intermediaries   Most of the macrofinance research has focused on the amplification mechanism generated by financial market frictions. The main hypothesis is that financial frictions exacerbate a recession but are not the cause of the recession (Quadrini 2011). However, as pointed out by, among others, Adrian and Shin in the *Handbook of Monetary Economics*, financial frictions can cause output cycles and, in the extreme case, a systemic crisis with strong real effects.

The way that DSGE macrofinance models have generally dealt with financial frictions is to introduce *exogenous* credit or financial shocks. Because of the exogenous disruption in financial markets, fewer funds can be channeled from lenders to borrowers. As a result of the credit tightening, borrowers cut on investment and consumption, and this generates a recession. Financial frictions emerge when trade in certain assets cannot take place (incomplete markets that limit the feasible range of intertemporal and intratemporal trades) or when certain actions cannot be contracted upon (either due to imperfect information or contracting). Agents are then unable to provide the adequate incentives to curtail excessive risk-taking, while anticipating or postponing some spending for consumption or investment, or insuring against uncertain events (to smooth consumption or investment).

In incomplete contracts and markets these frictions are relevant only if agents are heterogeneous (Quadrini 2011; Allen and Gale 2004a). If all agents are homogeneous, there is no reason to give incentives from a principal to an agent or to trade claims. Therefore, contracting and market incompleteness (including problems of imperfect information) and heterogeneity are crucial for modeling systemic risk. A number of new macrofinance models have gone in this direction, such as the models by Brunnermeier and Sannikov (2011), Gertler and Karadi (2011), Gertler and Kiyotaki (2010, 2013), and Jermann and Quadrini (2012).

Although these models incorporate shocks to financial markets and intermediaries, these shocks are treated as exogenous. However, as we explain in detail in this book, the ex ante endogenous buildup of excessive risk is crucial to explain and understand systemic risk. And importantly, the preventive ex ante role of macroprudential policy is crucial when risks are endogenous. If risks were exogenous, ex post crisis management policies would suffice.[9]

2. No excessive credit supply If one reads surveys of macrofinance models such as those by Quadrini (2011) and Brunnermeier, Eisenbach, and Sannikov (2013), one might conclude that there are no DSGE models where credit supply is excessive. However, we argue that ex ante credit booms are crucial to explaining systemic risk, and affect both the likelihood and severity of financial crises.

In fact, Brunnermeier, Eisenbach and Sannikov (2013, p. 83) conclude their survey with: "[I]n almost all of the 'credit models' the level of credit is below first best. These models stress that financial frictions restrict the flow of funds. In crisis times these inefficiencies are amplified further through adverse feedback loops. The appropriate policy response requires the central bank to step in and to substitute the lack of private credit with public funding. This is in contrast to Minsky's and Kindleberger's lines of work. They stress that the level of credit can be excessively high, especially when imbalances and systemic risk are building up during a credit bubble. The bursting of these bubbles can then tie the central bank's hands and impair not only financial but also long-run price stability."

3. No network interactions (and complexity) As we explain in chapter 5, systemic risk cannot be fully understood without considering the network structure of financial connections. These connections can be in the interbank market, in wholesale markets, in derivative positions (e.g., CDSs), and in assets and liabilities. Moreover the network is not exogenous; rather, it depends on incentives such as those arising from policy (LoLR type of policies or the too many too fail bailouts) and may be extremely fragile in times of crisis (Allen and Gale 2000a; Freixas et al. 2000; Caballero and Simsek 2009, 2012; Caballero and Krishnamurthy 2008a, b; Acemoglu, Ozdaglar, and Tahbaz-Zalehi 2010).

A key issue is that depending on the network, systemic risk (the macro real effects) can be very different (as we explain in detail in chapter 5). However, DSGE models generally abstract from the existence of such a network among financial intermediaries, despite the systemic risk that such networks pose.

4. No true "general" equilibrium   In spite of the acronym, one may be skeptic as to whether DSGE models can capture the general equilibrium effects of systemic risk. In order to get some dynamic "general equilibrium" elements, such models leave out crucial financial frictions. In particular, apart from endogenous risk-taking, excessive credit supply, and financial networks, heterogeneity of agents is crucial. For example, the buildup of leverage may vary markedly across different sectors of the economy. In the recent crisis, high indebtnedness is a problem primarily for households in the United States, for nonfinancial firms and households in Spain, and for the sovereign in Greece, although for many other countries the locus of increased leverage was within the financial sector (notably banks). Moreover other important aspects which are not yet present in DSGE models are nonlinearities such as in threshold strategies in global game models, Knightian uncertainty, zombie lending, overinvestment (rather than underinvestment) problems, and adverse selection problems.[10]

To put it differently, a key concern we have is whether the DSGE models can incorporate the relevant financial frictions that matter for systemic risk, including the endogenous risk-taking that we will see in chapter 4, the contagion effects in network models that we will see in chapter 5, and the real effects within a crisis that we will see in chapter 6. We believe that some items in current core DSGE models have to be left out in order to incorporate certain crucial financial frictions. For example, Martinez-Miera and Suarez (2012) leave out some key elements of previous DSGE models in order to have a simple dynamic general equilibrium model where there is endogenous excessive risk-taking by banks.

A recent alternative to DSGE put forward by Goodhart et al. (2012, 2013) uses the framework of incomplete markets. It considers a model that includes both a banking system and a shadow banking system in a two-period framework where all contracts are money denominated and where heterogeneous households and firms can default on their loans. The fact that prices are endogenous in a simplified general equilibrium framework is crucial to the analysis as it allows us to understand when and why a fire sale from shadow banks can occur and the effects on the whole economy. Heterogeneity of agents with different endowments (durable good vs. consumption good) and the two-period dynamics are also important considerations. Compared with DSGE models, the radical two-period simplification has the benefit of focusing on specific market frictions, in this case, those related to shadow banking and households' bankruptcies. This way the model illustrates how market incompleteness distorts the different markets.

Such a framework allows for comparison of different banking regulatory rules (loan to value, haircuts, liquidity and capital requirements, dynamic provisioning) and compute their effects. Interestingly, the authors calibrate their model on parameter choices that trigger defaults in the bad state of the world, so as to be as close as possible to the description of a general equilibrium and dynamics of a systemic crisis. Compared with DSGE models, the model is more tractable and more intuitive, but it is still difficult to understand the underlying driving forces, as it integrates both heterogeneous agents and heterogeneous financial institutions (because of the modeling of shadow banking).

5. Black box DSGE models First, the generality and high degree of sophistication of the DSGE approach, which may be a strength of these models, has its drawbacks. The model can be adjusted until its calibration matches the data observed in the past. So it can partially explain the past but cannot help in devising the right policy for the future. In effect, nothing can be said about the next crisis if it is not identical to the previous one.

Second, because of their complexity, DSGE models appear as black boxes. While it is possible to understand the joint impact of the modeling assumptions, it is without a qualitative view of the underlying mechanisms (that could be helpful in preventing future crises). This negative view of DSGE models is also expressed by Sims (2007) who considers these models to be only "story-telling devices and not hard scientific theories." This is an important point: the main difference from VAR models is that DSGE models impose more structure so as to limit the number of free parameters.

While DSGE models have been helpful for central banks in forecasting and policy analysis, it is not clear that they are useful in predicting systemic crises or in assessing policies that can manage them. In view of this limitation, Sims raises the question of how rigorous it is to "require these models to match in fine detail the dynamic behavior of the accounting constructs and proxy variables that make up our data." If we take this criticism seriously, DSGE models are basically theoretical qualitative models whose empirical results should be taken with caution.

6.   No macroprudential policy analysis with DSGE   If DSGE models do not capture the relevant financial frictions and are to be considered mostly black boxes, then why use macroprudential policy analysis of externalities that depends on these models? Simpler micro-based banking/finance models offer a better understanding of the market failure and the problems that require intervention or more regulation. However, these finance models do not offer the quantitative aspect of DSGE models, so an integrated model of systemic risk should have some simple dynamic "general" equilibrium aspects, leaving out elements from DSGE models that are not useful so as to introduce relevant financial frictions and financial market failures.

As Caballero (2010) explains, focusing on a subset of markets, instead of general equilibrium effects, can offer crucial intuition as to how the spillovers operate and how financial and nonfinancial firms as well as households react, a dimension that is often absent in the direct analysis of the comparative statics of general equilibrium. This is crucial for policy: on the one hand, without knowing well the externality it is not possible to apply good public policy analysis to correct the market failure; on the other hand, without a quantitative model that incorporates relevant general equilibrium effects it is not possible to measure systemic risk and, hence, to do (macroprudential) supervision and regulation.

3.4   Toward an Integrated Model of Systemic Risk

When we put side-by-side the static, asymmetric information-based banking models and DSGE models, the difference is enormous. To be sure, the ultimate objective is the same: to identify financial frictions and understand the implications regarding systemic risk. Identifying the right model to assess the likelihood and the impact of a systemic event may appear as a more limited objective than the modeling of the whole financial market in a dynamic general equilibrium setting, but still the modeling of the financial-economic framework poses a dilemma: either the model satisfactorily explains the implications of a certain financial market imperfection, presumably asymmetric information based, or else it builds on representative agents and is susceptible to being calibrated.

Besides, the very idea of a systemic crisis seems to be associated with a discontinuity. If this is correct, then any calibration of the model in good times is of no use to understanding what happens in crisis times, so DSGE model calibrations are of limited help. In fact the modeling of systemic risk is far from being achieved. Nevertheless, through the multiplicity of both asymmetric information/imperfect contracting and DSGE models, our knowledge of financial imperfections has improved. This implies that it is now possible to use some building blocks of the micro-banking/finance models and use them in the DSGE approach. Alternatively we may generalize and introduce dynamics and general equilibrium aspects in banking/finance models. So partial convergence is possible, but—as we have explained—this implies that some aspects of DSGE models should be left out. That is the good news; the bad news is that such a synthesis is not yet there.

3.5 Conclusions

There is no generally agreed-upon model or framework of systemic risk. This chapter has reviewed the existing multiplicity of modeling approaches and perspectives in the macro and finance literatures to sketch what the ideal model of systemic risk should look like and which elements it should include. We have emphasized that DSGE models, which are appealing because they operate in a general equilibrium framework and therefore are better suited than partial equilibrium models to draw policy recommendations, thus far have not embedded realistic depictions of financial frictions. We call for a middle of the road approach whereby existing partial equilibrium models developed in the banking and finance literatures, which provide a rich description of the different types of financial frictions and systemic risk in the financial system, are generalized by introducing dynamics and general equilibrium aspects, such that implications for the real economy and policy recommendations can be drawn.

4   The Buildup of Financial Imbalances

In 2007 the economies of the United States and Western Europe were overwhelmed by a financial (notably banking) systemic crisis, which was followed by a severe economic recession. This sequence of events was not unique: financial crises are recurrent systemic phenomena, often triggering deep and long-lasting recessions.[1] In fact systemic financial crises are typically not random events triggered by exogenous events, but they tend to occur following periods of rapid credit growth and other financial imbalances—notably asset price bubbles—within the financial sector. Conditional on a crisis, these ex ante financial imbalances are associated with higher ex post systemic costs. Therefore it is important for policy makers, supervisors, and academics to understand the ex ante determinants of systemic crises. This chapter offers an overview of the drivers of financial fragility stemming from the buildup of imbalances in the financial sector and its relation with systemic risk.

Because systemic crises arise from the buildup of imbalances in the financial sector, the ex ante prevention of excessive risk-taking and avoidance of the buildup of excessive financial imbalances (not just ex post crisis management and resolution) should be a crucial objective of macroprudential policy. As we explain in this chapter, systemic risk normally arises from ex ante correlated risk choices by individual financial intermediaries (i.e., endogenous systemic risk), not because of risks outside of the financial system (i.e., exogenous risk); therefore, ex post crisis interventions, such as central bank liquidity injections or government recapitalizations fail to address the root causes of the systemic crisis, and can even cause higher ex ante risk-taking by disregarding moral hazard and thereby increasing the likelihood of a systemic financial crisis (Goodhart and Perotti 2012). While ex post policies are important to support the liquidity and capital positions of financial institutions, the flow of credit to the real economy, and asset prices in crisis times, as we will see in subsequent chapters, macroprudential policy applied in booms should be the crucial line of defense to combat systemic risk.

A critical question for policy is therefore *why*—in the first place— excessive endogenous risk-taking and buildup of imbalances in the financial sector occur. Excessive risk-taking in financial (notably banking) markets has been interpreted as stemming from either of two root causes (see Stein 2013a). The first is risk-taking based on time-varying risk appetites—which we term the *preference* channel. To some market commentators, academics, and central bankers, credit and asset price bubbles arise from investors being guided by behavioral finance: not fully rational thinking, such as being overoptimistic in good times and neglecting tail risks or limited memory of previous crises (see Shleifer 2012). Yet some of the fluctuations in the preferences for risk-taking can be fully rational, as in habit-formation models where good times make financial intermediaries less risk averse, and so they search for yield.

The second explanation for the credit and asset price bubbles is pervasive incentives for excessive risk-taking of banks and other financial intermediaries arising from limited liability and high leverage.[2] This alternative view we label the *agency* view of risk-taking.

We believe that one cannot understand systemic risk without this agency view of excessive build up of financial imbalances. First, the basic agency problem stems from the fact that most financial intermediaries operate under limited liability and are highly leveraged, notably in the banking sector. Consequently there are strong incentives for excessive risk-taking. Second, risk-taking could increase because of the presence of explicit and implicit government guarantees and subsidies (e.g., deposit insurance), which imply that financial gains are privatized but losses are in large part socialized.

Indeed the excessive credit boom and lending standards softening in the US mortgage market before the recent crisis could be partly blamed on the financial innovation of an unregulated shadow banking system funded by securitization (including foreign liquidity) to arbitrate (evade) capital regulation, on very loose monetary policy, and on the expectation of bailouts by policy makers (see Pagano 2012 among others). The potential central bank and government bailouts, including a lack of market disciplining by creditors in not imposing losses on unsecured debtholders, lowered the cost of financing for financial intermediaries. Therefore the main deficiencies arise from agency problems not only in the private sector (financial intermediaries) but also in the public sector (central banks, governments and regulators and supervisors), which implies that the political economy of financial regulation is critically important.

It is important to stress that depending on which one is the most important view of the determinants of excessive risk-taking (preferences vs. agency channel), measurement of systemic risk and optimal prudential policy will be different. For example, higher capital requirements would have positive effects whether one subscribes to the agency or the preferences channel by increasing buffers in a crisis. However, it is only in the agency case that higher capital requirements would also reduce ex ante risk-taking.

Financial intermediaries that take excessive ex ante risks increase collectively the systemic risk in the financial system. But what are the specific factors and decisions that cause excessive risks? The main channel is excessive credit and leverage. These variables show the strongest ex ante correlate with the incidence of financial crises in the empirical literature analyzing large historical and cross-country episodes of systemic financial crises. Credit acceleration notably increases the likelihood of financial crises, and conditional on a crisis occurring, it increases its systemic nature and the negative effects on the real economy associated with the crisis. Credit booms, however, can also result from (and promote) sound economic fundamentals (credit demand-driven) and therefore be part of the equilibrium growth path, without contributing negatively to systemic risk. For example, research has shown that since the 1970s two-thirds of the credit booms did not produce financial crises (Dell'Ariccia et al. 2012). Therefore a key interest in our analysis is to identify the determinants of the bad credit booms that cause financial instability.

Credit booms that increase systemic risk generally stem from correlated risk exposures by financial intermediaries that develop into asset price bubbles in real estate and other asset classes. This herding behavior by financial intermediaries can make even small banks (those that do not enjoy too big to fail subsidies) become systemic as a group, since the government may, ex post, bail them out in order to cope with a *too many to fail* situation. Executive compensation based on relative performance, with stock options and lack of claw-back options, and a corporate governance of banks that promotes the maximization of shareholder value—instead of other stakeholders such as debtholders—also encourage this type of excessive risk-taking.

In this chapter we describe the determinants of asset price bubbles. Banks are often important buyers of these assets with market prices above fundamentals. Consequently an important policy issue is whether these risky assets should be financed with deposits and other funds protected by deposit insurance and implicit guarantees from governments, or whether the core deposit-taking and lending activities of banks should be separated from risky financial investments. This has motivated new regulations such as the US Dodd–Frank Act (with the so-called Volcker rule), the UK ring-fencing proposal known as Vickers report, and the structural reform proposals by the European Commission following the Liikanen report in the European Union; we discuss them in more detail in the last chapters of the book.

The rest of the chapter proceeds as follows. First, in order to document that systemic crises are not exogenous phenomena, we review empirical evidence on the ex ante correlates and determinants of systemic financial crises. Given that financial crises are not high-frequency events, we draw mainly on empirical studies using historical data (more than a hundred years) and a large number of countries. Second, as the overall result from these historical and cross-country empirical analyses is that credit growth generates the best predictive signals of strong financial instability, we proceed to analyze the determinants of credit (including debt and leverage) booms and other financial imbalances. We offer explanations of systemic risk based on both distorted incentives of financial intermediaries (agency) and behavioral reasons (preferences). We then discuss and provide micro evidence on the main factors in the agency channel that explain excessive systemic risk: competition, financial deregulation (liberalization) and political economy constraints, corporate governance of the banking sector and the lack of market discipline, financial innovation (securitization), and the macroeconomic environment. Finally, we analyze the determinants of asset price bubbles, and we then provide concluding remarks.

4.1 Ex ante Correlates of Systemic Financial Crisis

The global financial crisis of 2008 is described as being the worst global financial crisis since the Great Depression. The evidence supports this characterization because, seven years after the start of the crisis, many countries have not reached pre-crisis levels in terms of aggregate output per capita, and others face persistent problems of unemployment.

Because there is a great time gap between systemically important financial crises (i.e., financial crises are rare events), an empirical analysis requires the use of datasets that span across many years and countries (see Gorton and Metrick 2012).[3] Moreover crises tend to occur in waves, sharing many phenomena. Therefore it is important to empirically analyze long historical time series and long cross-country episodes over the last forty years to pin down the ex ante correlates of systemic financial crises. We explain in this section the ex ante correlates that are the potential drivers of systemic risk.

4.1.1 Large Historical and Cross-country Datasets

Reinhart and Rogoff in a set of papers and Schularick and Taylor (also with Jordà) (2012, 2014) in another set have analyzed long historical time series about credit, where Reinhart and Rogoff focus on public and private debt and Schularick and Taylor on bank credit. These papers show a strong correlation between ex ante credit booms (as well as debt and leverage) and the likelihood of subsequent banking crises. Moreover, conditional on a crisis, ex ante credit booms make the ex post systemic costs higher.

Reinhart and Rogoff (2008) define a banking crisis by the occurrence of bank runs with some failures or if there are no runs, the closure, merging, takeover, or large-scale government assistance of an important financial institution (or group of institutions) that marks the start of a string of similar outcomes for other financial institutions.[4] They find that the historical incidence of banking crises is about the same for high-income economies as for emerging markets, and that the incidence varies strongly over time. For example, in the period between 1945 and 1975 there are basically no banking crises in high-income countries as this was a period of extreme financial regulation after the Great Depression. Reinhart and Rogoff find that on average banking crises follow strong external debt increases and that banking crises often lead to sovereign debt crises. The results suggest that ex ante private leverage stepped up the banking crises, and that public debt crises were just a consequence rather than a cause of banking crises.

Schularick and Taylor (2012) discern another aspect of systemic financial crises in analyzing aggregate bank credit growth and financial

crises. They build an excellent 140-year panel dataset over the 1870-
2008 period for fourteen developed countries.[5] Their dataset is unique
in that they assess the structure of bank credit and bank-asset series for
each country.

They find that prior to the Great Depression, money and credit
aggregates were stable with relation to GDP. All three increased sharply
just before the Depression and then collapsed in its aftermath. As
pointed out by Schularick and Taylor, prior to 1950 the stability of these
series would be consistent with the monetarist view, and would not
suggest any need to analyze broader credit aggregates. Credit is just
the asset item in the balance sheets and money is the liability counterpart. This is the view that most central banks would hold until recently,
even though the authors show that the post-1945 era was characterized
by bank loans and assets increasing relative to GDP, while broad money
relative to GDP remaining stable. As credit began to be disengaged
from broad money, it could grow rapidly, via increased bank leverage
and nonmonetary funding.

Schularick and Taylor also explore the likelihood and severity of
financial crises. They use financial and macro variables in an *early-
warning signal* approach to predict a financial crisis. The results show
that bank credit booms are a strong predictor of financial crises. Instead,
broad money aggregates do not have the same predictive power,
notably in the post-WWII period. The historical evidence presented by
Schularick and Taylor implies that pre-crisis bank credit booms are the
most important ex ante correlate of financial crises.

Given the importance of credit booms for financial crises, what is
the role of credit in business cycles, and do crises that were preceded
by strong credit booms have worse economic outcomes? As we
explained in the two introductory chapters of the book, it is important
to know whether financial crises are just a consequence of business
cycles, or whether they shape business cycles and can cause economic recessions and depressions. Moreover macroprudential policy
is justified by the strong negative externalities from the financial to the
real sector associated with banking crises. Do these strong systemic
costs depend on the credit and leverage booms preceding banking
crises?

Jordà, Schularick, and Taylor (2013) analyze these questions with a
focus on private credit overhang. Based on 200 recession episodes in
their sample of 14 advanced countries over 140 years, they document
that financial crises as compared to normal recessions are more costly

in terms of aggregate output lost, and for both types of recessions, larger ex ante credit expansions tend to be followed by deeper recessions and slower recoveries.[6] They indeed show that "credit bites back."

Financial factors play an important role in the modern business cycle, as they show that the financial imbalances built up in the period preceding the crisis are important drivers of the strong negative real effects to the economy during the crisis. Not only do ex ante credit booms affect the likelihood of a financial crisis, but conditional on a crisis, the real effects are worse when the crisis is preceded by a credit boom. In this regard their historical analysis corroborates the view that ex ante financial imbalances are a first-order determinant of systemic risk.

Their findings that credit dynamics shape the business cycle suggest that credit is not merely a secondary phenomenon. If credit were to just follow strong economic fundamentals (credit demand-driven), then models that omit banks and credit supply may be sufficient. However, these historical findings suggest that credit plays an independent role in driving the aggregate economy, and thus that more sophisticated macrofinance models are needed, as we argued in chapter 3.

Jorda, Schularick, and Taylor (2013) also analyze the effects of leverage in normal and financial crisis recessions. The latter ones are more painful, as the aftermath of leveraged booms is associated with worse growth, investment spending, and credit growth. If the recession coincides with a financial crisis, these effects are compounded and typically accompanied by marked deflationary pressures.

They find that the buildup of credit in the boom increases financial fragility, though their results are not about the causes of credit booms, nor can they make strong causality inferences on the net effects of credit. Nevertheless, their overall results are generally supportive of the idea that financial factors play an important cyclical role. Potential explanations for these effects, as the authors argue, include financial accelerator effects, debt-overhang problems or that shifts in expectations have more negative effects when credit booms have risen in a more extreme way. We review the different channels later in this chapter and in other chapters of the books (especially in chapter 6 on the costs of systemic financial crises).

The same set of authors present another interesting study (Jorda, Schularick, and Taylor 2011) in which they use the same dataset to explore whether ex ante external imbalances increase the risk of financial crises or only ex ante credit booms. They find that ex ante credit growth is the single best predictor of financial crises, but the correlation between credit booms and current account imbalances has grown much tighter in recent decades.[7] Moreover loan growth is significantly higher before national ("isolated") crises and before global crises. The current account deteriorates in the run-up to normal crises, but the evidence is inconclusive in global crises, possibly because both surplus and deficit countries are involved in a global crisis. Importantly, the interest rate was low in the run-up to the four global crises in their sample.

The final part of the Jorda, Schularick, and Taylor paper addresses the question of whether widening external imbalances constitute a warning signal for policy makers that financial instability risks are on the rise. Just as we noted earlier, ex ante credit growth—not the current account—proved to generate the best predictive signals of financial instability. In a globalized economy with free capital mobility, credit cycles and foreign capital flows have the potential to reinforce each other more strongly than otherwise. A strong and sustained credit boom cannot be financed with local increase of deposits and wealth (especially if not driven by very strong fundamentals); foreign liquidity, or liquidity stemming from expansive monetary policy or financial innovation (e.g., securitization), needs to be present and to interact with the credit cycles.

The historical data indeed show that high rates of credit growth in conjunction with widening imbalances pose risks to financial stability. In the recent crisis the credit booms and large current account imbalances in many countries, low levels of short-term (monetary) and long-term rates, and increasing recourse to securitization combined to capital inflows generated substantial systemic risk. Maddaloni and Peydró (2011) analyze these trends with a survey of lending conditions and standards for the euro area countries and United States that the national central banks and regional Feds request from banks. In particular, they explore the determinants of soft lending conditions and standards for the financial crisis that started in 2007. They find that countries with worse economic performance during the crisis are those with ex ante softer lending conditions. They find that current account deficits or lower long-term interest rates do *not* correlate with softer lending conditions.

The historical evidence on financial crises exists only for a relatively short panel of countries, heavily dominated by high-income countries. Large cross-country analyses albeit over a shorter period of time are also important to analyze financial crises. Laeven and Valencia (2008, 2013) provide a comprehensive database on systemically important banking crises during the more recent period 1970 to 2011 and some stylized facts associated with these banking crisis episodes. They propose a methodology to date banking crisis episodes based not only on subjective measures of financial distress in the banking system (as in Reinhart and Rogoff 2008) but also on objective measures of policy responses to support the financial sector, including deposit freezes and/or bank holidays, bank nationalizations, bank recapitalizations, and other restructuring costs, liquidity support, government guarantees, and asset purchases. They further examine the robustness of this approach to modifying the thresholds applied to policy interventions and by comparing their dating methodology with credit and output growth realizations. Their database on banking crises episodes is complemented with dates for sovereign debt and currency crises during the same period. In total, they identify 147 banking crises, 211 currency crises and 66 sovereign debt crises over the period 1970 to 2011.

Besides dating banking crisis episodes, they present information on the economic costs and policy responses associated with banking crises for a subset of the 147 episodes identified, allowing for a comparison of the policy mix used to resolve banking crises and an assessment of the real effects of banking crises. The information on crisis policy responses differentiates the Laeven and Valencia (2013) database from the historical datasets of Reinhart and Rogoff (2008) and Schularick and Taylor (2012) both of which have a longer time series but do not contain such information.

The data collected by Laeven and Valencia (2013) point to significant differences in policy responses between advanced and emerging economies. The authors find that monetary and fiscal policies are used more extensively during banking crises in advanced economies than in emerging and developing economies. One explanation is that advanced economies have better financing options to use countercyclical fiscal policy and more flexibility to use expansive monetary policy. Moreover they find that fiscal outlays associated with financial sector interventions (including bank recapitalizations with public funds) in advanced economies are about half those in emerging and developing economies, despite relatively larger banking systems in advanced economies. This is consistent with the greater reliance on expansive macroeconomic policies in advanced economies, which indirectly also support the financial sector.

They also find that advanced and emerging economies tend to experience larger output losses than developing economies. These larger output losses are to some extent driven by deeper banking systems, which make a banking crisis more disruptive (see also Kroszner, Laeven, and Klingebiel 2007 who use a shorter sample). Advanced economies also experience larger increases in public debt than emerging and developing economies, which may be associated with a greater use of countercyclical fiscal policy. Although expansionary macroeconomic policies indirectly support banks by enhancing their growth prospects, such policies can slow down actual bank restructuring.

Laeven and Valencia also compare the output losses across different types of financial crises and find that sovereign debt crises tend to be more costly than banking crises, and these in turn tend to be more costly than currency crises. Moreover output losses associated with twin crises are more severe than those corresponding to standalone crises.

The recent global crisis has also sparked interest in the relationships among income inequality, credit booms, and financial crises. Rajan (2010) and Kumhof et al. (2015) suggest that a rising income inequality led to a credit boom and eventually to a financial crisis in the United States in the first decade of the twenty-first century, as it did in the 1920s. However, Bordo et al. (2001) using data from 14 advanced countries between 1920 and 2000, suggest that the previous findings on those two crises for the United States are not universal. The results suggest that credit booms heighten the probability of a banking crisis, but not a rise in income inequality. Instead, they find that low interest rates and economic expansions are the only two robust determinants of credit booms, namely the familiar boom–bust pattern of declines in interest rates, strong growth, rising credit, asset price booms, and financial crises.

Using a sample of 57 emerging market economies and 22 advanced economies over the 1973 to 2010 period, Gourinchas and Obstfeld (2012) also find that the rapid buildup of leverage is important for the likelihood of financial crisis. They find that domestic credit expansion and real currency appreciation have been the most robust predictors of financial crises, regardless of whether a country is emerging or advanced. For emerging economies moreover, higher foreign exchange reserves predict a sharply reduced probability of a subsequent crisis.

Credit booms are clearly a critical ex ante correlate of financial crises. But do all credit booms end up in a crisis? Dell'Ariccia et al. (2012)

analyze credit booms for 170 countries over the last forty years of data. Their study does not condition on the occurrence of crises; instead it analyzes all countries and all credit booms, both with and without crises.

A key initial question for this study and more generally is how to define credit booms. Credit booms are episodes with abnormal positive deviations in credit over economic activity.[8] Most methodologies in the literature compare a country's credit-to-GDP ratio to its trend.[9] A definition of credit booms that can be more easily used in real time should be based on absolute thresholds for credit growth (Dell'Ariccia et al. 2012). Of course, another way to analyze credit booms is one based on asset pricing (Stein 2013a) where the key variable is the variation in the pricing of credit risk over time. However, prices could be low and still there may not be a boom, and then there is the problem that asset prices for credit-related claims are not readily available for many countries.

Dell'Ariccia et al. (2012) identify credit boom episodes by comparing the credit-to-GDP ratio in each year t and country i to a backward-looking, rolling, country-specific, cubic trend estimated over the period between years $t - 10$ and t. They classify an episode as a boom if either (1) the deviation from trend is greater than 1.5 times its standard deviation and the annual growth rate of the credit-to-GDP ratio exceeds 10 percent, or (2) the annual growth rate of the credit-to-GDP ratio exceeds 20 percent. Because only information on GDP and bank credit to the private sector available at time t is used, this definition can be made operational in real time. They apply this definition to their 170-country, 40-year sample, identifying 175 credit boom episodes, which translates into a 14 percent probability of a country experiencing a credit boom in a given year.

Dell'Ariccia et al. (2012) find the following stylized facts: (1) the median boom lasts three years, with the credit-to-GDP ratio growing at about 13 percent per year; (2) credit booms are not a recent phenomenon, but the fraction of countries experiencing a credit boom in any given year has seen an upward trend since the financial liberalization and deregulation of the 1980s (reaching an all-time high in 2006 in the run-up to the last global financial crisis); (3) most booms happen in middle-income countries, consistent with the importance of catching-up effects, yet high-income countries are not immune to booms, suggesting that other factors are also at play; (4) more booms happen in relatively undeveloped financial systems; (5) Eastern Europe stands out in the later period with a disproportionately higher frequency of booms relative to other regions, reflecting the expansion of the European Union and the associated integration and catching up that fueled booms in many of the new or prospective member states, and pointing to the possibility of financial integration as a driver of credit booms; and, importantly, (6) one in three credit booms end up in financial crises.

Contrary to the aforementioned analyses using historical data, Claessens et al. (2010b) perform a cross-country analysis of the global financial crisis of 2008, studying 58 advanced countries and emerging markets in total. Their main conclusion is that the crisis rooted in a number of factors, some common to previous financial crises and others new. Factors common to other crises, like credit booms, asset price bubbles, and current account deficits, help explain cross-country differences in the severity of economic impacts. New factors, such as increased financial integration and dependence on wholesale funding, help account for the amplification and global spread of the crisis.

They find that those countries with a closer link with the US financial system (or direct exposure to the MBS market) were the first to be affected. Moreover those countries with home-grown imbalances such as rapid credit and high leverage growth, asset price bubbles, and current account imbalances, were the most severely hurt. Their results suggest early warning indicators such as asset price bubbles (especially if fueled by credit growth), accumulation of credit and debt, increasing dependency on external and wholesale funding, and failure to build up fiscal room in good times.[10]

4.1.2 Limitations of Historical and Cross-country Datasets

Because financial crises are relatively rare events, we looked at long historical time series and long cross-country analyses. Credit booms are crucial for systemic crises, but—as the literature shows—many credit booms do not end up in crises. The drawback with the research methodology thus far is that only aggregate data are used based on long historical or cross-country datasets. As a result the excessive risk-taking or "bad" credit booms are not isolated from "good" credit booms based on solid economic fundamentals (good investment opportunities).

We therefore reviewed studies that consider a few systemic crisis episodes and depend on disaggregated micro datasets, which allow a better understanding of the determinants of dangerous credit booms: disentangling credit supply and demand; compositional changes in credit (including excessive risk-taking); lending standards including conditions related to loan volume, spread, maturity, covenants, and collateral; correlation among the different loans (diversification or lack thereof); liability-based leverage—in particular, short-term wholesale leverage—and the network of (direct and indirect) exposures among financial institutions.

Understanding the determinants of potentially dangerous credit booms and excessive risk-taking is crucial not only for academics (testing the different theories) but for policy makers as well, since causality is needed to design the best preventive policy tools. Disaggregated micro data help in identifying empirically the causes of credit cycles and other financial imbalances, as we will see in this chapter. Credit booms are not random phenomena; the financial imbalances built up in the financial sector are largely based on endogenous risk decisions taken collectively as a response to changes in the macro, financial, and regulatory environment, which change the explicit and implicit incentives of financial intermediaries on excessive risk-taking.

Disaggregated credit data (coupled with exogenous shocks) are used to distinguish between causality and correlation. Research based on long historical or cross-country datasets delivers evidence based on suggestive correlations but not conclusive evidence based on causal inference. For early warning signals, correlations are enough as they help predict systemic risk. However, to change pervasive incentives, the policy maker needs to know what the exact determinants of the excessive risk in the financial institutions are. For example, whether an increase of capital requirements reduces ex ante excessive risk-taking or instead reduces credit supply can only be answered with micro level analysis.

In the next sections, where we discuss the determinants of credit booms and other financial imbalances that policy makers and academics have proposed, we provide a summary of the main empirical research papers using micro data.

4.2   Determinants of Credit Booms and Other Imbalances

The general result from large historical and cross-country empirical analyses is that excessive credit growth generates the best signals of impending financial instability. This observation in turn raises the question of why there are credit booms and why lending standards and conditions vary over the cycle.

Again, we need to consider the interactions of preference (beliefs) and agency (incentives) views to understand the dynamics of excessive risk-taking in credit markets. Then again, there can be agency problems between banks and debtholders, as banks are highly leveraged and benefit from implicit and explicit government guarantees.

4.2.1 The Preference Channel

Lending standards change over time and reflect fluctuations in the preferences and beliefs of financial intermediaries' managers and also final-investors such as households, where beliefs concerning economic prospects may or may not be fully rational. Credit is abundant and cheap when managers' and households' risk tolerance is high, which could be due to a recent run-up in wealth. Habit-formation models have this property (Campbell and Cochrane 1999; Stein 2013a). And credit is also abundant and cheap when managers and households extrapolate current good times into the future and neglect low-probability tail risks as in theories of behavioral finance.[11]

Campbell and Cochrane (1999) develop a model in which investors have time-varying risk aversion, stemming from the assumption that investors' utility functions depend on the past history of aggregate consumption, whereby their motive may be "to keep up with the Joneses." Investors become risk averse in recessions, when their consumption is low relative to past aggregate consumption. They are less risk averse in booms, when consumption is high, and risk-taking may feel less intimidating. These pro-cyclical movements in risk tolerance allow investors to be compensated for holding risky assets in recessions. Thus the model generates expected returns that are high in recessions and higher risk-taking in booms. A lending boom may occur in a period where returns on credit claims are too low (Stein 2013a).

Manganelli and Wolswijk (2009) analyze spreads between euro area government bond yields before the Great Depression under the Campbell–Cochrane model. They find that spreads are related to short-term monetary interest rates, market liquidity, cyclical conditions, and investors' incentives to take low-risk spreads when liquidity conditions are abundant. Chen, Collin-Dufresne, and Goldstein (2009) also apply the Campbell–Cochrane model but in their case to corporate bond markets. Yields on Baa-rated bonds are substantially higher than those on Aaa-rated bonds, despite that the default probabilities of Baa are only slightly higher than Aaa bonds. A model with time-varying risk aversion can account for high Baa-Aaa spreads, as defaults of Baa bonds are more likely to happen in recessions, when risk aversion is high. Therefore investors want to be compensated with high yields.

If we depart from fully rational agents, the field of behavioral finance that builds on research in psychology shows how excessive risk can be obtained in booms – as in Robert Shiller's so-called irrational exuberance.[12] The representativeness theory of Kahneman and Tversky (1982) provides a natural means of extrapolating the expectation of investors that trends will continue (see Barberis 2012). Likewise the direct evidence on investor expectations of stock returns suggest extrapolative component (e.g., Vissing-Jorgensen 2004). Extrapolation has also been used to understand asset price bubbles (Kindleberger 1978) and also overvaluation and subsequent reversal of high-performing growth stocks (De Bondt and Thaler 1985; Lakonishok, Shleifer, and Vishny 1994). Data across securities and markets show that price trends continue over months, the so-called momentum, but that prices revert over longer periods (Cutler, Poterba, and Summers 1991). More precisely, investors put money into well-performing mutual funds and into stock funds after the stock market has performed well (Frazzini and Lamont 2008; Yagan 2014). Such phenomena have been described as investors "jumping on the bandwagon" believing that "the trend is your friend," and failing to realize that "trees do not grow to the sky," that "which goes up must come down" (see the review by Shleifer 2012). In the next subsection we discuss different theories of asset price bubbles where behavioral finance may provide the best explanations for their occurrences.

Gennaioli, Shleifer, and Vishny (2013) present a model of shadow banking in which banks originate and trade loans, assemble them into diversified portfolios, and finance these portfolios externally with riskless debt. In their model, outside investor wealth drives the demand for riskless debt and indirectly for securitization. The authors show that the shadow banking system is stable and welfare improving under rational expectations. Things however change when investors and intermediaries neglect downside tail risks because they cannot imagine bad outcomes during quiet times. Systemic risk then dramatically increases.

Gennaioli, Shleifer, and Vishny (2013) argue that the neglect of tail risk is critical to understanding aspects of the recent financial crisis. There is some suggestive evidence that even sophisticated investors prior to the crisis did not consider the likelihood of sharp declines in real estate prices (Gerardi et al. 2008), and have reliable models for pricing securitized debt (Coval, Jurek, and Stafford 2009a). Gennaioli, Shleifer, and Vishny (2013) consider investors who neglect downside risks which means that these investors believe that the payoffs on the collateral in the worst-case scenario are higher than they actually are, so they buy more debt thinking that it is riskless. When financial intermediaries and investors realize that a worse state of nature than they had previously anticipated might occur, intermediaries face massive exposure to that downside risk, which they must bear because they sold "riskless" bonds to investors. Systematic risk becomes systemic in the sense that exposure to macroeconomic risk causes all intermediaries to fail together.

Gennaioli, Shleifer, and Vishny (2013) therefore show that financial innovation provides false substitutes for truly safe bonds when investors neglect downside (tail) risks and that, as a consequence, financial innovation may decrease overall welfare. Systemic risk increases as securitization promotes the expansion of balance sheets of banks and increases financial links among banks, and with changes in investor sentiments, extreme financial fragility arrives.

There are other interesting theories in between psychology and sociology that can, in part, explain financial crises. For example, Benabou (2013) investigates collective denial and willful blindness in groups, organizations, and markets—that is, group think.[13] He shows that wishful thinking (denial of bad news) is contagious when it is harmful to others, self-limiting when it is beneficial, and that contagious exuberance can also seize asset markets, generating investment frenzies and crashes.

For the recent crisis there is evidence of collective overoptimism by the groups who had the most at stake in the housing bubble (consistent with Benabou's model), and against standard views of moral hazard or even herding. Cheng et al. (2014) show that mid-level managers in the mortgage securitization business were more likely to buy a house at the peak of the bubble, and slower to divest as prices started falling, than either real estate lawyers or financial analysts covering commercial property companies. Foote et al. (2012) document how banks and dealers issuing mortgage-backed securities kept a lot of them on their books, resulting in huge losses, and moreover they assigned very low probabilities to adverse outcomes, even after prices started falling.

Berger and Udell (2004) analyze empirically a behavioral hypothesis more closely related to banking that we believe partly explain the pro-cyclicality of bank lending. The institutional memory hypothesis is driven by a deterioration in the experience of loan officers over the bank's lending cycle that results in an easing of credit standards.[14] Specifically, over time banks tend to forget the lessons they learned from their last crisis. The deterioration in loan officer experience is partly due to a proportional increase in officers that have never experienced a loan bust and partly due to the attrition over time of experienced officers who could train them. The deterioration in loan officer experience may result in an easing of credit standards as officers become less able to differentiate lower quality borrowers from higher quality borrowers.

The authors test this hypothesis using data from US banks over the 1980 to 2000 period using over 200,000 bank-level observations on commercial loan growth, over 2,000,000 loan-level observations on interest rate premiums, and over 2,000 bank-level observations on credit standards and loan spreads from bank management survey responses. The empirical analysis supports Berger and Udell's institutional memory hypothesis.

4.2.2 The Agency Channel

While the preference channel is very interesting and there is compelling empirical and anecdotal evidence to support its existence, we believe that—at least for banking—the key driver of excessive risk-taking is the agency channel. The reason is that banks operate under limited liability and high leverage, generating steep incentives for bank management to design contracts that promote risk taking. For example, in Spain before the 2008 crisis (as well as in other countries), loan officers' compensation structures were based on loan volume. This implied an incentive to over-lend to cash in short-term profits even at the expense of future loan defaults. Agarwal and Wang (2009) and Agarwal and Ben-David (2014) apply a model with an exogenous change in the compensation structure of a bank in the United States to show that loan volume incentives encourage excessive risk-taking and increase defaults.

But why do banks choose compensation structures that promote excessive risk-taking by managers such as loan officers? Why is corporate governance deficient in banking? These questions can only be answered with an agency explanation, not with a preference channel explanation (see Stein 2013a).

We believe that the excessive softening of lending standards cannot be explained without considering the agency view. Because credit decisions are almost always delegated to agents inside banks and other financial intermediaries, to identify the causes of excessive risk-taking one has to analyze the incentives of the intermediaries, which are shaped by regulations, central bank policies, accounting standards, financial competition and innovation, and corporate governance (including compensation structures). Many of the incentive problems had already been noticed before the crisis (e.g., see Rajan 2005; Freixas and Rochet 2008) and by others after the crisis (e.g., Stein 2013a).

In financial intermediation, many quantitative rules are vulnerable to agents who act to boost measured returns by selling insurance against unlikely events—that is, by writing deep out-of-the-money puts (see Rajan 2005; Stein 2013a). This implies short-term immediate profits with a long-term risk. Since credit risk in bank loans involves put-writing (as in long-term balloon loans with initial fees), one can postpone defaults by simply renewing or lengthening the loan maturity (loan evergreening or zombie lending). Moreover these agency problems may be exacerbated by competitive pressures among intermediaries and by relative performance evaluation.

The main example comes from the mutual funds literature, where even a small superior performance over the competitors can attract large inflows of new assets under management, which implies higher short-term profits (given that compensation is linked to total assets under management). And if these yield differentials do not reflect managerial skill, but just higher excessive tail risk-taking, then competition to attract assets will only make excessive risk-taking worse (see Chevallier and Ellison 1997 and Stein 2013a).

The classical example in banking comes from Rajan (1994), who asks why bank credit policies fluctuate and why changes in credit policy are correlated with changes in the condition of those demanding credit. As he explains, in a rational profit-maximizing world, banks should maintain a credit policy of lending if and only if borrowers have positive net present value (NPV) projects. Therefore a change in the level of bank credit should be a consequence only of a change in the credit quality of borrowers (the fundamentals, credit-demand driven). In the absence of central bank's monetary policy changes, bank supply of credit should not exert an independent influence on the level of credit.

Rajan argues that rational bank managers with short horizons will set credit policies that influence and are influenced by other banks and demand side conditions. As he shows, this leads to a theory of low frequency business cycles driven by bank credit policies. In addition to maximizing the bank's earnings, the bank manager is concerned with his reputation. A key realistic assumption is that the composition of bank loan portfolios as well as the specific performance of borrowers is not easily observable by the market, but only the bank's earnings.

Consequently bank managers may attempt to shape the market's perceptions by manipulating current earnings in Rajan's model. This is easily done if the bank alters its credit policy. For example, by concealing the extent of bad loans originated by extending the term of loans or by lending new money so that insolvent borrowers can pay their current loans, or weakening covenants so as to avoid recognizing default, namely loan evergreening or zombie lending.[15] Similarly the bank may pursue a soft credit policy that generates substantial up-front fees at the expense of future credit quality.

These credit policies boost current earnings at the expense of future earnings. The market is more forgiving of a bank's poor performance if it knows that the entire economy has been hit by a systematic adverse shock. When multiple banks lend to a sector, the market learns something about the systematic component of uncertainty from each bank's earnings. This informational externality makes bank credit policies interdependent. A bank's reputation is less sensitive to poor earnings when other banks admit to poor earnings. Because true earnings are less likely to be high when the borrowing sector is distressed, banks collectively coordinate—meaning they herd—on an adverse shock to borrowers to tighten credit policy. In addition, as we explain in chapter 9, banks are more eager to declare loan defaults when other banks do so because there may be too many banks to fail and thus a bailout is easier to obtain. This theory therefore yields systemic risk through credit supply cycles that stem from financial intermediaries' limited liability, compensation structure, and governments' policies.

4.3   Factors That Increase Excessive Systemic Risk

For prudential policy we cannot just list each of the possible ways that the agency channel can lead to excessive systemic risk. In this section, we provide general factors affecting systemic risk, both in the time-varying dimension (credit and asset price cycles) and in the cross-sectional dimension, which are: competition, deregulation (financial liberalization) and political economy considerations, corporate governance and lack of market discipline, financial innovation, and a change in the economic environment (including monetary policy that we analyze in chapter 10).

4.3.1 Competition

Several theories of banking predict that an increase in bank competition increases risk-taking, jeopardizing financial stability. In Rajan's (1994) model, bank competition is crucial for driving the excessive credit supply and risk-taking, as executive compensation is based on relative performance. High levels of competition in banking may be detrimental for financial stability as they reduce the charter value of banks (through reducing oligopoly rents), thereby reducing the negative impact of bad realizations of risks. Keeley (1990) analyzes the US Savings and Loan crisis of the 1980s and finds that the bank failures stemmed from several deregulation measures that reduced banks' monopoly rents, increasing the value of their put option on the deposit insurance fund. Similarly Edwards and Mishkin (1995) argue that the excessive risk-taking observed in the 1980s in the United States also stem from the erosion of profits due to competition from financial markets.

Other models predict the opposite relation between bank competition and risk-taking. A lack of competition apart from bringing inefficiencies can lead to high loan rates to nonfinancial firms, which may react by choosing excessive risk to gamble for resurrection.[16] Moreover, when banking competition increases, it may be an optimal strategy to be prudent to gain market power when competitors take excessive risk and fail (see Perotti and Suarez 2002; Inderst 2013).

In general, the effects of banking competition on financial stability can therefore be positive or negative (Martinez-Miera and Repullo 2010). In fact many financial crises follow episodes of financial liberalization, including increased competition in the banking sector and financial markets, that have influenced banking regulators and supervisors: "The legislative reforms adopted in most countries as a response to the banking and financial crises of the 1930s shared one basic idea which was that, in order to preserve the stability of the banking and financial industry, competition had to be restrained. This fundamental proposition was at the root of the reforms introduced at that time in the United States, Italy, and most other countries." (Padoa-Schioppa 2001).

Competition also affects the screening by banks of potential borrowers. By screening out borrowers that do not meet adequate lending standards, banks reduce adverse selection, which is crucial to avoid excessive bank risk-taking. However, as Dell'Ariccia and Marquez (2006a) explain, since screening is costly, banks' adherence to adequate lending standards must be compensated by benefits stemming from reductions in the losses associated with bad loans. The authors present a model where banks have private information about the riskiness of some ("known") borrowers but not about others ("unknown" borrowers). Banks screen borrowers when there are low proportions of unknown borrowers in the market as banks are afraid of lending to borrowers known by their competitors and rejected by them—which is to say, there is a winner's curse for a bank obtaining a borrower as this borrower may have been rejected by all the other banks, in particular their bank-relationship banks. In this case screening leads only good borrowers to obtain credit.

However, there is also a pooling equilibrium when the proportion of unknown borrowers is high. In this case banks are not afraid of other banks rejecting known bad borrowers, as many of the new borrowers are unknown to all banks. This may be the case in credit booms when new applicant borrowers enter into the market. In this case, because of bank competition, banks may switch to not screening to maximize profits. The softening of lending standards will bring a credit boom with ex post credit defaults and financial instability. Ruckes (2004) also shows in a related model that in very good times banks do not have an incentive to screen, thus getting a time variation of lending standards over a cycle.

Beck, Demirguc-Kunt, and Levine (2003) and De Nicolo et al. (2003) analyze bank competition and stability. Both papers use concentration ratios as their measure of bank competition, assuming that a country constitutes a banking market, and analyze the likelihood of banking crises, not of individual bank failures.[17] Beck, Demirguc-Kunt, and Levine (2003) use a Logit probability model to explain the probability of a banking crisis as a function of the bank concentration ratio (and several macro and structural control variables). Using a panel of 70 countries over the period from 1980 to 1997 they find that the concentration ratio is negatively associated with the probability of a banking crisis. However, other measures of competition have the opposite effect on crisis probability, as they find that restrictions on new bank entry significantly increase crisis probability, which leads the authors to question if concentration ratios are a good proxy for bank competition (see also Claessens and Laeven 2004 for evidence questioning the usefulness of concentration ratios as measures for competition).

De Nicolo et al. (2003) use a continuous crisis probability measure for the five largest banks in a country through a "z-score" measure, which they use to determine the probability that the largest banks will experience combined losses great enough to destroy their combined capital. The z-score denotes the number of standard deviations that the bank's return on assets must fall to make the bank insolvent, computed over the period 1993 to 2000 for 97 countries, and they measure competition with a five-bank concentration ratio. The authors find that a more concentrated banking industry is more prone to banking crises, similar to Boyd and De Nicolo (2005) using different data and empirical strategy, but the exact opposite result of that obtained by Beck et al. (2003).

Taken together, the existing empirical evidence on the link between bank competition and the incidence of banking crisis is inconclusive.

4.3.2   Financial Deregulation and Political Economy

Many financial crises throughout history are preceded by financial liberalization and deregulation.[18] These could imply similar excessive risk-taking as in the case of excessive bank competition. Over the last thirty years there has been a significant liberalization of the financial system allowing an increase in competition both geographically (within a country and between countries via financial globalization) and across financial products (through the removal of the Glass–Steagal and other related regulations, almost all financial intermediaries compete in loans, investments, insurance, deposits and other financial margins).

Financial globalization measured by cross-border gross positions has increased enormously over the last decades, especially in the OECD countries. Lane and Milesi-Ferretti (2006) showed an increase from 100 percent in 1976 to 600 percent in 2006 of gross external assets and liabilities over GDP for the high-income countries, whereas for the middle- and low-income countries the increase is more modest. The main reasons are the liberalization of the capital account and important financial market reforms. For example, in Europe the single market for financial services (including the Financial Service Action Plan) and the adoption of the euro have been important institutional changes driving cross-border flows (Kalemli-Ozcan, Papaioannou, and Peydró 2010).

Moreover, in the decade prior to the start of the crisis, the increase in financial globalization was the highest in recent history, and in particular, cross-border banking has become a major source of financial integration (see Kalemli-Ozcan, Papaioannou, and Peydró 2010; Claessens et al. 2010a).

Financial globalization may increase or decrease systemic risk (Kalemli-Ozcan, Papaioannou, and Peydró 2013). From an ex ante (before a crisis) point of view, the positive effects of financial globalization are to allow international risk sharing (diversification), increase competition and efficiency, and boost "good" risk-taking (specialization of countries in their competitive advantages). The negative effects are that potentially dangerous credit booms are more easily financed as local wealth and deposit increases do not become constraints for the local credit boom. In principle, the credit boom will be financed with external short-term wholesale funding, thereby increasing financial fragility.[19] There is significant evidence of these effects for those countries that were hit severely in the 2008 global financial crisis (e.g., Iceland, Ireland, the Baltic countries, Spain, United Kingdom, and United States). Moreover, once the crisis has started, systemic risk may increase due to financial contagion and other effects, as we will see in chapters 5 and 7.

A key risk factor that we have seen giving rise to systemic risk is the increase in leverage, which in part was spurred by financial globalization over the last decades. In many European banks, leverage stood at more than 30 to 1 at the beginning of the crisis, with a substantial part on short-term leverage consisting mainly in short-term claims from other financial intermediaries in the (international) wholesale market. Not only does such high short-term leverage make each financial intermediary financially fragile at the individual level, but the dense short-term financial connections among intermediaries—both nationally and, since the 1990s, internationally—make systemic risk very high. These risks are not only taken through direct financial linkages among financial intermediaries, but also indirectly, for example, by financial intermediaries holding similar correlated risky assets. These correlated risks may be endogenously chosen by intermediaries so that in case of negative shocks, there will be too many institutions to fail.

But why have there been so many financial deregulation measures? It is interesting to note that there were few banking failures in the thirty-year period after 1945, probably stemming from the strict regulations during the Great Depresion (see Bordo et al. 2001 and chapter 6 of this book). However, some of these regulations may have been inefficient and clearly some financial risk is beneficial for long-run growth. For instance, Ranciere et al. (2008) show that countries that suffer financial crises tend to experience higher growth rates subsequently while Jayaratne and Strathan (1996) find that the removal in the 1980s of some of the US banking restrictions stemming from the 1930s spurred rapid economic growth. A key motivation of financial deregulation is therefore to increase financial sector efficiency.

Another explanation could be that there has been powerful lobbying by the financial system for deregulation. Johnson and Kwak (2010) and Acemoglu (2011) clearly explain the experience of financial deregulation over the past thirty years in the United States as a salient example of the importance of the financial system's lobbying in shaping financial reforms. On the one hand, the regulations may be necessary because they address market failures by removing distortions arising from agency problems. On the other hand, deregulation tends to strengthen the already powerful financial sector (see Acemoglu 2012).

Financial deregulation started with small changes such as ending fixed commissions on stock trading in 1975, and then became larger with the eradication of Regulation Q in 1980 (which limited interest rates on savings accounts).[20] Moreover financial institutions grew ever larger thanks to deregulation. The 1994 Riegle–Neal Interstate Banking and Branching Efficiency Act and the 1999 the Gramm–Leach–Bliley Act led to a wave of mergers and acquisitions that created very large and powerful financial institutions.

During the period of deregulation and financial innovation, the financial sector size and profits grew enormously, as shown by Johnson and Kwak (2010), Acemoglu (2011), and Philippon (2009). For example, the financial sector profits grew 800 percent during 1980-2005, while nonfinancial profits rose by 250 percent, and the size of the financial sector grew from 3.5 percent to almost 6 percent of GDP. As banks became larger, they substantially increased lobbying and contributions to political campaigns: by 2006 they gave $260 million, while the next largest donor, health care, gave $100 million and there was also a revolving door between Wall Street and the government (Johnson and Kwak 2010; Acemoglu 2012). As Acemoglu (2012) explains, likely more important than deregulation was the lack of new regulations on the new risks stemming from financial innovation. For example, regulations would have altered the valuation and risk perception of collateralized debt obligations based on mortgage-backed securities and credit default swaps, and as such would have tempered risks in the financial system. This regulatory void and deregulation, in conjunction with the other agency problems that we explain in this chapter, created an environment that favored the excessive risk-taking that created the 2008 financial crisis.

The size of the financial system was viewed as positive for economic growth before the crisis, but this view has been questioned since the crisis in part because of the recent problems in countries with large banking systems relative to the size of the economy (Cyprus, Iceland, Ireland, Netherlands, and Switzerland). Moreover, despite an extensive body of empirical literature that finds a positive relationship between economic growth and financial deepening, recent evidence suggests that the positive effect of finance on growth tapers off at high levels of financial development (e.g., see Beck, Degryse, and Kneer 2014).

Credit cycles and excessive risk-taking can also arise through political economy channels. A notable example is given by Agarwal et al. (2012). They find that the passing of the US Community Reinvestment Act (CRA) led to risky lending. The authors use exogenous variation in banks' incentives to conform to the standards of the CRA around regulatory exam dates to identify the causal effect of the CRA on credit supply. They find that adherence to the act led to riskier lending by banks (substantial higher credit volume with subsequent defaults) and that the effects are strongest during the period when the market for private securitization was booming.

Fernández-Villaverde, Garicano, and Santos (2013) identify another interesting channel that links credit cycles and political economy. They argue that the adoption of the euro delayed rather than advanced economic reforms in the euro area periphery and led to the deterioration of key institutions in these countries. They convincingly argue that the massive reduction in exchange-rate risk and interest rates imply that the budget constraints that the periphery countries faced were loosened, as these countries could cheaply borrow thus delaying potentially painful reforms. This created a credit boom while weakening economic fundamentals in the periphery countries, paving the way for the euro area crisis.

An important aspect of systemic risk is clearly the quality of banking supervision, and specifically the institutions that supervise the banks.

For example, an important part of the banking union in Europe is that the ECB became the new bank supervisor for medium and large banks as of November 2014 (in cooperation with national banks, who before 2014 were the main supervisors for euro area banks). Who is the better supervisor and why? Agarwal et al. (2014) study supervisory decisions of US banking regulators and, for empirical identification, exploit a legally determined rotation policy that assigns federal and state supervisors to the same bank at exogenously fixed time intervals. The authors find that federal regulators are systematically tougher, downgrading supervisory ratings almost twice as frequently as state supervisors. They argue that the discrepancy in regulator behavior arises from differences in how much regulators care about the local economy as well as differences in human and financial resources involved in implementing the regulation. Their results have important implications for the design of banking regulators not only for the United States but also for Europe and other parts of the world.

4.3.3 Financial Innovation, Market Discipline, and Corporate Governance

Several key differences distinguish the corporate governance of banks from that of nonfinancial firms, as we also discuss in chapter 8 on microprudential policy. Banks have many more stakeholders and are substantially more leveraged, and the (on and off balance sheet) assets and liabilities of banks are opaque and complex and can shift risks rather quickly.[21]

Most banks have more than 90 percent of debt to total assets ratio in contrast to 40 percent (or even lower) for nonfinancial firms (where capital ratio is without risk adjustment, i.e., a pure leverage ratio). Banks have more stakeholders than nonfinancial firms. The stakeholders in a bank include debtholders, the majority of which are the retail depositors and other debtholders that are normally other financial intermediaries. The deposit insurance authority therefore has an interest in the bank's health.

Because a bank's insolvency can have negative consequences for the financial system as a whole and even for the broad economy at large (more relevant for more connected, larger financial institutions), the government is yet another stakeholder in the bank. Borrowers such as firms and households of a bank are stakeholders as well, as it is difficult for them to switch to new banks in the event of bank problems (credit supply reduction) especially in the midst of a crisis (e.g., due to the

winner's curse of Shaffer 1998). But borrowers and depositors in connected (related) banks become stakeholders as failures in a bank are
passed to other connected banks (e.g., through the interbank market),
and in turn to their borrowers and depositors. Indeed Iyer and Peydró
(2011) show that the social costs of a bank failure are larger than the
private costs associated with the bank that fails. Moreover, as retail
depositors are generally small and subject to free-riding issues in monitoring, the importance for market disciplining of other debtholders
increases. Finally, a small part of stakeholders are shareholders, who
in some banks, notably European, could only represent around 3 to 4
percent of total assets.

Despite this complexity of stakeholders, the board of a bank typically only represents the views of shareholders, subject to regulatory
constraints (with the exception of countries where boards have fiduciary duties also to other stakeholders, such as in Germany's
co-determination system where labor representatives also sit on
company boards). Bank shareholders' risk-taking incentives may
diverge substantially from those of other stakeholders. One could see
the payoffs for (bank) shareholders as a call option written on the bank
assets, with a strike price equal to the level of debt (Merton 1973). As
option pricing shows (e.g., Black–Scholes), the higher the volatility,
especially with huge leverage, the higher is the value of the call, which
is to say, the higher is the bank stock price.

While debt and equity are equally costly under a Modigliani–Miller
world, in banking this is not the case as depositors have access to the
explicit and implicit deposit insurance, they do not demand compensation for substantial risk, which implies that debt is a cheaper source of
funds and biases banks' funding choices toward more leverage.[22] In
effect, because of the high levels of moral hazard in banking, short-term
wholesale debt is the next cheapest source of finance, whereas long-
term borrowing (or equity) is more expensive as a source of bank
finance, as shown by Calomiris and Kahn (1991) and Diamond and
Rajan (2001).

The evidence shows that both the boards and the compensation
package for CEOs represent the shareholders' preference for high risks.
Laeven and Levine (2009) and Ellul and Yerramilli (2013) show that the
presence of institutional investors increases bank risk. This preference,
however, is in conflict with the preference of other stakeholders, in
particular, debtholders and taxpayers. Recent evidence shows the need
for reform and for strengthening the risk management roles of banks

and there is suggestive evidence that linking executive pay to the price of debt (as opposed to equity) can reduce excess risk, as in recent years some banks have paid their executives in debt, instead of equity, to diminish their risk appetite.[23]

Market discipline by debtholders could reduce the excessive appetite for risk-taking by bank shareholders. Yet banks have increased their size, scope, and complexity, making market discipline less effective. Banks are both opaque and complex. As Levine (2004) notes, "Banks can alter the risk composition of their assets more quickly than most nonfinancial industries, and banks can readily hide problems by extending loans to clients that cannot service previous debt obligations" (for models on these two issues, see Rajan 1994; Myers and Rajan 1998). Morgan (2002) shows that rating agencies disagree substantially more over ratings on bonds issued by banks than over those issued by nonfinancial firms (with bank data before 2000).[24] Additionally the business of securitization has increased substantially opacity, thus making these opacity problems even bigger. Moreover, large banks face little market discipline because the market expects bailouts in case of distress, as in the Irish crisis. Credible banking resolution mechanisms can be a partial solution to this problem, as we discuss in chapter 8 of this book. An important step into this direction is the new EU directive (that follows the Cyprus resolution) that will promote bail-ins from shareholders, debtholders, and even depositors with more than 100,000 euros.

Higher capital requirements could also be a source of market discipline as shareholders' skin in the game would increase, thereby reducing the appetite for excessive risk-taking. Another complementary way is to regulate the corporate boards of banks such as to stipulate that boards have fiduciary duties not only to shareholders and should attach more weight to preventing defaults, including by reviewing and scrutinizing management's risk-related programs and activities, and to increase the presence of other stakeholders, thereby aligning the incentives of bank CEOs and other managers better with those of other stakeholders. However, as much as the development of the shadow banking system was a way for US banks to arbitrage capital regulation (Acharya and Schnabl 2009), banks may find new ways to get around new capital requirements, diminishing the effect of market discipline. For example, the arbitrage of bank capital regulation was crucial to the development of the shadow banking system as, under Basel rules, credit risk was penalized by capital requirements, but off-balance sheet liquidity risks were not. Given the private incentives at play in banking and the lack of market discipline, strict regulation and supervision is of utmost importance for the proper functioning of banks and other financial intermediaries.

Finally, financial innovation is also important, as Kindleberger (1978) already emphasized the link between financial innovation and bubbles, arguing that excessive credit creation often results from the development of substitutes for what previously had been the traditional monies. The role of financial innovation in precipitating credit booms and subsequent financial crises through the financial intermediary system is emphasized by numerous economic historians (e.g., White 1996; Calomiris 2009; Bordo 2008; Kindleberger and Aliber 2005). More recently Kohn (2009) notes the tendency for financial crises to be preceded by bubbles spurred by financial liberalization or innovations.

There is an emerging literature on the effects of securitization on bank lending and risk-taking. For example, Keys et al. (2010) empirically examine this issue using a dataset on securitized subprime mortgage loan contracts in the United States and, for identification, they exploit a specific rule of thumb in the lending market (i.e., there exists a threshold in borrower credit scores below which internal lending rules would prevent GSEs from lending and therefore the probability of being securitized is greater for loans just above compared to just below this threshold) to generate exogenous variation in the ease of securitization and compare the composition and performance of lenders' portfolios around the ad hoc threshold. Conditional on being securitized, the portfolio that is more likely to be securitized defaults by around 10 to 25 percent more than a similar risk profile group with a lower probability of securitization.

Securitization has therefore been associated with lax lending and excessive credit creation in mortgage markets during the 2000s (Mian and Sufi 2009), and in business loans (Jiménez et al. 2014b; Maddaloni and Peydró 2011). We review part of this literature in chapter 7 on how to measure systemic risk (in this case credit cycles) and in chapter 10 on monetary policy and credit cycles.

4.3.4 Economic Environment
We now consider how changes in the economic environment alter the risk-taking incentives of banks and other intermediaries making credit decisions. For example, a prolonged period of low short- and long-term

interest rates can create incentives to take on greater liquidity or credit risks, or to employ additional financial leverage, in an effort to reach for yield (see Rajan 2005; Diamond and Rajan 2012; Stein 2013a; Allen and Rogoff 2011). For example, an insurance company with a guaranteed minimum rate of return on some of its products increases its insolvency risk when exposed to a long period of low rates, which therefore increases its incentives to take on higher risk (see Rajan 2005 and Stein 2013a for this and other examples).

An important stylized factor of bank credit cycles is that observed measures of loan performance problems are pro-cyclical with loan defaults, past due loans, provisions and charge-offs being very low during most of the expansion and rising exponentially during the downturn (Laeven and Majnoni 2003).[25]

Consistent with these stylized facts, Alan Greenspan when he was Chairman of the Federal Reserve noted that regulators agree that "the worst loans are made at the top of the business cycle." (Chicago Bank Structure Conference, May 10, 2001). In fact Jiménez and Saurina (2006) show that banks take significantly more risks during the expansion, but these risks are revealed only later. As Berger and Udell (2004) note, practitioners also echo these findings: "Human nature being what it is, lenders and borrowers frequently assume that strong growth will continue unabated. Loans made towards the end of an economic cycle are often underwritten based upon unrealistic assumptions concerning growth" (Furth 2001, p. 31). These explanations are related to the behavioral view that we saw earlier in this chapter. Moreover Greenspan also noted that at the bottom of the cycle, "the problem is not making bad loans...it is not making any loans, whether good or bad, to credit-worthy customers," consistent with the credit crunches in recessions.

These stylized facts are also consistent with data from the Federal Reserve's Senior Loan Officer Survey (SLOS) and euro area Bank Lending Survey (BLS). US and euro area banks ease their lending standards in good times and tighten them in downturns, even after controlling for changes in demand (Lown, Morgan, and Rohatgi 2000; Jordan, Peek, and Rosengren 2002; Lown and Morgan 2002; Maddaloni and Peydró 2011). Finally, Maddaloni and Peydró (2011), as we will see in chapter 10, show that several of the main factors that we have discussed in this section interrelate to each other in explaining soft lending standards (notably low monetary rates, weak banking supervision, and high levels of financial innovation).

4.4 Asset Bubbles

Pre-crisis periods tend to experience not only credit booms but also asset price bubbles (Kindleberger 1978; Reinhart and Rogoff 2009a). Moreover the worst credit booms are normally accompanied by asset price bubbles, including in real estate and equity prices. Therefore, one way to prevent future systemic financial crises may be to design policies that ensure that asset price bubbles are minimized. However, just like with credit booms, not all asset price bubbles have negative effects, in the sense that either they trigger financial crises when they burst (even assuming that one can identify them ex ante) or that they may even have instead a positive impact on economic growth. Therefore, as we argued in the previous chapter, we need tractable models of bubbles that incorporate externalities within the financial sector (and to the real sector) associated with the bursting of bubbles and that can be used as a basis for policy analysis, but developing such theories has so far proved a challenging task.

As explained in the review by Allen and Rogoff (2011), the early theoretical models showed that asset price bubbles do not arise in standard models. For example, Tirole (1982) shows that with finite horizons or a finite number of agents, bubbles in which asset prices deviate from fundamentals are not consistent with rational behavior; in fact Santos and Woodford (1997) showed that the conditions under which bubbles arise in standard general equilibrium frameworks are very special. Moreover, building on the overlapping generations model of Samuelson (1958), Tirole (1985) showed that bubbles could exist in infinite horizon models in which all agents are rational. A large literature based on developments of this model has developed, where recent contributions include Caballero and Krishnamurthy (2006), Farhi and Tirole (2012b), and Martín and Ventura (2012).

For example, Martín and Ventura (2012) show that financial bubbles could be beneficial by increasing borrowing capacity when underinvestment (not overinvestment) is the main problem in the financial sector. They develop a model of economic growth with bubbles, where changes in investor sentiment lead to the appearance and collapse of macro bubbles. They show how these bubbles mitigate the effects of financial frictions. During bubbly episodes, unproductive investors demand bubbles while productive investors supply them. These transfers of resources improve the efficiency at which the economy operates, expanding consumption, the capital stock and output. When bubbly episodes end, the transfers stop, and consumption, the capital stock, and output contract.

As explained by Allen and Rogoff (2011), a critical problem with these models is the extent to which their framework is consistent with the bubbles in real estate and stock markets that are documented in Kindleberger (1978) and Reinhart and Rogoff (2009a), where bank credit plays a prominent role, notably in bubbles associated with systemic crises.

Another strand of the bubble literature, therefore, builds more realistic models based on asymmetric information where everybody rationally believes that they may be able to sell the asset at a higher price even though it is above its fundamental. Allen, Morris, and Postlewaite (1993) develop a discrete-time, finite-horizon model where the absence of common knowledge led to bubbles in asset prices.[26] Abreu and Brunnermeier (2003) also show in a model that an asset bubble can persist despite the presence of rational arbitrageurs. The resilience over time of the bubble stems from the inability of arbitrageurs to temporarily coordinate their selling strategies. This synchronization problem together with the individual incentive to time the market results in the persistence of bubbles over a substantial period.

There is another part of the literature on bubbles that uses behavioral finance models with distorted beliefs. As explained in the review of behavioral finance by Barberis (2012), a bubble can form when investors disagree sharply about an asset's future prospects and there are short-sale constraints (Miller 1977; Harrison and Kreps 1978; Scheinkman and Xiong 2003; Hong and Stein 2007).[27] The rationale is that the positive investors will buy but the negative ones cannot short in the presence of short-sale constraints, thereby the asset price will only reflect the positive views, and in consequence it will be overvalued.

Fostel and Geanakoplos (2008) also assume agents are divided into (a small group of) optimists, representing the natural buyers of the assets, and (a large group of) pessimists. Both groups are completely rational, forward looking, and expected utility maximizers, but with different priors. Heterogeneity and market incompleteness are important because then the valuation of an asset can depend critically on what a potentially small segment of the economy thinks of it. With these assumptions, they show how leverage cycles can cause contagion, flight to collateral, and issuance rationing in a frequently recurring phase they call the anxious economy.

Bubbles may also appear because investors extrapolate past outcomes (returns, or default rates) into the future (Lakonishok, Shleifer, and Vishny 1994; Barberis, Shleifer, and Vishny 1998). As explained by Barberis (2012), this assumption is motivated by Kahneman and Tversky's (1974) representativeness heuristic, where people expect small samples of data to reflect the properties of the population, thus potentially leading to overextrapolation. Barberis and Shleifer (2003) show a bubble formation based on overextrapolation of past returns, which is itself motivated by representativeness. Moreover bubbles can also form based on overconfidence—notably, on the precision of people's forecasts (Daniel, Hirshleifer, and Subrahmanyam 1998). When investors obtain and analyze information to estimate an asset's fundamental value, they may become overconfident about the usefulness of this information, leading them to overvalue the asset price.

While the previous behavioral models of bubble formation are based on distorted beliefs, there are also some preference-based models with similar mechanisms to the Campbell–Cochrane model that we discussed earlier in this chapter. For example, after investors experience gains in their holdings of an asset, they may become less risk averse because future losses can be cushioned by the prior gains, thereby reducing their risk aversion thus increasing the asset price even further (Thaler and Johnson 1990; Barberis, Huang, and Santos 2001). Moreover, as shown by Barberis and Huang (2008), bubbles are likely to occur in stocks related to a new innovation or technology as investors may view these stocks as a kind of lottery, where a strong preference for lottery-like payoffs may stem from how the brain overweighs low probabilities (Kahneman and Tversky 1979).

Probably the best model for understanding the real estate bubble in the United States and other advanced economies with housing price booms is the representativeness heuristic model that argues that bubbles occur because people tend to overextrapolate the past when making forecasts about the future, thus home buyers overextrapolated the past growth in the real estate prices; thus overpaying for their homes. But then for a bubble to grow you need also the external investors that provide mortgages to overextrapolate as well. Another branch of the literature develops agency theories of bubbles.[28] These models seem to be particularly relevant for financial intermediaries such as banks where, as we have seen earlier, agency conflicts are substantial. Allen and Gorton (1993) construct a continuous time, finite horizon model where an agency problem between investors and portfolio managers can create bubbles even though all participants are rational. Allen and Gale (2000c) develop a model with an agency problem where bubbles arise as a result of an expansion in credit, and Barlevy (2014) extends it to allow for more general debt contracts and dynamics. Allen and Gale (2003, 2004c, 2007) and Adrian and Shin (2008b) explicitly focus on the relationship between lending and asset price bubbles, which we review in chapter 10 of the book. Banks that pay a price higher than fundamentals enter into negative net present value investments, and thus engage in a form of risk shifting that increases with the asset bubble, spurred by the protection on the downside from limited liability combined with high leverage.

4.5 Conclusions

Systemic financial crises are not random events triggered by exogenous events; they tend to follow periods of strong credit growth. Credit (and with it debt and leverage) acceleration notably increases the likelihood of financial crises, and conditional on a crisis occurring, it significantly increases its systemic real negative effects for the broad economy. Moreover the worst credit booms are accompanied by asset price bubbles, including in real estate and equity prices.

Financial globalization and current account deficits are also important correlates with the occurrence of systemic financial crises. In an increasingly globalized economy, with free capital mobility, credit cycles and foreign capital flows have the potential to reinforce each other more strongly than before. External debt increases sharply in advance of banking crises, and banking crises tend to lead sovereign debt crises. For emerging economies, higher foreign exchange reserves also predict a sharply reduced probability of a subsequent crisis.

Deficient banking corporate governance and executive compensation, lack of market discipline, banking competition, financial liberalization and deregulation, deficient financial regulation (also stemming from political economy problems), financial innovation, and good macrofinance environment are important drivers of too soft lending standards and the buildup of other endogenous financial imbalances such as asset price bubbles. Therefore, despite the relevance of the preference channel in understanding credit and asset booms, we conclude that the incidence and ramifications of systemic credit and asset booms cannot be explained without the agency channel for excessive risk-taking of banks and other financial intermediaries.

Because systemic crises are not exogenous events, but come from the buildup of imbalances in the financial sector due to pervasive incentives of financial intermediaries, the ex ante prevention of excessive risk-taking and buildup of financial imbalances should be a critical mission of macroprudential policy, not just ex post crisis management and resolution. Therefore ex post intervention alone would fail to address the root causes, and it could even cause higher ex ante systemic risk through moral hazard. Therefore ex ante macroprudential policy is of utmost importance to contain systemic risk and avoid costly financial crises.

5   Contagion

In this chapter the issue of contagion among financial institutions is considered. Contagion from one financial intermediary to the other is at the core of banking and financial regulation because it is the main externality caused by a bank's distress. This is why the efficient handling of a banking crisis requires a perfect understanding of the channels of contagion, so as to minimize the cost to taxpayers of liquidating some financial institutions while building the necessary firewalls to protect the others. Moreover macroprudential policy can be applied to the externalities that increase systemic risk only if the channels of contagion are fully understood.

Contagion, in a strict sense, refers to a "domino effect" that a failure of one bank has on other banks and financial intermediaries. Thus contagion either precipitates the failure or increases the probability of failure, and, more generally, increases the fragility of the banking system as it increases banks' cost of funds and reduces their margins. Because banks are central to the financial system, and even are the main prime brokers of hedge funds and engage in cross-border financing, contagion can spread also to all financial intermediaries. That is to say, a contagion in the banking system could cause failure in other parts of the financial system, as occurred in the 2007 shadow banking system. The intensity of such an effect depends, of course, on the overall macroeconomic and financial environment.

Let us draw a simplistic comparison with epidemiology. In flu epidemics contagion also corresponds to the classical domino effect, yet the epidemic and the contagion will be much more severe in cold weather, the equivalent of a fragile macrofinancial environment. This comparison also allows us to observe the difference: to consider the epidemic equivalent of a banking crisis, we would have to take into account the notion that a large number of ill people will lead to colder weather, thus amplifying the effect. The same as people can be quick to change their activities to avoid exposure to the flu (e.g., a child not going to school), financial intermediaries can be quick to endogenously change financial links as most of these links are short term. So we have to take into account that the banking (financial) network is endogenous and time varying. From this comparison we gain two insights: first, the importance of the domino effect will depend on the overall fragility of the banking system; second, the overall fragility of the banking system depends on the extent of the domino effect, as the aggregate health of the banking system affects banks' financial fragility and the domino can change the structure and connections of the banking network.

A clarification between contagion and macro fragility is in order. Banking crises are characterized by the joint failure of a large number of banks. Yet, strictly speaking, this need not be due to contagion. Macro fragility could result from banks facing the same exogenous shock, for example, because they implemented poor investment strategies (as discussed in chapter 4). Then it would be the failure of these risky investments, not contagion per se, that causes systemic risk. To better illustrate the domino effect, we will consider the case in which the banking crisis is triggered by a macrofinancial shock, and the financial fragility is unrelated to contagion. Unlike stock markets, we will not focus on comovements in banks' profitability but rather on the interdependence in their returns.[1] This is necessary in order to define precisely the contagion phenomenon, because, in theory, a banking crisis will occur at the same time as a decrease in the prices of assets (real estate, stocks, corporate bonds) and a "flight to quality" (i.e., a move away from risky to safe assets by investors). In practice, it is seldom the case that contagion occurs in a perfectly safe financial environment or that a macrofinancial shock simultaneously affects all banks, as the borders between contagion and financial fragility are somewhat blurred. For these reasons the task of identifying and measuring contagion with nonexperimental data is challenging, and especially in a financial crisis when the overall fundamentals of the banking system are weak. (For another perspective on financial fragility, e.g., the strengthening of credit standards, see Lown and Morgan 2006 and Maddaloni and Peydró 2011; we addressed the lack of coincidence between business cycles and credit cycles in chapter 4.)

The magnitude of contagion depends on the characteristics of the banking industry. Of course, when banking regulatory standards are set high, the spread of contagion will be much smaller. However, the successive waves of financial deregulation may operate in the opposite direction and increase the likelihood of contagion. This is clearly illustrated in the case of shadow banking.

In this chapter we review contagion generated by changes in expectations, by counterparty default, by liquidity shortages, by the reduction in credit supply, by the feedback effect of other markets, by information disclosure, and by cross-country effects. In section 5.1, we discuss the mechanisms of contagion; in section 5.2, we discuss how these mechanisms interact and reinforce each other. Finally, section 5.3 focuses on the structure of networks as determinants of the contagion risk.

5.1   Mechanisms of Contagion

The discussion begins by considering the different channels of contagion, starting with the classic ones and finishing with the new channels that have been at work during the recent crisis. It is important to emphasize that the distinction between different channels is somewhat academic in the following sense: first, it is often quite difficult to distinguish one channel from the others as they all operate simultaneously and reinforce one another. Second, because regulatory authorities are swift in intervening and preventing contagion, it is difficult to identify a smoking gun and to point out which of the channels of contagion is at work. For example, after studying more than 100 bank failures, Goodhart and Schoenmaker (1995) conclude: "It has been revealed preference of the monetary authorities in all developed countries to rescue those large banks whose failure might lead to a contagious, systemic failure."

For the sake of exposition, we cover each channel in isolation in each subsection, thus examining the seven following channels: (1) expectations, (2) counterparty default, (3) liquidity, (4) credit supply, (5) contagion to other markets, (6) disclosure, and (7) cross-country contagion, before turning to the study of their connection and their reinforcement.

Prior to the analysis of each channel it may be helpful to visualize how the different channels interact. The diagram of figure 5.1 shows the interactions between macroeconomic and financial environment, banks' results and balance sheet situation, their ability to obtain funding, and the impact on asset prices. The presentation introduces not one but two feedback effects from the banking sector to the

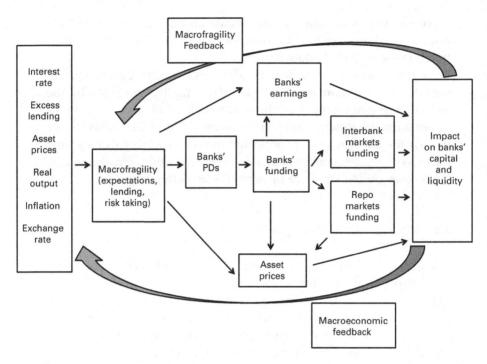

Figure 5.1
Channels of contagion

macrofinancial environment, emphasizing a distinction between the classical macroeconomic variables, that can be seen as exogenous in the short run, and those that are characteristic of macro fragility, such as expectations, banks' cost of funds, leverage and risk-taking, that react immediately to the particular circumstances of the banking industry and are directly related to financial stability. The feedbacks could affect one or the other and sometimes both: thus, changes in banks' credit standards have an effect on real output only with a lag, while banks' losses increase immediately their leverage and overall macrofragility.[2]

5.1.1 Contagion through Expectations and Bank Runs

The mechanism of contagion that was the raison d'être of Central Banks in their role as lender of last resort in the mid-nineteenth century in Europe is extremely simple. Because depositors know that banks' bankruptcies are positively correlated, the failure of a bank leads them to update their beliefs regarding the solvency of other banks. As they are holding demand deposits, their reaction is the withdrawal of their deposits, as this assures them to have their par value in gold or as a claim on the central bank. In other words, as Chen (1999) shows, contagion due to a bank failure gives information on the returns of similar assets to depositors of other banks.

The mechanism could work even if the banks' assets are uncorrelated. It is sufficient that depositors perceive a higher probability of a bank run for this to be a self-fulfilling prophecy, just as in the Diamond–Dybvig (1983) model. Of course, as established by Gorton (1988) using nineteenth-century data, the empirical evidence shows that the purely speculative bank runs on solvent institutions were the exception and that the majority of runs concerned fragile institutions close to insolvency in periods of weak macroeconomic fundamentals. In fact global games models, notably those of Goldstein and Pauzner (2005), show that coordination problems (panics) are stronger when bank fundamentals are weaker.

From a theoretical perspective, in today's fiat money world, pure contagion through expectations in solvent banks should never occur. Indeed withdrawals from one bank will be redirected to another bank, and the solvent bank will then lend it back to the bank suffering the bank run through the interbank market. Also, as the central bank is able to manage the aggregate amount of liquidity supplied, it allows for the convertibility of deposits into cash at the aggregate level. Still, the whole argument hinges on the necessary condition of a perfect functioning of the interbank market that is required to allow the reallocation of liquidity from one bank to another, thus compensating the erratic movements caused by irrational depositors.

It is well known that deposit insurance and suspension of convertibility immediately stop contagion through expectations. Suspension of convertibility is seldom used, but retail depositors are typically protected by deposit insurance. Hence, the main channel of contagion in a well-developed financial system is the unsecured interbank market or, in general, wholesale markets. As wholesale funds are mainly short term, they can be transferred from one bank to another almost instantly, thus creating huge liquidity problems in some financial institutions. Of course, this mechanism can be seen from the positive side as "market discipline." Still, in the recent crisis, it was a cause of concern that led regulatory authorities to be quite cautious and provide implicit or explicit insurance to unsecured liability holders, as was the case after Lehman failed or in the euro area crisis, and in particular, in Ireland and in Spain.[3]

5.1.2   Contagion through Counterparty Risk

As experts in risk management, banks trade risks as insurance companies do in the reinsurance market. The implication is that any banking system has in place a network of assets, liabilities, and off balance sheet contracts that banks hold one against another.[4] A well-functioning payment system requires banks to be able to transfer liquidity, defined here as central bank reserves, in a quick and efficient way from one bank to another. In addition to liquidity concerns, banks may also hold important positions against one another because of their role in risk management, which may imply using derivatives both for hedging a given position and for speculation.

Prior to the 2007 crisis, this network of counterparty risks was supposed to be the main channel of contagion. It simply states that if bank A goes bankrupt, all banks that had a counterparty risk with bank A will suffer losses. If the extent of these losses is high enough, the creditor banks' capital is reduced beyond some critical threshold, which leads the creditor bank to its bankruptcy. Whether the mechanism goes through the unsecured interbank market or through the derivatives market is here of secondary order in so far as banking contagion is concerned. The only relevant fact is that the losses generated by the bankruptcy of bank A are so large that they trigger the bankruptcy of some other banks. Of course, some other financial intermediaries were crucial in some of these markets in the 2008 crisis; for example, the insurance company AIG wrote many CDS contracts, and thus its failure could have precipitated a massive loss for many financial intermediaries, notably banks.

The issue of counterparty risks has been modeled by Allen and Gale (2000a) who show how the very same mechanisms of cross holding of deposits among banks, that are an efficient solution to cope with idiosyncratic liquidity risk, may be the origin of a full-fledged systemic liquidity crisis, if the banking system is affected by global liquidity shortage.[5] The Allen and Gale (2000a) model has multiple equilibria and the ex ante contagion probability is zero, which is not good to make any policy analysis. Dasgupta (2004) overcomes these two problems with a model of interbank contagion based on global games. The possibility of contagion reduces the incentives for banks to use the interbank market to cope with idiosyncratic liquidity problems. Brusco and Castilglionesi expand the Allen and Gale framework to take into account moral hazard in the form of excessive risk-taking.

Iyer and Peydró (2011) test financial contagion due to interbank linkages. For identification they exploit an idiosyncratic, sudden shock caused by a large Indian bank failure in conjunction with detailed data on interbank exposures. First, they find robust evidence that interbank exposure to the failed bank leads to large deposit withdrawals; and even more in banks with higher interbank exposures that are at a greater risk of contagion. Second, the magnitude of contagion is higher for banks with weaker fundamentals, suggesting that contagion is stronger when overall bank fundamentals are weak as in a crisis. Third, interbank linkages among surviving banks further propagate the shock—that is, they find second-round effects over and above the first (direct) round effects of the initial contagion. Finally, they find that there are negative real economic effects. All in all, their results suggest that interbank linkages act as an important channel of contagion.

Freixas, Parigi, and Rochet (2000) take a slightly different road in modeling the network of counterparty risks in the interbank market. Their argument is that depositors may choose to hold liquidity rather than to rely on the interbank market in order to transfer their deposits from their original location to the location where they want to consume. When depositors choose to withdraw the interbank market freezes, leading to an inefficient "gridlock equilibrium."

An important issue in this context is to consider the aggregate liquidity the monetary authorities inject so as to cope with financial instability (an issue we examine in chapter 10). The aggregate supply of liquidity determines interest rates, the supply of credit, the projects that have to be liquidated before reaching maturity, and the efficiency costs this early termination implies (Holmstrom and Tirole 1998, 2011; Allen and Gale 2000a), so that an adequate management of the liquidity supply may solve the crisis. Yet, contrasting with this view, Freixas, Parigi, and Rochet (2000) argue that it is not only injection of liquidity that is critical but also where this injection takes place, as their framework is inspired by a spatial setup.

The policy implications are quite different because, in the first case, open market operations will suffice to restore financial stability while, in the second, it will be essential to direct liquidity to the institution that is confronted with the liquidity shortage, so as to avoid the gridlock equilibrium. Notice that this does not imply that it is the bank in distress that has to be provided with liquidity. On the contrary, it might imply that the bank in distress is declared bankrupt while all its counterparts having short maturity claims on it will obtain the liquidity they require in order to avoid a market gridlock. For example, in Iyer and Peydró (2011), the public liquidity should be directed toward the banks directly linked with the failed bank, as the second-round effects in the form of interbank dry-ups did not allow the private liquidity to flow easily.

The extent of the web of reciprocal obligations among banks and its complexity has been one of the major channels of contagion. The increase in the market for derivatives and explosion of the CDS market has led to a situation where the bankruptcy of a key player, like AIG, can jeopardize the whole banking system and amplify the crisis by multiplying banks' losses. This can occur because a loan whose credit risk is hedged with a CDS is considered a very low risk, and therefore it has a very low capital requirement. In the recent crisis it became evident that these hedges were far from perfect because of the counterparty risk of the seller of protection in the CDS contract. This outcome was the direct result of over the counter (OTC) contracting, and the same derivative transactions conducted through a centralized clearinghouse in an organized market, with complete transparency, adequate margin calls, and circuit breakers would have led to a much lower risk, a point the recent regulatory reform takes into account.

5.1.3   Contagion through Liquidity Shortages

One of the main lessons of the current crisis has been that contagion can also occur through liquidity shortages. The failures of Bear Stearns and Lehman Brothers indeed happened while these institutions were sufficiently capitalized according to Basel II criteria, although this could be attributed to the delayed inflow of accounting information. At any rate, the fulfillment of capital requirement by these institutions at the moment of their financial distress proved that the speed and depth of the liquidity crisis was crucial in precipitating their fall. Of course, the academic literature had long emphasized the difficulty in distinguishing illiquid from insolvent banks. Still it was thought that a liquidity crisis would only affect a limited number of banks, as was the case with Northern Rock , and not the whole banking system that had access to the Central Bank liquidity supply.

Because one of the major functions of banks is maturity transformation, as exemplified among others by the Diamond–Dybvig (1983) model, a single bank offering demand deposit and the corresponding access of their customers to the payment system faces the risk of being liquidity short as it is holding illiquid assets. To cope efficiently with this risk, apart from general wholesale markets where other financial intermediaries operate as money market funds, the modern banking system provides banks with access to two main markets for liquidity where banks holding an excess of central bank reserves lend them to those that are in short supply. The first of these two markets is the repo market where the loans are fully collateralized and the solvency of the counterpart is a minor issue (with the exception of counterparties that are on the verge of going bankrupt in which case a repo operation may have administrative and legal costs).[6] The second of these markets is the unsecured market where the solvency of the counterpart is a key issue and where banks are expected to play a role in monitoring each other, thus imposing market discipline on one another through peer monitoring (Rochet and Tirole 1996). In addition the market for securities, and in particular, the money market, constitutes an additional mechanism for banks facing a liquidity shortage to raise funds. As a consequence, prior to the crisis, the consensus on liquidity was that if indeed a bank was solvent in a developed financial system, the interbank market would allow the bank to cope with a bank run because the bank would be able to obtain liquidity at the market interest rate. Of course, some previous experiences were there to show that this was not always the case.[7]

Diamond and Rajan (2005) show that bank failures can be contagious, not just because of depositor panics or contractual links between banks but because bank failures can also shrink the common pool of liquidity, creating or exacerbating aggregate liquidity shortages, potentially leading to a contagion of failures and a total meltdown of the system.[8]

The discussion on the buildup of financial fragility has already emphasized the critical importance of fire sales, and the amplifying effect of collateral prices in the reduction of the credit supply. We now turn to consider the mechanisms that lead to a failure in the three markets for liquidity, starting with the unsecured interbank market and then turn to the behavior of banks in the other two markets and how a shortage of liquidity or a decrease in asset prices might lead banks to sell their assets, thus collectively facing the consequences of fire sale prices. As we will see later, the injection of liquidity by the central banks would solve this problem but would also provide the incentives for banks to take additional ex ante liquidity risks (Diamond and Rajan 2012).

Asymmetric Information in the Unsecured Interbank Market   Absent huge liquidity management errors, a bank will face a liquidity shortage only if the three sources of liquidity (the repo, the unsecured interbank, and the securities market) fail simultaneously, which prior to the current crisis appeared as quite a remote possibility. Yet this was an incorrect perception of the link between the three markets. Indeed many of the assets that the banks held (ABS, CDOs, etc.) were highly complex and agents had difficulties in assessing the true probabilities of a default. As pointed out by Holmstrom (discussion of Gorton's paper), provided that all agents in the market are symmetrically informed or that risk is negligible, this does not prevent agents from transacting in the market. But once the assets were considered risky, some agents could have better information than others (the ABACUS structured fund story created by Goldman Sachs following Paulson's instructions is a good illustration).[9] Once some agents have better information, uninformed agents become suspicious of any transaction and the liquidity in the market suddenly dries. This explains the liquidity dry-up in the market for ABS and CDOs. But then the repo market immediately followed up in becoming illiquid, as these "toxic assets" could not be used as collateral. In fact, as agents become more and more worried about the real cash flows and risks underlying structured securities, the haircuts on repos were increased until they could no longer be used in a repo transaction. Figure 5.2, borrowed from Gorton and Metrick (2012), shows this phenomenon.

Krishnamurthy, Nagel, and Orloz (2014) obtain different results from Gorton and Metrick (2012). They analyze in detail which short-term debt markets suffered from runs during the financial crisis with a novel dataset of repurchase agreements (repo) between nonbank cash lenders and dealer banks. They find that the collateral backing these repos prior to the crisis was largely composed of government securities rather than riskier private sector assets. The subsequent contraction in repo with private sector collateral was relatively small in the aggregate, and relatively insignificant compared with the contraction in the asset-backed commercial paper market, but its effects were concentrated on a few most exposed dealer banks.

The third market, the unsecured one, was then bound to become illiquid for two reasons. First, every bank preferred to hoard liquidity in order to prevent a possible liquidity shock rather than to lend in the interbank market except for the overnight market whose volume of transactions increased. Second, the "peer-monitoring" function could

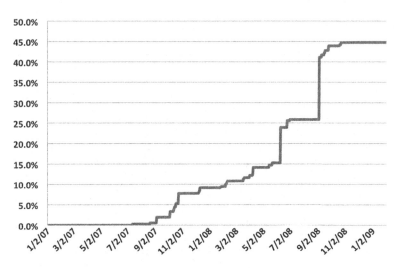

Figure 5.2
Repo haircut index Source: Gorton and Metrick (2012)

not be properly performed as every bank was suspected to hold large amounts of "toxic assets" of difficult valuation. Figure 5.3, borrowed from Heider, Horoeva, and Holthausen (2004), shows how the inter-bank market rate, based on quotes (Euribor) not on actual rates, included a risk premium (measured by the difference between the three-month interbank market and the three-month EONIA swap market that has no principal risk) from the beginning of the liquidity crisis in August 2007 and how this risk premium increased after the Lehman Brothers bankruptcy. It also shows how banks reacted in depositing their liquidity at the ECB facility despite the existence of other alternatives such as placements in the interbank market. Inter-bank deposits offered a higher rate than ECB deposits but were deemed a riskier alternative because of the counterparty risk of dealing with another bank.

Afonso, Kovner, and Schoar (2011) examine the importance of liquid-ity hoarding and counterparty risk in the US overnight interbank market during the financial crisis of 2008. Their findings suggest that counterparty risk plays a larger role than does liquidity hoarding: the day after Lehman Brothers' bankruptcy, loan terms become more sensi-tive to borrower characteristics. In particular, poorly performing large banks see an increase in spreads of 25 basis point and borrow, on average, 1 percent less.

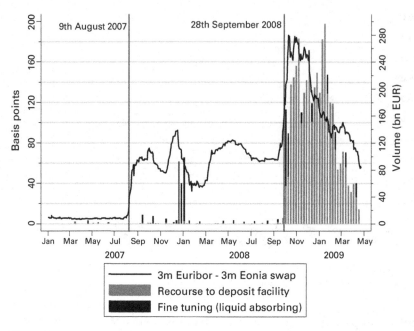

Figure 5.3
Turbulence in euro interbank markets. Interbank spread and excess reserves (recourses
to the ECB deposit facility and liquidity-absorbing fine-tuning operations), daily average
per week, January 2007 to April 2009 Source: Heider, Horoeva, and Holthausen (2004)

Abbassi et al. (2015) using target 2 data for the euro area show that
access to term deposits massively decrease after the Lehman failure.
Afterward the dry-up concentrated in overnight deposits' access,
maturity, and cost. In the sovereign crisis there was a liquidity dry-up
in cross-border loans. In this period, as in the term and overnight
deposits in the Lehman's period, relationship lending in the interbank
market, especially for smaller banks, helped alleviate interbank
illiquidity.

Freixas and Holthausen (2006) and Malherbe (2014) provide models
showing how adverse selection can lead to multiple equilibriums in
the interbank market, even more in the case of cross-border transactions. The argument is related to the idea of self-fulfilling prophecies.
An interbank market can be liquid if the majority of banks use it for
liquidity reasons, and only a minority of banks uses it to borrow when
they know they are insolvent so that adverse selection is a minor issue.
Yet the same market can become illiquid if the majority of banks instead
use the repo market or sell their liquid securities to obtain liquidity

leaving the unsecured interbank market to insolvent borrowers so that it becomes a lemons' market.

Taken literally, pure liquidity risk is not a major channel of contagion, as regulatory authorities should be able to cope with the simple task of lending to each of the illiquid and solvent banks. Unfortunately, as mentioned before, this ideal situation never occurs. Lending to banks by the central banks is risky (e.g., in 2012 the eurosystem was lending more than 400 billion euros to Spanish banks, which is an exposure higher than 40 percent of the Spanish GDP!). We have therefore to envision liquidity contagion in the context of a solvency crisis, with serious banks counterparties risk and aggravated by fire sales in the asset market that fully justify the pessimistic expectations of the banks' creditors regarding their solvency.

Cash in the Market and Fire Sales   One of the main basic principles of financial economics is that the price of assets is the value of the future cash flows discounted at the correct interest rate, so that asset prices are based on fundamentals and not on liquidity. Allen and Gale (2004a), on the contrary, develop the simplest possible model of cash shortages by assuming, at the antipodes of the usual perfect market and net present value analysis, that the supply of cash available in a market is fixed. This implies that the total revenue from asset sales is always constant, so that no matter how large the increase in the quantity of assets sold, the corresponding price decrease leads to the same aggregate revenue.

When confronted with a liquidity shortage, a bank forced to sell its assets will provoke a decrease in the price that will affect all banks and may force other banks to sell additional assets. When banks' aggregate demand for liquidity is higher than the available demand, there is no equilibrium in a Walrasian market (there would be a non-tâtonnement equilibrium if banks were to sell sequentially), so only additional cash coming from outside investors may lead to a floor in the decreasing price spiral.

Acharya and Yorulmazer (2008a) model this phenomenon in a simple framework and show how banking crises are amplified by a cash in the market type of financial rigidity through the interaction of liquidity shortages and fire sale prices. A simple way of explaining the mechanism they consider is to assume that banks that go bankrupt have to liquidate their assets and only successful banks are able to buy these assets. When this is the case for a sufficiently large number of

bank bankruptcies, fire sale prices will trigger additional bank bankruptcies, thus causing a systemic crisis.

Adrian and Shin (2010) observe, based on data for investment banks
in the United States, that another mechanism may come into play fostering banks' asset sales, even if it does not originate in a bank's liquidity shortage. It is related to the banks' behavior regarding their choice
of leverage. They remark that banks that manage their risk with a value
at risk (VaR) approach will have to deleverage when the price of assets
is low (and have incentives to increase their leverage when prices are
high). Their empirical analysis shows that such an approximation to
investment banks' behavior is consistent with the observed positive
correlation between asset prices and leverage of investment banks.
Notice that the analysis is based on book values not market values of
equity (and leverage), but this is the measure of equity to be considered
because capital requirement regulation is based on book values of
equity. Now, when all banks behave in the same way, a decrease in
prices will generate losses and banks will de-lever, thus generating a
massive sale and the beginning of a downward cycle.

Mian, Sufi, and Trebbi (2014a) obtain evidence on fire sales prices in
the recent crisis. Banks located in states without a judicial requirement
for foreclosures are twice as likely to foreclose on delinquent home-
owners. Comparing zip codes close to state borders with differing
foreclosure laws, they show that foreclosure propensity and housing
inventory jump discretely as one enters nonjudicial states.[10] The increase
in foreclosure rates in nonjudicial states persists for at least five years.
Using the judicial/nonjudicial law as an instrument for foreclosures,
they show that foreclosures lead to a large decline in house prices, residential investment, and consumer demand.

Repo Markets   The repo market allows banks to borrow with all the
guarantees of holding good collateral and legal certainty of immediate
repossession. From that perspective, it appears as a perfect instrument
to raise liquidity in the market. Nevertheless, its well-functioning could
have induced financial institutions to underestimate its risk and promoted short term borrowing backed by long-term assets, creating what
ex post had appeared as an excessive maturity mismatch. The possibility of borrowing in the repo market could have led, as shown by Brunnermeier and Pedersen (2009), to two types of liquidity spirals, as
during a crisis, haircuts on repos will increase and their prices will
decrease. This will suddenly deprive banks funded in the wholesale

market from access to liquidity and force them to sell their assets, thus increasing downward pressure on prices.

Before explaining Brunnermeier and Pedersen's argument, consider the role of haircuts. As an extreme example, consider a financial institution that is funding itself in the wholesale market while holding 5 percent equity. Interest on the assets are sufficient to repay interest on the funds borrowed on the repo market, the difference between long-term interest rate and short-term interest rate allowing for the higher remuneration of the equity. If an endogenous shock occurs and increases the volatility of the securities that are repo'ed, the market will require a higher haircut of, say, 10 percent. The resulting situation will be one where the financial institution will be unable to roll over its repo positions. In our example, it will force the financial institution to sell 50 percent of the assets.

In quite a similar way a decrease in asset prices will make it impossible for a financial institution to raise the funds required to roll over its repo liabilities in the wholesale market. With a 5 percent decrease in the price, the rollover of repos would allow the financial institution to raise only 85.5 in the wholesale market, which is insufficient to repay its liability of 90.

Brunnermeier and Pedersen (2009) consider these two effects in a dynamic model, where some agents (customers) are faced with a liquidity shock in their endowment and have to sell their assets. These customer trading needs are accommodated by investment banks that

Table 5.1

Initial 5 percent haircut		Subsequent 10 percent haircut	
Assets	Liabilities	Assets	Liabilities
ABS 100	Repo 95	ABS 50	Repo 45
	Equity 5		Equity 5
100	100	50	50

Table 5.2

Initial price: 100 Haircut 10 percent		Subsequent price: 95 Haircut 10 percent	
Assets	Liabilities	Assets	Liabilities
ABS 100	Repo 90	ABS 50	Repo 45
	Equity 10		Equity 5
100	100	50	50

act in the traditional role of speculators, smoothing price fluctuations and making profits out of the difference between the market price and its fundamental value. If investment banks have access to as much funding as they might need, this will make all price deviations from fundamental vanish. Yet investment banks need funding liquidity, as they have to finance their trades through repo operations, borrowing from financiers who set the haircuts as a function of the volatility of the assets and might infer the risk from the price distribution rather than from fundamentals, creating a market imperfection.[11] If this is the case, price-smoothing investment banks may be liquidity short and may be reluctant to take positions in high haircut securities. The decreasing market liquidity that results will lead to higher price volatility for the asset and direct prudent financiers to demand a higher haircut, thus reducing the investment bank access to funding liquidity.

A destabilizing liquidity spiral emerges, where market liquidity and funding liquidity are mutually reinforcing. The destabilizing liquidity spiral spreads from one security to another, leading to a generalized liquidity dry-up as speculators are forced to de-lever their positions across assets (Covitz et al. 2009; Duygan-Bump et al. 2013).

5.1.4   Contagion through Aggregate Credit Supply

A typical characteristic of a systemic crisis is the drop in assets' values, sometimes over and above fundamentals; that is, assets are liquidated at fire sale prices. This has two effects. On the one hand, it generates losses and thus reduces banks' capital, since banks hold the assets.[12] On the other hand, it decreases the value of the assets that borrowers are susceptible to pledge in order to obtain credit. These two different effects lead to the same result: in both cases the bank's response will be to decrease its supply of credit, as we will see in more detail in the next chapter.[13] A temporary reduction in the supply of credit is not, per se, a cause of contagion, even if it generates a real effect (Peek and Rosengren 2000) as it is not easy for firms to substitute one bank for another. Yet, as this occurs in the aggregate, it leads to a decrease in firms and households' investment, and consequently to a decrease in the rate of growth of the economy.

This throttles firms, reduces activity, and generates unemployment, thus amplifying the feedback effect on banks and other financial intermediaries. Still, in terms of the time span, it should be noted that market contagion is often instantaneous while the feedback effects through the real sector (that sometimes is even protected by the existence of credit lines) can take months.[14]

Credit Crunch   At the start of the 1990s the US economy was confronted with a new phenomenon: rather than making traditional industrial and commercial loans or mortgage loans, banks tended to invest in safe assets, particularly US Treasuries. This, of course, had critical macroeconomic implications, as it reduced the aggregate amount of investment. This phenomenon, referred to as "credit crunch," was first diagnosed as an unintended consequence of Basel I capital regulation by Bernanke and Lown (1992). Since the beginning of the 1990s, banks had to comply with the new Basel I capital regulations (agreed upon in 1988). The banks which capital had been eroded by losses had to choose between issuing additional capital at a huge cost (as these costs are high in crisis times) or rebalancing the portfolio by investing more in assets with a low risk weight at the expense of their loan making activity. As issuing additional equity implied excessive dilution costs, banks chose to invest in Treasuries with its implication of reducing aggregate private investment.

Credit crunches have been observed also in the aftermath of the Asian crisis of 1997, and more recently in the recent crisis. In fact, although it is quite reasonable to think that Basel I capital regulation was the main cause of the credit crunch, it should be emphasized that a model of efficient capital management by banks should lead to the same prediction: when banks' capital is depleted, banks' optimal behavior will depend on the relative risks and returns on their assets and liabilities, so that if their cost of equity is too high, they will choose to restructure their portfolio so as to decrease their overall risk, and comply with capital requirements from the market by reducing the size of their portfolio of risky loans.[15] This approach can be envisioned in a more rigorous way by modeling the banks' optimal capital decisions, as for instance in Holmstrom and Tirole (1997) who assume that a minimum capital requirement guarantees that banks perform their monitoring role. Jiménez et al. (2012) show, using loan application-level data, evidence consistent with a reduction in the supply of credit (a credit crunch) during the recent crisis in Spain due to low levels of bank capital.

Debt Deflation   The concept of debt deflation was one of the key ideas put forward by Irving Fisher (1933) when confronted with the crisis in the 1930s. Observing the correlation of credit supply with economic growth and asset prices, Fisher suggested a causal link: as asset prices go down, the amount of credit that is backed by collateral has to decrease; this reduces the rate of growth and subsequently asset prices. It is only when asset prices decrease sufficiently that this vicious circle stops. A rigorous model of debt deflation has been more recently developed by Kiyotaki and Moore (1997). Their model assumes that loans have to be 100 percent collateralized (in this case, by land) so that the amount of credit that nonfinancial firms can get today depends on the price of land tomorrow, which is rationally anticipated. Cycles in the price of land then generate cycles in credit and in economic activity.

Of course, when considering contagion through asset values it is difficult to draw a clear-cut line distinguishing it from a classical business cycle aggravated by financial sector imperfections. From this perspective, the concept of "financial accelerator" that originated in the beginning of the twentieth century and was rigorously modeled by Bernanke and Gertler (1989) should also be related to contagion through asset values.[16] Here is where the coexistence of the other channels of contagion is critical. It is mainly because of contagion through liquidity that contagion through asset values takes a life of its own. With the crisis, the combination of the two has been analyzed, suggesting contagion mechanisms where the decrease in asset prices reinforces banks' shortage of liquidity and forces them to sell their assets at fire sale prices. Three main liquidity-driven contagion channels—contagion through reduced participation of market makers (as in Brunnermeier and Pedersen 2009), contagion through fire sale triggered drop in collateral, and contagion through fire sale triggered insolvency expectations—have received attention in the recent literature in an area where additional contributions are to be expected.[17]

5.1.5 Contagion to Nonbank Financial Institutions and Feedback Loops

One important dimension of the impact of a bank's bankruptcy is its contagion to other nonbank financial institutions, such as insurance companies, finance companies, mutual funds, hedge funds, equity funds, and the shadow banking sector. The issue is particularly relevant in some countries, as in the United States, where nonbanks are more important quantitatively than banks, and many of these nonbank intermediaries are subject to less regulation and supervision than banks.

Whenever the banking industry is distressed, the contagion it generates on real activity implies a decrease in the price of assets. Besides overall real activity and asset prices, bank bankruptcy has a general impact on the stock market and on loans. The liquidity problems that result can lead to fire sales that affect the solvency of other financial institutions. Also nonbanking financial institutions' market share might increase at the expense of a banking industry that is in trouble to serve its usual goals and keep its customers.

In this section we will not consider the impact of the banking crisis on each different nonbanking institution but rather focus on the direct impact on the liquidity and solvency of these financial institutions and on possible feedback effects. The outcome will, of course, depend on the degree of sophistication of the financial markets and institutions. If the banking industry is ring fenced, a possibility recently raised in the UK banking regulation proposal, or if there are firewalls, the impact will be much lower.

The recent crisis has shown that contagion to the nonbanking financial institutions can be dramatic in some specific cases. Three channels of direct impact are worth mentioning: shadow banking, money market mutual funds, and the government sponsored banks, Fannie Mae and Freddie Mac.

Shadow Banking   Shadow banking has made the issue of contagion particularly relevant. With the development of shadow banking, a part of traditional banking activity is now being outsourced to other financial institutions. In particular, both bank and nonbank financial institutions partner in the process of securitization as well as in the provision of credit protection through CDS. The contractual obligations between the originating bank and the vehicle holding the asset is crucial in terms of contagion.

First, regarding securitization, in the United States as in the United Kingdom, banks have provided liquidity facilities to the special purpose vehicle (SPV) or conduit that acquired the banks' securitized loans, in order for the SPV to be able to issue asset-backed commercial paper (ABCP).[18] This liquidity line turned out to involve a very high risk that capital requirements fail to take into account. Indeed, in 2007, when delinquencies on subprime loans soared and investors shunned the liabilities issued by SPVs, the banks were forced to buy it from investors, thus absorbing it back onto their balance sheets, and faced additional losses to their capital.

Second, as we learned from the AIG crisis, CDS operations connect a bank and the seller of protection, in this case an insurance company. Lehman's bankruptcy caused huge increase in credit risk and a credit downgrade of AIG. Under the CDS contracts, the downgrade required AIG to post additional collateral that the insurance company did not have. As a consequence, AIG would have been in breach of contract, which, in turn, would have implied a sudden sharp increase in risk weighted assets for those banks using the CDS protection and a need for additional capital. This would have led to a capital shortage for the banking industry, so the Federal Reserve and the US government had to step in with a credit facility to prevent the company's collapse. Indeed the AIG bailout was preferred to the crisis its bankruptcy would have caused.

Money Market Mutual Funds   Without being part of the shadow banking, in buying assets and liabilities from banks, money market mutual funds (MMMFs) provide a regular source of liquidity to banks, particularly by buying ABS/CDOs.[19] From the perspective of an investor, MMMFs constitute a substitute for a deposit; from the perspective of the bank, it is the natural buyer of short-term AAA security.

The contracts offered in a MMMF are such that the redemption of shares is guaranteed by the sponsoring institution at $1 per share. This is possible because the fund invests in low risk, highly liquid securities that minimize the risk to the sponsor. On September 15, it was clear that all MMMFs that had a significantly large part of their securities invested in Lehman Brothers would have a share value below $1, and consequently redeemed their investment. This wave of redemptions constituted a run on MMMFs, which according to Duygan-Bump et al. (2013) led to a $400 billion decrease of the total assets managed by institutional prime funds in just a few days. Because MMMFs (in contrast to banks) are not backed by deposit insurance or lender of last resort facilities, the only protection investors have is the implicit guarantee of the sponsoring bank (or other financial intermediary). This is why when some MMMFs "broke the buck" (i.e., their net asset values dropped below $1), the Fed decided to provide liquidity through an Asset-Backed Commercial Paper Money Market Mutual Fund Liquidity Facility, thus taking on a role similar to that of a classic lender of last resort function for banks.[20] Moreover in both the United States and Europe there have been policy proposals to limit systemic risk stemming from these funds.[21]

Government-Sponsored Specialized Financial Institutions The 2008 financial crisis affected government-sponsored financial institutions in different ways depending on the extent of their commitments and their missions. In some financial institutions providing loans to small firms, the general reduction in banks' credit supply gave them an important role in providing funds to the firms, which were rationed by the combination of strict terms of lending and a credit crunch. Nevertheless, institutions that were committed to buy securities in the market were forced to take huge losses.

The crisis of Fannie Mae and Freddie Mac, whose role was to securitize loans by buying them from banks, bundling them and reselling them, illustrates the previous point. Once the originate-to-distribute business model collapsed, these two institutions did not stop securitizing but understood their mandate as supporting the market. According to Ashcraft et al. (2010), Freddie Mac played the role of lender of last resort until the piling up of its losses required it was put under conservatorship on September 6, 2008.

5.1.6   Contagion through Information Disclosure

It has been argued that during the recent crisis the use of full fair value based accounting has aggravated contagion. The amplifying effect of marking to market would work in the following way: banks suffer losses, this is immediately reflected in their accounts, capital is therefore decreased, and consequently bank debtholders require a larger additional premium to continue financing the entity; this premium squeezes the bank's margin, leading to additional losses. The mechanism is even more pronounced and perverse in the presence of a fire sale of assets (as it occurred with the so-called toxic assets during the recent global financial crisis). Indeed in this case the losses on these securities led banks to sell them, thus creating additional losses. The key to this argument is that the value of the asset in a malfunctioning market does not reflect the discounted cash flow of this asset and therefore marking to market leads to an overstatement of reported losses. While this argument may be valid in theory,[22] the current state of research does not seem to provide a clear-cut answer as to whether fair value accounting information increases contagion, so the argument is incomplete and open to a number of criticisms (see Laux and Leuz 2010; Freixas and Laux 2012).

To begin, the argument seems to ignore the rational expectations of investors. The implicit assumption is that in the absence of information, investors expect banks to be solvent. While this may be true in normal times, the assumption is incongruous in a banking crisis framework: the opposite assumption of pessimistic investors interpreting the lack of information as evidence that the outcome is worse than expected seems to make more sense, especially, as in the last crisis, when adverse selection proved to be a big part of the problem. Yet it is not clear that in the midst of a banking crisis, investors trust the content of banks' financial accounts, even if based on historical values, nor that banks will report the truthful value of their losses, even if mark to market is to be applied. Illustrating this point, Huizinga and Laeven (2009) find that investors discounted the reported values of banks real estate loans by over 15 percent and of mortgage-backed securities by some 13 percent in 2008. Clearly, investors realize the possibilities of manipulation arising from the fair value accounting and discount the book values accordingly.

Second, the argument is based on a misconception of the equivalence between mark to market accounting and fair value accounting. In fact mark to market is applied to securities, referred to as "level 1" inputs, that are traded in liquid markets. This is a valid practice for investment banks but not for commercial banks that hold a large fraction of their assets (some 69 percent according to the IMF Global Financial Stability report) as level 2 assets, whose valuation is based on models that use observable inputs, and level 3 assets that are valued by the bank according to internal models. In addition, held to maturity securities are reported at amortized costs, so historical cost accounting applies.

Third, fair value accounting offers banks substantial discretion. During the crisis, banks argued that losses related to mortgage-backed and other securities were temporary, and were allowed to use models to value these assets. Citigroup reported losses on available for sale and held to maturity of $2.8 billion in the fourth quarter of 2008 when the decrease in fair values of these assets was about $19 billion. Because of this, the general view is that fair value accounting left sufficient degrees of freedom to banks as to avoid the direct impact of marking to market on their income and equity (Huizinga and Laeven 2009; Laux and Leuz 2010).

Fourth, in October 2008 banks were allowed to reclassify their assets using July 2008 prices that did not reflect the impact the Lehman bankruptcy had on the securities market prices. So, although from a theoretical perspective the argument could be correct, further research will be needed to refine it and confirm its validity.

5.1.7 Cross-country Contagion

While it is obvious that changes in exchange rate affect banks' returns, this is not directly related to any type of cross-country contagion[23] but part of the macroeconomic environment generating financial fragility. So, as before, the analysis focuses on the mechanisms of contagion, while taking the macroeconomic environment as given, with the understanding that the two effects can reinforce one another during a crisis.

With the crisis, the consensus on the role of multinational banks in limiting the extent of the banking crisis has changed completely. The reason is that prior to the crisis the standard paradigm was the one-country banking crisis. If anything, cross-country banking would provide the benefits of channeling liquidity from a country with excess liquidity to another that is liquidity short (Kalemli-Ozcan, Papaioannou, and Peydró 2010, 2013). The crisis has confronted economic analysis with a simultaneous multiple-country crisis, showing that there are striking differences between a systemic crisis in a single small country and a worldwide systemic crisis—or involving several countries that are key in the financial markets—a difference that should be attributed to the difference in focus between partial equilibrium and general equilibrium.

Systemic Crises in a Single Country From a theoretical perspective, the standard neoclassical view suffices to illustrate why the presence of foreign banks may help in reducing the impact of a systemic crisis in a single country.

Indeed a systemic crisis in a single country implies a reduction of the credit supply, whether because of lack of banking capital or because of restricted funding availability for financial institutions. One way or another, the implication is an increase in the risk-adjusted return on capital in that country. This is an opportunity for foreign banks and foreign subsidiaries (whether foreign or domestic) that are not subject to the same liquidity and capital depletion. As such, cross-border banking has a very positive impact in a crisis situation as it plays the role of shock absorber.

Morgan, Rime, and Strahan (2004) develop a multiple-economy variant of the canonical banking model of Holmstrom and Tirole (1997) and test it using cross-state banking exposure data across US states. They show that if firms in certain states are hit by positive shocks that increase the value of their collateral, then under financial integration they receive more credit both from in-state and from out-of-state banks. As a result output increases in the affected region relatively more as compared to output in other regions, making cycles diverge.[24] The model of Morgan, Rime, and Strahan (2004) also predicts that banking integration may lead to more, rather than less, synchronized output cycles. This occurs if the shock is on the banking sector rather than on firm's productivity/collateral. If there is a negative shock to banks' capital, the induced contraction of credit supply has negative real effects for the domestic economy. If the domestic credit supply reduction is significant, under banking integration, the business cycles of the two interconnected regions/economies will become more synchronized, since banks that operate in financially interconnected regions pull out funds from the nonaffected region to continue lending in the affected region.

The empirical evidence corroborates the theoretical argument. De Haas and Van Lelyveld (2010) show how during single country crises, subsidiaries of financially strong parent banks were able to use their internal capital and liquidity market and did not reduce their supply of loans, unlike domestic banks.

Of course, this could have the unintended consequence of reducing the credit supply in the foreign bank's home country. This effect is negligible when large international banks lend to a small country confronted with a banking crisis, but it could be relevant when it affects large countries. The pioneering contribution of Peek and Rosengren (1997) indeed establishes how the Japanese crisis affected the US financial market.

Cross-border Banking Effects in a Worldwide Systemic Crisis   The study of a worldwide systemic crisis is somehow reminiscent of the analyses of Allen and Gale (2000a) and of Freixas, Parigi, and Rochet (2000), provided that one abstracts from currency issues and considers countries instead of individual banks. Indeed the same mechanisms of cross-country liquidity insurance that are provided by banks in the Allen and Gale framework could be originating cross-country contagion in a global liquidity crisis, with every multinational bank tending to retrench to its own domestic market.

On the behavior of foreign banks, the contribution by De Haas and Van Lelyveld (2014) shows that "multinational bank subsidiaries had to slow down credit growth about twice as fast as domestic banks," while domestic banks had access to a larger core deposit basis that made their funding and the lending more stable. Laeven and Giannetti (2012a) further show that during financial crises global banks tend to retrench to their home markets, even when those home markets are also experiencing financial crises.

Cetorelli and Goldberg (2011) examine the behavior of US bank branches across the world and show, using data before the 2007 crisis, that large globally oriented banks rely on internal capital markets with their foreign affiliates to help smooth domestic liquidity shocks so that a domestic liquidity shortage is also matched by a repatriation of liquidity toward the parent company. Symmetrically, in a second paper, Cettorelli and Goldberg (2012) establish a similar pattern for foreign bank branches that, on average, experienced a 12 percent net internal fund "withdrawal," and a sizable effect on their lending.

Kalemli-Ozcan, Papaioannou, and Perri (2013) study the effects of financial integration (through banks) on the transmission of international business cycles. In a sample of twenty developed countries between 1978 and 2009, the authors find that, in periods without financial crises, increases in bilateral banking linkages are associated with more divergent output cycles. This relation is significantly weaker during financial turmoil periods, suggesting that financial crises induce comovement among more financially integrated countries. They also show that countries with stronger, direct and indirect, financial ties to the United States experienced more synchronized cycles with the United States during the recent 2008 financial crisis. They then interpret these findings using a simple general equilibrium banking model of international business cycles with shocks to banking activity. The model suggests that the relation between integration and synchronization depends on the type of shocks hitting the world economy, and that shocks to global banks played an important role in triggering and spreading the 2008 financial crisis.

Ongena, Peydró, and van Horen (2013) study the international transmission of shocks from the banking to the real sector during the global financial crisis. For identification, they use matched bank-firm level data, including many small- and medium-size firms, in Eastern Europe and Central Asia. They find that internationally borrowing domestic and foreign-owned banks contract their credit more during the crisis than domestic banks that are funded only locally. Firms that are dependent on credit and at the same time have a relationship with an internationally borrowing domestic or a foreign bank (as compared to a locally funded domestic bank) suffer more in their financing and real performance. Single-bank relationship firms, small firms, and firms with intangible assets suffer most. For credit-independent firms, there are no differential effects. Their findings suggest that financial globalization has intensified the international transmission of financial shocks with substantial real consequences.

A new interesting dimension of cross-country banking is introduced in the analysis of their risk-taking behavior. Do banks that are more strictly regulated at home export their cautious behavior abroad? According to Ongena et al. (2012) it is precisely the opposite phenomenon that takes place. Their results show that banks that face strict regulation—namely with greater barriers to entry, tighter restrictions on bank activities, and higher minimum capital requirements in their domestic markets—choose to take more risk in the host country where regulatory standards are less stringent. In other words, their conclusion is the existence of a channel for exporting risk-taking.

5.2   Reinforcing Loops

Although for expositional reasons we have presented the different channels of contagion separately, it is obvious that all the channels combine and reinforce one another as illustrated in figure 5.1, so the partial equilibrium analysis may hide critical issues that will only become apparent once an overall general equilibrium approach is introduced.

Banks' liquidity shortages lead them to de-lever and to sell their assets, which triggers fire sales and decreases in asset prices. The fire sales generate losses, and the consequent capital depletion in financial institutions causes an increase in counterparty risk, which in turn sets off a dry-up in the unsecured interbank market (and also in the secured market, which uses as collateral the assets under fire sales). Thus more and more banks begin to be financially distressed. At this stage the bankruptcy of any financial institution would initiate a panic through the network of interbank exposures. In the case of AIG, the bankruptcy would have triggered losses in all the financial institutions that had bought credit risk protection from it. This made AIG a systemically important nonbank institution. In addition other negative effects can be at work such as international contagion and credit supply effects.

One would be tempted to consider a global model that combines the different channels of contagion. This is obviously the right way to go. Nevertheless, the existence of multiple equilibriums and nonlinearities should be taken into account. More specifically, this means that the economy could be subject to a sudden, discontinuous change of state that triggers a change in the values of all elasticities, which would make the task of simulating and calibrating the contagion channels much more arduous. In considering the joint impact of the different channels of contagion, the analysis is brought quite close to the challenges of measuring systemic risk, a point we fully develop in chapter 7.

There are two basic methodologies that measure systemic risk. Option theory allows computing a bank's probability of default (PD) out of the movements in its stock prices. Although this approach has a more solid theoretical foundation and has the benefits of considering the joint movements of all sources of financial instability, it appears as a black box because it is difficult to identify the sources of the main problems financial institutions face, and therefore it is impossible to define the best regulatory and macroprudential policy. Additionally the option valuation framework is adequate only if financial markets are close to perfect, which is not the case during a systemic crisis. This may be the reason why a number of central banks have put forward the alternative approach based on the balance sheet.

The balance sheet approach takes into account the structure of banks' balance sheets and attempts to measure how default probabilities (PDs) are affected by the macroeconomic factors. The macroeconomic variables are real output, inflation, real equity prices, overnight nominal interest rate, a long-term interest rate, and possibly some critical exchange rates.

The Bank of England's Risk Assessment Model for Systemic Institutions (RAMSI) emphasizes the risk over and above those taken into account by financial institutions themselves. It considers the channels of interbank exposures, as well as the interaction between balance sheets and asset prices and uses several rounds to solve for the joint bankruptcies. The integration of these channels allows identifying financial threats that would otherwise be ignored. This approach allows obtaining evidence on discontinuities and nonlinearities. Alessandri et al. (2009) argue that it provides a more rigorous modeling of the distribution of individual and systemic losses and of the value of banking assets as "bimodal in character, with a main peak associated with a healthy banking sector and a considerably smaller second peak in the extreme tail associated with outbreaks of contagious defaults."

5.3   The Magnitude of Contagion

To begin with, the extent of contagion depends on the banks' financial fragility. The ex ante profitable strategies of lending, herding, and risk-taking developed in good times will determine how important contagion effects will be when a crisis occurs. These issues have already been discussed in chapter 4.

Nevertheless, a second important issue is to be considered, since banks do not operate in perfectly anonymous markets but establish relationships among them and with other economic agents. As a consequence the magnitude of contagion will also depend on the networks linking financial institutions one to another as well as to other economic agents, a structure sometimes referred to as "the architecture of the financial system." This is why identifying the existing networks can help us understand the likely impact of a bank default on other economic agents and plan for such a contingency.

A network can be defined as a collection of nodes and links between nodes representing relationships between agents. The theory of networks has been successfully applied to other areas of economic analysis, and the formation of networks has been an interesting and relevant part of the analysis. When it comes to financial contagion, the theory of networks provides a more rigorous perspective on contagion and a clearer view of possible systemic risks, even if has limited results regarding the identification ex ante of network formation (see Allen and Babus 2009 and also Cocco et al. 2009, who show that interbank markets networks are such that the liquidity shocks of the participants have a low correlation). Applied to contagion, the ex ante formation has not provided highly relevant insights into financial contagion.

As a network represents a structure of contracting between economic agents, it is clear that the nodes and links will depend on the specific type of contract the agents are trading. In addition the size of economic agents is crucial, as shown in any graphical representations. This is an important element, as the contagion effects of bank A on bank

B will be proportional to the size of the asset that bank B holds as a proportion of its own assets. Consequently banks' networks may differ depending on the size of participants, on whether we analyze counter-party risk, liquidity risk, or OTCs reciprocal positions, and on both for historical reasons and technical reasons.

Existing banks' networks could be the result of different financial structures, such as a larger percentage of firms obtaining funds directly from the financial markets as in the United States while banking is more prevalent in Europe, or the result of banking regulation (the Glass–Steagall Act limited banks' operations in the equity market). It could also be the result of the access to a central securities depository or a clearing facility. Whatever the reason, this architecture will be criti-cal in determining the extent of contagion.

The main network we are interested in is the network of banks' reciprocal assets and liabilities. Its structure will allow determining what will be the banks that will be affected by a bank default. From a theoretical perspective, papers by Allen and Gale (2000a) and Freixas, Parigi, and Rochet (2000) both emphasize the importance of financial architecture of the unsecured interbank market for contagion and financial stability. The following diagram from Freixas, Parigi, and Rochet (2000) illustrates this point by considering three banks of equal size: in the first case lending operates clockwise, so that each bank funding depends on the solvency of another bank, while in the second, bank 1 is pivotal, representing the centrality of a money center, while banks 2 and 3 are peripheral.

The implication is that despite the three banks being identical, the two architectures are different. They differ in their resilience because the bankruptcy of one of the banks may or may not affect the others. They also differ in the centrality of the nodes or agents in the financial

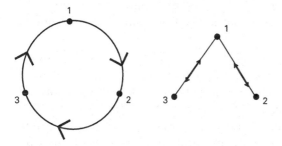

Figure 5.4
Banking network structures and financial contagion

system, as the critical liquidity shocks that will trigger a systemic panic are not the same, and they will be different because in the second graph, bank 1 may be systemic if it is too interconnected to fail.

As the main risk of contagion was thought to be the domino effect, research on the network of interbank counterparty risks was developed in central banks to assess the impact of the failure of one bank on the rest of the banking system. This required the use of detailed data on banks' counterparty risks that allowed a simulation of the impact of a given bank's bankruptcy.[25] The simulation has to take into account several rounds as the impact of bank A might affect bank B that in turn affects bank C, and the impact of joint bankruptcies initiated by A, but now including B and C, on other banks have to be considered. Overall, the results were quite reassuring, showing that except for large too-big-to fail banks, there was no serious systemic risk threat stemming from the network of interbank counterparty risks (see Upper 2007 and Iyer and Peydró 2011 for a critical review).

The results from this line of research were open to criticism for three reasons. First, loss given default (LGD) during a systemic crisis could be higher than in normal times. Second, the research took the channel of contagion through the network of interbank counterparty risks acting independently of any other channel. Third, these simulations take banks' actions to be very passive, whereas endogenous reactions of banks (e.g., runs) are crucial in wholesale markets.

This line of research has evolved to moderate these criticisms. Cifuentes et al. (2005) took into account declining asset prices due to banks' fire sales. Eisenger et al. (2006) included macroeconomic shocks. Other contributions include funding risk (Chan-Lau 2010). The Bank of England RAMSI model may be the most complete one as it integrates all possible contagion channels (Aikman et al. 2009). Nevertheless, the variability of LGD can be taken into account by assuming it to be a random variable. Memmel et al. (2011) use this approach and show that under the assumption of a stochastic LGD simulation, results show a more fragile banking system.

The analysis of networks is also interesting to establish how liquidity is channeled among banks. The usual assumption is that the interbank market is an anonymous market where participants have a negligible counterparty risk. However, Rochet and Tirole (1996) argue that the unsecured interbank market allows banks to monitor one another, so that banks can avoid duplication of monitoring costs by interacting mainly with the same counterparties. According to Cocco et al. (2009), this is precisely the case: banks create lender-borrower networks and are therefore more likely to borrow funds from banks with whom they have a relationship, obtaining funds at a lower interest rate than otherwise. This is particularly useful for smaller banks and banks with more nonperforming loans that tend to have limited access to international markets. Abbassi et al. (2015) analyze the interbank market in the euro area during the 2008 to 2012 crisis and find that relationship lending is crucial. Exploring the evolution of the interbank network, Mistrulli (2005) finds that the interbank market structure changed from an almost "complete" network (where all banks are symmetrically financially linked) to a "multiple money center" structure.

Obviously the unsecured interbank market is not the only one where financial architecture will be essential. Indeed the analysis extends to any type of counterparty risk. Hence the centrality of AIG in the network of bank CDS' contracts was critical in generating the CDS crisis in September 2008.

Another important network in determining the extent of contagion works through relationship banking. The network is here extremely simple, as a firm obtaining funds under relationship banking has only a link with its main bank while a firm using arm's length finance has a potential link to any bank. The implications regarding contagion through the reduction in the supply of credit are then quite different for the different types of firms. If all banks restrict their credit, they will tend to give better terms on the loans to those firms with which they have a lending relationship (Berlin and Mester 1999; Bolton et al. 2013). If instead a bank goes bankrupt, it will be the firms that maintain a relationship with the bankrupt bank that will suffer the most as it will be more difficult for them to prove their creditworthiness to other banks.

Slovin et al. (1993) establish this last point by showing how Continental Illinois' failure had a 2 percent negative effect on their US corporate clients' share prices. His findings are confirmed by Djankov (2005) who analyzes the impact of 31 bank failures in the East Asian crisis and concludes that "bank relationship adds value to a firm, and that investor confidence in bank-related firms depends on investors' certainty in the continuity of the banking relationship" (p. 2095).

This difficulty for firms to substitute one lending relationship for another can further be seen when some banks reduce their supply of loans. In a world of arm's-length banking, this should have a limited impact. Instead, in a world of relationship banking, it will have a dramatic effect on the firms borrowing from the banks in difficulties. Peek and Rosengren provide evidence on this effect by using the Japanese banking crisis as a natural experiment where the reduction in credit supply is unrelated to the US business cycle and are able to establish conclusively that loan supply shocks emanating from Japan had real effects on economic activity in the United States.

A particular type of network is the one where the whole banking and financial system depends on the survival of a systemically important financial institution, either, as it was well known with a too big to fail bank or, more recently, with a too big, too complex, or too interconnected nonbank, as was the case for the AIG crisis.

According to the Financial Stability Board, systemically important financial institutions (SIFIs) are "financial institutions whose distress or disorderly failure, because of their size, complexity and systemic interconnectedness, would cause significant disruption to the wider financial system and economic activity" (Financial Stability Board 2011). Global SIFIs (G-SIFIs) have additionally strong cross-country activities so that their bankruptcy affects financial stability in several countries.

Almost by definition, too big to fail banks' bankruptcies are infrequent, since typically they are rescued in case of financial distress. It is quite exceptional that an institution like Lehman Brothers goes down given that it is systemic and the market expects its bailout. In such a case, where individual solvency risk and systemic risk are one and the same, the impact is immediate, with a dramatic fall in the stock market, and in the corporate bond market, and a generalized increase of counterparty risk. Though, as we argue in this chapter and other parts of the book, the 2008 crisis was not caused simply by contagion by the Lehman failure, it was a signal that the correlated strong risks that Western banks took in the 2000s (loans in real estate and wholesale short-term finance) were being realized.[26]

A bank like Continental Illinois that was in financial distress in 1984 acted as correspondent bank for nearly 1,000 banks at the time. According to Schoenmaker (1998), 66 banks had uninsured deposits in excess of 100 percent of their capital, and another 113 banks had deposits between 50 and 100 percent of their capital. Conceivably, if the uninsured deposits in Continental had not been protected by the Federal Reserve and the Federal Deposit Insurance Corporation (FDIC), its failure would have caused a chain of bank failures.

5.4   Conclusions

Our discussion in this chapter showed that contagion has multiple dimensions. It can arise from multiple sources and operate through multiple mechanisms, and these mechanisms tend to interact and reinforce each other. However, actually measuring contagion is a challenge, both because some of its effects operate indirectly and through feedback loops and because data on network structures and direct exposures is limited. Going forward, supervisors and maroprudential policy makers need much better data to monitor these networks and measure systemic risk arising from contagion channels.

6 Systemic Risk and the Real Costs of Financial Crises

Financial crises can be highly damaging not only for the financial system but also for the real economy, as the impairment of the financial system reduces the intermediation of savings to the real economy and the deleveraging of financial institutions puts undue pressures on asset prices and credit flows. Additionally financial crises tend to follow periods of high leverage for households and nonfinancial firms, and the ensuing debt overhang problems reduce aggregate consumption and investment. Moreover a decline in aggregate demand feeds back into the financial system by depressing asset prices and collateral values, creating a vicious cycle whereby weaknesses in the financial sector and real economy reinforce each other.

Financial crises not only have a strong immediate negative impact on aggregate output and employment, but their negative effects tend to persist over a prolonged period of time, with a recovery to pre-crisis levels of economic activity and wealth often taking several years. A crucial question is therefore what explains the persistency of these financial shocks. Why is it that several countries today have still not recovered to their pre-crisis levels of GDP per capita?

Country experiences in handling financial crises have been met with mixed success, with government policies sometimes aggravating rather than alleviating problems. Some government policies only target the financial system, such as the creation of a bad bank or bank recapitalization, whereas other policies are more macro oriented, including expansive monetary and fiscal policies. Expansive policies may be beneficial to minimize the short-term impact of a crisis but have important intergenerational consequences and may plant the seeds for the next bubble. Other interventions such as forcing banks to hold more capital may be more effective in good times rather than in crisis times. Structural public policies can also play an important role in restoring financial and economic stability, for instance, policies that foster a more diversified financial system or that increase the flexibility of labor markets.

This chapter reviews existing evidence on the impact of financial crises on the real economy, with particular emphasis on the impact of systemic crises. Notice that although we address here the cost of financial crises in isolation, this is only part of an overall cost–benefit analysis of financial development, and therefore the benefits of financial liberalization and financial deepening should be kept in mind.

The real costs of financial crises can be measured in terms of output losses, increases in unemployment, asset prices, fiscal costs associated with bank support measures, and increases in public debt. We abstract here from the social costs associated with loss of employment and debt overhang problems (e.g., see Atkinson et al. 2013).

Output losses and the increase in public debt capture the overall real and fiscal implications of the crisis. Laeven and Valencia (2013) find that the average banking crisis since 1970 costs the taxpayer a staggering 12.4 percent of GDP in terms of fiscal outlays committed to the financial sector, with a high of 56.8 percent in the case of Indonesia in 1997 (figure 6.1).[1] They estimate average output losses of 30.1 percent of GDP, with cumulative output losses for Ireland and Latvia in 2011 standing out at over 100 percent of potential GDP. The average increase in public debt for countries with public debt increases amounts to 26.0 percent of GDP, with highs of 108.1 percent of GDP in the case of Guinea-Bissau in 1995, 83.3 percent of GDP in the case of Uruguay in 1981, and 72.8 percent of GDP in the case of Iceland in 2008. But there are also many countries for which public debt does not increase during banking crisis episodes.

These cost estimates are conditional on potential policy action taken and are therefore not directly comparable in a strict sense. Also, such estimates do not include taxpayer money put at risk to contain the crisis (including from government guarantees on bank liabilities and subsidized deposit insurance), nor do they capture any wealth transfers associated with accommodative macroeconomic policies to save the banking system (e.g., from creditors to debtors via inflation or low interest rates, or from young to old via increases in public debt). Output losses will differ depending on the size of the initial shock, differences across countries in how the shock was propagated through the financial system, and the intensity of policy interventions (Laeven and Valencia 2008).

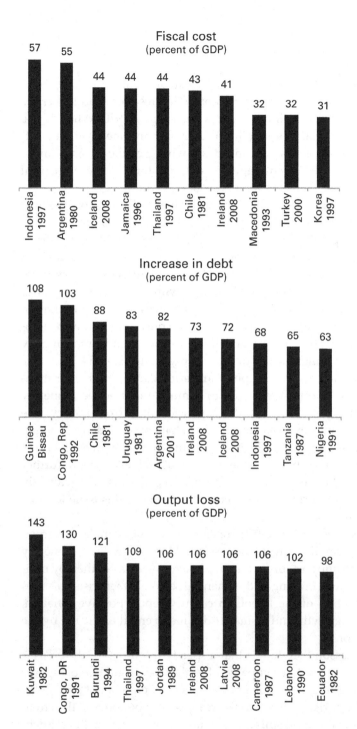

Figure 6.1
Costliest banking crises since 1970. Increase in debt is increase in public debt. Fiscal cost
is fiscal outlays associated with bank restructuring policies. Output loss is cumulative
loss in GDP relative to trend GDP. All outcomes are expressed relative to GDP. Source:
Laeven and Valencia (2013)

The analysis of financial crises in Laeven and Valencia (2008, 2013) is very detailed, especially in terms of policy responses and of crises around the world, but limited to the period post-1970. What do we know about financial crises going further back in time? Are they different from the recent crises, and if so, why? Schularick and Taylor (2012) and their subsequent papers with Oscar Jordà analyze financial crises for the past 140 years for 14 developed countries.[2]

The authors find that the impact of financial crises on the real economy was more muted in the post-1945 era in absolute numbers, but was of comparable magnitude relative to trend.[3] Measured in terms of output declines, financial crises remain severe during the post-1945 period. The maximum decline in real investment activity was more pronounced before World War II, though with a sharp recovery after four years. The two eras show strong differences in terms of inflation during financial crises. Financial crises in the prewar period were associated with deflation and a stagnation of narrow and broad money growth (these findings are not driven simply by the Great Depression). Instead, financial crises in the postwar period came with higher inflation relative to normal times due to a much more active monetary policy response, as shown by the expansion of narrow money. The more activist stance in monetary policy helped avoid a debt–deflation vicious cycle (Fisher 1933), which was a common feature of earlier crisis episodes. Deflation, by increasing the real value of debt, further increases the debt overhang and credit crunch problems, which already tend to be severe during banking crises. (We turn to this issue in more detail in the next section.)

Schularick and Taylor (2012) conclude that policy makers learned the lessons from the Great Depression. More aggressive monetary policy and fast support for the financial sector were used, thereby mitigating strong deleveraging of the financial sector. In fact crisis episodes in the second half of the twentieth century report positive inflation, higher money growth, and a smaller decline in credit extension by the financial sector.[4]

A general lesson therefore is that a speedy resolution of the crisis is of the essence, even if accompanied by high fiscal outlays to support the financial sector. A postponement of such action will not only delay the recovery but risks adding to the real costs by prolonging the credit crunch and the negative spirals associated with slow growth and debt overhang problems (Calomiris, Klingebiel, and Laeven 2003; Laeven and Valencia 2008). However, active monetary policy by providing liquidity to weak banks and governments can also delay necessary policies to restructure the financial system.[5]

Turning to real effects, it is interesting to observe that despite the much more aggressive policy response in the postwar period, the cumulative real effects of financial crises have been somewhat stronger in the postwar period. In the aftermath of postwar financial crises, output dropped a cumulative 6.2 percent relative to trend, and real investment by more than 22 percent. Moreover the prewar output decline effect is largely an artifact of the Great Depression of the 1930s. The lower observed real effects of financial crises during the pre-1930 era is consistent with the idea that financial sectors played a less central role in the economy at the time. It is also consistent with the view that economies suffered less from nominal rigidities, especially before 1913, as compared to the 1930s, and hence were better able to adjust to nominal shocks such as crisis-induced debt deflation (Chernyshoff et al. 2009).

Why are output losses so large nowadays despite the more expansive central bank and government policies? On the one hand, governments and central banks learned the 1930s lessons that activist policies are needed to prevent negative feedback loops in the economy. On the other hand, the financial sector has grown in size and leverage, as we have seen in detail in chapter 4. Therefore shocks hitting the financial system now have a larger impact on the real economy. Moreover explicit and implicit government guarantees on bank liabilities have fostered the growth of excessive leverage and risk-taking within the financial system. Although the deleveraging process following the crisis has led to some shrinkage of the financial system in some advanced economies, financial systems by and large remain highly leveraged and concentration has increased through mergers and acquisitions. Indeed the costs of systemic risk could be even higher nowadays compared to earlier periods when the financial system was smaller, less leveraged, and less complex, and thus the role for macroprudential policy in curbing these systemic risks has grown.

Reinhart and Rogoff (2009b) analyze the aftermaths of financial crises.[6] These aftermaths share three characteristics. First, they involve deep and prolonged asset market collapses, with real housing price declining on average 35 percent over six years and equity price collapsing on average 55 percent over three and a half years. Second, they are associated with strong declines in output and employment, with the unemployment rate rising on average 7 percentage points over the down phase of the cycle. Output falls from peak to trough an average of over 9 percent, though the duration of the downturn, averaging two years, is shorter than for unemployment. Third, the real value of government debt tends to balloon, rising an average of 86 percent in the major post–1945 crisis episodes. A substantial part of debt increase is not due to the costs of bailing out and recapitalizing the banking system, but to the collapse in tax revenues associated with economic recessions, as well as often ambitious countercyclical fiscal policies aimed at mitigating the downturn (Laeven and Valencia 2012).

6.2   Transmission Channels

The financial system performs several important functions for the real sector, and therefore its overall impairment creates several substantial costs for firms and households—for example, the smooth functioning of the payment system, risk sharing, and saving products. The main transmission channel from financial sector distress is the impairment of the allocation of funds from savers to firms for investment and to households for consumption. This allocation of funds mainly takes the form of bank credit, though in some countries such as Germany and Japan banks also take equity stakes in firms. Moreover in some countries financial markets constitute important alternative sources of finance, and can act as a "spare tire" for firms in need of external finance when the banking sector is in distress.

A reduction in credit is an important negative spillover from financial crises. Credit is reduced in a crisis partly because of lack of credit demand as economic perspectives are worse and thus investment opportunities and consumption needs are reduced. However, as firm cash flows are lower in crisis times, the need for external finance in a bust can be higher. Moreover, as collateral and asset prices are lower, agency costs of borrowing are higher, and therefore credit is reduced despite a potential demand for credit. This is also known as the (firm or household) balance sheet channel effect.

Furthermore systemic crises tend to follow periods of strong credit growth and increasing leverage, and thus debt overhang problems associated with the crisis and a collapse in asset prices may lead to a reduction of aggregate investment and consumption, including through reduced access to external finance. Likewise there may be a strong reduction in risk appetite by financial intermediaries and investors, thus lowering access to external finance for risky projects in particular, including those needed for a strong recovery of economic growth. Finally, although firms and households may continue to have a positive demand for credit and be solvent, they may not be able to obtain the necessary credit because bank illiquidity and insolvency may create a reduction of the supply of credit, namely a credit crunch. Contagion within the financial system can further aggravate bank capital short-ages and liquidity problems, with funding and market liquidity prob-lems reinforcing each other. In extremely severe systemic crises, the financial system can be so impaired that it is no longer able to perform its main function of attracting savings and channeling them to their most productive use to support investments and consumption, thus implying large real costs.

Banks collect private information from borrowers to make valuable relationship loans, thereby enhancing borrowers' welfare (Sharpe 1990; Rajan 1992; Bhattacharya and Chiesa 1995; Boot 2000). This information would be lost if banks fail (Bernanke 1983). For example, Bae et al. (2002) show that firms with closer relationships to their banks benefited from easier access to credit from their banks during the Korean finan-cial crisis of 1997. Bank failures therefore create negative externalities for the failed bank's clients through an increase in borrowing cost or credit rationing.

Moreover firms that lose their main bank relationship during the crisis may suffer disproportionately because surviving banks are at an informational disadvantage and will therefore be reluctant to lend to such firms, especially when these firms are small and opaque. Prob-lems in the banking system thus change production decisions of bor-rowers and this has real effects.

A large empirical literature has shown that financial conditions have real consequences (King and Levine 1993; Rajan and Zingales 1998; Levine 2005). Bernanke (1983) and Calomiris and Mason (2003) find that the US banking crisis during the Great Depression reduced the efficiency with which credit was allocated, and that the resulting higher cost and reduced availability of credit acted to reduce domestic output by depressing aggregate demand. Though less studied, the real conse-quences of the European banking crisis in 1931 might have been equally worse, following the collapse in Vienna of Kreditanstalt, which was taken over by the Austrian government, and which shook confidence not only in other Austrian but also in German banks, and was followed by a number of bank failures and corporate bankruptcies resulting in high unemployment in Germany.

Bernanke and Lown (1991), Peek and Rosengren (1995), and Hancock and Wilcox (1994) using US banking data each present evidence consistent with the hypothesis that bank lending is curtailed—a credit crunch—when bank capital is low or when the banking sector has suffered significant capital losses. However, a deterioration in the quality of borrowers during crises also implies a decrease in bank lending, and thus causality is not clear. Klein et al. (2002) and Peek and Rosengren (1997, 2000) exploit the losses faced by Japanese banks from the collapse of the Japanese stock market as an exogenous shock to the lending by Japanese banks' subsidiaries in the United States to show that negative shocks to bank capital have real effects by curtailing credit. Ashcraft (2005) uses the closures of healthy subsidiaries of a failed banking holding company as an exogenous disruption to the supply of credit and finds important negative economic effects in the corresponding local county income. However, firms borrowing from weak banks may also have worse investment opportunities, and thus causality is not clear.

Jiménez et al. (2012) analyze the credit crunch in the 2008 crisis in Spain using a dataset consisting of loan applications.[7] To establish a causal link between bank balance sheet strength and credit supply, they focus on the set of loan applications made in the same month by the same borrower to different banks of varying balance-sheet strengths. Within this set of loan applications, for which the quality of potential borrowers is constant, they study how economic conditions affecting the granting of loans vary with bank capital and liquidity conditions. Moreover they analyze whether firms that get rejected in their initial loan application can undo the resultant reduction in credit availability by successfully applying to other banks. (If that was the case, then it would imply that the real effects associated with credit crunches are minimal.)

They find that lower GDP growth reduces the probability that a loan application is granted, particularly during crisis times. The negative effect on loan granting is statistically stronger for banks with low capital, implying that a bank capital crunch leads to a credit crunch. They also find that firms that get rejected in their initial loan application cannot undo the resultant reduction in credit availability by applying to other banks, especially in periods of tighter economic conditions.[8]

Jiménez et al. (2013) analyze how variation in bank capital stemming from loan loss provisioning rules affects credit supply and real effects during the recent crisis in Spain. They find at the loan level that banks with ample dynamic loan loss provision funds (which constitute part of tier 2 capital) at the onset of the crisis maintain their supply of committed credit to the same firm after the crisis shock to a larger extent than banks with less loan loss reserves. At the same time banks with more provisions shorten loan maturity and tighten collateral requirements, possibly to compensate for the higher risk taken by easing credit volume during the crisis.

In terms of real effects, they find that the changes in loan level credit are binding at the firm level, with credit contracting especially for those firms that borrowed more from banks that had lower ex ante dynamic provision funds, suggesting that firms cannot substitute for the lost bank financing. Consistent with this interpretation, they find that firm's total assets, employment, and survival probability are negatively affected as well. These results imply that the existence of large bank capital buffers (built up prior to the crisis) helps banks absorb shocks during a crisis with strong real effects.[9]

Frictions in bank lending can also impact employment outcomes. Chodorow-Reich (2014a) analyzes banking relationships and employment in the United States during the 2008 crisis and uses the dispersion in lender health following the collapse of Lehman Brothers as a source of exogenous variation in the availability of credit to borrowers. He finds that firms that had pre-crisis relationships with less healthy lenders had a lower likelihood of obtaining a loan following the Lehman bankruptcy filing, paid a higher interest rate if they did borrow, and reduced employment by more compared to pre-crisis clients of healthier lenders. These effects vary by firm type, being much larger for smaller, more informationally-opaque firms. The withdrawal of credit accounts for between one-third and one-half of the decline in employment at small and medium firms in the sample in the year following the Lehman bankruptcy.

Results for large firms are insignificant. Is this because large firms have access to financial markets, so that they can substitute bank credit with other sources of finance? Kashyap, Stein, and Wilcox (1993) provide evidence that capital markets can act as a "spare tire" to bank loans for firms when monetary conditions are tight. Tighter monetary policy leads to a rise in commercial paper issuance by firms and a fall in bank loans to firms. Becker and Ivashina (2013) analyze firms' substitution between bank debt and nonbank debt (public bonds) using firm-level data. Any firm that raises new debt must have a positive demand for external funds. The authors interpret firm's switching from loans to bonds as a contraction in bank credit supply. They find strong evidence of substitution from loans to bonds at times characterized by tight bank lending standards, high levels of nonperforming loans and loan allowances, low bank share prices and tight monetary policy.

These results suggest that there are variations of credit supply around the business and monetary cycle, but also, similarly to Adrian, Colla, and Shin (2012), these results suggest that other sources of finance (in this case market debt) can partly neutralize the negative impact of bank credit crunches. This evidence supports the view that a more diversified financial system, where markets operate alongside banks, may limit the negative impact of financial crises. At the same time, the mingling of banks and markets can also elevate systemic risk if the risks arising from the interconnections between banks and markets are not closely monitored and controlled. The extent to which firms depend on external sources of financing (from banks or markets) matters especially during a crisis. In a cross-country setting, Kroszner, Laeven, and Klingebiel (2007) and Dell'Ariccia et al. (2008) examine the real effects of banking crises and find that economic sectors more dependent on external finance suffer more during banking crises. Kroszner, Laeven, and Klingebiel (2007) also find that these effects are more pronounced in developing countries, in countries with deeper financial systems, and in countries with more severe banking crises. Moreover Raddatz (2006) provides evidence that financial development reduces economic volatility. He finds that sectors with larger liquidity needs are less volatile and experience smaller crises in financially developed countries.

Bank failures, as we have discussed in detail in chapter 5, also generate negative externalities for other banks in the form of a loss of confidence in the stability of the financial system as a whole, losses from interbank and derivative exposures to failed banks, and losses from assets that the failing bank is forced to sell at fire sale prices. This is different in other industries, where competitors generally gain from the failure of another firm. These negative externalities associated with bank failures offer the main rationale for financial regulation: to prevent socially costly bank failures (Dewatripont and Tirole 1994;

Bhattacharya et al. 1998; Gorton and Winton 2003; Freixas and Sant-omero 2004). The recent global financial crisis is a prime example of intensified counterparty risk placing undue stress on interbank markets and other wholesale markets, with negative ramifications for the flow of bank funds. Moreover Allen and Gale (2004a) show that bank fail-ures have important welfare implications as banks provide consumers with insurance against idiosyncratic liquidity shocks, a role that markets generally do not perform equally.

Iyer et al. (2014) analyze whether a freeze in the interbank market creates a reduction of credit supply for firms, and whether central banking policy can reduce such a squeeze. They study the effects of the 2007 to 2009 banking crisis on credit supply to businesses. For empirical identification, they use loan-level data for the entire Portuguese banking sector, matched with firm and bank balance sheets, and exploit the unexpected freeze of the European interbank market in August 2007. They analyze lending before and after the crisis by banks with different susceptibility to the interbank shock, based on their interbank exposure prior to the crisis. For the same borrower, they find that banks that rely more on interbank finance before the crisis decrease their lending more severely during the crisis. The credit supply reduction is stronger for riskier banks. Overall, they find limited positive impact of central bank liquidity assistance on credit supply, but banks with higher depen-dence on the interbank market hoard liquidity.

Moreover the credit supply reduction is stronger for smaller, younger firms, with weaker banking relationships. Importantly, they show that the firms cannot compensate the reduction in supply via obtaining credit from other, less affected, banks, nor from other sources of debt, including trade credit and bonds. Finally, they find no credit crunch for large firms.[10] Their results suggest that the liquidity shock of the finan-cial crisis of 2007 to 2009 affected smaller, more opaque, younger firms more severely than larger, more established firms. To the extent that these firms also tend to be the most entrepreneurial firms, these results imply that the liquidity shock has substantial negative ramifications for economic growth.

On firm characteristics that proxy for quality and risk, such as firm return on assets and loan interest coverage, Iyer et al. (2014) find that banks cut credit supply across the board with respect to firm profits. However, somewhat surprisingly, they find that banks do not cut—in fact, support—credit supply to weaker firms in terms of low loan inter-est coverage. A possible explanation is loan evergreening or "zombie" lending, namely the rolling over of bad loans to distressed borrowers to avoid loan write-offs. A credit reduction to these firms might increase potential loan defaults, which could in turn increase capital requirements for banks and/or the likelihood of firing the banks' top managers.

Albertazzi and Marchetti (2011) present evidence consistent with loan evergreening by Italian banks during the recent financial crisis. In this case, loan evergreening occurred by lengthening the maturity of existing loans to distressed firms, preventing these firms to default on their loans and allowing bank managers to hide bad loans in their balance sheet by rolling them over.

The term "zombie lending" was originally coined in the context of the Japanese banking crisis of the 1990s. Caballero, Hoshi, and Kashyap (2008) show that the zombie lending caused extremely negative effects in Japan, prolonging the period it took to overcome the financial crisis and increasing the associated costs. The authors show that zombie lending keeps artificially alive firms that instead should exit the economy and reduces the credit to more productive, newer sectors. These changes in the composition of credit supply therefore reduce GDP growth and thus increase the costs over time of financial crises and systemic risk. Some commentators even argue that the recent policies in the euro area are keeping zombie banks artificially alive through a combination of regulatory forbearance and easy lending by the eurosystem of central banks.[11] In this case "zombie" refers to the distressed bank rather than the non-financial borrower. Not only does the failure to remove zombie banks (or bad assets) from the financial system delay restructuring and economic recovery, but zombie banks also have an incentive to "gamble for resurrection": distressed banks that enjoy limited liability have an incentive to choose a risky asset portfolio that pays out high profits if the gamble succeeds but leaves debtholders and depositors, and taxpayers, with the losses if the gamble fails. Such risk shifting behavior is optimal for the distressed bank because if the gamble pays off, the bank returns to solvency, and if not, the bank continues being insolvent, without significant losses for shareholders or the manager.[12]

Kane (1989) and Cole et al. (1995) document the existence of gambling for resurrection during the US S&L (saving and loans bank) crisis in the 1980s. Rising interest rates in the late 1970s following the appointment of Volcker as chairman of the Federal Reserve reduced bank profits (and thus capital) for S&Ls as they had existing portfolios dominated by long-term, fixed rate mortgages that paid lower rates than rates on (short-term) deposits. S&Ls expanded into riskier activities (e.g., commercial real estate) to gamble with high risk, high return lending opportunities, which turned into huge bank losses and eventually fiscal costs for the taxpayers.

There is also evidence consistent with gambling for resurrection during the 2007 to 2008 crisis. Baldursson and Portes (2013) analyze gambling for resurrection in the Icelandic banking crisis, where in October 2008 the three major banks collapsed. The banks had expanded at a rapid pace and reported seemingly healthy balance sheets until their collapse. In August 2007 wholesale liquidity dried up and the Iceland banks, as the authors show, gambled then on resurrection, expanding their balance sheets and refinancing the investments of their owners and other big borrowers even more. The banks also prevented their share prices from collapsing by purchases of their own shares in the stock market. Only a month before the collapse of October 2008 the banks all reported strong liquidity positions. Baldursson and Portes (2013) show that these reports were misleading, that all this went on apparently unnoticed by regulators, and also how bank funding unraveled over few days and the banking collapse became inevitable. Unlike other advanced economies, Iceland did not have the resources to bail out its banks, which ex post may have reduced the overall costs of the financial crisis.

For the recent euro area crisis, Acharya and Steffen (2015) show evidence of a "carry trade" behavior of banks in the market for sovereign bonds, consistent with gambling incentives. Estimates from multifactor models relating equity returns to GIIPS (Greece, Ireland, Italy, Portugal, and Spain) and German government bond returns indicate that banks have been long peripheral sovereign bonds funded in short-term wholesale markets, a position that generated "carry" until the GIIPS bond returns deteriorated significantly inflicting significant losses on banks. They show that banks that were more vulnerable to funding pressures, such as banks with more wholesale funding and poorly capitalized banks, that have greater incentives to gamble through carry trade, had particularly large exposures and even increased their exposures between the two European stress tests of March and December 2010, taking advantage of a widening of yield spreads in the sovereign bond market.

As the crisis progresses, the authors find that there is an increase in "home bias"—greater exposure of domestic banks to its own sovereign's bonds.[13] On balance, their results are supportive of moral hazard in the form of risk-taking by undercapitalized banks to exploit low risk weights and central bank funding of risky government bond positions.

To deal with large-scale distressed banking assets, governments have often resorted to establishing so-called bad banks that acquire distressed assets from otherwise healthy banks. An important potential benefit of removing distressed assets from bank's balance sheets is that this can free up lending capacity to more productive borrowers, and thus reduce the zombie lending. However, country experience with the setting up of bad banks or asset management companies to manage distressed banking assets have been met with mixed success, in part because of governance problems that plague the management of such government controlled entities or because of the difficulty in recovering value from these bad assets in distressed asset markets. The more successful cases were those that were giving sound incentives to maximize the recovery value of the assets acquired (Calomiris, Klingebiel, and Laeven 2003).

Another important effect of financial crises is their impact on public debt. This effect occurs because of the fiscal costs associated with both the repair of the financial system (e.g., bank recapitalizations and asset purchases) and the decline in aggregate economic activity. What are the effects of the resulting increases in public debt on the economy? Is there a crowding out of private investment? Why do domestic banks increase their positions in domestic public debt as compared to foreign investors? In 2007 countries in the euro area periphery were enjoying stable growth, low deficits, and low spreads. Then the financial crisis started and pushed them into deep economic recessions, raising their deficits and public debt levels. By 2010 they were facing severe sovereign debt problems. Spreads increased and so did the share of sovereign debt held by domestic creditors. Credit was reallocated from the private to the public sectors, reducing investment and deepening the recessions even further. This created a vicious cycle between weak banks and weak sovereigns, whereby weak banks increased their holdings of sovereign paper and sovereign stress reduced the value of banks' holdings of such paper.

To account for these facts, Broner et al. (2013) propose a model of sovereign risk in which debt can be traded in secondary markets. The model embeds creditor discrimination and crowding-out effects.

Creditor discrimination arises because, in turbulent times, sovereign debt offers a higher expected return to domestic creditors than to foreign ones (domestic are favored over foreign investors in case of default, or domestic banks in case of government failure would equally lose even without public bonds as the implicit guarantees would be lost). This provides incentives for domestic purchases of debt.

Crowding-out effects arise because private borrowing is limited by financial frictions. If private credit markets would work perfectly, the purchases of sovereign debt by domestic creditors could be financed by borrowing from foreign creditors. However, there are agency costs in private borrowing, especially for smaller firms with limited collateral. As a result purchases of sovereign debt by domestic creditors may crowd out productive investment. Crowding-out is welfare reducing because even though creditors might benefit from the high returns of domestic debt, the economy as a whole loses because of the forgone private investment opportunities.[14]

Banking crises are often associated with a collapse in the value of collateral, normally in real estate, triggering sharp declines in credit availability for firms and households, which are also reinforced by the lower net worth and risk of non-financial borrowers.[15] Bernanke and Gertler (1989) and Bernanke et al. (1996) show that credit market conditions can propagate and amplify negative shocks to nonfinancial borrowers' wealth in the presence of asymmetric information between borrowers and lenders. Therefore private sector balance sheet channels can be important in driving the real effects of credit (Bernanke and Gertler 1995). Kiyotaki and Moore (1997) show that shocks to asset prices that lower the value of collateral can lead to downward spirals in asset prices by reducing the amount that can be borrowed against this collateral. Caballero and Krishnamurthy (2001) argue that such negative spirals are especially severe in emerging markets because firms need to maintain large amounts of collateral to borrow internationally, which limits the amount of collateral they can use to borrow locally.

Mian and Sufi (2014a) analyze the household balance sheet channel (Mishkin 1978) during the recent recession in the United States. They find that a drop in aggregate demand driven by shocks to household balance sheets is responsible for a large fraction of the decline in US employment and consumption from 2007 to 2009. Moreover they find that job losses in the nontradable sector are higher in high-leverage counties that were most severely impacted by the balance sheet shock (a debt overhang problem), while losses in the tradable sector are distributed uniformly across all counties. They find exactly this pattern from 2007 to 2009. Their estimates suggest that the decline in aggregate demand driven by household balance sheet shocks accounts for almost 4 million of the lost jobs from 2007 to 2009, or 65 percent of the lost jobs in the data.

All in all, the evidence suggests that each of the bank and nonfinancial sector (firms and households) balance sheet channels play an important role, causing negative real effects during a financial crisis. Maddaloni and Peydró (2011 and 2013) show with US and euro area loan survey data that credit conditions vary over the business cycles, partly reflecting variations in credit supply (i.e., the bank lending channel), but also variations in credit demand and firm and household net worth and collateral (i.e., balance sheet channels). Both channels operate alongside each other, and reinforce each other, in the sense that weaker firm and household balance sheets negatively impact the balance sheets of banks, and this in turn reduces the willingness of depositors and markets to fund banks.

These two channels are thus stronger when the debt overhang problems in the economy are more severe (Myers 1977; Bernanke and Gertler 1995). Debt overhang problems can contribute to a reduction of credit in systemic crises: good investment opportunities (projects with positive net present value) are not executed because of high firm leverage, thus reducing economic growth. As a result the higher the ex ante leverage, the higher not only the likelihood of a financial crisis (as we saw in chapter 4), but also the worse the negative effects on the real economy when a crisis occurs (see the evidence by Schularick and Taylor 2012).

An overhang of illiquid assets, often associated with banking crises, can also cause a credit market freeze. Banks that hold large quantities of illiquid assets may trigger sales at fire sale prices when faced with negative liquidity shocks. Diamond and Rajan (2011) argue that impaired banks that may be forced to sell illiquid assets in the future have private incentives to hold, rather than sell, those assets, even though this depresses the current value of their assets. The reason is that by selling the asset the bank will sacrifice the returns that it would get if the currently depressed value of the asset recovers. At the same time potential buyers of these assets (including healthy lenders) will demand higher returns in anticipation of a potential fire sale, reducing their incentive to lend. The result is a worse fire sale and a larger drop in lending than is necessary. Holmstrom and Tirole (1998) show that economies may suffer efficiency losses when credit markets are disrupted such as during banking crises and are no longer able to provide funds to firms that are hit by liquidity shocks and need to raise external funds to avoid bankruptcy. Such bankruptcies cause significant negative real effects. Consistent with this, Jiménez et al. (2014b) find that banks with higher proportion of illiquid assets such as real estate provide less credit supply to firms.

Banks suffering severe losses tend not only to see rising costs but may also face a reduction in their liabilities. This could be a mechanical effect of the downsizing of the whole balance sheet, but it may also be the consequence of the impossibility of obtaining funding in the market (which, on the bright side, is a welcome form of market discipline). Such a rationing may be the result of depositors, at risk of losses, preferring to place funds elsewhere. Banks, in turn, will transmit their liquidity shortages to their borrowers in the form of a contraction of credit availability (Valencia 2014). Credit will become more costly, making financial distress of borrowers and banks more likely. Iyer et al. (2014) provide evidence that liquidity rationing can create a credit crunch for firms.

In contrast, Acharya and Mora (2015) find that worse banks may react by increasing deposit rates to obtain retail liquidity. They study the behavior of bank deposit rates and inflows during the 2008 global financial crisis. Their results suggest that banks facing a funding squeeze seek to attract deposits by offering higher rates. Banks offering higher rates are those most exposed to liquidity demand shocks (as measured by their unused commitments, wholesale funding dependence, and limited liquid assets), and have also weaker balance sheets (higher nonperforming loans). Such rate increases have a competitive effect in that they lead other banks to offer higher rates as well.

Banking crises often have important distributional consequences, because central bank and government policies that attempt to save the financial sector generally imply wealth transfers from taxpayers to banks and, in general, from savers to creditors. For example, recapitalizations of insolvent banks constitute a wealth transfer from taxpayers to banks and expansive monetary policy (including higher inflation or lower interest rates) implies a transfer from creditors to debtors. These distributional changes affect systemic risk in a financial crisis. Moreover, there are other ex-post effects in systemic risk for income and wealth inequality following financial crises, as for example, through a reduction in aggregate consumption in highly leveraged households (Mian and Sufi 2014a). But systemic risk may also have ex ante effects, as policy makers may want to push credit to reduce consumption inequality, in turn causing credit booms to riskier borrowers that might end up in costly financial crises (Rajan 2010).

Finally, banking crises in one country can also imply externalities on other countries, through foreign bank presence and interbank markets. Such contagion risk has increased due to the internationalization of banking and the growth of cross-border banking (Laeven and Valencia 2008). Regulatory arbitrage across countries and competition for safety nets across countries also creates externalities. Peek and Rosengren (1997, 2000) find that loan-supply shocks to Japanese banks in Japan that were exogenous to economic conditions in the United States spilled over to the United States through the US-based subsidiaries of Japanese banks and led to a contraction in credit and economic activity in the United States.

Kalemli-Ozcan, Pappaionannou, and Perri (2013) study the effect of financial integration (through banks) on the transmission of international business cycles. In a sample of twenty developed countries between 1978 and 2009, they find that in periods without financial crises, increases in bilateral banking linkages are associated with more divergent output cycles. This relation is significantly weaker during financial turmoil periods, suggesting that financial crises induce contagion (positive comovement) among more financially integrated countries. They also show that countries with stronger direct and indirect financial ties to the United States experienced more synchronized cycles with the United States during the recent 2008 financial crisis. At the same time Cetorelli and Goldberg (2012a) show that multinational banks can act as a buffer against liquidity shocks by relying on their internal capital markets. They show that the lending of US banks with a global presence is much less sensitive to changes in liquidity conditions induced by monetary policy than the lending of globally active US banks.

6.3 Positive Effects of Financial Crises

We have focused so far on the real costs of systemic risk and financial crises, but is there a trade-off between economic growth and financial stability? By screening and funding risky investments with positive net present value, banks contribute to economic growth (King and Levine

1993; Levine and Zervos 1998). Therefore when banks are in distress such as during banking crises this negatively impacts economic growth. However, banking crises can also have a cleansing effect, forcing the exit of unviable banks. For example, Calomiris and Kahn (1991) argue that bank runs can be beneficial in that they salvage some of the bank value. Other theories on business cycles and banking crises find that financial crises can be optimal (Allen and Gale 1998) and that crises allow Schumpeterian creative destruction.

Ranciere et al. (2008) indeed confirm that countries that have experienced occasional financial crises have, on average, grown faster than countries with stable financial conditions. Because financial crises are realizations of downside risk, they measure their incidence by the skewness of credit growth. Unlike variance, negative skewness isolates the impact of the large, infrequent, and abrupt credit busts associated with crises. They find a positive effect of systemic risk (measured as the skewness of credit growth) on growth in a large sample of countries over the period 1960 to 2000. To explain this finding, they present a model in which contract enforceability problems generate borrowing constraints and impede growth. In financially liberalized economies with moderate contract enforceability, risk-taking is encouraged and increases investment. This leads to higher average economic growth but also to greater incidence of financial crises. In the data the link between skewness of credit growth and GDP growth is strongest in such economies.[16]

6.4 Conclusions

Financial crises tend to be associated with large economic costs, even in the presence of large-scale government interventions and expansive macroeconomic policy. Yet financial crises can also have some cleansing effects, and in the long run there is some suggestive evidence that financial crises may not negatively affect economic growth. Indeed, since Schumpeter it has been acknowledged that crises trigger the exit of inefficient firms and the entry of new ones. This implies that crisis management policies (including macroprudential policy) face important trade-offs, including the need to avoid ex ante moral hazard and planting the seeds for the next systemic financial crisis. Prolonging the resolution of a financial crisis tends to add to the eventual cost of the crisis, as low growth and weak balance sheets cause debt overhang problems and generate downward spirals in aggregate investment and consumption that prolong the financial crisis, postponing recovery and adding to the real and fiscal costs of the crisis.

From a macroprudential perspective, a key issue is how to design a consistent set of regulatory rules so as to lower the macroeconomic costs (e.g., in terms of economic growth), while decreasing the probability of financial crises as well as their economic cost. Of course, macroprudential policy will be in place because the benefits of prevention are higher than the costs of systemic crises. After all, there are significant ex ante costs associated with regulations to avoid financial crises, stemming from regulatory distortions that misallocate capital and reduce financial sector efficiency (see chapter 9 on the ex ante costs of some macroprudential regulations) and some financial crises (the non-systemic ones) are not very costly. We believe that the new measures of preventive macroprudential policy are in many cases justified to contain systemic risk, because strong *systemic* crises have high ex post real costs. Our view is therefore that macroprudential policy should not only deal with crisis management but also be used to prevent crises by reducing the buildup of systemic risk during boom periods.

7 Measuring Systemic Risk

We have analyzed what systemic risk is, its sources, and the consequences of its realization. But how can we measure systemic risk?[1] For example, regarding inflation, central banks have a precise objective regarding price stability and know how to measure it.[2] However, for financial stability and for macroprudential policy purposes, supervisors and central banks need to measure systemic risk, and as we have seen in previous chapters, this is a difficult task, as systemic risk is an endogenous risk based on multiple, time-varying externalities within the financial sector as well as from the financial to the real sector. As there is not a full understanding of these endogenous risks, the existing measures of systemic risk are still at the early stages. Not only do we lack an adequate measure of systemic risk but also all necessary data to properly measure systemic risk. With these caveats in place, we provide a summary of the main existing measures of systemic risk.

What should we look for in a measure of systemic risk? First, as we have shown in chapter 4, systemic risk often starts with the building up of excessive risk-taking during good times, when credit (leverage and debt) booms and asset price bubbles are being created. Moreover, given their perverse incentives, financial institutions take excessive correlated risks (e.g., herding) and establish short-term wholesale connections, implying that systemic risk changes endogenously over boom episodes together with the network linkages of financial institutions. Therefore a good measure of systemic risk should capture this (endogenous) time variation of systemic risk, thus providing early warning signals of the excessive buildup of financial imbalances.

Second, because some financial institutions are more systemic than others, both due to their size and financial linkages with the rest of institutions, a measure of systemic risk should also provide information on such cross-sectional variation of systemic risk, thus allowing the supervisors to know in real time which financial intermediaries are contributing the most to the riskiness of the system (e.g., a ranking of the most "systemic" financial intermediaries).

However, as explained in this chapter, there are significant limits to existing measures of systemic risk from a conceptual and data availability perspective. Greenspan (2002) in fact argued that while a central bank cannot identify asset price bubbles in real time, it can clean up the burst. There are several layers of uncertainty: is the asset price or credit boom based on fundamentals or is it a bubble? And if it is a bubble, is it going to cause a financial crisis or recession?

One of the central messages in our book is that given that the real costs of systemic risk stemming from credit and asset price bubbles are huge (output and employment losses), intervening early on during the credit and asset price booms may be justified. Central banks and supervisors would then trade higher type I errors (i.e., the risk that there is no bubble while they have acted preventively against the credit and price increase) in exchange for lower type II errors (i.e., there is a bubble, but there is no preventive ex ante action).[3]

We believe that supervisors should focus on leveraged bubbles, that is, credit booms in conjunction with asset price booms, as financial crises throughout history show are particularly dangerous. For example, the dot-com bubble, which was funded largely through equity, was much less damaging than the real estate and credit bubble that led to the 2007 to 2009 crisis. Apart from moral hazard issues, the reason is that equity acts as a buffer to absorb asset losses, while leverage intensifies asset price shocks by reducing the amount of equity that can offset asset losses, thus generating debt overhang and risk-shifting problems. Moreover, as we show in this chapter, there are potential real time measures of excessive supply of credit and risk-taking by financial institutions that can be used to identify credit bubbles in real time. Furthermore not only do positive asset price bubbles matter for systemic risk but also the negative ones, namely fire sales and excessive asset price reductions in crises (Allen and Gale 2007). Therefore measurement of systemic risk is not only relevant before financial crises but also during the crises, as in this period negative spillovers are huge and gambling for resurrection type of strategies of weakest institutions are possible. Thus, macroprudential policy also has an important ex post crisis management role.

It is important to stress what the differences are between systemic risk and other types of financial risk (credit, liquidity, and market risk). Systemic risk is not orthogonal to other forms of risk traditionally faced by financial institutions. Risk qualifies as being systemic when it is extreme, thus affecting a substantial part of the financial system (and in turn, the economy at large). Moreover systemic risk is, of course, not idiosyncratic risk faced by a financial institution, but neither is it equal to systematic risk, since variation within the business and market cycle (when systematic risk changes) do not necessarily imply strong changes in the impairment of a substantial part of the financial system. Moreover systemic risk has a substantial component of correlated risk exposures among financial institutions.

We provide an overview of existing measures of systemic risk, highlighting their strengths and weaknesses, and offer considerations for measuring systemic risk in practice. Importantly, in practice, data limitations are of first order. For example, we do not have a detailed map of all the financial connections among all the financial institutions. As the financial system is in great part globalized, this map of micro-financial connections is extremely difficult to obtain, but even worse, the majority of countries do not have it at the national level.[4]

Moreover, even if the data were available, it is important to have data collected at very high frequency because financial institutions, as compared to most nonfinancial firms, have assets that are highly liquid, and given their moral hazard problems discussed in earlier chapters, they can quickly change their liquid financial assets into higher, excessive risk (Myers and Rajan 1998). Therefore the objective is to provide guidance on how supervisors should measure systemic risk in practice, including in environments with data limitations, such as emerging markets and OTC markets, and when some financial interconnections among financial intermediaries such as financial assets, credit exposures, repos and uncollateralized interbank market transactions are missing.[5] We cover the underlying assumptions and data requirements for each existing measure of systemic risk and, when possible, evaluate each measure's relative performance in forecasting negative economic outcomes.

Broadly speaking, research on systemic risk measurement is primarily focused on the two objectives we previously mentioned: (1) the development of indexes summarizing the systemic risk of the financial system as a whole and (2) the identification of individual institutions posing systemic risk threats. This is done while paying close attention to the new financial regulations that were being developed in the aftermath of the crisis, including attempts to identify the so-called systemically important financial institutions (SIFIs). The first type of measures capture a time-varying dimension of systemic risk faced by the overall financial and economic system, whereas the second type of measures capture the cross-sectional dimension across financial inter-mediaries, including SIFIs but also clusters of financial institutions linked via asset and liability financial connections. Both types of mea-sures are correlated, because risks from financial contagion are higher when the overall financial system is weak (Iyer and Peydró 2011), and most cross-sectional measures can also be computed over time to capture time-series variation in systemic risk.

A challenge to comparing different empirical measures of systemic risk is that their definitions vary considerably. Several competing defi-nitions of systemic risk have been put forward in the literature and no universal consensus has emerged yet. The common feature shared by most systemic risk definitions is the risk that can put in jeopardy the functioning of the entire financial system and that generates substantial negative externalities to the real economy (see our definition of sys-temic risk in chapters 1 and 2).

Measures of systemic risk can be based on fundamentals or be directly derived from market data. With respect to the first, one could derive measures based on the theoretical models that we saw in the previous chapters (e.g. interlinkages of financial institutions or corre-lated risk exposures in securities), but the measures could also be based on evidence from previous systemic financial crises. For example, unsustainable levels of leverage for households, nonfinancial firms, and banks could be derived from historical data of LTV ratios or debt to income ratios prior to the crises.

Measures of systemic risk can also be directly derived from market data (based on the view that market prices reflect a substantial part of all the information available at each moment of time). Because financial markets are deep and complex, statistical information on financial prices, such as the correlation of returns, provides crucial information to supervisors. Indeed, if we assume a strong form of market efficiency (Fama 1965, 1970), these measures could, in principle, detect and measure systemic risk in a superior way. However, deviations from market efficiency, such as those arising from asset price bubbles, or the incorporation of policy expectations, such as potential bailouts (and thus lack of market discipline in banks), can limit the attractiveness of these market-based measures.

In particular, when market prices incorporate potential bailouts by governments and financial sector interventions by central banks, measures of systemic risk based on market prices will reflect the systemic risk cures attempted by public policy and will thus underestimate systemic risk. Recent policy measures related to bail-in bonds and contingent capital for financial institutions not only can improve incentives for financial institutions but also provide market information that can be used to measure systemic risk more precisely. Moreover, because market prices may be distorted, one should not rely only on market-based prices but supplement these with quantity-based measures of systemic risk, including early warning signals based on credit and short-term leverage booms and the interconnectivity of the financial system—which is to say, measures based on fundamentals.

Moreover, even if these measures incorporate all market information, the supervisor may not know why some banks are more systemic than others. That is, without very precise micro data (e.g., financial interlinkages), the policy maker would not know whether the systemic risk problem is just due to size or to the type of financial interlinkages (e.g., derivatives vs. interbank exposures). To implement the adequate prudential policy, it is crucial to know the mechanism underlying systemic risk, so that regulation can tackle the externality that is causing the systemic risk.

Additionally measures derived from fundamentals may suffer from the Lucas critique (Lucas 1976). For example, lending surveys are very useful to detect credit booms not due to strong economic fundamentals. Still, once the banks know that the central bank uses that information to supervise lending, they may not provide truthful information. Therefore systemic risk measures derived from both fundamentals and market data are necessary, though all the previous caveats should still be kept in mind.

The rest of the chapter proceeds as follows. We first summarize and review the different approaches to systemic risk. Second, we examine the relative performance of systemic risk measures. Third, we discuss systemic risk in practice and the challenges (both in models and data) to the measurement of systemic risk. Finally, we provide some concluding remarks.

7.1 Measures of Systemic Risk

The literature has proposed many approaches for measuring systemic risk. We can classify existing approaches either based on the nature of the systemic risk they intend to capture, or based on the types of data they use to measure systemic risk.

Taking the first approach, we can distinguish three sets of indicators to assess the buildup of systemic risk: (1) aggregate measures of financial soundness, (2) measures of individual institution risk, and (3) measures of systemic interlinkages among financial institutions (IMF 2009; Gerlach 2009).

Aggregate indicators of financial soundness focus on changes in the behavior of quantities and prices of financial assets to gauge vulnerabilities in the financial system as a whole, including asset prices, interest rates, credit growth, capital flows, lending surveys, and macroeconomic indicators. These indicators have proved vulnerable in previous financial and economic system crises. Moreover these vulnerabilities are partly related to the business cycle, with financial excesses being built up during boom periods to potentially end up in financial crises or recessions. For example, several papers by Jorda, Schularick, and Taylor that we discussed in chapter 4 have shown that the highest correlate with financial recessions are large credit booms in conjunction with large asset price booms, notably in real estate.

Though readily available, these indicators provide little information about the state of individual financial institutions or the interlinkages among institutions and therefore cannot protect against systemic risk arising from financial contagion. For example, because US regulators and supervisors focused primarily on developments in the US mortgage market as a whole, they mostly missed the systemic risk arising from the securitization process in the subprime mortgage market, which constituted only a small portion of the overall US mortgage market. So it is important to calculate the previous statistics for subsets of markets.

In general, it is difficult to separate supply from demand effects when measuring broad credit of financial sector trends. This is important as credit growth may reflect strong economic fundamentals. In fact many credit booms do not end up in a financial crisis (Dell'Ariccia et al. 2012). A key issue in identifying the drivers of systemic risk is whether finance follows the economic cycle or partly causes the economic cycle, which is to say, whether problems in the financial sector cause strong economic recessions or financial crises are just a by-product of large economic recessions. Some recent work has focused on separating demand from supply effects, with the aim to assess the contribution of individual banks to the systemic risk of the financial system. For example, credit registers present in more than 100 countries allow compositional changes in credit supply to be analyzed and measured with regard to excessive risk-taking and thus the banks to be singled out that are mainly causing the excessive risk-taking (see Jiménez et al. 2012, 2014a, b).

Measures of individual financial institution risk have been fairly well developed from either accounting information or market prices. Included are CAMELS (capital, assets, management, earnings, liquidity, and sensitivity) measures as well as market-based measures of asset volatility and leverage. Nevertheless, the current crisis has shown the limitations of such measures as they are based on assumptions that may seldom be fulfilled during a crisis. For instance, the capital ratios of individual banks could be quite different depending on whether AIG, which was selling CDS protection, was solvent or bankrupt.

Methods to assess interlinkages among financial institutions have been less developed until recently. They include network models that track the transmission of financial distress across the financial system via linkages (e.g., in the interbank market) and interdependency models that study how the default risk of an institution depends, through linkages, on those of other financial institutions (IMF 2011). Stress tests could analyze these issues, but the tests carried out so far by the EBA and the Fed are mainly microprudential in nature without a substantial focus on the interconnections among financial intermediaries and also between the financial and real sector in taking a macroprudential view (see the excellent critical review of the stress tests by Greenlaw et al. 2012).

Most of the models to assess interlinkages are about measuring systemic risk arising from contagion. In general, they do not measure externalities associated with bank failures that are not priced by the market or spillovers arising from interconnectedness among banks and other financial institutions that are not captured by interbank exposures. Examples of such spillovers include pecuniary externalities from fire sales of assets, derivative counterparty exposures, and the strategic interactions among banks that induce them to take correlated risks ex ante or to use the aggregate pools of liquidity (De Nicolo, Favara, and Ratnovski 2012).

Indeed the state of the literature reflects the general difficulty of developing measures and empirical tests that can make a clear distinction between contagion in a strict sense and systemic risk arising from correlated risks, including common shocks or revisions of investor expectations when information is asymmetric and uncertainty high (De Bandt and Hartmann 2000; De Bandt, Hartmann, and Peydró 2015).

Regarding the types of data used for measurement, we can group measures of systemic risk as either fundamentals or market-based measures. Measures based on fundamentals, on the one hand, attempt to measure systemic risk using (1) a structural model of risk that identifies specific channels of risk in the economy or indirectly based on a finance and/or macro model or (2) empirical evidence from previous systemic financial crises. These measures can be further refined by applying more aggregated macro information or more precise micro-level information. Market-based measures, on the other hand, infer risk from the empirical distribution of returns and asset prices. They are based on the assumption that market prices reflect all available information and attempt to extract such information to construct indices of financial distress that measure systemic risk.

Measures based on fundamentals using macro data include traditional macro measures of the buildup of financial imbalances, such as excessive credit growth, leverage, and asset price booms. These can be computed for the economy as a whole or for specific sectors, such as real estate, households or cross-border exposures. Moreover, if data availability permits, excessive credit supply booms can be identified using micro information such as credit register data. Other systemic risk measures that tend to measure fundamentals include (1) network models of interbank liquidity contagion that track the transmission of liquidity shocks throughout the financial system based on a network analysis of a matrix of inter-institution liquidity exposures, (2) stress tests that measure the ability of the financial system's capital and liquidity buffers to withstand extreme but plausible shocks based on economic and financial scenario analysis, and (3) contingent claim analysis that considers risk adjustments to sectoral balance sheets using market prices.

Measures that rely mainly on market data include (1) tail measures that capture the probability of extreme negative returns for a set of banks conditional on one or more banks being in distress, or tail measures that capture an individual financial institution's contribution to the financial system as a whole being in distress, and (2) comovement measures that capture the interrelatedness among financial institutions' returns, including financial networks.[6]

7.1.1 Measures Based on Fundamentals

Sectoral Measures: Credit, Leverage, and Asset Price Booms In chapter 4 we saw that the buildup of financial imbalances on certain specific sectors are the main sources of systemic risk, such as excessive credit growth and (short-term wholesale) leverage in correlated assets that generate asset price (including real estate) booms. Measures of systemic risk that can provide early warning signals on these sectors' imbalances are thus based on fundamentals.

Traditional measures of financial imbalances operate mostly at the macro-level, and include measures of credit growth, financial leverage, and asset price booms (e.g., Kaminsky and Reinhart 1998). Some of these measures can also be constructed at the sectoral level (e.g., real estate price booms or household leverage) or at the institution level (e.g., leverage or margin requirements at the institution level). However, macro-aggregate measures, despite being informative and even crucial, are too imprecise to measure systemic risk. For example, credit growth has been the best predictor of financial crises, but as we saw in detail in chapter 4, if aggregate measures of credit are chosen, then only one in three credit booms end up in banking crises (Dell'Ariccia et al. 2012).

Credit booms can be caused by strong economic fundamentals (credit demand-driven) and therefore not cause systemic risk. Separating credit supply from demand is important because if changes in bank credit were driven by genuine demand-side factors, such as productivity shocks, then policy intervention based on the premise that the fault lies on the credit supply side (e.g., banks' moral hazard problems) can be totally counterproductive. Therefore it would be incorrect to intervene solely on the basis of aggregate credit growth as an indicator of systemic risk.

However, there is a methodology that can help policy makers better understand the extent to which credit supply side factors generate aggregate fluctuations in credit, but this methodology depends on the access to timely and comprehensive loan-level data such as those obtained from a credit registry (see Khwaja and Mian 2008; Jiménez et al. 2012, 2014a, b; Mian 2014). While such credit registry data are available in many countries, there are major countries such as the United States that do not have public credit registers or equivalent data. Moreover the level of detail of credit registry information varies a great deal across countries; therefore, to avoid limiting the applicability of this approach, we describe it for the most general case where data on loan volume is available at the borrower–lender time period level.

The methodology outlined here derives from Jiménez et al. (2014b).[7] The basic purpose of the methodology is to test certain hypotheses about the role of supply-side factors in generating observed changes in bank credit. The methodology offers two advantages from an econometric standpoint. First, it provides an unbiased estimate of the supply-driven bank lending channel. Second, it takes into account general equilibrium adjustments made at the borrower level in reaction to the bank lending channel effect and provides a bias-corrected net effect of the bank lending channel at the borrower level. We will briefly illustrate the methodology below with some applications.

Consider an economy with banks and firms indexed by i and j respectively. Firm j borrows from N banks at time t. For simplicity, let's assume that it borrows the same amount from each of the N banks. The economy experiences two shocks at t: a firm-specific credit demand shock η_j (reflects changes in the firm fundamentals affecting the demand for credit) and a bank-specific credit supply shock δ_i reflecting changes in the bank's funding and solvency situation).

Let y_{ij} denote the log change in credit from bank i to firm j, then the basic credit channel equation in the face of credit supply and demand shocks can be written as

$$y_{ij} = \alpha + \beta \times \delta_i + \eta_j + \varepsilon_{ij}. \tag{7.1}$$

Equation (7.1) assumes that the change in bank credit from bank i to firm j is determined by an economy-wide secular trend α, an observable credit supply shocks δ_i, unobserved borrower fundamentals (that proxy for credit demand shocks) η_j, and an idiosyncratic shock ε_{ij}. Though equation (7.1) is reduced form in nature, it can be derived as an equilibrium condition by explicitly modeling credit supply and demand schedules.

In a frictionless world, bank lending is independent of credit supply conditions and only depends on firm fundamentals (credit demand factors). Financial intermediaries in such a world have no impact on the economy, and hence there is no bank transmission channel, that is,

$\beta = 0$, in equation (7.1). The presence of financing frictions, however, may force banks to pass on their credit supply shocks δ_i to borrowing firms, thus making $\beta > 0$.

A positive coefficient β is often referred to as the existence of a bank lending channel, and is the key supply-side parameter of interest. It cannot be estimated with OLS if one suspects that there is a correlation between the credit supply shock and unobserved demand shock.[8] Khwaja and Mian (2008) resolve this issue by focusing on firms with $N_j > 2$ and absorbing the firm fundamentals' shock through firm fixed-effects—that is, the demand shock in the equation is eliminated with the firm fixed effects, and therefore the estimated coefficient with fixed effects provides an unbiased estimate of β.

However, the previous estimator does not give a complete picture of the net effect of the (credit supply) bank lending channel on the economy. In particular, individual firms affected by some banks due to a negative bank supply shock may seek funding from new banking relationships to compensate for any loss of credit. An unbiased estimate of the net (or aggregate) effect of supply-side banking shocks on borrower j can be estimated using the equation

$$\bar{y}_j = \bar{\alpha} + \bar{\beta} \times \bar{\delta}_j + \eta_j + \bar{\varepsilon}_j \,, \tag{7.2}$$

where $\bar{y}_j$ denotes the log change in credit for firm j across all banks.[9] It is not a simple average of y_{ij} from (7.1) because a firm can start borrowing from new banks as well. $\bar{\delta}_j$ denotes the average banking sector shock experienced by firm j at time t from the n_j banks lending to firm j previous to the shock. The aggregate impact of the credit supply channel is captured by the coefficient $\bar{\beta}$. If there is no adjustment at the firm level in the face of bank-specific credit channel shocks, then $\bar{\beta} = \beta$, but normally the coefficient in equation (7.2) is lower in absolute value as firms can substitute credit with other less affected banks (or other sources of finance). Moreover, one can construct an unbiased estimator of $\bar{\beta}$, with an adjustment term correcting for the otherwise unobserved covariance between credit supply and demand shocks (see Jiménez et al. 2014b).

A key advantage of the proposed methodology is that it can be implemented in real time. Another advantage is that it relies on credit registry (or comparable loan level) data that exist in many countries. We next provide an example of the application of this methodology in the case of Spain. However, there are many examples in the literature using this methodology in other countries as well.[10]

Jiménez et al. (2014b) apply the methodology above to the case of Spain and test whether the boom in real estate securitization during the 2000s enabled banks with large real estate assets to expand credit supply by securitizing their real estate portfolio. They estimate equation (7.1) with borrower fixed effects separately for each quarter t. y_{ij} is defined as the log change in loan volume from bank i to firm j. The change is computed from a fixed quarter (2004Q4 in their case as the time of expansion of securitization) till quarter t. The credit supply shock is defined as the ex ante (year 2000) variation in real estate holdings for bank i, and real estate exposure proxies for the capacity of banks to securitize assets during the securitization boom. The analysis utilizes the comprehensive quarterly loan-level credit registry data from the Bank of Spain that covers a period from 1999Q4 to 2009Q4.

Starting in 2004 (when securitization in Spain shoots up), their estimation of equation (7.1) yields a strong positive credit supply effect for banks with real estate exposure due to improved access to wholesale financing. The positive credit supply effect turns negative in 2008, however, when the global securitization market collapsed. The net (aggregate) impact of securitization at the borrower level (derived from estimating equation 7.2) is muted due to a crowding-out effect. Interestingly, these effects could have been obtained in real time during the pre-crisis period 2004 to 2007

Even when a public credit registry does not exist, as in the case of the United States, the methodology can be applied as long as detailed loan-level data is available such that lenders can be paired with borrowers. Using loan-level data from the Fed's SNC program, and absorbing demand and supply shocks through borrower and lender fixed effects, Mian and Santos (2011) show that the increase in drawn lines of credit is not unique to the 2007 to 2009 crisis, but the same pattern is seen in each of the previous two recessions of 1990-91 and 2001 (though in the latter one there was no banking crisis). Similarly Ivashina and Scharfstein (2010), De Haas and van Horen (2012), and Giannetti and Laeven (2012a) use commercially available syndicated loan-level data to identify credit supply shocks.[11]

As all this research suggests, using available information at the time, an excessive credit boom could have been identified by the central bank well in advance of the first failures of subprime lenders in 2007. Credit went especially to subprime borrowers, despite an increasing differential over time in household income of prime over subprime borrowers, and especially in geographical areas with more securitization and in areas in which real estate prices were not increasing (Mian and Sufi 2009). Moreover the credit boom was not driven just by strong economic fundamentals, nor was it entirely driven by real estate prices (see Dell'Ariccia, Igan, and Laeven 2012).[12]

Of course, there is the benefit of hindsight to these arguments, since we now know to look at securitization, credit growth, and risks arising from lending to subprime borrowers. However, policy makers understood that some risks were evolving in real estate, securitization, and credit (Bank of Spain 2003; Rajan 2005; ECB's Financial Stability Review 2006). Moreover, historically, analyses of financial crises show that credit booms, excessive risk-taking, and financial innovation have been considered key drivers of systemic financial crises before (e.g., Kindleberger 1978).

Detailed loan-level data that allow a matching of borrower and lender better identify credit supply. Therefore, in the case of credit bubbles, it would be possible to significantly decrease type I and II errors associated with the occurrence of financial crises and act preventively to avoid financial crisis. For asset price bubbles, identification would, of course, be more difficult than for credit booms. However, if apart from aggregate data on the price dynamics, there are transactions where the buyer, seller, and the terms of the transaction are known, a supervisor could obtain useful information on the people buying and riding the bubble, and make inferences regarding excessive risk-taking.

Not only does the overall size of a credit boom matter for financial stability but also its allocation (e.g., its concentration across sectors of the economy or the risk taken). The previous papers analyze the average effects of credit supply, but a crucial issue is to identify in the data compositional changes in credit supply. An example of such heterogeneous effects can be found in bank risk-taking, which is an important determinant for systemic risk. Jiménez et al. (2014a) analyze the effects of monetary policy on credit risk-taking with an exhaustive credit register of loan applications and contracts in Spain. They separate the changes in the composition of the supply of credit from the concurrent changes in the volume of supply with a substantial set of fixed effects to control for unobserved time variant heterogeneity in firm and bank fundamentals, and quality and volume of demand using a two-stage model that analyzes loan applications in the first stage and loan outcomes for the loans granted in the second stage. They analyze whether the composition of credit supply favors borrowers with higher ex ante (and ex post) risk.

They also show the potential biases that can arise when estimating the credit channel with outstanding credit only, namely without a two-stage model of credit supply. Their estimates show that without controlling for the first-stage sample bias (i.e., the granting of loan applications), the estimates of risk-taking in the second stage are considerably smaller in absolute value because risk-taking in loan outcomes is not independent from risk-taking in the granting of loan applications.[13] Therefore systemic risk in bank lending should ideally be measured using data on loan applications and outcomes for the granted loans, though these data are not always available.

Lending survey data collected by central banks also convey very useful information about credit cycles, the change in lending conditions and standards, and loan demand changes. For instance, prior to the recent global financial crisis, the Bank Lending Survey (BLS) of the euro area and the Senior Loan Officer (SLO) Survey for the United States provided very useful information to assess whether lending standards were softening or not, and the reasons behind such changes (see Dell'Ariccia, Laeven, and Suarez 2013 for an analysis of the impact of monetary policy on risk-taking of US banks using confidential loan-level results from the SLO survey).

Euro area national central banks and regional Feds request banks to provide quarterly information on the lending standards and conditions that they apply to firms and households. The detailed information reported in the surveys is quite reliable, not least because the surveys were carried out by central banks whose bank supervisors could cross-check the quality of the information received with exhaustive hard banking data. In fact Del Giovane et al. (2011) show an example of publicly available cross-checking for the lending survey using detailed supervisory data on bank lending in Italy. Consistent with this finding, the lending standards from the surveys have been shown to be not only correlated with actual credit spreads and volume (see Ciccarelli et al. 2013) but also to be good predictors of credit and output growth (see Lown and Morgan 2006 for the US evidence and De Bondt et al. 2010 for the euro area).

For the pool of all borrowers, including the rejected applications, lending surveys provide information not only on whether lending conditions change (and how much) but also on why loan conditions change.[14] For example, they provide information on whether a tightening of lending conditions is due to an increase in nonfinancial borrowers' risk or due to changes in bank capital, liquidity, or competition (supply side).

Both the US and euro area lending surveys show a large heterogeneity over time and between states and countries in lending conditions and standards. In particular, lending conditions for both firms and households softened in the good times and tightened in the bad times. With regard to the euro area countries, there is also a stark contrast between core and periphery countries in the development of lending standards. For example, while in Germany there was a softening of lending conditions and an increase in loan demand during the crisis, in Italy there was a strong tightening of lending conditions due to both firm risk and bank balance sheet weaknesses.

The analysis of lending surveys shows that when loan volumes and prices soften, other loan conditions—such as loan maturity, covenants, and collateral—soften as well. Therefore high leverage or low margin requirements can be seen as complementary signs of a buildup of systemic risk, thus leading to a leverage and credit cycle (see Fostel and Geanakoplos 2008; Geanakoplos 2010; Geanakoplos and Pedersen 2014). All in all, the lending surveys can provide early warning signals of excessively lenient lending standards. However, unfortunately, if banks knew that central banks would use this information to assess financial stability, their incentives to report the true values could change. In a sense, the ideal supervisory measures should be "Lucas critique proof."

Credit booms also affect asset prices. Under the (demand) fundamentals' based view, asset prices are not affected by credit supply but only reflect the discounted value of future cash flows. However, assets are often financed through leverage (credit), as it was the case in the 1920s stock market bubble when stocks were largely bought on credit as well as in the 2000s US real estate bubble. Therefore a softening of lending conditions could potentially increase asset prices, notably real estate, thus potentially generating credit and asset price booms. Conversely, during a crisis a credit crunch could induce fire sale prices. So spirals of funding and price movements could reinforce each other because of collateral-based lending (Kiyotaki and Moore 1997) or because of market illiquidity (Brunnermeier and Pedersen 2009).

Empirically, however, it is difficult to identify (and thus quantify) the impact of credit supply on real estate prices, as higher real estate prices by increasing borrowers' collateral can also increase credit availability—that is, a reverse causality identification problem.[15] Favara and Imbs (2011), using branching deregulation in the 1990s to identify the causal link between credit supply and house prices, find that US states that deregulated subsequently experienced larger house price increases. Interestingly, these results could have been obtained without much delay in the 2000s to assess whether a real estate bubble was being created to some extent by the credit supply.

Adelino, Schoar, and Severino (2012) using exogenous changes in the conforming loan limit as an instrument for lower cost of financing (and higher credit supply) show that easier access to credit in the United States significantly increased house prices.[16] They find that houses that become eligible for financing with a conforming loan show an increase in house values of 1.1 dollars per square foot (for an average price per square foot of 224 dollars) and higher overall house prices, after controlling for a rich set of house characteristics. These coefficients are consistent with a local elasticity of house prices to interest rates below 10.

Yet, in a crisis, a reduction of credit supply (in general funding liquidity) can force financial intermediaries to sell assets to obtain liquidity at prices lower than fundamentals (fire sales). These effects are especially strong when assets are information based (and adverse selection problems are important) and if financial intermediaries who can buy those assets are liquidity constrained. Brunnermeier and Pedersen (2009) show theoretically how market liquidity and funding liquidity are mutually reinforcing, giving rise to liquidity spirals, fragility, flight to quality, and systemic risk.

The funding in repo markets also poses substantial systemic risks, as seen in the last crisis in the United States, where counterparties increased margin requirements following a fall in asset prices of securitized mortgages, forcing banks to sell assets at fire sales to meet margin calls. This in turn reduces collateral values, encouraging additional margin calls, starting a negative liquidity spiral, and transmitting negative externalities on to the other financial intermediaries that hold similar assets (Garleanu and Pedersen 2011; Brunnermeier and Pedersen 2009; Gorton 2009). Consistent with these theories, Gorton and Metrick (2012) find that changes in the spread between Libor and OIS interest rates, a proxy for counterparty risk, were strongly correlated with changes in credit spreads and repo rates for securitized bonds, implying greater uncertainty about the solvency of banks and lower values for repo collateral.

Competition among financial intermediaries can also affect fire sales during a contraction, and thus systemic risk.[17] Favara and Giannetti (2015) show that in mortgage markets with low concentration, lenders have a higher propensity to foreclose defaulting mortgages. Foreclosure decisions by individual banks may increase aggregate losses in the economic system because they generate a pecuniary externality as higher forecloses may cause house price to drop. In concentrated markets, instead, as lenders have a substantial exposure to the real estate sector, they internalize the adverse effects of mortgage foreclosures on local house prices, and thus are more disposed to renegotiate risky mortgages. Favara and Giannetti (2013) provide empirical evidence consistent with this hypothesis using mortgage data on US counties during the 2007 to 2009 housing market collapse.

All in all, there are ex ante real time indicators to measure credit booms, including supply changes and softening of lending standards. Loan-level data from public credit registries or from private sources are needed. Lending surveys by central banks are also useful. Credit growth in turn can affect asset prices and often is a precursor to financial crises. Indeed the worst asset price bubbles in history tend to be those based on credit (leverage). Finally, it is important to monitor fire sales, funding illiquidity, and credit crunches to stave off systemic crises.

Interbank Liquidity Networks   Contagion arising from interbank linkages is an important source of systemic risk that has been researched extensively. A key insight from the seminal papers on financial contagion by Allen and Gale (2000a) and Freixas et al. (2000) is that the possibility for contagion depends on the precise network of the interbank market. There is a stream of literature that studies the possibility of financial contagion due to interbank linkages via simulations depending on the network of the interbank market.[18]

An important contribution by Furfine (2003) uses exposure data on overnight interbank federal funds to simulate the risk of financial contagion. He constructs the overnight interbank exposures via the actual payments of banks among each other: for example, if bank A pays X to bank B at day t, then if B pays $X \times (1+r)$ to bank A on day $t + 1$, it is possible to infer that there was an overnight interbank loan with interest equal to r. Most supervisors have in this way access to overnight interbank data. However, other direct financial connections of banks as medium- and long-term claims or derivative positions are not available. If we want to properly measure systemic risk, these data are crucial, so that we have a complete exposure of direct (and indirect) links between banks and other financial intermediaries.

Furfine (2003) finds contagion to be negligible. In contrast, Humphrey (1986), using data from the Clearing House Interbank Payments System (CHIPS) to simulate the impact of a settlement failure of a major participant in the payment system, shows that this failure could lead to a significant level of further settlement failures.

Upper and Worms (2004) study contagion arising from interbank exposures in the German interbank market. Through a counterfactual simulation, they find that the failure of a single bank could lead to the breakdown of 15 percent of the banking system. Elsinger et al. (2006a) use detailed data from the Austrian interbank market and study the risk of contagious failures due to an idiosyncratic shock. In their simulations they find the probability to be low. They also find that although the probability of contagious default is low, there are cases in which up to 75 percent of the defaults are due to contagion.

Although the above-mentioned works explore the issue of financial contagion due to interbank exposures, they do not capture the *endogenous* responses of (wholesale and retail) depositors and creditors during a crisis, a key issue in contagion (the propagation of idiosyncratic shocks).[19] Many of the mentioned studies on interbank markets are from before the recent crisis and downplay the importance of interbank contagion. A recent study by Cont, Moussa, and Santos (2013) of the Brazilian banking system takes a different approach from these earlier network papers. Cont, Moussa, and Santos find that contagion significantly contributes to systemic risk in Brazil. As the authors argue, their results do not contradict previous findings but present them in a different way: while most of the earlier studies use indicators averaged across banks, the Brazilian case shows that given the heterogeneity of the systemic importance across banks, the sample average is a poor representation of the degree of contagion, and therefore conditional measures of risk should be used instead. Moreover they argue that most of the studies mentioned above are based on too generous recovery rate assumptions (assets recovered at pre-default value), whereas recovery rates could be close to zero for short-term uncollateralized interbank deposits in crisis times.

Moreover, with the exception of Elsinger et al. (2006a, b), the precrisis papers measure only the impact of the idiosyncratic default of a single bank, whereas Cont, Moussa, and Santos (2013) include stress scenarios where balance sheets are subjected to common shocks—this is consistent with Iyer and Peydró (2011) who show that contagion is stronger when overall banking system is weaker. As in Elsinger et al. (2006a, b), Cont, Moussa, and Santos (2013) find that while the probability of contagion is small, the loss resulting from contagion can be very large in some cases.[20]

Chan-Lau et al. (2009) argue that to identify and quantify systemic risk, several complementary approaches should be used: (1) the network approach, which relies on intermediary-level data to assess how interconnections can cause unexpected problems, (2) the co-risk model where co-risk is measured as the increase in credit default swap (CDS) spreads of a "recipient" institution that would result when the CDS spread of a "source" institution is very high, and (3) the default intensity model, designed to capture the effect of contractual and informational systemic linkages among institutions, as well as the behavior of their default rates under different levels of aggregate distress.[21] The authors argue that each approach has its limitations, but together these methods can provide systemic risk monitoring tools.

Battiston et al. (2012) argue that there is no widely accepted methodology to determine the systemically important nodes in a financial network. To fill this gap, they introduce DebtRank, a novel measure of systemic impact inspired by feedback centrality. As an application, they analyze a dataset on the USD 1.2 trillion FED emergency loans program to global financial institutions during 2008 to 2010. They find a group of 22 institutions that received most of the funds and form a strongly connected graph where each of the nodes becomes systemically important at the peak of the crisis. The results suggest that the debate on too big to fail institutions should include the equally important issue of too central to fail.

All in all, the majority of the mentioned papers takes the network of wholesale connections as given, and analyzes risks in an exogenous way (e.g., contagion given a network). However, financial networks are endogenous as some recent literature has modeled, and a crucial factor is the endogenous risks, for example, withdrawals and liquidity dry-ups.

Stress Tests   Stress tests have been an important measure in identifying financial risk since the crisis. For example, the Dodd–Frank now requires the Federal Reserve to regularly perform stress tests, or in Europe through the European Banking Authority (EBA) in collaboration with national supervisors, and in October 2014 the EBA published the results of its first Asset Quality Review, as the euro area central supervisor.

As Greenlaw et al. (2012) show, the recent stress tests for both the United States and Europe were mostly microprudential in nature rather than macroprudential, as they mainly focused on the solvency of individual financial intermediaries rather than the financial system as a whole.[22] For example, a crucial issue in order to assess systemic risk is the interbank exposures that we analyzed in the previous subsection with the counterfactual simulations. However, stress tests do not deal with these issues, despite that they could require the data and stress test wholesale liquidity dry-ups and contagion.

In 2011 the largest financial intermediaries in the United States were required to provide the Federal Reserve with a comprehensive capital plan based on a stress testing framework that considers a range of economic and financial scenarios, including very severe ones. The stress capital estimates were evaluated relative to regulatory minimums and a tier 1 common to risk-weighted assets supervisory reference level of 5 percent. As Greenlaw et al. (2012) highlight, the stress tests did not allow for feedback effects between different financial institutions and between the financial and the economy at large. Interlinkages of credit restrictions to the real sector or short-term wholesale positions among financial intermediaries were not considered, though they pose crucial externalities for systemic risk.

Also in 2011 the EBA published its second stress test of 90 EU banks from 21 countries. As Greenlaw et al. (2012) explain, the objective was to assess their capital resilience against an adverse but plausible scenario, such as the substantially worse GDP, unemployment and house prices, and some modest sovereign stress (despite of the Italian and Spanish problems), with haircuts applied to sovereign exposures in the trading book and increased provisions for these sovereign exposures in the banking book.

Despite that in Europe wholesale liquidity from the interbank market is significant and a crucial part is cross-border, the stress tests focused on assessing the solvency of individual banks in the face of shocks to the asset side, as in the US case. Therefore stress tests were mainly microprudential. In any case, the main criticism of the early European stress tests was the lack of credibility as Dexia and Irish banks passed the test, although they had huge problems afterward (Dexia failed in the following months despite passing the stress test with a core tier 1 ratio of more than 10 percent—above the 5 percent threshold).

Macroprudential stress tests should focus on the whole financial system, and also its connections with the economy at large. A key lesson from the 2008 global financial crisis is that runs on systemic banks by wholesale depositors can lead to a credit crunch to the real economy. As Greenlaw et al. (2012) argue, to avoid aggregate deleveraging in crises, policy measures should focus on raising new capital measured in total dollars or euros, rather than on capital ratios, as otherwise banks cut on credit or sell too many assets, potentially causing strong negative externalities to economy and other financial institutions, such as credit crunches or fire sales. All in all, stress tests are particularly useful for the measurement of systemic risk, but unfortunately, they have been mainly microprudential so far.

Contingent Claim Approach Lehar (2005) measures overall risk at the financial system level rather than at the level of individual intermediaries using standard risk management tools. Following Merton (1974), he interprets equity as a call option on a bank's assets. There are three key parameters: (1) correlation between the values of banks' asset portfolios to measure the probability of multiple simultaneous defaults, (2) financial soundness to measure the probability of failures, and (3) volatility of the bank's assets also to measure probability of default. Lehar uses data on a sample of international banks for the 1988 to 2002 period and estimates the dynamics and correlations between bank asset portfolios. To analyze systemic risk, he models the individual bank failures as contingent claims on the bank's assets, taking into consideration the correlated failures. He finds risk especially high during the Asian crisis starting in 1997.

Gray and Jobst (2011) introduce a new framework for macroprudential analysis using a risk-adjusted balance sheet approach and linkages among financial intermediaries. The systemic contingent claims analysis (CCA) framework helps quantify the magnitude of general insolvency risk and government contingent liabilities by combining the individual risk-adjusted balance sheets of financial institutions and the dependence between them. They present results from stress tests of systemic risk using their framework with applications to European banks.

Hovakimian, Kane, and Laeven (2012) propose a measure of systemic risk of financial institutions by extending the Merton (1974) model of safety net subsidies for individual banks to a portfolio of banks. Specifically, they express the value of banking–sector losses from systemic default risk as the value of a put option written on a portfolio of aggregate bank assets whose exercise price equals the face value of aggregate bank debt. An individual bank's systemic risk is then computed as its contribution to the value of this potential sector put on the financial safety net. Because the explicit deposit insurance premiums that banks generally pay in return for the safety net protection, they enjoy are minimal (prior to the recent crisis, 97 percent of FDIC-insured institutions in the United States paid zero premia to the FDIC), these put value estimates can in most cases be interpreted as the subsidy a bank extracts from the safety net.

This approach is akin to a contingent claims approach but incorporates the value of the safety net subsidy, including any value that accrues to the bank from lender of last resort policies, the presence of too big to fail policies, and other implicit government guarantees. Applying their model to quarterly data on US banks over the period 1974 to 2010, they find that systemic risk for the US banking sector as a whole reached unprecedented highs during the financial crisis years 2008 to 2010, and that bank size, leverage, and asset risk are key drivers of systemic risk.

7.1.2 Measures Based on Market Data

To measure systemic risk, it is important to have data on financial linkages, such as the interbank exposures and loan-level data that we described in the previous sections, though such data are not always available. As externalities are crucial for systemic risk, precise transmission mechanisms are difficult to measure without detailed information on financial linkages. In contrast, bank-level data on equity and bond prices are generally available, thus a part of the literature has measured externalities indirectly through market-based indicators. For example, Aharony and Swary (1983) and Swary (1986) measure spillovers in bank equity prices using an event study methodology to identify the effects of specific bank failures or bad news for certain banks on other banks' stock prices.[23]

Many market-based measures of systemic risk analyze the degree of interconnectedness of banks and other intermediaries, where interconnectedness is based on measures of dependence between pairs of intermediaries' equity, CDS, and bond prices. A very simple but limited approach is to compute linear correlations. As return data display time-series dependence (e.g., due to momentum), correlation does not necessarily imply dependence across variables. Moreover, as highlighted by Hartmann, Straetmans, and de Vries (2007), systemic risk is about dependence in the left-tail risks, which has implied measures based on tail dependence, computed using extreme value theory (EVT) or quantile regressions.

The crisis has also motivated new ways to measure systemic risk, such as the CoVaR and SRISK measures (Adrian and Brunnermeier 2009; Brownlees and Engle 2015). These measures of systemic risk use market data to quantify the loss of capitalization of the financial system in case of large shocks, rather than just identifying systemic risk with high levels of interconnections in the financial system. These measures try to infer the potential capital losses from equity prices and balance sheet data.

As noted in the start of this chapter, market-based measures exploit the information available from market participants, who are the ones with a keen interest in acquiring and processing information, though there are important market inefficiencies and distortions to market prices, including the market incorporating potential bail-outs in some key financial intermediaries. Moreover, without very precise micro data on financial interlinkages, it would be impossible for the supervisor to know whether a financial firm's contribution to systemic risk is due to its size or due to the type and size of its interlinkages with the financial system. Nevertheless, we do believe than these market-based measures on systemic risk are crucial. With these caveats in mind, we proceed to explain the main approaches.

Extreme Value Theory   Hartmann, Straetmans, and de Vries (2007) make an early and critical contribution on systemic risk measurement based on market data. They study the probability of extreme returns of a set of banks conditionally on other banks being in distress. Their approach is based on extreme value theory (EVT), a statistical approach to quantify the joint occurrence of rare events such as severe banking problems, and which was previously applied by Hartmann, Straetmans, and de Vries (2004) and Poon, Rockinger, and Tawn (2004) to estimate the strength of banking system risks.[24] More precisely, to measure systemic risk, they estimate the probability of crashes in bank stocks, conditional on crashes of other bank stocks or the market.

Their approach allows them to estimate the probabilities of spillovers between banks, their vulnerability to aggregate shocks, and changes in those risks over time.[25] They define a bank in a critical situation when there is a dramatic collapse of its stock price, and then identify the risk of a problem in one or several banks spilling over to other banks ("contagion risk") with extreme negative co-movements between individual bank stocks. They also identify the risk of banking system destabilization through aggregate shocks using the "tail-β" proposed by Straetmans, Verschoor, and Wolff (2008), which is measured by conditioning their co-crash probability on a general stock index (or another measure of systematic risk) rather than on individual banks' stock prices. Based on the estimated individual co-crash probabilities and tail-βs, they can analyze systemic risk over time.

They estimate this measure of systemic risk using data for the 50 most important banks in the US and euro area for the period 1992 to 2004. The results suggest, first, that the risk of multivariate extreme spillovers among US banks is higher than between European banks. Hence, despite higher interbank exposures in the euro area, the US banking system is more prone to spillovers among banks. Second, the lower spillover risk among European banks is mainly due to weaker cross-border linkages. Results could be different in the 2000s due to the massive increase in banking integration in Europe (Kalemli-Ozcan et al. 2010). Third, cross-border spillover probabilities tend to be smaller than domestic spillover probabilities. Fourth, structural stability tests for their indicators suggest that systemic risk, both through interbank spillovers and aggregate risk, has increased over time, and the break points are on the second half of the 1990s.

As the authors acknowledge, there are limitations to this approach, as important financial intermediaries are not listed (thus have not equity prices) and one needs to observe some negative shocks to analyze the contagion to others, but in good times, when systemic risk is building, we may not see negative shocks. Moreover this approach assumes that equity (and also bond) prices are aggregators of all private and public information, however, as we have shown in previous chapters, banks often lack market discipline (in part because of regulatory distortions, including public subsidies through, e.g., LoLR or TBTF). Nevertheless, despite these caveats, the EVT approach is an important tool to measure systemic risk.

Tail Networks Hautsch et al. (2014a, b) also associate systemic risk with extreme events using tail networks. They evaluate financial intermediaries' risk of financial distress on the basis of stock price information and base their measure on extreme conditional quantiles of corresponding return distributions, quantifying the risk of distress of individual intermediaries and the entire system respectively. In this sense, their framework builds on the concept of conditional value at risk (VaR), which is a widely accepted measure for tail risk. For each intermediary they identify its so-called relevant (tail) risk drivers as the minimal set of macroeconomic fundamentals, intermediary-specific characteristics and risk spillovers from competitors and other companies driving the company's VaR.

Detecting with whom and how strongly each institution is connected allows them to construct a tail risk network of the entire financial system. A company's contribution to systemic risk is then defined as the induced total effect of an increase in its individual tail risk on the VaR of the entire system, conditional on the firm's position within the financial network as well as overall market conditions. The underlying statistical setting is a two-stage quantile regression approach. In the first step, institution-specific VaRs are estimated and tail risk spillovers of other banks are captured by loss exceedances. To shrink the high-dimensional set of possible cross-linkages between all intermediaries to a feasible number of connections, they make use of the least absolute shrinkage and selection operator (LASSO) techniques (see Belloni and Chernozhukov 2011), that allows them to identify the relevant tail risk drivers for each institution. The resulting identified risk interconnections are best represented in terms of a network graph for the system (that they apply to the 57 largest US financial companies).

In the second step, for measuring an institution's systemic impact, they individually regress the VaR of a value-weighted index of the financial sector on the institution's estimated VaR while controlling for other variables. They determine a financial firm's systemic risk contribution as the marginal effect of its individual VaR on the VaR of the system. Their empirical results suggest high tail risk interconnectedness among US financial institutions, as these network risk interconnection effects are the dominant drivers of the individual risk of financial institutions. Importantly, the detected channels of potential risk spillovers contain fundamental information for supervision authorities. Based on the estimated network, they can categorize institutions into: main risk transmitters, risk recipients, and companies that both receive and transmit tail risk, which are very useful for macroprudential supervision and regulation.

Principal Components and Granger Causality   Billio et al. (2012) use principal components analysis (PCA) and Granger-causality networks to measure interconnectedness and apply them to the monthly returns of hedge funds, publicly traded banks, broker/dealers, and insurance companies. They use PCA to estimate the common factors driving the returns of these intermediaries, and the pairwise Granger-causality tests to identify the network of statistically significant Granger-causal relations among the intermediaries.[26]

For banks, broker/dealers, and insurance companies, they use the 25 largest listed firms in each of the four sectors and use monthly equity returns. For hedge funds, which are private partnerships, they use monthly reported net of fee fund returns. Their empirical results show that linkages within and across all four sectors are highly dynamic. Over time, all four sectors have become highly interrelated, increasing the channels through which shocks can propagate throughout the system.

Their results also show that the returns of banks and insurers seem to have more significant impact on the returns of hedge funds and broker/dealers than vice versa. This asymmetry became highly significant prior to the 2008 financial crisis, suggesting that these measures may be useful out of sample indicators of systemic risk. Moreover this pattern suggests that banks are more central to systemic risk than the so-called shadow banking system, possibly as banks tend to be prime lenders to other financial institutions.[27]

Variance Decompositions   Most asset returns exhibit nonlinear dynamics, especially time-varying volatility. Diebold and Yilmaz (2014) analyze the future volatility of returns through a VAR framework panel of realized volatility measures. They measure interconnectedness among financial intermediaries with variance decompositions, which can decompose the total prediction error variability in the contributions of the different components of the system. The authors show how variance decompositions can be mapped into networks and propose a number of network metrics based on such decompositions.

They apply their methodology to measure the degree of interconnectedness and systemic risk in the US financial system during the recent financial crisis. Results suggest that the volatility of large US financial institutions has a high degree of interconnectedness. Importantly, the analysis also yields that the largest commercial banks have the highest level of interconnections to the other sectors in the network. Moreover the time series shows that interconnectedness increases in periods of distress. All in all, the previous two papers using Granger-causal approach and variance decompositions show that banks are the most important financial institutions for systemic risk, even in market based financial systems as the United States.

CDS Structural Form   Credit default swaps (CDS) are contracts that insure against a default event and in general are traded in over the counter markets. These are usually traded by large financial institutions, which buy and sell CDS against the default of nonfinancial firms, banks, and countries. As explained in Giglio (2012), because the bank that sells the CDS contract can default, the buyer of the CDS is also exposed to counterparty risk. Therefore the CDS price reflects the joint probability that the credit event happens *and* the seller of the insurance also defaults.[28] Such counterparty risk can significantly lower the value of the insurance during systemic risk episodes. However, as explained in Giglio (2012), bank bond prices are not affected by counterparty risk as they only reflect individual default probabilities. Therefore bond prices in conjunction with the prices of CDSs written by banks against other banks contain information about individual and pairwise default risk of these banks.

Giglio (2012) shows how to use CDS and bond price data to infer the probability of joint default of several banks. However, individual and pairwise default probabilities alone do not identify the probability that many banks default together, which generates financial instability. To obtain an estimate of systemic risk using bond and CDS prices, we would need to make strong functional form assumptions about the joint distribution function of defaults. Giglio (2012) instead shows how to construct bounds on the probability that several banks default together derived without imposing any assumption about the shape of the joint distribution function.[29]

Ang and Longstaff (2013) develop a multivariate CDS model that allows them to capture systemic as well as individual default risk and apply it to analyze the default risk of individual US states treasuries and major European countries. Their results suggest that systemic risk in Europe is higher than in United States. Moreover systemic sovereign risk is strongly related to financial variables, more than to macroeconomic fundamentals.

CoVar, SES, and SRISK   A key lesson from the crisis is that a substantial drop in the level of capital in the financial system implies negative externalities to the broad economy. CoVaR, SES, and SRISK indexes try to measure the drop in the value of assets of the financial system following a systemic event. CoVaR, SES, and SRISK differ in the estimation strategy employed as well as the definition of what constitutes a systemic event.

CoVaR is a systemic risk measure proposed by Adrian and Brunnermeier (2009). The CoVaR of institution i is defined as the VaR of the market conditional on its returns being at a level C:

$$\Pr\left(R_{tm} \le CoVaR_{ti}^{p} \mid R_{ti} = C\right) = p,$$

where p denotes the confidence level of the VaR. The systemic risk measure proposed by the authors is based on $\Delta CoVaR$, which is defined as the difference between the CoVaR for institution i when C equals to VaR_{ti}^{p} (i.e., i is in distress) and when C equals its median (i.e., normal times). The institutions with the largest $\Delta CoVaR$ are the institutions classified as being the most systemic.

Quantile regressions are used to estimate the CoVaR and the authors show how to estimate unconditional CoVaR as well as time varying CoVaR using state dependent variables. They apply their methodology to a sample of US financial institutions for the 1986 to 2010 period. The authors show that contagion effects are stronger in crisis times, and that CoVaR is weakly correlated with VaR, and therefore captures a different risk dimension.

Acharya et al. (2010) develop a model in which capital shortages of individual financial institutions in periods of distress generate systemic risk in the economy. Their measure is called the systemic expected shortfall (SES), and is a linear combination of the marginal expected shortfall (MES) and leverage. The SES of a financial institution is its propensity to be undercapitalized when the system as a whole is undercapitalized. The idea is the following: if a financial institution experiences capital shortages when the overall financial system is in distress, then this institution generates strong negative spillovers to the real economy as other financial intermediaries will not be able to substitute for example its credit and liquidity to the private sector, as the financial system overall is weak, and therefore deleverage from this institution will be costly for the economy and financial system at large.

Building on Acharya et al. (2010), Brownlees and Engle (2015) propose an SRISK index that attempts to measure the future expected capital shortage a financial intermediary would experience in case of a downturn in the market. Let D_{it} be the book value of debt and W_{it} the market value of equity of institution i at period t. Also let k be a capital buffer parameter which determines the fraction of market valued assets that the financial institution is required to hold for regulation. The capital buffer of the firm is defined as

$$CB_{it} = W_{it} - k \, (D_{it} + W_{it}).$$

If we assume that the capital buffer is positive, then the financial institution can operate properly; however, if the capital buffer is negative, the institution is going to experience distress. If a financial institution experiences a capital shortage during a market downturn, this is going to generate systemic risk because when the market is down, several institutions will be distressed simultaneously and this may impair the whole financial and economic system.

Thus it is of interest to compute the expected shortage an institution would suffer in case of a substantial market correction. The SRISK index is simply the expected capital buffer conditional on a market drop lower than a threshold C, where R_{it+1} is gross stock price return one period ahead:

$$SRISK_{it+1} = k \, D_{it} - (1-k) W_{it} \; E(R_{it+1} | R_{mt+1} < C).$$

In the practical implementation of the index, Brownlees and Engle (2015) consider a k of 8 percent and a C of 20 percent over a one-month horizon. The authors then use the SRISK index to rank financial institutions: the higher the expected capital shortage in case of a crisis, the more systemically risky a financial institution is (the cross-sectional dimension of systemic risk). Moreover the aggregate level of SRISK of the whole financial system can be used as an aggregate time-varying index of systemic risk (the time dimension of systemic risk). Importantly, the empirical application to a set of large US financial institutions in the 2000-10 period shows that the SRISK rankings significantly predict the amount of capital injected by the Fed to individual financial institutions and that an increase in aggregate SRISK predicts downturns in real activity.[30]

7.2 Relative Performance of Systemic Risk Measures

The systemic risk measures discussed in the previous section each have their own specific advantages and limitations. Moreover these measures differ substantially in their predictive power to forecast key

World Financials -Total SRISK (US$ billion)

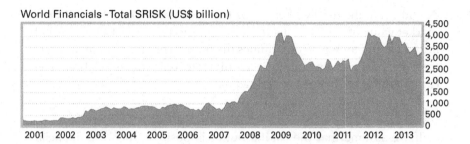

Figure 7.1
SRISK for the world financial system, in US$ billion for the period June 2000 to June 2013
Source: V-Lab, NYU Stern

variables of finance-macro variables of interest. A first look at the two
best-known measures of systemic risk—CoVaR and SRISK—shows a
notable increase in measured systemic risk prior to and during the
crisis period 2007 to 2009 (figures 7.1 and 7.2). This suggests that these
measures do a fairly good job in picking up the time-series dimension
of systemic risk.

Moreover these measures point to sizable differences across financial
institutions, with large institutions on average contributing more to
systemic risk, consistent with their relative importance in terms of size
and financial interconnections. Indeed size appears to be an important
correlate of both CoVaR and SRISK (figure 7.2 and table 7.1). This suggests that these measures also capture some of the cross-sectional variation in systemic risk.

However, when estimated over longer periods, CoVaR also points
to significant systemic risk during earlier periods, such as during the
year 1997 (see figure 7.2), which is not consistent with the widely held
view that the recent crisis was unprecedented since the great depression of the 1930s. Moreover the evolution over time of both CoVaR and
SRISK may mask that the underlying process is driven by a common
risk factors, and so could have little bearing on the predictive power
of either measure. An assessment of the relative performance of various
systemic risk measures, including CoVaR and SRISK, requires a more
detailed analysis of their predictive power, both in and out of sample.

A crucial issue concerning systemic risk measures is their ability to
produce useful early warning signals. Again, the literature on the
assessment and comparison of the different measures proposed in the
literature is still in its infancy. Moreover a challenge of the assessment
of these measures is that systemic events are, fortunately, rare and this

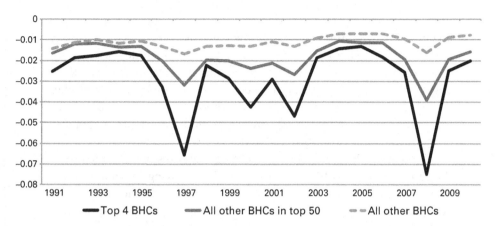

Figure 7.2
ΔCoVaR estimates of the contribution to systemic risk by bank size, in a sample of US bank holding companies over the period 1991 to 2010. Note that bank i's ΔCoVaR is the VaR of the banking system conditional on bank i being in distress compared to when bank i is in its median state, and this indicates the marginal contribution of bank i to the banking system's overall systemic risk. Note that more negative values of ΔCoVaR denote higher contribution to systemic risk. Averages across large banks (top four in terms of assets), medium-size banks (top five to top fifty in terms of assets), and small banks (below top fifty in terms of assets). Source: Adrian and Brunnermeier, Federal Reserve Bank of Chicago (US BHC Call reports); authors' calculations

Table 7.1
US financials with largest systemic risk (SRISK), June 2013

TOP 10	SRISK%
Bank of America	16.4
JP Morgan Chase	16.1
Citigroup	14.9
MetLife	8.3
Morgan Stanley	7.9
Prudential Financial	7.8
Goldman Sachs	6.2
Hartford Financial Services	3.1
Capital One Financial	2.8
Lincoln National Corp	2.5

Source: V-Lab NYU Stern, data as of June 20, 2013
Note: SRISK as percentage of total SRISK for US financials, top ten in terms of SRISK%.

makes drawing inference harder. The rest of this subsection provides an empirical evaluation using quantile regression analysis of the ability of alternative systemic risk measures to forecast quantiles of key variables of macroeconomic activity, drawing entirely on the work by Giglio, Kelly, and Qiao (2014). Indeed, as our definition of risk implies the systemic event has a significant downward impact on real activity, the link between systemic risk measures and extreme reductions in economic activity could be exploited.

Giglio et al. (2014) examine 18 existing measures of systemic risk in the United States and 10 measures for the United Kingdom and Europe. They use the longest possible data history, back in some cases to the entire postwar sample in the United States. The authors show that taken individually, these measures reveal low predictive ability for macroeconomic downturns. However, an index that aggregates them using their proposed methodology (based on reductions of aggregating the different measures) consistently outperforms them both in and out of sample.[31] Moreover their empirical results reach a positive conclusion regarding the systemic risk measures. When taken altogether, systemic risk measures have useful predictive information about the probability of future macroeconomic downturns. Importantly, their conclusion is based on out-of-sample tests and is robust to permutations, samples, and controls. This is after policy makers endogenously react, as the authors find that systemic risk indicators predict policy decisions, in particular a rise in systemic risk predicts an increased probability of a large drop in the Federal Funds rate, suggesting that the Fed takes preventive action at elevated risk levels.

Their results show that systemic risk is a multifaceted phenomenon, as we argue throughout this book. First, a few systemic risk measures, such as measures of financial sector equity volatility, possess significant predictive power in a variety of specifications; other variables, including leverage and liquidity measures, perform well only in some specifications. Second, systemic risk measures are more informative about macroeconomic shocks' lower tail than about their central tendency, where macroeconomic performance is measured on innovations in industrial production or the Chicago Fed National Activity Index.

Another important contribution showing related results is Allen, Bali, and Tang (2012). They attempt to assess the usefulness of micro versus macro aggregated systemic risk measures. Their paper investigates whether a simple aggregated measure of systemic risk in the financial sector predicts a drop in real activity. Their answer is yes (though micro measures of systemic risk do not predict macro effects). They also show that it is the risk in financial firms that drives systemic risk rather than the risk of nonfinancial firms, as adding an equivalent index of systemic risk for nonfinancials does not enhance predictive power.

7.3 Using Systemic Risk Measures to Monitor Systemic Risk

Measuring systemic risk poses a number of challenges, including data limitations and how to distinguish systemic risk from other factors such as uncertainty and systematic risk. Existing approaches require detailed data that are frequently not available, especially for banks that are not listed, emerging market economies and bank to bank direct and indirect financial linkages, as well as for the unregulated parts of the financial system, such as the shadow banking sector, OTC derivatives markets, and hedge funds. Though we have covered some of these issues in previous sections when talking about the data requirements, we turn in this section to possible ways to estimate systemic risk with data limitations.

Most existing approaches to measuring systemic risk require detailed data that are not readily available, be it high-frequency data or financial institutions' level exposures. For example, network models require detailed data about interinstitution exposures that are generally not available (e.g., derivatives or interbank positions for each pair of banks). A solution is to use a market-based approach to measure systemic risk, but unfortunately, not all financial institutions issue traded securities, limiting the application of models that require market prices as inputs. Nevertheless, extrapolation methods can be applied, and large interconnected financial institutions are usually traded in markets. As a result market data limitations are less severe for the subset of financial institutions that are likely to pose the most systemic risk.

Brunnermeier, Gorton, and Krishnamurthy (2012) conceptualize and design a risk topography that outlines a data acquisition and dissemination process to inform about systemic risk. They emphasize that systemic risk (1) cannot be detected based on measuring balance sheet items and income statement items, (2) typically builds up in the background before materializing in a crisis (as discussed in chapter 4), and (3) is determined by market participants' response to various shocks (as discussed in chapters 5 and 6). They propose that regulators elicit from market participants their (partial equilibrium) risk as well as liquidity sensitivities with respect to major risk factors and liquidity scenarios. They persuasively argue that general equilibrium responses and economywide system effects could be calibrated using this panel dataset.

As explained in the first part of this chapter, if, for example, supervisors used lending standards as a measure in central bank surveys, then supervisors would have seen evidence of the "Lucas critique" as banks would try to mask their potential excessive soft lending standards by reporting little softening in the survey. Moreover, as systemic risk measures are always partial as we have explained in this chapter, once banks and other financial intermediaries know that supervisors use certain measures, then banks' shareholders and managers (potentially other employees) would have an incentive to take excessive risk by adjusting their risk-taking behavior to measures that are less monitored by supervisors and reduce those that are actually used by regulators.

Of course, as important to the systemic risk measures are market data. However, as we discuss extensively in chapters 4 and 9, there is too little market disciplining in banking, at least until recently as the market expected bailouts and liquidity assistance; therefore the measures of systemic risk using market data could reflect little risk as they also incorporate the potential bailouts from taxpayers and the liquidity assistance from central banks.

Each of the systemic risk measures discussed in this chapter has their own specific advantages and limitations. Taken individually, the predictive power of existing measures of systemic risk is poor at best (Giglio et al. 2014). In practice, and data permitting, it is therefore typically advisable to employ a combination of measures to track different aspects of systemic risk over time and across institutions and markets. Individual measures have low predictive ability for macroeconomic downturns but an index that combines and aggregates them consistently outperforms them both in and out of sample (Giglio et al. 2014).

Yet these measures differ substantially in their predictive power to forecast key variables of macroeconomic activity and other variables of interest. The choice of systemic risk measure will therefore depend also on which aspect of systemic risk one intends to track, be it over time or across institutions, markets, or countries. Having said this, systemic risk may appear in unexpected places, and it is therefore advisable to employ a broad set of indicators to track various aspects of systemic risk over time and across space.

Indeed, as there are many systemic risk measures, as compared to price stability and inflation for central banks in their normal monetary policy measures, there may be conflicting signals in the measures and some rankings of importance should be developed. We believe that in the short term supervisors should pay attention to all the different measures. They should aggregate different measures into a more global measure, but they should also pay attention if a particular measure is giving a red signal.

The measurement of systemic risk should not be considered in isolation but within a macroprudential policy framework. In particular, the Systemic Risk Board (or the regulatory body in charge of tracking systemic risk in the country) should decide how it informs the market about the state of systemic risk, given the different measures of systemic risk being used. Supervisors should not only care about the (financial) stability of the financial sector but also about the real effects to the economy at large, as this is a crucial element of systemic risk and motivation for macroprudential policy.

Simplified approaches could be useful if data are an issue. For example, Duffie (2014) presents and discusses a "10-by-10-by-10" network-based approach to monitoring systemic risk in the financial system. Using this approach, a regulator would analyze the exposures of a core group of systemically important financial firms to a list of 10 stressful scenarios (the number "10" can be adjusted to fit circumstances). For each scenario, the designated financial institutions would report their gains (or losses) and also provide the identities of the 10 counterparties with whom the gain (or loss) for that scenario is the greatest in magnitude relative to all counterparties. The gains or losses with each of those 10 counterparties would also be reported, scenario by scenario.

Gains and losses would be measured in terms of market value and also in terms of cash flow, allowing regulators to assess risk magnitudes in terms of stresses to both economic values and liquidity. Exposures would be measured before and after collateralization. One of the scenarios would be the failure of a counterparty. The "top ten" counterparties for this scenario would therefore be those whose defaults cause the greatest losses to the reporting institution. With such a monitoring system in place, a supervisor charged with systemic risk would have crucial information, though without hard data, it is not clear whether financial institutions have the incentive to truthfully answer all the details.

7.4   Conclusions

It is difficult to construct a perfectly reliable measure of systemic risk in real time, because all necessary data are not available and because systemic risk is a complex, endogenous and multifaceted risk that depends on multiple externalities and endogenously correlated decisions by financial intermediaries. Nevertheless, there are partial measures that can help overcome many of these problems, thus allowing measurement of systemic risk. As we explained in this chapter, it is crucial to cross-check measures based on both fundamentals and market data, as well as on both prices and quantities, and to rely not only on macro-aggregate variables but also on micro-based measures using data on single financial institutions or multiple interlinkages among institutions. However, we do believe the measurement of systemic risk is an area (along with the finance-macro models explained in chapter 3 and the effectiveness of macroprudential policy in chapter 9) that needs to advance more in order to provide macroprudential policy makers with adequate tools to monitor systemic risk.

Measurement of systemic risk is crucial for macroprudential policy as macroprudential supervision is, by definition, impossible without reliable measures of systemic risk. As explained in this chapter, by giving the strengths and weaknesses of the different measures, we have shown areas in which there has been a lot of advancement and other areas in which little progress has been made. Aggregation of different measures can give fewer false positives, measurement of asset price bubble based on credit is feasible, even in environments without excellent data, and there is a significant progress in market-based measures and networks. A central advance will also come from more data available. Macroprudential policy needs a precise identification of the main externalities at work in each moment, and precise data are crucial for this measurement, and thus for policy.

8   Systemic Risk and Microprudential Regulation

One of the major lessons of the current crisis has been the failure of traditional banking regulation. It failed because of unforeseen spill-overs, as it happened between the market for asset-backed securities and the interbank market, with the collapse of the former leading to the freezing of the latter and because general equilibrium effects, such as the impact of banks' distress on economic activity and firms' solvency, were disregarded while their monitoring was essential to preserve financial stability. The major error regulatory authorities incurred was to assume that building model-based seemingly rigorous capital regulation complemented by supervision and market discipline at the individual level would ensure overall financial stability. This lack of a macroprudential perspective on banking risks constituted the main shortcoming of banking regulation. Still, microprudential regulation also failed, including by allowing banks to operate at very high levels of leverage, by permitting regulatory arbitrage through weak supervision, and by the absence of a properly functioning resolution framework for failing financial institutions. The lessons from financial crises, and especially from the current one, will help in analyzing the particular role of every single piece of the regulatory structure either in reducing or in amplifying the effects of the crisis. This is all the more important because the links between macroprudential and microprudential policy are not obvious, with macroprudential risks being an input for microprudential regulation and microprudential buffers and firewalls being an input for macroprudential regulation.

Some aspects of systemic risk, such as those associated with individual banks not internalizing their actions on the riskiness of the overall financial system and the procyclicality of financial regulation, can only be addressed through macroprudential regulation. However, other aspects of systemic risk can in part be reduced by microprudential regulation. Effective microprudential regulation, by limiting the probability of individual bank failures, by boosting available buffers to absorb the shocks from failures, and by facilitating a quick and orderly resolution of failing institutions, will go a long way to reduce the systemic risk arising from the negative spillovers and contagion risk associated with bank failures. By fixing the microprudential regulatory framework for financial institutions and making individual financial institutions more stable and less leveraged, we may need less macroprudential regulation (assuming that the reduced risks in the regulated sector are not replaced by even greater risks in the nonregulated parts of the financial sector) and will make any macroprudential regulation more effective. In this sense, fixing microprudential regulation can be seen as a complement to macroprudential regulation. A discussion of the need for a new macroprudential regulatory framework should therefore start with the role of traditional microprudential regulation.

This chapter will discuss the rationale for a microprudential regulatory framework and its impact on the reduction (or aggravation) of systemic risk. It will describe the limitations traditional microprudential regulation faces in managing systemic risk, and discuss the impact of the new regulation framework issued by the Basel committee and the Financial Stability Board in response to the G20 initiative, as well as its implementations in the Dodd–Frank Act and the new European Directives.

As we have already argued in chapter 1, the ultimate goal of banking regulation is to create a framework for financial stability as the necessary condition for stable economic growth. As a consequence both macroprudential and microprudential regulation are not an objective per se, but constitute intermediate targets. Even if economic stability promotes growth, there is a trade-off between growth and the costs of financial regulation that will affect the design of both micro and macroprudential regulation. Such a trade-off is never explicitly stated in the justification of banking regulation, although it is present, as it is clear that banking regulation intends to strike a balance between two extremes: perfect financial stability with high levels of capital, zero risk of banks' bankruptcy, costly loans and reduced banking activity or low capital levels, highly competitive loans in a large banking industry with high levels of systemic risk. The trade-offs between the size of the credit market and its stability are relevant only once the efficient frontier between risk (for stability) and return (for market size) is reached. Thus the improvement upon current regulatory practices aims at increasing financial stability without reducing long-term economic growth. This is why well-designed micro and macroprudential policy is essential for long-term stable growth.

Microprudential regulation considers mainly the individual bank bankruptcy risk, even if some elements of the social cost of a bankruptcy may be taken into account. Macroprudential policy measures and monitors the overall levels of risk that the banking system has to face and identifies sources of risk, such as contagion, spillovers to financial markets and bubbles in some assets that are ignored by risk managers because they are invisible at the level of an individual bank risk model.

The distinction between microprudential and macroprudential policy is complex because it is multidimensional, as the two differ in their objective, their focus, the type of externalities, and the inputs required. The main differences between microprudential and macroprudential policy are as follows:

1. *Different objectives* By definition, microprudential regulation is concerned with the risk of failure of an individual bank and its consequences, while macroprudential regulation is concerned with overall systemic risk.

2. *Differences in focus* Microprudential regulation considers a partial equilibrium framework where the social cost of a bank's bankruptcy is contemplated, taking into account possible contagion and externalities on the bank's customers but where the impact on prices and markets (including a possible market collapse) is disregarded. Macroprudential regulation takes the opposite and complementary view and focuses on general equilibrium issues, thus avoiding the composition fallacy of assuming that what is efficient at the individual level will be efficient at the collective level.

3. *Different targeted distortions* The microprudential view considers the social cost of an individual bank failure without taking into account indirect effects. The macroprudential view instead takes into account the impact of bank failures on asset prices and economic activity as well as its feedback on banks' risks, so that it is concerned with the business cycle, the financial accelerator mechanism that causes business cycles to be amplified by financial market imperfections, the procyclical nature of the banks' strategies (which themselves depend upon banking regulation), and the impact of changes in asset prices.

4. *Different necessary inputs* Microprudential regulation is based on exogenously given probability distributions for asset prices (and the cost of funding or the price of liabilities in perfectly rigorous models) as well as their correlations. The macroprudential approach is based on a completely different view, as the risk is, at least partly, endogenous. Consequently, while the microprudential approach may take, for instance, the price distribution of real estate as given, the macroprudential approach will consider equilibrium prices to be determined by herding behavior and the buildup of bubbles.

As a consequence of these multidimensional differences between the microprudential and the macroprudential approach, there are not only important discrepancies but also multiple areas of overlap.

Obviously our notion of risk is completely different depending on whether the economy is functioning normally (even if it is in a downturn) or if it is in the middle of a systemic crisis. But, more important, the macroeconomic and macroprudential perspective on financial stability should be a key input in the regulatory process in order for banks to use a risk assessment (internal) model that takes into account the building up of imbalances as well as the probability of a systemic crisis. This has an implication that some clearly microprudential tools have important macroprudential consequences. Thus limiting the loan to value or the loan to income ratios are both microprudential and macroprudential measures. Even consumer protection that prima facie is clearly microprudential could have strong positive implications on the financial stability front (e.g., as illustrated by the systemic risks posed by mortgage lending in foreign currency).

With this delicate and somewhat blurred distinction in mind, we would like to explore in this chapter why the traditional microprudential regulatory framework failed and whether the currently proposed microprudential remedies are likely to create an improved financial environment where systemic crises will be averted or, at least, where their effects will be minimized. The role of macroprudential regulation will be taken up in the next chapter. Our analysis will consider both the public interest view of regulation as well as the private interest view.

8.1 Why Financial Regulation?

The analysis of prudential regulation at the individual bank level requires a justification of why banks do not fulfill their efficient role in resource allocation. In the case of banks, why is it that the shareholders choice of capital (or leverage) is inadequate. And, once we agree financial regulation is required, what view of regulation should we adopt? Should regulation maximize general welfare or be the outcome of an equilibrium among different interest groups?

8.1.1 Market Failures in the Banking Industry

The first question we need to address regarding microprudential regulation is why, in the first place, regulation is required. In the absence of market imperfections a competitive market leads to the optimal allocation where profit-maximizing banks would select to finance all positive net present value projects because the structure of their liabilities is irrelevant, as the Modigliani–Miller conditions hold (see Fama 1980).

Banking regulation exists precisely because this is not the case and the bankruptcy of a financial institution generates an externality. Indeed the bankruptcy of a financial institution leads to contagion (as we saw in chapter 5) and destroys the value of the relationship between banks and their clients. Banks' prudential regulation is therefore aimed at (1) limiting the probability of a bank's bankruptcy and (2) limiting the impact of a bank's bankruptcy. The complexity of this issue is aggravated because once banks' liabilities become safe (e.g., through deposit insurance), debtholders' market discipline vanishes, providing incentives for excessive risk-taking, which in turn requires additional regulation.

Consequently, from a microeconomic perspective, the objective of regulation is the efficient allocation of funds to potential borrowers, which implies, in particular, setting the right level of risk (and the potential costs for taxpayers in case of a bank bankruptcy), through the combination of markets and financial intermediaries, whether as equity or debt, to all investment projects with a positive risk-adjusted net present value computed at the equilibrium interest rates and internalizing bankruptcy externalities. This way the arbitrage in the risk-return frontier that is to be reached by the market subject to regulation will reflect all the social costs of both an individual bank failure and a systemic crisis, a point that we will examine below in connection with the failure of the safety net.

In contrast to this idyllic view of financial markets, anyone intending to grasp the quintessence of the crisis and identify its regulatory roots will agree that there has been a deficit of macroprudential and shadow banking regulation. In hindsight, it is clear that the current financial crisis has its origin in defective banking regulation.

8.1.2 The Public and Private Interest Views of Microprudential Regulation

As carefully and convincingly explained by Barth, Caprio, and Levine in their book *Reforming Banking Regulation: Till Angels Govern*, in order to understand banking regulation, it is essential to distinguish between two views of the world: the public and the private interest view.

The Public Interest View of Microprudential Regulation   The basic assumption of the public interest view is that regulatory authorities intend to define and implement banking regulation in order to maximize some measure of welfare. This approach may take into account a number of restrictions, such as a given institutional structure or limited information, but will nevertheless consider that the regulatory authorities' objective is to improve welfare by improving the allocation of firms in the most efficient way.

The Private Interest View of Financial Regulation   Contrasting with the welfare-maximizing view of regulation, Stigler's (1971) seminal paper suggests that regulation should be seen as a commodity with its demand by consumers and producers and its supply by the regulatory agency. Because producers are a much stronger well-organized interest group than consumers, "as a rule, regulation is acquired by the industry and is designed and operated primarily for its benefit" (Stigler 1971, 1973). This led to the private interest theory, rent-seeking, and capture theory view of regulation, where regulation is used by the industry to increase the rents it is able to capture (Peltzman 1976). For producers, the cost–benefit of lobbying is quite favorable as the government can produce subsidies (e.g., banks' bailouts), reduce competition by restricting entry, or decrease production costs (e.g., by considering a loan hedged with a CDS as AAA). To some extent the regulatory capture theory states that we will only observe self-serving regulation even if it is implemented by regulatory agencies. The overall implication is that many types of regulation do not serve a public interest but simply boost the rents of a particularly powerful interest group within society.

According to the private interest view, the effective regulation will result from the collusion and rent redistribution between the regulatory agency and the interest groups. Consequently the incentives for regulatory agencies to collude should be made explicit. On this account two theories coexist. Using the terminology of Barth et al. (2006), it is possible to distinguish "systematic corruption" whereby the politicians' gain comes from buying political support through their access to funds for their campaigns and for the investment projects and "venal corruption" where the career of the regulatory agency directors may lead to a highly profitable position in a regulated firm. One way or the other, the incentives for collusion between politicians and regulatory agency managers exist, thus providing a rigorous basis to the regulatory capture theory.

Still, a number of caveats have to be considered:

First, the public interest and private interest views are extreme polar cases, and quite possibly we will observe something in between. This will change in time with the type of institutions, with the political structure of the country that allow for more or less weight for the interest groups, and even with public opinion (presumably the Enron scandal did not leave much option for collusion in the drafting of the Sarbanes–Oxley Act).

Second, it is important to keep in mind the possibility of a tautological snag: there will always be winners and losers from a regulatory reform, so that identifying the winners as "powerful interest groups" does not gives any support to the theory of regulatory capture, but is a simple ex post description of the impact of the reform.

Third, we may expect interest groups to change through time, to discover loopholes and create new products that avoid the regulation protecting other interest groups, leading to re-regulation, so that there are complex dynamics in the regulatory game.

The ultimate issue is whether the private interest view of regulation is relevant, and for that we have to put it to the test. Testing this theory is difficult because of the three caveats we mentioned. Ideally we should define ex ante the interest groups and test whether they are the main beneficiaries of the regulatory reform, although we should also check that this is not a win-win situation where consumers have also benefited from the reform.

Two interesting contributions are provided by Kroszner and Strahan (1999, 2001). In their first paper, they consider the timing of the de-regulation of branching restrictions and show that the de-regulation was delayed in those states where small banks had a more preeminent role. In their 2001 paper they analyze the voting behavior in the US Congress to show that the passage of regulation (1991 Federal Deposit

Insurance Corporation Improvement Act) was partially explained by how important the small and big banks were, as well as insurance and banks in each constituency. A similar analysis is performed by Stratmann (2002) for the enactment of the Gramm-Leach-Bliley Act that repealed the Glass–Steagall Act of 1933. The evidence is also valid for Europe where Heinemann and Shüller (2004) have used the private interest approach in explaining bank regulation and supervision across countries.

Overall, the evidence is there. Yet, if it does not prove welfare has diminished for some interest group, it is not a definite proof. It seems obvious that in some cases the private interest of some type of regulation will dominate, but this will not always be the case. Consequently it will be important to consider the private interest view of regulation as a possible force in play and regulation as the equilibrium result of a bargaining game, while considering that neither a pure public interest nor a pure private interest approach to regulation will be a realistic representation of the world.

8.2 Implementing Regulation

The implementation of regulation implies a delegation of power to a specific regulatory authority. Such a procedure requires clarifying, first, what has to be regulated, and second, how it has to be regulated, by specifying the powers of the regulator as well as its limits so as to protect the regulated banks from arbitrary regulatory decisions.

8.2.1 Types of Regulation

Traditionally a distinction is made between two types of regulations: conduct regulation and structural regulation (Kay and Vickers 1990). As implied by the names, "conduct regulation" is used for regulating the behavior of the agents operating in the market; "structural regulation" is instead implemented in order to regulate market structure and promote competition.

Conduct of Business   The conduct of business regulation establishes rules about how firms treat their customers. The existence of such rules and the penalties in case of lack of compliance is critical in the financial area where customers have limited information and financial institutions have conflicts of interest as they often perform the functions of both sellers of financial products and financial advisors. Regulating conduct of business is not restricted to banking but encompasses all financial operations between a financial institution and its customers. It establishes how financial institutions should conduct business with integrity and in compliance with the customers interest, exerting due diligence in providing financial services to customers.[1]

In the recent crisis, inconsistent conduct of business regulation has been critical in the excessive risk taken by holders of subprime mortgages that were induced to believe that the combination of a low initial "teaser" interest rates and the increase of real estate prices were sufficient to guarantee safe profitable operations. Similar conflicts of interest have been observed in other markets where subordinated debt or short-term uninsured debt was sold to banks' customers as a substitute for deposits. In Eastern European countries, and in particular, in Hungary, banks' customers have been granted Swiss franc denominated mortgages with lower interest rates without being duly informed of the risks of revaluation of the Swiss franc.

As these examples show, conflicts of interest should not be underestimated. There are two key implications of the lack of adequate conduct of business: first, at the ex ante stage, funds are channeled to inefficient use at the expense of other projects that will not be financed. Second, at the ex post stage, the fact that customers are unable to fulfill their repayment obligations constitutes an element of systemic risk.

Structural Regulation   Structural regulation is necessary in a market when its competitive structure is threatened. This is true for the banking market, but a number of additional considerations have to be taken into account.

First, to prevent banks' bankruptcies, entry and mergers have to be regulated.[2] Second, both the theoretical and empirical literature have emphasized that there might be a trade-off between competition and financial stability.

As it is intuitive, if banks have higher margins because they are enjoying monopolistic rents, the chances of going bankrupt decrease. Also this provides banks with an incentive to behave in a more prudent way because in the case of bankruptcy they would lose their charter value, which is defined as the present value of their future rents.[3]

Prudential Regulation   Because the main externality in the banking industry is the bankruptcy of a bank, the major concern of regulatory authorities will be to reduce the likelihood of a bank bankruptcy or, if a bank is to fail, to limit its impact on the payment system, on public confidence, on the rest of the banking industry, and on economic activity. Microprudential regulation is defined as all regulatory measures that reduce the probability of a bank bankruptcy as well as its impact on other banks and economic agents.

8.2.2 The Legal Infrastructure

A specific law (usually part of the banking law) defines both the powers that are delegated to the regulatory authority and their limits. The law establishes the characteristics of the regulatory authority, and in particular, its degree of independence, its access to information (e.g., auditing information), and its ability to impose sanctions on the institutions that do not comply with current regulation.

Prior to the current crisis, the law allocating powers to the regulatory authorities was designed so as to cope with banking institutions exclusively. As the problems in shadow banking backfired, it became clear that this was a mistake, but the process of adapting laws to a new economic environment is slow and costly so the changes in regulation are limited and implemented with an important delay. Nevertheless, it should be mentioned that the United Kingdom reacted swiftly, changing its banking law in 2009, and in particular, defining a new regime for banks' bankruptcies. In the United States the process was almost as fast, but the degree of complexity of the Dodd–Frank Act and the powers that it delegates to different committees or the Securities and Exchange Commission are so broad that it is difficult to assess its future impact.

Because the delegation of powers has to be based on national legislation, regulation can only be national. Institutions such as the Basel committee draw their power from the countries' incentives to commit to high regulatory standards. Indeed it is in the interest of the countries to show that their banks are duly regulated and abide by international standards. Nevertheless, the legal structure of regulation is always determined at the national level, and, consequently, this might lead to important cross-country differences.

The Regulatory Institutions   The evolution of the banking industry and its integration with financial markets through the creation of financial conglomerates has led a number of countries to reexamine what was the traditional structure of financial regulation. The traditional approach, often referred to as the "institutional approach," is based on the legal status of the regulated financial entity. The firm's legal status, typically a bank, a broker-dealer, or an insurance company determines which of the three corresponding regulatory authorities will be in charge. This model, based on the specialization of each type of regulation, was progressively abandoned in favor of a unified approach that could deal more easily with financial conglomerates. This was the structure chosen by the United Kingdom where the functions of the Financial Services Authorities were complemented by those of the Bank of England in charge of overall financial stability, that is, of systemic risk.[4] The failure of Northern Rock showed possible weaknesses in the UK model of financial regulation and prompted a revision of the role of the two institutions, with the Bank of England taking over the FSA.

Nowadays it is clear that the institutional structure of regulation matters and that it has to be reviewed so as to take into account macroprudential regulation. As macroprudential regulation is built upon the central bank information, the "systemic risk council" or "systemic risk oversight board," even if independent from the central bank, will draw all its information from this institution. Similarly, as the role of macroprudential regulation is to assess hidden risks, whether bubbles, maturity mismatches, or other, the microprudential institutions rely on the macroprudential input in computing the actual banking risks.

8.2.3 The Safety Net

As the main externality generated by the banks' operations has its origin in the social cost of banks' bankruptcy, countries with a well-developed banking industry have progressively put into place a number of mechanisms to prevent bank failures and to limit the worst of their effects. The safety net is constituted by the articulation of, at least, the six following elements:

1. Strict definition of banking activities
2. Banking supervision
3. Deposit insurance
4. Capital requirements
5. Lender of last resort
6. Bailout and bank closure policy

As is clear, since the safety net decreases the probability of each individual bank's bankruptcy as well as the impact and the contagion it causes, it is not only a mechanism to reduce the social costs of an individual bank bankruptcy but also the main determinant for the containment of contagion and systemic risk. Nevertheless, it would be erroneous to consider the safety net as the only determinant of systemic risk, as it ignores macroprudential policy (see chapters 9 and 10).

One of the lessons of the crisis has been that the different components of the safety net may help contain the crisis or, on the contrary, generate the wrong incentives and creating a culture of overconfidence for agents in markets and financial institutions, aggravating the tail risks and amplifying the effects of a crisis.

8.3 Risk Assessment and Capital Regulation

In order to assess the performance of the safety net during the crisis, we have to address two different questions. First, whether the safety net as it was designed performed adequately in the extreme conditions of the crisis. The second question goes beyond that and considers whether the design of the safety net itself was fit to cope with systemic risk.

On the positive side, deposit insurance and monetary policy (see chapter 10) were instrumental in limiting a generalized bank panic on behalf of depositors and in reducing fire sales and the corresponding banks' losses. Both in the United States and in Europe the limits of deposit insurance were increased, and a depositors' "flight to quality" was avoided in this way. Also central banks reforming the lender of the last resort function provided liquidity and extended currency swaps that prevented a global run.

On the negative side, it must be acknowledged that other components of the safety net failed. First, banks' supervisors, despite the running of stress tests, were clearly underestimating the risks faced by banks, and in particular, the risk related to shadow banking, securitization, and credit default swaps.

Second, capital regulation also failed, not only because of the underestimation of the required risk weights but because of the definition of capital in Basel I that overestimated the role of tier-2 and tier-3 capital and, even, within tier-1 capital assigned too limited a role to common stocks and retained earnings. Finally, the bankruptcy procedures at hand were ineffective in dealing with distressed banks in a quick and orderly way. In particular, this was a key issue concerning banks operating across borders. The Icelandic banking crisis is sufficient to illustrate this point: it shows how in a crisis cross-border banks become national, and regulatory and fiscal authorities care only about minimizing the cost to national taxpayers. Indeed Iceland declared its deposit insurance company bankrupt, issued emergency legislation to protect Icelandic depositors and left UK and Dutch depositors unprotected.

8.3.1 Capital in the Logic of Basel II

Bank capital plays a number of roles. One is controlling bank risk-taking: shareholders with more skin-in-the-game have lower incentives to take risk (Marcus 1984; Keeley 1990). Another is to promote risk sharing: capital acts as a buffer to absorb losses and helps avoid bankruptcy costs and spillovers of bank distress onto the rest of the financial system and the real economy, including by allowing for the orderly liquidation and disposal of assets in the event of financial distress (Gale and Ozgur 2005). Also, banks with higher capital can better attract funds, increasing the amount of lending in support of the economy (Holmstrom and Tirole 1997),

In a Modigliani–Miller world, banks should be financed only by equity so that their probability of going bankrupt is zero and the associated externality vanishes. According to Admati et al. (2013) this point has not been sufficiently taken into account both by bankers and by policy makers who have overestimated the cost of banks' equity by disregarding the decrease in equity that a lower leverage implies. Nevertheless, once financial imperfections are considered, equity has a higher cost than debt. This may be for several reasons. One is taxes. For instance, equity is double taxed while debt is not (Modigliani and Miller 1958). Another reason is asymmetric information, such as the costs associated with the dilution of equity when incumbent investors and managers have information about the firm that new equity investors do not have (Myers and Majluf 1984). Agency conflicts can also raise the cost of equity relative to debt, for instance, by reducing managerial incentives for efficiency (Jensen and Meckling 1976). There could also be economic agents that value bank debt (notably deposits) for its high liquidity and safety (DeAngelo and Stulz 2013; Allen et al. 2014). Whatever the reason, it implies that there is an optimal balance to be found between the cost of bank loans and the probability of a bank failure that will determine the socially optimal level of capital.

In spite of these costs of imposing higher capital requirements, the high level of leverage at which many global banks were operating prior to the 2008 global financial crisis left many banks with wafer thin margins to deal with the shocks from the systemic risk that was built up in the system, with as a result that many banks had to be rescued using taxpayer money. A reduction in leverage through higher capital requirements (including more emphasis on the quality of capital), by curtailing risk taking by financial institutions and increasing their buffers in the event of distress can go a long way to reduce systemic risk. However, high bank capital may trigger a migration of activities from banks to the less regulated and thus potentially riskier non-bank sector, amplifying the boundary problem in financial regulation (Goodhart 2010; Martin and Parigi 2013; Plantin 2015) and increasing systemic risk. The balance of these forces has to be carefully weighted in designing bank capital regulation.

The One-Factor Merton Model   A second point to emphasize is that if the risks of individual loans are independently distributed, the law of large numbers assures that the probability of bankruptcy tends toward zero when the number of loans tends to infinity, provided that the expected return on the loan is larger than the average cost of capital, that is, that banks are profitable ventures. This means that in such a world of independently distributed losses, the expected losses are covered by the interest rate charged on the loan.

This academic exercise allows us to define capital as differing from provisions. Indeed risks related to the independent risks of each loan, the *expected* losses, should be covered by the interest rate charged on the loan and accounted for as provisions. Capital should, instead, be defined as the amount to cover unexpected correlated risks. [5]

The independently distributed losses case implies that any realistic model of banks' risks should be based on common factors simultaneously affecting all loans. The Basel approach takes the simplest possible model when it postulates the existence of a single (macroeconomic) factor that, as a first approximation, could be thought of as GDP growth. This is the rationale for having banks' capital requirements that constitutes a buffer against the risk in this single systemic factor and is different from provisions.

In a world of specialized banks there is no unique measure of risk for each asset, as the portfolios the banks hold are different and have sector-specific risk. The risk of a specific Irish mortgage for an Irish bank that has 60 percent of its portfolio invested in this type of loan is therefore higher than for a German bank that has 2 percent of its portfolio invested in Irish mortgages. So the single-factor model cannot take this feature into account. Finally, notice that the single-factor model is an approximation. If there were several macroeconomic factors, the risk weights for each financial product would depend on the proportion of the different macroeconomic factors a bank portfolio embodies (Gordy 2003).

Regulatory Capital   Basel II's definition of regulatory capital was inherited from Basel I without any significant modification. Yet the capital of any firm is different depending on whether one considers the firm as a going concern or as a gone concern. In the first case, we are able to include elements related to the future cash flows of the firm; in the second, those elements should be excluded.

A clear example of this is the accounting of tax credits on future profits that was considered part of capital for Japanese banks during the Japanese banking crisis (Skinner 2008). Obviously, if the bank is to continue as a going concern, this is an asset. Nevertheless, were the bank to fail, this has no value whatsoever. This confusion led to limiting the transparency of the disclosed figure for banks' capital and as a reaction emphasizing high-quality capital in Basel III.

In addition the mechanism of Basel II implied the procyclicality of banks' supply of credit: as assets are downgraded, capital had to be increased so that banks required more capital precisely at the point in time when they could not issue new equity successfully and reacted by cutting down their loans.

So the very mechanism that was aimed at allowing for a soft landing of banks in distress at the individual level generated an amplification loop when the crisis developed. As put forward by Hanson et al. (2011), the issue with the capital requirements ratio is that it can be satisfied by increasing the numerator (capital) or by decreasing the denominator (risk-weighted assets). While the former has a positive overall impact on financial stability, the latter translates into asset sales and a reduction in credit, with the risk of leading to damaging fire sales and a credit crunch. The capital requirement should therefore be satisfied to a large extent by increasing the numerator (capital), not by decreasing the denominator (risk weighted assets). This is particularly relevant during periods of crises, when asset sales and credit reductions by banks can add to already damaging downward spirals in the financial system. As it turns out, this difference has been critical in the different ways that the United States and Europe have approached the crisis. While stress tests in the United States resulted in large capital injections in US banks, including through the government-sponsored TARP program, no such counterpart was found in Europe where banks were largely left to decide for themselves whether to meet capital requirements through capital injections or asset reductions. The deleveraging process by European banks that ensued has likely contributed substantially to the lackluster growth performance of European countries in recent years, in addition to the negative impact from depressed demand.

8.3.2 Supervision and the Failure of Internal Risk Models

Supervision constitutes an essential input for regulatory action, as it is the channel through which information reaches the regulator, is verified, and possibly triggers regulatory action. The Basel Committee of Banking Supervision has emphasized the crucial role of supervision in Basel II by making it the second pillar and by issuing a reference document stating the "Core Principles of for Effective Banking Supervision" (1997, revised 2006, 2012) that are the *"de facto* minimum standard for sound prudential regulation and supervision of banks and banking systems" (p. 1, 2012). Because their implementation is monitored by the IMF and the World Bank in their Financial Stability Assessment Program, countries have the right incentives to adopt the 29 core principles. The Basel II second pillar and the "core principles," although with different emphasis, are complementary and open the door to a consistent worldwide supervisory framework.

While the Basel documents serve its objective to improve worldwide supervision, the increased complexities of Basel II led to some concerns regarding the accurate assessment and measurement of risks (as illustrated by the existing cross-country disparities in its measurement[6]). These concerns became fully justified, in a dramatic way during the crisis. The supervision of banks' returns and their fulfillment of existing regulation is already a complicated exercise involving the rigorous use and interpretation of financial firms' reporting and external auditing. The assessment of risks is a very complex issue, as risk will never be fully observed. It is only its materialization in the balance sheet and profits and losses that will be observed, presumably too late, possibly in the middle of a crisis. Nevertheless, both the riskiness of assets and of the asset-liability structure as well as off balance sheet can be measured and, with hindsight, it is clear that they should have been measured more accurately or in a more cautious way.

In defense of banks' risk managers and their regulators, it should be stated that banks' individual risks cannot be accurately measured in the absence of a macroprudential framework that allows every bank to understand the effect of the overall financial environment (firms and banks leverage ratio, excessive credit growth, bubbles, exchange rate risk, etc.) on its own risk. As mentioned before, because macroprudential regulation is one of the insights from the current crisis, it cannot be retrospectively applied to find fault with the behavior of the main economic actors. So our assessment of the mistakes made before the crisis must center on the aspects that could have been identified before the crisis.

The Failure of Internal Risk Models The Basel II second pillar establishes that the responsibility for holding sufficient capital lies with the banking firm (principle 1), but that supervisors should review and validate the process (principle 2). The crisis has shown that this validation was not correctly done.

Both risk managers and supervisory authorities were accepting sophisticated internal rating models to measure risk in an accurate way, but the approach was delusory for a number of reasons. To begin with, the objective of internal models in a world where bank managers are expected to deliver shareholders value must be to decrease regulatory capital so as to benefit from high leverage while abiding by the capital regulation rules. Second, as suggested by Haldane (2013), the internal rating model was a critical innovation that increased complexity and consequently banks' opacity. This complexity found its way in the denominator of the capital ratio but also in the numerator with hybrid instruments that could be computed as capital (tier 1 or tier 2) according to the regulatory rules of Basel II.

The first consequence of this overconfidence in the internal rating models was insufficient capital to cope with the actual risks banks were facing. This subsequently led to a generalized lack of trust in the banking industry and the collapse of the interbank market. The second consequence is that banks measuring their profits on the basis of their "safe operations" obtained large profits as measured by the spread of their returns over the risk-adjusted cost of capital (the so-called fake alpha). The huge profitability of banks led to a policy of large payouts, in terms of generous dividends and bonuses. Current changes in banking regulation are aimed at correcting these mistakes.

Errors in Risk Weights Considering risks as purely determined by internal rating models implies denying any role for overall benchmarks. Here consultation with the regulatory authorities, banking industry lobbies and reference to the standardized approach had a role in coordinating the industry models. With hindsight it becomes clear that some risks were underestimated as in Basel III they have been more clearly defined and measured:

1. *Credit valuation adjustments* Under Basel II, the risk of counterparty default and credit migration risk were addressed but mark to market losses due to credit valuation adjustments (CVA) were not. During the financial crisis, however, roughly two-thirds of losses attributed to counterparty credit risk were due to CVA losses and only about one-third were due to actual defaults. This resulted not only in delayed reporting of the actual losses but also to increased opacity in a market where the bank accounts were known to reflect only part of the effective losses.

2. *Trading book and complex securitization exposures* The risks of so-called re-securitizations in both the banking and the trading book were understated.

3. *Counterparty credit exposures* Banks' derivatives, repo, and securities financing activities were not duly assessed.

4. *OTC exposures* OTC rules regarding collateral management and initial margining were considered to have the same risk as exposures to central counterparties recognized by the Committee on Payments and Settlement Systems (CPSS) and the International Organization of Securities Commissions (IOSCO).

5. *Rating inflation* Rating agencies combined with the overconfidence in the ratings issued structured products that led financial intermediaries to limit their effort (due diligence) and invest on the basis of ratings and risk returns rather than on the analysis of the expected cash flows from the investment.

8.3.3 Market Discipline, Rating Agencies, and Fair Value Accounting

Disclosure of accurate reliable information is crucial for the market to assess the risks a financial institution is taking and to exert market discipline, thus adjusting the cost and availability of funding to each financial institution's risk-taking strategy. A bank that is taking more risk should have a higher cost of funds. This principle is enthroned as the third pillar of Basel II.

Its justification is straightforward. Under fair competition a bank's cost of funding should reflect its risks. Disclosure is therefore essential for markets to allocate funding in an efficient way and to decide which banks are to expand and which ones are to shrink or simply disappear. Market discipline improves the efficiency of the banking industry, and lame ducks are eliminated in good times so that in bad times the crisis is less severe. An alternative complementary justification focuses on disciplining bank managers. As explained in chapter 2, bank runs can discipline bank managers and be an efficient way to preserve banks' assets, as in the Chari–Jagannathan (1988) or Calomiris–Kahn (1991) models. In addition market discipline complements supervision because market signals constitute a valuable input for regulators.

Because of the existence of deposit insurance, there is no market discipline on deposits below some threshold,[7] so the responsibility of the adjustment of funding costs relies on uninsured liabilities, and, in particular, on subordinate debt as this liability has a higher downside risk and is therefore more sensitive to changes in a bank's risk level.

The empirical literature has shown that market discipline does operate in the banking industry. As expected, banks taking higher risks have a higher cost of funding (see Flannery 1998). Nevertheless, investor's faith in market discipline was shattered in the financial crisis.

Would Full Fair Value Accounting Aggravate Banking Crises? Because the banking crisis occurred right after the implementation of full fair value for banks, assuring investors that a higher proportion of assets were marked to market, some pundits, like Steve Forbes or Brian Wesbury, have argued that marking to market was one of the amplifying effects of this new accounting regime (see Pozen 2009). In fact, as mentioned in chapter 5, the argument is very weak for two reasons: first, it hinges on the fact that full fair value is tantamount to marking to market the banks' assets; second, it is based on an implicit assumption that uninsured liability holders would be more optimistic. The alternative view, that in the absence of disclosure the investors' view of banks in the middle of a crisis would be more pessimistic seems more realistic.

Nevertheless, there is an argument to be made recommending caution in the banks' payout decisions regarding dividends and bonuses once the new accounting rules are applied. Indeed, as fair value accounting increases the volatility of financial institutions' profits and losses (Bernard et al. 1995), the dividend setting rules that constitute a signal of future profitability should adjust for this higher variability and be set in a more conservative way. Unfortunately, it seems that the banks' boards of directors did not change their bonuses or dividend policy. Acharya et al. (2008) observe that banks were paying huge dividends and bonuses while observing signs that the crisis was brewing. A similar point is made in the De Larosière report that states how accounting has provided incentives for "the banks to act short term" (De Larosière 2009, p. 21) and how it provides an element of procyclicality if the behavior of the agents does not adapt to the new accounting rules, so that the relation of dividends to more volatile profits is kept unchanged.

Credit-Rating Agencies Reporting and Market Discipline   Not only firms themselves can provide valuable information, including financial statements, to investors to support market discipline. Third parties can also do so and contribute to the accuracy of the market price of risk. While the term "gatekeeper" has been applied to all types of economic agents performing this function, auditing firms play a role in the control of accounts, more as a back office desk, while it is credit-rating agencies that are closer to assessing firms' risks, as a front office desk, and therefore have a more direct impact on market discipline.

In hindsight, it is clear that credit-rating agencies did a poor job in rating CDOs in the year before the crisis. Possible causes are (1) the inaccurate statistical models based on pre-crisis real estate prices' statistical behavior, (2) excessive growth of the CDOs market for ratings, or (3) conflicts of interest as the issuers' demand depended on the CRA providing favorable ratings, which boosted CRAs short-term revenues even if it could jeopardize their long-run reputation (on February 4, 2013, the US Department of Justice Civil Division filed a civil lawsuit against Standard and Poor's regarding its ratings in 2007 of some US collateralized debt obligations).

Whatever the reason, the pre-crisis ratings of CDOs led to investors' overconfidence in those ratings and, quite possibly, to a lower level of due diligence by investors in their choice of portfolio investment strategies. The sudden downgrade of CDOs between February and July of 2007 alone, when Standard & Poor's took 637 negative actions on ratings (250 downgrades and 387 credit watch negative actions) on 2006 vintage subprime RMBS, led to huge unexpected losses and the illiquidity of the CDO "toxic assets" market.

The investors' excessive confidence in the agencies ratings of ABS and CDOs, possibly combined with the excessive appetite for AAA securities resulted in low funding costs for banks and thus confirmed the profitability of the securitization and tranching process, causing the excessive growth of the mortgage market. The sudden downgrading of CDOs in 2007 led to the opposite extreme: a generalized diffidence of both ratings and financial products resulting from securitization.

Market Discipline during a Systemic Crisis The disclosure of true reliable information by banks as mandated by the third pillar of Basel II depends on the impact it has on the banks' share value. In normal times higher or lower profits will be reflected in the price of shares without implying that the bank is in distress. However, in a crisis, the public confidence on the banks' solvency may be jeopardized by the release of important losses. Consequently banks, and particularly, banks in distress, may lack the incentives to disclose their losses.

It is important to note that the reasons for the lack of market discipline in a boom and in a crisis may be very different. As Freixas and Laux (2012) state, "In the boom it is quite likely that the major problem was a lack of market participants' incentives to use or demand information. In contrast, in the bust, the dominant problem seems to be that transparency is most difficult to achieve when it is needed most."

According to Morgan (2002), banks' assets are more opaque than those of nonfinancial firms' and hiding losses should therefore be easier. It seems reasonable to assume that when a bank is close to distress the numbers that are disclosed are unreliable, as suggested by anecdotic evidence. One of the recent examples is the use of the 105 rule on the accounting of repos by Lehman Brothers prior to its default. In addition, as shown in Aghion, Bolton, and Fries (1999) and Mitchell (2000), because banks have the possibility of rolling over loans to bad borrowers, a practice referred to as evergreening, the regulatory information is reliable only if reporting losses are lower when the loan is called back, but when the alternative is to declare the bank's insolvency, evergreening is clearly a way to postpone the worst while gambling for resurrection.

Overall, while empirical evidence shows that in good times market discipline allows for discrimination between different types of financial intermediaries, in bad times investors withdraw from funding banks altogether without distinguishing between levels of risk or competence across banks. Market discipline has a positive role in eliminating "lame ducks" during good times but when markets are malfunctioning, they facilitate investors' panics and their coordination on the inefficient equilibrium as it happens in the classical Diamond–Dybvig (1983) model.

8.4 Complementary Safety Net Regulatory Instruments

8.4.1 Deposit Insurance
The 2008 global financial crisis has illustrated how important a careful design of deposit insurance is. While the idea of introducing market discipline through co-responsibility was implemented in the UK deposit insurance scheme so that depositors would bear part of the cost of a bank's failure (a 10 percent cut from deposits between £3,000 and £33,000), it did not survive the failure of Northern Rock and the first bank run's queues observed since the 1930s its failure triggered. The importance of respecting the deposit insurance rules were also evident in the 2013 Cyprus crisis, when the government proposed to tax small depositors below the €100,000 coverage limit rather than increase the tax on larger uninsured deposits. The contagion effect to other European countries was instantaneous.

The fragility of the deposit insurance system was, however, exposed by the Icelandic crisis. The lack of cross-country monitoring led the Icelandic banks to an unprecedented expansion, so that the moment their banking system was hit by the crisis, the deposit insurance company went bankrupt and deposit insurance was void of any content. This was in striking contrast to what happened previously in other countries or during the Savings and Loans (S&L) crisis in the United States where the Treasury (and thus the taxpayer) provided the funds to pay for deposit insurance. Yet, in the US case, the size of the banking industry was so large in comparison with Iceland's GDP that there was no other feasible solution available. The lesson is that the deposit insurance scheme is only valid if the deposit insurance company is backed by the government and its commitment to take over the deposit insurance claims. These experiences have led to a complete restructuring of deposit insurance in Europe, with equal coverage limits across countries and a proposed common deposit insurance fund.

8.4.2 Lender of Last Resort and Liquidity Provision
On the positive side, central banks did respond effectively as lenders of last resort. Their reaction to the liquidity crisis was quick, and

involved creative thinking as well as learning by doing. Indeed the simultaneous collapse of inside liquidity and the interbank market required the injection of outside money to prevent a complete gridlock. The banking and financial chaos that central banks were submerged in had no precedent, and some of the early mechanisms that were designed to inject liquidity failed. For instance, the US discount window was ineffective in providing liquidity to banks, as its use was affected by a stigma that hurt the potential user's reputation.

8.4.3   Bank Resolution Procedures

When a bank is in financial distress, facing high funding costs, difficult access to funding, and restrictions on its usual operations, supervisory and regulatory authorities, as well as the Treasury, need to become involved to help determine the extent of the bank's losses and the best way to put an end to its crisis. We will refer to such regulatory action that results in the bank being restructured or declared bankrupt as a *bank resolution procedure*.

The resolution procedure has multiple dimensions, as it concerns who will pay for the bank's losses, and what are the effects of the bank failure and its resolution on financial stability. It has a crucial impact on systemic risk because it affects contagion, and when not appropriately placing losses on shareholders and unsecured debtholders, on moral hazard. Short term debt holders at other banks will update their perception of risks and may choose to stop financing the bank.

Designing the correct bank resolution procedures from the financial stability perspective requires a consistent framework to assist banks in distress in minimizing the externalities their financial condition is generating. The externalities to be considered are, first and foremost, the contagion types we discussed in chapter 5:

- Contagion through expectations
- Contagion through direct cross-bank holdings (interbank lending, OTC derivatives)
- Impact on asset prices caused by fire sales
- Illiquidity
- Feedback through decreased credit supply and lower economic activity

More generally, a bank bankruptcy will have an impact on the banking industry through the general loss of confidence in banks.[9] This is particularly compelling for a banking system operating in a world of free capital flows where investors can choose to transfer their funds to another country. In order to minimize contagion, we will argue that an efficient bank resolution procedure has to be orderly, speedy, and minimize the burden on public finances, so as to avoid generating false expectations of a bailout.

The analysis is complicated because the regulator objectives and its assessment of the costs of the banks' crisis will depend on the following characteristics: what is the extent of the capital shortage, what is the cost to the deposit insurance company in case of liquidation, whether the financial institution is systemic, and whether liquidation can trigger a systemic crisis because of financial fragility and extensive contagion.

The Legal Preconditions   A key part of the bankruptcy procedure is the banking law. The legal structure will determine the protection of the different types of shareholders and, consequently, will affect the resolution delays and the uncertainty regarding the extent of the losses that will be borne by each category of claimholder. To reduce uncertainty, legal certainty will be a preliminary condition. Indeed, it is essential to have a clearly defined banking resolution procedure known by investors and regulators. Nevertheless, even if there is legal certainty, long delays will imply more losses and there might be uncertainty regarding the issue of litigation.

The United States has a clearly defined banks' bankruptcy procedure since 1991 when the FDICIA act was adopted. It allows for prompt corrective action. More recently, in 2009, the UK introduced a well-structured banking resolution toolkit as part of the reform in its banking law that was triggered by the Northern Rock crisis. It draws on the experience of other countries and gives the regulator the four following powers (Brierley 2009): (1) the power to transfer part or all of the bank business to a private sector purchaser, (2) the power to create a bridge bank controlled by the Bank of England to manage all or part of the failing bank business, (3) the power to place a failing bank into temporary public ownership, and (4) the power to close the failing bank and facilitate the fast and orderly payout of depositors' claims or transfer their insured deposits to a healthy private sector bank. These rules are in line with the principle of protecting the creditors' rights, so that all netting arrangements and secured credit are protected, and more generally, a "no creditor worse off" safeguard protects stakeholders (the comparison here is not with a generous bailout but with the standard insolvency proceedings that has a much higher cost for the defaulting financial institution's stakeholders). Another interesting example is the Danish resolution framework, which we examine in section 8.7.2.

Still, the task of legislators is not an easy one, as there must be enough tools available and sufficient provisions for possible contingencies, such as might involve distinguishing between a small and a too big to fail bank, to prevent a speedy nonnegotiable solution, and this should be consistent with the main legal structure for investors' protection.

Bankruptcy Bankruptcy law is important in that it defines the worst-case scenario for regulatory authorities when confronted with a financial institution in distress.

From a legal perspective, because banks are corporations, liability holders' claims (being property rights) should not differ no matter whether the corporation is a nonfinancial corporation or a financial entity, and this point of view was accepted in the majority of countries until the 1990s. This corresponds to the *lex generalis* bankruptcy code and does not distinguish between financial and nonfinancial firms. The *lex specialis*, that defines a specific bankruptcy code for financial institutions, was then the exception and is now becoming the rule.

The reason why a special bankruptcy treatment for financial institutions is vital is because the objectives in case of a bank bankruptcy are not the same as in case of a nonfinancial corporation. Indeed, the latter requires a strong investor protection measures while the former has to balance these with the need to prevent a systemic crisis.

Investor protection requires that the bankruptcy procedure aim is to guarantee fairness and efficiency, with (1) the fair treatment of all liability holders according to their rights as contractually established, and (2) the maximization of the value to creditors, by choosing between liquidation or continuation of the firm as a going concern. These are typically the objectives legislation intends to achieve in a non-financial firm's bankruptcy procedures.

The objectives of banking regulation differed in that the principal aim is to contain contagion. So the bankruptcy procedure has to be orderly and speedy in order to prevent contagion and preserve financial stability. In particular, an orderly and speedy procedure implies, in addition to legal certainty, that it is renegotiation free, and informationally feasible.

Orderly Resolution   Because contagion occurs through a change in expectations, a bank resolution should allocate losses in a way that is perfectly in line with investors' expectations. Such a transparency may be difficult to achieve as regulatory authorities tend to emphasize the fact that banks are safe rather than informing investors of the risks they face. Still, an orderly resolution procedure allows investors to compute the extent of their losses and the illiquidity of their assets (as some claims will only be paid after a number of legal battles). In addition, a clearly defined bankruptcy procedure will tie the regulators' hands and force them to act, thus limiting the losses associated with forbearance.

An orderly resolution that allows to use the bank's 8% capital buffer to cover its losses with no loss to its subordinate debtholders would be impossible under the general bankruptcy regime, because there is no legal mechanism to declare a bank bankrupt if it has a positive equity and is able to carry on its operations, even if it continues accumulating losses. Notice the buffer of 8 percent in fact turned out to be lower in practice as the tier 2 component of bank capital could not absorb losses. In some countries, such as Germany, the holders of subordinated debt entered into lawsuits and declared their rights to coupons held by banks that had not declared bankruptcy. Moreover, for many banks, a significant part of regulatory capital did not constitute capital that could actually absorb losses, such as deferred taxes or subordinated debt. This, of course, added to the mood of uncertainty.

The US FDICIA prompt corrective action is a good example of an orderly bank resolution procedure, where a number of rules leave limited discretion to the bank's manager and to the regulator, thus reducing the uncertainty surrounding the resolution. The bank will progressively face more restrictive conditions as their capital ratios deteriorated.

Speedy Resolution   When a bank is in distress, access to funding is either expensive or impossible. Depositors distrust and the high funding costs it implies will cause the bank to have negative margins. In other words, the bank will be destroying value by the day. This is why regulatory authorities have to intervene quickly to restore the bank's access to funding in normal conditions by reestablishing the market confidence.

From a theoretical perspective, the distress of a bank can be thought of as a bargaining game where the objective of the regulator is to limit contagion while the objective of the firm is to maximize shareholders value. As in any bargaining game, the fallback solution in case of disagreement is important, and this is why a bank-specific bankruptcy procedure constitutes a prerequisite for an orderly and speedy solution to banks' financial problems. An orderly and speedy resolution will put the regulatory authorities in a much better position in the bargaining game to protect taxpayers' interests. The speedy resolution will also preserve the banks' assets value, so that claimholders are also better off. Still, a lengthy bargaining for a larger share of the assets may be the best strategy for each category of claimholder even if the size of the assets continues shrinking.

A lengthy resolution procedure would also increase the uncertainties and raise the risk premia of bank debt as well as the banking sector's ability to raise funds in the market. In addition, when confronted with a traditional bankruptcy process, the holder of a liquid asset on the bankrupt bank would be suddenly stuck with an illiquid liability with a maturity and a value that depends on the court's decisions. This is a serious problem for a nonfinancial firm, but it can be catastrophic for a financial institution that deals with short delays and highly liquid assets in order to manage its liquidity risks. If the deposit insurance is not adequately managed, this illiquidity dimension can even affect perfectly insured depositors (especially when the government does not provide a backstop to the deposit insurance scheme in the event of a shortfall) as safe deposits would be frozen while the Deposit Insurance Company takes full responsibility of the administration and the payment to depositors. The recent crisis in Cyprus illustrated these uncertainties, as it constituted not only a threat of withdrawing *de facto* the full deposit insurance through a tax on insured deposits, but also led to a freeze of bank accounts for ten days, which halted the well-functioning of the payment system.

Resolution or Restructuring?   Whether an orderly and speedy resolution procedure is in place or not, the regulatory authorities will have to take a quick decision on whether to liquidate the bank or restructure it by inject fresh capital. Of course, the costs and benefits depend upon the bankruptcy law as well as the institutions in place and the information available.

When solvency is at stake, the first line of rescue is, of course, the private finance arrangement. In a perfect Modigliani–Miller world, a debt–equity swap would allow the bank to avoid the crisis and to restore investors' confidence. Still, the problem is that of coordination: debtholders are better off if other debtholders swap their debt for equity while they keep their debt whose value will then increase. Consequently a debt–equity swap, even if efficient, will never occur and will have to be forced by the regulatory authorities. If debtholders commit ex ante to swap their liabilities for equity should a well-specified credit event occur, the coordination problem is avoided. This is the logic of the new liability structures that are currently proposed for the speedy and orderly resolution of banks' bankruptcies (see section 8.7).

Private Finance Resolution   If the banking law permits the regulatory authorities to auction out the defaulting bank, thus forcing its takeover, the injection of taxpayers' money will be avoided and the ex ante incentives to invest in risky assets because in case of distress a bailout is expected, will be reduced. If the value of the bank's equity is still positive, so that the market value of the bank as a going concern is larger than the face value of its debt, a purchasing bank simply buys all the assets and takes over all the liabilities. Debt holders will then recover the full value of their claims and only shareholders will suffer a loss. The existence of a speedy and orderly bank bankruptcy procedure is here critical, as usually shareholders would prefer to use all possible lines of litigation to bargain for more time and better conditions for the sale or dilution of their shares (see Dewatripont and Freixas 2012). The forced takeover will allow the merged bank to continue as a going concern.

Alternatively, the bank could be liquidated, and if the value of the assets that are not pledged as collateral is larger than the amount of debt there will be no cost for the Treasury. In a similar vein, if the banking law permits it, the regulatory authorities may threaten to force the recapitalization of the banks in conditions that are less favorable than the market ones. Faced with such a credible threat, the bank will look for a private recapitalization that is clearly preferred to the regulatory recapitalization though it may confer a loss to shareholders. This mechanism has proved to be efficient in recapitalizing banks in the United States once the initial part of the banking crisis was over. In both cases, debtholders' rights are not diluted and, consequently, there should be no contagion effect caused by the bankruptcy procedure.[10]

If the contagion effects are expected to be limited, which occurs because (1) the bank is not systemic, (2) the banking industry benefits from a good financial environment, and (3) the bank in distress has invested in different assets, the regulatory authorities may decide to liquidate the bank. The liquidation cost will then affect unsecured liability holders and there will be contagion with a negative externality for other banks which funding conditions will deteriorate. So the impact becomes larger the more confused and slower the bank resolution procedure is.

Alternatively, despite large contagion effects, a bank may have to be liquidated, as was the case for Lehman, because no other way out is available. In this case it is the legal and institutional structure that forces the liquidation with the negative effects of contagion.

Assisted Resolution As a result of the cost-benefit analysis, regulatory authorities may be willing to restructure the bank through a number of mechanisms that quite often constitute an implicit or explicit capital injection. Such a bailout may be justified for both good and bad reasons. Indeed, the bailout may be the result of a rigorous cost benefit analysis or the outcome of a lobbying process, agents having the wrong incentives and objectives (e.g., those arising from career concerns) or simply overoptimistic expectations regarding the (low) cost and (high) benefit of a bailout.

A clear, good reason is to avoid triggering a systemic crisis, whether the institution in distress is a SIFI or the fragility of the banking industry has reached such a high level that even a non-systemic bank could cause a bank panic. Another good reason is cost efficiency: once we take into account the cost to the Deposit Insurance Company for the reimbursement of depositors in the event of a bank failure, it may be less costly to inject funds in a bank and then sell it as a going concern rather than liquidate it, as the losses on a bank that is liquidated are higher[11].

Unfortunately, the support to a financial institution in trouble could also be justified for bad reasons. First, as mentioned, the opacity of banks' assets may mislead regulatory authorities who can have an overoptimistic view of the bank's crisis (possibly combined with the absence of disclosure by the bank of some key elements of its portfolio of investments), seeing it as a Diamond–Dybvig speculative crisis rather than a fundamental solvency crisis. This may especially be the case if the regulatory authorities are not fully independent and the government prefers to postpone the bank's crisis for political reasons. Second, the government may intervene because it fears that the implementation of the bankruptcy procedure will have a high political cost.

This is presumably why, in 2011, Spain injected first large amounts of funds into its "cajas" while later on, in 2012, forced by a European Commission Memorandum of Understanding it accepted to implement a bank specific resolution procedure.

To complicate matters, the distinction between "good reasons" and "bad reasons" is blurred. So, for example, the rescue of the non-systemic Northern Rock bank to avoid a panic was based on the information provided by the Financial Services Authority, according to which Northern Rock was perfectly solvent and was only facing a temporary liquidity problem due to the dry-up of the securitization market. Subsequently it became clear that Northern Rock was in fact insolvent.

Because the injection of public funds into distressed banks usually results in a high cost for the Treasury and ultimately for taxpayers, it is essential that the containment of contagion is done at minimal cost. This can be achieved by using different instruments that, depending on the specific characteristics of the crisis, will be more or less effective and will imply higher or lower costs to taxpayers. In particular, we can identify four different types of instruments:

1. *Liabilities guarantees* A first simple way to restore public confidence in the banking system is for the regulatory authorities to intervene and put an end to a banking crisis by guaranteeing all banks' liabilities. As this happens in a systemic crisis situation, the government guarantee may be particularly costly. This was the case in the recent Irish crisis of 2008, where it had a direct impact on the fiscal deficit of the Irish government, increasing the Irish sovereign risk premium. In addition, as banks were holding Irish sovereign debt, the subsequent downgrading of sovereign bonds led to losses in the Irish banks, with sovereign risk and bank risk interacting in a vicious circle or deadly embrace.

2. *Regulatory capital injection* To support the bank, the government may buy subordinated debt, preferred equity, or equity shares the bank is forced to issue. These are ways to increase the banks' equity or to reduce the bank's financial cost in the case of preferred equity. Of course, at the initial stage the regulatory authorities jointly with the Treasury may buy debt or subordinated debt, but this will not improve the bank's solvency as it increases its leverage. An extreme form of equity injection is the banks' nationalization, which is usually met with strong criticisms as private management is seen as more efficient. Because of this criticism, the nationalization is often temporary with

the creation of a bridge bank that will be privatized again once public confidence has been restored.

3. *Asset revaluation interventions* The government may intervene by buying assets in the markets, a solution envisaged but never implemented in the United States.

4. *"Good bank/bad bank" restructuring* Presumably the most important lesson of the multiple crises around the world and their management is the importance of the so-called good bank/bad bank separation. The bank in distress is divided in two and the bad assets are allocated to the so-called bad bank, an asset management company that may either be common to all banks or be specific to each bank in distress, and the bad assets are held to maturity under a passive management or sold to the market as market conditions improve. A good bank/bad bank restructuring will reduce the banks' incentives to gamble for resurrection, because the good bank will have enough capital and sufficient skin in the game while the bad bank will be under passive management and cannot take risky investments. Once separation is realized, the good bank will be allowed to a fresh start without the burden of the bad assets. The key issue is how the liabilities are distributed among the good bank and the bad bank.

Cross-border Bank Resolution The decision whether a multinational financial institution should be bailed out or liquidated raises quite difficult legal issues.

First, if a bank is systemically important, the intervention is costly and the issue of how the cost is to be split among the different beneficiaries or "burden sharing" arises. This may be illustrated by the Lehman Brothers case, whose bankruptcy implied a huge global cost for many countries around the world but whose rescue was to be borne exclusively by the US Treasury. In the absence of an ex ante agreement, every country will try to free-ride on the home regulatory authorities, leading to inefficient decisions and chances that a systemically important institution may go bankrupt triggering a global systemic crisis. The two possible ways out have occurred during the recent crisis. At one extreme, the Irish authorities chose to guarantee every single claim on their banks, and consequently had to inject an amount of capital that led them to a spectacular budgetary deficit and to a sovereign crisis. The other extreme was the decision made by the Icelandic authorities that chose to declare their banks and deposit insurance company bankrupt, and then to issue legislation to protect only domestic depositors.

The inconsistency of the financial regulatory framework has been mentioned by Freixas (2003) and Goodhart and Schoenmaker (2009). Generalizing this analysis, Schoenmaker (2011) forged the concept of the "financial stability trilemma." The financial stability trilemma states that a stable financial system, an integrated financial system, and a national financial stability policy cannot be simultaneously achieved. This is so because stability in an integrated financial system will require the recapitalization of systemic banks in times of distress and this may not be feasible or desirable by the home country if there is no fiscal integration. Therefore, if we want to have an integrated financial system and national financial stability policies, then financial stability as a whole cannot be attained.

Second, cross-border bankruptcy raises complex issues, as different jurisdictions may have different bankruptcy codes. The most relevant issue here is the confrontation of two types of approaches to cross-border bankruptcy, the universal approach and the territorial one. In the universal approach, all assets and liabilities of a bankrupt bank are considered jointly, regardless of the legal jurisdiction where they originated. Alternatively, in the territorial approach, each country considers the assets and the liabilities that are held in the country. As a consequence there is a conflict if a country has a territorial approach and the bankrupt bank is in a jurisdiction where the universal approach prevails.[12]

A third important issue is how a multinational bank operates in different countries. A bank can expand by opening branches or by creating subsidiaries. When a bank is structured as a unique legal entity with branches in different countries, the bankruptcy of the unique bank implies the liquidation of all its branches. If instead the entity is structured with a parent company and a subsidiary in the foreign country, it is possible for the parent company to declare bankruptcy but the subsidiaries in each country to survive, or alternatively for one subsidiary to become insolvent while the parent company survives.

To sum up, there are multiple ways to restructure or liquidate a bank and the regulatory authorities should combine them in order to limit the access to public funds. Still, beyond the issue of the fiscal cost of a crisis, the design of the legal and institutional framework so as to allow regulatory interventions in an orderly and speedy way is essential to contain contagion and prevent systemic crises.

8.4.4 The Safety Net in an International Environment

The growth of multinational banks operating across multiple markets as well as the development of the international interbank operation has raised the issue of international coordination of banking regulation and supervision. Historically, this has led the Basel committee to propose a set of minimum standards for banking supervision, namely the Basel I, II, and III frameworks. It seems quite intuitive that setting minimum standards should increase overall international financial stability. Still, Morrison and White (2009) show that the issue is more complex by simply comparing a laissez faire policy with the imposition of standards characteristic of a level playing field. They show that a laissez faire policy favors a better regulated economy, whereas imposition of standards benefits the economies with worse regulation, a paradoxical effect that points out at the costs of setting uniform standards that annihilate the reputational benefits for a country by imposing tougher regulation.

A second issue to be taken into account in the analysis of international regulation is that the creation of an international safety net that is jointly determined by several noncooperative countries constitutes a problem of financing a public good. With each country deciding on its level of regulation and supervision, banks' and regulators' incentives are distorted. In each country, setting less stringent regulatory requirements allows banks to diminish their funding costs, obtain a competitive advantage, and expand in other countries. Consequently domestic regulators are tempted to reduce the level of regulation. Yet, by doing so, they generate a negative externality for other countries that now face a lower level of financial stability as well as a lower market share for its own banks[13] (see Dell'Ariccia and Marquez 2006b; Hardy and Nieto 2008).

To avoid the underprovision of international banking regulation and supervision, it seems natural to increase coordination among regulators. This means setting the basis for exchange of information and putting in place similar rules. Nevertheless, because this is a noncooperative game, the first-best efficiency will not be reached unless the interests of the countries are perfectly aligned (Holthausen and Rönde 2002).

The limitations of the safety net in an international context can become dramatic, however, as evidenced by the European sovereign risk crisis, when there is some degree of integration. Indeed this is the case stated in the EU second banking "single-passport" directive of

December 1989, that a bank obtaining a charter in any of the European countries was allowed to operate in any other country by opening branches so that the supervision of every bank is the responsibility of the home country and that supervisors trust one another in their criteria to monitor banks operating in Europe. In this way, a single market for banking services was being created even if some differences remained (notably differences in regulation, supervision, and deposit insurance schemes).

The consequence of this incomplete financial integration is that while the mandate of every supervisory and regulatory authority in each country is to protect financial stability at the domestic level as well as to promote the development and efficiency of the financial industry again, let us emphasize, at the domestic level, the European objectives were misaligned and implied cross-country externalities. Consequently it was in the interest of the national supervisory authorities (e.g., those of Cyprus, Iceland, Ireland, and Spain) to foster the growth and development of the banking industry that was crucial for their economic growth. Whether this is the result of some lack of independence of the supervisory bodies from political pressure is irrelevant. The issue is that the incomplete integration let to what appears, with hindsight, as an excessive growth of the banking industry, thus planting the seeds for a crisis that would affect other countries.

8.5 Financial Innovation and Regulation: The Rise of Shadow Banking and Regulatory Arbitrage

Because the mandate of banking regulatory authorities' focus is to prevent or limit the impact of banking institutions' failure, prior to the current crisis the boundaries of banking regulation were identical as those of the banking industry. The very idea that the benefits of a bailout could be extended to other institutions, thus providing them access to inexpensive funding through an implicit guarantee, was associated with deliberately increasing moral hazard problems in nonbanking institutions. Nevertheless, some banking activities, such as performing maturity and/or liquidity transformation, undergoing credit risk transfer and using repo operations, were being performed by nonbanks in the shadow banking industry.[14] The experience proved that this view of the banking industry was incorrect. The bankruptcy of Lehman and the bailouts of Bear Stearns and AIG showed that large nonbanking financial institutions could have a huge impact on the whole banking industry. The lesson of the 2008 events is that every single systemically important institution should be under the supervisory responsibility of banking authorities. The modified terminology and the current reference to systemically important financial institutions (SIFIs and G-SIFIS for the global ones) reflects this change in the overall perspective. In what follows we would like to clarify, first, why the existence of shadow banking could, in principle, improve overall efficiency; second, under what conditions this efficiency is reached; and third, why inadequate regulation leads to an inefficient use of shadow banking.

8.5.1   Framework for the Efficient Use of Shadow Banking

The Basel I capital requirements imposed a uniform 8 percent capital independently of the risk of the loans with a limited number of exceptions (e.g., sovereigns, financial institutions, and mortgages). This "one size fits all" view of risk, later corrected in Basel II, opened the door to both an efficient and an inefficient reallocation of capital (in the presence of securitization). In the first place, because some institutions are not subject to capital requirements, the transfer of banks' assets to those institutions (whose bankruptcy does not imply any social cost) is efficient. Yet, since the 8 percent charge is independent of the asset's risk, it is worth it for a financial institution to engage in regulatory arbitrage, packaging and securitizing its safest loans while keeping the high risk ones. This implies tranching the securitized loans and keeping the subordinated tranche or the first loss tranche. It is correct to state that by keeping the first loss tranche the financial institution has the right incentives to monitor and screen the loans so as to minimize the risk on this first tranche, thus reducing the moral hazard problems. Nevertheless, the 8 percent ratio was computed on the average portfolio of loans, not on the first loss tranche, and consequently regulatory arbitrage undermined the objective of providing a buffer of capital that is proportionate to the banks' risks. While the phenomenon we are referring to clearly leads to the undercapitalization of banks, securitization, when adequately regulated, is a perfect way to diversify risks away from the banking industry and transferring them to other institutions, thus increasing the efficiency of risk allocation.

Before the crisis, securitization and credit default swap operations were considered a step forward in the efficiency of the financial industry, as these financial innovations allowed to allocate banks' risks to institutions such as mutual funds and insurance companies, thus providing a higher diversification for those institutions while reducing banks' risks. Similarly credit default swaps (CDS) allow a bank to decrease its level of risk by transferring it to another institution, say, an insurance company. Through a credit default swap, a bank with, say, General Motors bonds in its portfolio, is able to buy protection against a default event of this company, an event clearly defined in the CDS contract, whether a downgrade in the rating or a straight bankruptcy of General Motors. Consequently CDS contracts constitute efficient financial innovations that allowed transferring risk to non-banking institutions.

8.5.2 Necessary Conditions for Shadow Banking

Two types of benefits can be reached from the existence of shadow banking. On the one hand, the transfer of the (risky) returns of a portfolio of loans to institutions with unrelated risks, such as insurance companies, increases the overall diversification and improves the risk-return frontier of the financial system. On the other hand, because capital is costly, by transferring banking risks to entities such as mutual funds, pension funds or households with a well-diversified portfolio that are not subject to capital requirements, banks need less capital while they provide the investor that buys the risks with a good opportunity in terms of risk/return.

This argument is perfectly valid provided that two implicit assumptions are met. First, the transfer of risks to the shadow banking sector should not distort in any way the risks taken by the originating banks. Second, the ultimate risk should be borne by well-diversified institutions that either cannot go bankrupt or whose bankruptcy has no social cost. This is because their default does not affect financial stability, and does not cause contagion or an increase in overall macroeconomic fragility.

The 2008 global financial crisis showed that neither of these two conditions was met, particularly in the United States, and this was true both for the securitization industry with the creation of asset-backed securities and collateralized debt obligations (CDO) as well as for the credit default swap (CDS) industries. In fact a large number of securitized issues were held by the banks themselves, especially by investment banks and were used to raise liquidity easily in the markets when these assets were liquid. The sudden collapse of the market for securitized loans severed bank's access to liquidity while jeopardizing their solvency.

Two characteristics of the CDS market implied a high systemic risk associated with CDSs. First, the volume of CDSs was much higher than the amount of debt it was supposed to hedge. Such a high volume implies that CDSs were not used for hedging but for speculation. Second, the CDS risks were not well diversified as the insurance company AIG was holding so large an investment in these contracts that its solvency could be jeopardized, as it became clear with its rescue in September 2008.

8.5.3   Incompetent Regulation of Shadow Banking

With hindsight, it is clear that the regulation of the securitization process in countries like the United States or the United Kingdom was inadequate. The regulation of securitization failed for several reasons but the most damaging one was the existence of liquidity lines provided by the originating bank that had very low risk weight and thus required very limited capital.

Because originating banks could extend liquidity lines to the buyers of their special purpose vehicles they could proceed to securitize their long-term assets and, instead of funding these assets in the special purpose vehicle with the corresponding long-term bonds, fund them with short-term claims. This maturity mismatch enabled the special purpose vehicle to obtain the spread between the long-term and the short-term interest rate in exchange for liquidity risk. In other words, one of the key functions of banks, the transformation of short term liabilities into long term assets was "outsourced" to the market. Of course, investors had to obtain some guarantee that they would get reimbursed at the end of the period even if no other investor showed up to roll over the short-term debt. Consequently, in order to issue these short-term claims on the special purpose vehicle, the originating bank had to provide a liquidity line guaranteeing the liquidity of the short-term securities: the originating bank would reimburse the claims at the maturity date while waiting for new investors to show up.

As credit lines did not require a high capital in view of their risk, especially in Basel I, this was an operation that allowed the bank to have a high expected return in exchange for a low capital charge. Still, as it was clearly seen later on, this meant that if suddenly no investor showed up the bank had to repatriate the assets of the SPV by buying the short-term claims and rolling them over so long as investors were not interested in this product. Thus this loophole in securitization regulation allowed the originating bank to hold very limited capital for what turned out to be a huge risk: the risk that the SPV assets turned out to be "toxic" and therefore had to be repatriated to the originating bank precisely in bad times. In other words, a bank could be perfectly capitalized in good times, but it could be suddenly undercapitalized in bad times because its assets grew in size at the moment when those assets were downgraded, and they therefore required a higher capital level.

Similarly the regulation of CDS was also inadequate. It is true that the existence of a credit protection should decrease the risk weight of the corresponding asset. Still, the decision by regulatory authorities to reduce the risk weight on a bank loan provided it was hedged with the corresponding credit–default swap was ignoring the bankruptcy risk of the counterparty offering protection. The crisis showed that this risk was far from being negligible. At the same time, once CDS were available, the incentives for a bank to monitor the company it was lending to were eroded, because the CDS price, being the cost of protection, reflected the effective risk. After all, whether the loan was safe or not, if it was to be hedged with a CDS, the only important issue was the cost of the protection. Hence the very existence of credit–default swaps provided the wrong incentive for the bank to lend with a lower level of diligence in the screening of the recipient of the loan. It may be the case that the counterparty risks were underestimated precisely because some counterparties such as AIG were considered too big to fail. From that perspective, banks were perfectly correct in expecting the Federal Reserve to bail out AIG to avoid a serious downgrade of all US banks.[15]

The crisis has shown that from a public interest perspective, regulatory authorities were wrong in allowing liquidity lines on short-term SPV liabilities. Moreover they were wrong in expecting the securitized assets to be held by agents such as insurance companies or mutual funds outside the banking industry. With hindsight, it is easy to see that while Basel capital requirements emphasized that capital should be computed at the consolidated level for a banking group, regulation simply omitted to consider consolidation at the level of the whole banking industry. As a consequence each bank assumed the other banks' securitized assets were safe while offering a relatively high interest rate on a supposedly safe AAA-rated security. This was clearly a mistake somehow related to the lack of macroprudential regulation and the absence of any consolidated measure of the securitization within the entire banking industry.

From a private interest perspective, it is true that a huge fraction of profits made by banks and by sellers of CDS as well as by credit-rating agencies originated in the transactions from the regulated commercial banking firms to the unregulated shadow banking institutions and markets. The risk-shifting that occurred between higher profits in good times and higher tail losses, helped by the lenient regulation, could not be adequately measured by each individual bank as it depended on the ill-functioning of the whole system.

To sum up, from a systemic risk perspective, securitization regulation at the microprudential level failed by allowing a combination of six factors:

1. Strong linkages between the regulated commercial banking sector and the unregulated shadow banking one.

2. Regulatory arbitrage based on an incorrect measure of risk (one size fits all and incorrect risk weight for the liquidity lines).

3. Consolidated risks in the commercial banking industry.

4. A buildup of risks in nonbanking institutions such as investment banks or insurance companies (e.g., AIG).

5. Information disclosure to be handled by credit-rating agencies that were supposed to serve as gatekeepers but whose mandate was to maximize the value of their shareholders' wealth, thus generating a conflict of interests.

6. The CDS market and some key institutions to take risks and OTC trading to continue with opacity and discontinuous thresholds.

With these effects combined, it was inevitable that there would occur an "interplay of market malfunctioning or even breakdown, fair value accounting and the insufficiency of equity capital at financial institutions, and, finally, systemic effects of prudential regulation created a detrimental downward spiral in the overall financial system" (Hellwig 2009, p. 7).

8.6 Corporate Governance

In a world with perfect information, firm managers would act in the best interest of the firms' claimholders. Unfortunately, once we depart from such a perfect world and acknowledge the agency problems between managers' and firms' stakeholders, we must question the role of the board of directors. Indeed, ideally, the board of directors monitors the firms' activities and, by so doing, guarantees that the managers act in the best interest of shareholders by maximizing the value of the firm's equity.

In recent years corporate governance has been the object of increased attention with a number of proposals aiming at more rigorous corporate governance, with the OECD, first in 1999, the Sarbanes–Oxley in 2002, and the Basel committee in 2006 being the most accepted, the first two considering the corporate governance of nonfinancial firms and the later the corporate governance of financial intermediaries.[16] Corporate governance in a bank faces the same challenges as in a nonfinancial firm, with two additional difficulties. On the one hand, banks operate with much higher leverage than nonfinancial firms, so that the role of debt and of debtholders is more preeminent. On the other hand, banks operate with the explicit insurance of the deposit insurance company and, more generally, with the implicit insurance of the regulatory authorities that convey the view that "banks are safe."

However, bank assets are opaque, and this makes it difficult for external investors to assess the financial condition of a bank; in other words, the possibilities of information manipulation and of acting on behalf of shareholders and at the detriment of debtholders are high. This is why the Basel committee has drafted a more restrictive corporate governance code than the OECD one, emphasizing the protection of stakeholders' rights rather than the ones of small shareholders.

It is true that bank capital regulation, by limiting leverage, requires a higher stake of shareholders and therefore alleviates the bank's agency problems. Nevertheless, capital requirements do not constitute a universal panacea as the agency problem is always potentially present and, in particular during a crisis, the issue becomes intensely worrisome (Laeven 2013).

From the recent crisis we learned some important lessons regarding corporate governance in banking firms:

1. Executive compensation, as the media has reported, was excessive. Some bank managers kept receiving huge bonuses while their banks were receiving public support. While this feature of executive compensation is of concern, it appears to have been of limited impact as it affected a small number of banks. In most cases bank managers are compensated with stocks and stock options, and because of that, on average, they were heavily penalized by the decrease in banks' stock values during the current crisis. Nevertheless, there is some evidence

that bank managers rushed to sell some of their stock prior to the crisis. For example, Cziraki (2013) reports that in mid-2006 insiders of high-exposure banks sold 39 percent more equity than insiders of low-exposure banks, while the two populations did not show a marked difference in the two previous years. It was with the first sign of decline in the US housing prices that insiders revised their assessment of their banks' investments and chose to sell.

2. While the general view regarding corporate governance in firms was that the number of independent shareholders should be increased so as to reduce the weight of managers in the board of directors, additional research by Adams and Mehran (2012) has shown that not only competence is a critical characteristic of banks' performance but also the board members' engagement level. Indeed banks where board members are members of several institutions performed worse than those where board members are fully engaged in the activities of a single bank.

3. While, in general, it is considered that shareholders activism will align a firm activity with shareholders' value maximization, in the banking industry this could be obtained at the expense of debtholders, at least in the short run. The analysis of Fahlenbrach and Stulz (2011) shows that banks with higher shareholder activism appear to have had higher losses during the crisis.

4. Risk management, with the identification of risk and its measure, is one of the key responsibilities of the board of directors. Consequently determining how important the risk management function is within the bank and within the risk culture of the bank constitutes a key decision of the board of directors. Considering this issue, Ellul and Yeralmilli (2010) examine the risk function in banks and show that banks where this risk management role was less important ended up with higher losses during the crisis. More precisely, Ellul and Yeralmilli consider multiple measures of the function of risk management within a banking firm (e.g., the ratio of the risk manager remuneration to the CEO remuneration) and obtain the same result: those firms that attached less importance to risk management ended up with higher losses. Bad luck cannot be invoked.

Overall, it is clear that the analysis of the risk taken prior to the crisis points to inefficient corporate governance of banks. To add to our concern, it must be noted that while the Basel committee has put a lot of effort in redesigning the capital requirement regulation, banks' corporate governance has not been the object of equivalent attention and no major regulatory reform has taken place in this area that is critical for the interests of banks' stakeholders.

8.7   The New Regulatory Framework

The G20 Seoul agenda for financial regulation (November 2010) set as objectives the improvement of effective supervision, the regulation of SIFIs, a peer review process through international agencies, and a stricter banking regulatory framework. This section will review the key aspects of the new financial regulatory framework that affect microprudential regulation, while its macroprudential dimension will be analyzed in the next chapter

8.7.1   Rethinking Basel III

Basel III Capital Requirements   The recent Basel document, referred to as Basel III, constitutes an attempt to improve banking regulation so as to prevent the worst effects of a systemic crisis. Basel III emphasizes the quantity and the quality of capital, requiring a higher fraction of tier 1 capital and consequently a lower fraction of tier 2 capital. It introduces a number of macroprudential time varying buffers.

Basel III improves the measures of risk as it incorporates in the process of risk assessment the lessons of the current crisis. It also introduces more transparency in the accounting of profit and losses These changes go in the right direction, but it is not clear that the additional capital is high enough, as the Icelandic crisis illustrates. After all, Lehman Brothers and Bear Stearns were satisfying Basel II capital requirements while going bankrupt.

Basel III also introduces a leverage constraint to complement these capital buffers. This introduction of a leverage constraint may improve market discipline if the absolute level of leverage is taken into account by the market when banks face strong pressures, as evidence on market discipline during a crisis seems to suggest.

Finally, besides these additional requirements on capital, Basel III has proposed two new liquidity requirements: the liquid coverage ratio (LCR) and the net stable funding ratio (NSFR) (more on this in the next chapter). However, there are alternatives to the imposition of liquidity ratios, and it has been suggested that a tax on short-term holdings could be more efficient than imposing these ratios. The liquidity coverage ratio also requires banks to hold high-quality liquid assets. One of the lessons of the crisis was precisely that liquidity can vanish suddenly, as happened to asset-backed securities, and later to sovereign Greek bonds. In such a reoccurrence the liquidity ratio will trigger a fire sale on the previously liquid security, thus aggravating the situation.

8.7.2 Rethinking Bank Resolution: Bail-in Policies and Contingent Capital

One of the lessons of the crisis was that bank resolution proposals have to address this issue more efficiently to provide a speedy and orderly recovery that avoids contagion. This is the case for Title II of the Dodd–Frank Wall Street Reform and Consumer Protection Act (Dodd-Frank Act) that specifies the Orderly Liquidation Authority (OLA) attributions, and that would be the resolution mechanism to cope with systemic financial firms in the United States. The idea of living wills submitted by the banks as a series of contingent operations if they face serious difficulties has been implemented in the United Kingdom and in the United States. The US Dodd–Frank Act requires all large bank holding companies to submit resolution plans.[17] These newly designed procedures should help reduce the cost of banks resolution while limiting contagion. Moreover living wills may improve risk management in normal times by forcing bank management to rethink the organizational structure of the bank.

The two main instruments that have been proposed are the issuance of contingent capital and the introduction of a bail-in clause in subordinated and senior debt. However, none of these measures in and of itself deals hands-on with the politics underpinning the too big to fail problem.

Bail-in Contrarily to contingent convertible debt instruments, the bail-in clause is in essence more akin to a bankruptcy process. The bail-in has to be initiated by regulatory authorities. It has to be clearly defined and can be based on accounting measures of capital. Once the bail-in clause applies, automatically liability rights are downgraded, equity rights are diluted, with equity holders obtaining a warrant in exchange for their stocks so that they will only obtain any revenue if the price of the stock reaches some threshold in the future. Subordinated debtholders become the new equity holders, and senior debtholders might become subordinated debtholders for a fraction of their debt, or they might simply have a reduction in the value of their principal. When these contracts are clearly designed and have legal certainty, they are contractually binding and have the advantage that they will be recognized as such across countries in any jurisdiction. This is a clear benefit of bail-ins as, in principle, they should avoid the complexities of cross-border bankruptcies.

Contingent Capital   Contingent capital entitles a company to issue new paid-in financial capital on or before some future date in exchange for a premium (called a "commitment fee"). The objective of these convertible securities is to provide capital automatically and quickly. The conversion of contingent convertibles can be triggered by:

1. A regulatory decision.
2. Regulatory capital falling below some threshold (accounting based).
3. The stock price of the bank falling below some threshold (market based).

An automatic and quick conversion of contingent convertible securities ("CoCos") into equity is only triggered by the third mechanism, that is, by a low market price for the bank's stock. The literature on this has pointed out a number of difficulties. For example, Sundaresan and Wang (2015) show that contingent capital with a market trigger, where stakeholders are unable to choose the optimal conversion policy, does not lead to a unique competitive equilibrium. Multiplicity of equilibria (and sometimes the absence of equilibrium) introduces not only price uncertainty but the possibility of market manipulation and inefficient capital allocation.

Contingent Capital and Bail-ins in Practice   Two contingent capital and bail-in frameworks have been adopted so far.

1. The Swiss capital regulation for large banks

On March 2012 the Swiss regulatory authorities undertook a radical transformation of the regulation of their two largest banks that are clearly G-SIFIs, Credit Suisse and UBS. The increase in capital the reform implies goes much beyond the one required by Basel III (see section 8.7) and is possibly motivated by a combination of a willingness to maintain the reputation of Swiss banks as particularly safe institutions. Moreover the size of the two SIFIs made their bail-out impossible given the amount of capital injection it would have implied in comparison with the Swiss GDP.

The reform consists in the following increase in capital and CoCos:

1. A capital buffer of 8.5 percent of risk-weighted assets beyond the Basel III 4.5 common equity requirement. Of this 8.5 percent, at least 5.5 percent must be in the form of common equity while up to 3 percent may be held in the form of convertible capital (CoCos). The CoCos would convert when a bank's common equity falls below 7 percent.

2. An additional contingent buffer of 6 percent of risk-weighted assets (RWA) consisting entirely of CoCos. Unlike the CoCos under the first buffer, the CoCos under the progressive component will convert when capital levels falls below 5 percent common equity.

The two G-SIFIs will therefore have a capital of 19 percent of risk-weighted assets (4.5 percent of minimum capital requirements under Basel III, the capital conservation buffer of the 8.5 and 6 percent surcharge).

2. The Danish Resolution Procedure

On June 25, 2010, the Danish Act on Financial Stability was amended so as to introduce a banking resolution scheme. The Act is of interest as it combines the idea of separation between the good bank and bad bank parts of the bank with a restructuring of liabilities characteristic of bail-ins. As part of the new resolution framework in Denmark, the Financial Stability Company will create a "good bank" with the assets of the old bank purchased at realization value in the event of a bank failure. Figure 8.1 illustrates its main features.

When a bank fails to meet the capital adequacy requirements within a given deadline, it may opt for bankruptcy. If it chooses not to declare bankruptcy, then its operational responsibilities are transferred to the financial stability company. The financial stability company will do the following:

1. Establish a new bank, the good bank. This new bank will have the assets of the old bank that are purchased at a realization value.

2. Transfer unsubordinated liabilities of the old bank to the new bank in proportion to the realized value of the assets. The remaining proportion will be kept in the old bank. (Of course, depositors are insured up to €100,000)

3. Give the new bank a capital injection.

4. Provide the new bank with liquidity either through access to the regular central bank refinancing operations and the interbank markets or, if this is not possible, through access to the financial stability company's liquidity.

5. Guarantee depositors in the new bank their deposits up to the amount of 100,000 euros if the proportional share of the assets is lower than this amount.

6. Adjust the realization value of the assets in two stages. During the first stage it entails a haircut in the valuation. In the second stage a due diligence process is conducted by two independent expert valuers. This will allow the haircut to be reduced if necessary.

7. Revert any earn-out in excess of "normal profits" of the new bank to the liability holders of the old bank.

The structure is innovative and worth observing, as it is a good example of how to minimize the outlay of taxpayers' money while, at the same time, limiting contagion. An interesting aspect to note is that the two stages in the determination of the realized value allow for a speedy restructuring in the first stage and a fair distribution of losses in the second stage.

8.7.3   Redefining the Limits of Banking Activity

Banking regulation has traditionally limited the scope of financial intermediaries by restricting the financial products they can invest in. Yet we observe huge variations in the regulation of banking restrictions both across time and across countries. The issue of what is the efficient form of regulation engenders a number of specific questions as to the priorities in today's regulatory reform. Are financial conglomerates a good thing? Should shadow banking be encouraged or limited? Should structural measures such as the Volcker rule[18]—"the Glass–Steagall Act of the twenty-first century"—, the European Commission's "Liikanen" proposal of January 2014,[19] or the UK's ring fencing recommendation of the independent Vickers commission be adopted by other countries?

This issue is directly related to the definition of banking. If we restrict banks to deposit taking institutions it may be efficient to restrict the degree to which they engage in high-risk investments, including securities insurance and real estate activities. If instead we adopt a broader definition of banks, the existence of the economies of scope may lead us to recommend permitting these activities. The theoretical

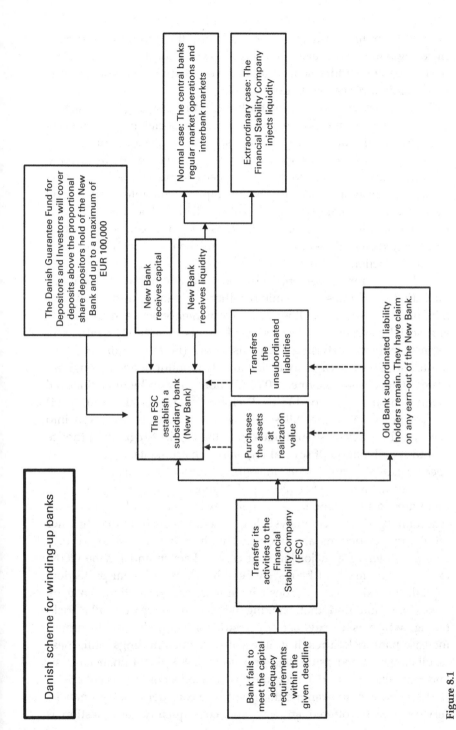

Figure 8.1
Danish bank resolution regime

models are of limited help in understanding this complex issue. Still, since regulation does exist, it is worth examining how the problem could ideally be addressed, using both the existing theoretical frameworks and empirical evidence.

The simplest way to examine the benefits of restricting banks' activities is to consider the divergence between the social and private cost and benefits of a bank investing in a specific financial instrument. To be sure, if there were no such divergence, there would be no reason to limit the bank activities. Nevertheless, because banks are financed by insured deposits and because of the implicit guarantees offered by these safety nets, banks tend to free-ride on debt, and because of limited market discipline, safety nets are insensitive to a bank's risk-taking strategies. It may therefore be efficient to separate the "casino" and "utility" functions of financial institutions.

A clear case for a divergence between social and private cost is when the activity generates a systemic risk that is not taken into account by the financial institution. Other cases of divergence between the private and social assessments of costs and benefits include (1) conflicts of interest in banks advising their customers (Bolton et al. 2007), (2) limited supervisory capacity to adequately monitor financial conglomerates (Laeven and Levine 2005), (3) politically influential financial institutions that are "too big to discipline" (Barth et al. 2006), or (4) market power. Yet, once all social costs and benefits are taken into account, the analysis should determine the efficient regulation (notice that the combination of several regulatory instruments, e.g., imposing specific capital requirements on some instruments, is possible).

According to Barth et al. (2006, p. 48) "most of the literature suggests there are positive benefits from permitting broad banking powers." Additionally their own analysis leads them to conclude that "greater regulatory restrictions are associated with a higher probability of a country suffering a major banking crisis." Laeven and Levine (2009) examine the impact of banks' ownership, investors' legal protection, capital, the existence of deposit insurance, and restrictions on bank risk-taking and find that banking restrictions increase banks' risk-taking, which is to say, activity restrictions and deposit insurance increase bank risk, a result in line with previous findings. Still, these results are obtained using data prior to the 2008 global financial crisis and may alter when including the systemic effect of this recent crisis.

A second way to examine this point is to consider that the financial services will be offered anyway, and consequently the question is whether it is more efficient for these services to be supplied by two different, separate institutions, one of which is a depository institution, or by a single bank. Surprisingly, from this perspective, the same theoretical framework can be used to address the issue of financial conglomerates and the issue of securitization with the creation of SPVs as separate institutions. It is nevertheless the best starting point to rigorously define the problem of how best to organize the provision of financial services, as it allows us to state the issue in terms of the degree to which losses are shared. For small shocks, a merged institution is much more resilient. However; for large shocks, a holding company with separate subsidiaries so that the failure of one subsidiary does not ruin the other is more stable.

Within this framework a number of issues can be addressed. First, a financial conglomerate would be more resilient in the event of small shocks, but if a large shock occurs, it could go bankrupt and cause a systemic crisis. Second, Freixas et al. (2007) show that once the distortion created by deposit insurance (or, more generally, the lack of market discipline) is explicitly modeled and the result justifies capital regulation, the structure of a holding with separate bank (with deposit insurance) and nonbank (with no access to deposit insurance and therefore no capital requirement) would improve the capital allocation process by reducing the cost of funds. The implication from a policy perspective would be that financial conglomerates structured as a unique legal entity are inefficient while those that are structured as a holding are efficient. This analysis appears to justify a separation of banking activities into different subsidiaries, and to affirm the UK ring fencing proposal and the Volcker rule.

Also there is justification for limits on activities where economies of scope pose substantial systemic risk, such as proprietary trading. However, beyond the specific cases we noted, we view the argument for broad limits and restrictions to be weak because such rules tend to be easy to circumvent through regulatory arbitrage.

8.7.4 Regulating OTC Risks

The previous framework allows us to address the issue of shadow banking that is now part of the regulatory reform agenda (see Financial Stability Board 2013). First, regulatory authorities need to identify clearly the risk and expected return of the investments that firms and households are to undertake. Second, they need to allocate these risks in an efficient way to the agents that are willing to bear them.

Although these issues are intertwined, we will attempt clarify them successively.

Regarding the first issue, regulatory authorities must take responsibility in consumer protection to ensure that full disclosure is made to investors as to the risk/return trade-offs of investments, to demand the highest standards of transparency, and to limit the potential moral hazards that can arise at the banks' level.

Regarding the second issue, regulatory authorities must take responsibility to allocate risks among agents. That is, they must consider the optimal amount of risk that society is ready to take and find the optimal way to allocate it. In effect, reducing banks' risks means increasing some other agents' risks and that in turn might increase banks' cost of funding. From an economic efficiency point of view, this is not a zero-sum game: bankruptcy costs erode part of the overall expected return. As a consequence a simple way to analyze the optimal level of shadow banking is to minimize bankruptcy costs. From that perspective it is clear that securitized loans that are held by mutual funds or by pension funds decrease bankruptcy costs while those that remain within the banking industry do not change the consolidated bankruptcy costs even if, at the individual level, they happen to mislead supervisory authorities into thinking that bank solvency and liquidity risk are under control.

8.8   Conclusions

In this chapter we have reviewed the failures of microprudential regulation and the current reforms to the microprudential framework for banks, with special emphasis on the new Basel III framework. Although the Basel III proposal goes in the right direction, it focuses excessively on capital requirements and lacks a rigorous analysis of the microfoundations of banks' excessive risk-taking, a point that may be more related to the quality of supervision and corporate governance than to a precise estimation of risk weights and capital requirements. Also, although Basel III is designed to decrease banks' risk, more research is needed on the costs and benefits of banking regulation, and in particular, the regulation of shadow banking, liquidity requirements, and information disclosure.

We suggest that microprudential regulation should complement and be subordinated to macroprudential regulation in that risks have to be contained by focusing not only on the risk of individual financial institutions but by taking into account all possible spillovers, reinforcing loops, and general equilibrium effects that contribute to systemic risk. Indeed, it is only on the basis of a strong macroprudential perspective that a rigorous appraisal of banks' internal risk models can be performed. This does not mean, of course, that microprudential regulations should only be enacted on macroprudential grounds. Ensuring that banking supervisors safeguard the stability of individual financial institutions and intervene early on in failing banks is critical to protect depositor and consumer rights, and will go a long way to boosting overall financial stability and containing the cost to taxpayers of a financial crisis.

9   Systemic Risk and Macroprudential Regulation

This chapter describes the "new" regulatory and supervisory framework that relies on macroprudential regulation to manage systemic risk. It gives an overview of possible macroprudential tools, including their strengths and weaknesses, and discusses the trade-offs involved in choosing an optimal policy mix. We emphasize the preventive role of macroprudential policy in limiting the likelihood of a financial crisis and the impact on the economy; and we analyze the ex post role of macroprudential policy during crisis management. We argue that regulatory policies need to include both the time and the cross-sectional dimensions of systemic risk, and that the appropriate measures for these two dimensions are likely to be different. The implementation of macroprudential policy will need to be fitted to the type of systemic risk. For example, more intensive oversight will need to be used when the incentives for excessive correlated risk-taking are higher and be directed more toward systemically important financial intermediaries.

To administer a macroprudential framework, it is critical that the systemic risk be measured in real time, as explained in chapter 7. While, in general, macroprudential policies are variations of microprudential policies, we discuss their different roles, and complementary policies that could limit both the likelihood and the cost of systemic crises, especially policies that automatically limit *both* the attractiveness of leverage during credit and asset price booms and the negative effects of crises.

This chapter also elaborates on the potential costs of excessive regulation. One direct cost of regulation is that the regulatory measure boosts financial stability but hurts the real economy. For example, measures that limit "healthy" credit booms may hurt economic growth. Other regulatory measures may reduce systemic risk but increase the cost of financial intermediation and even hurt financial stability. And there is a risk that regulatory measures, by limiting systemic risk in one segment of the market, increase systemic risk for the market as a whole when these measures displace activity to less tightly regulated segments of the market. Furthermore there is a risk that a tightening of prudential measures will induce a reduction in credit supply, with banks compensating for the loss in profits by taking on higher risk (in search for a higher yield), with negative implications for financial stability. Therefore, we cover in this chapter the positive and (potentially) negative aspects of macroprudential policy.

While the risks associated with the buildup of financial imbalances and other types of systemic risk were in great part known before the global financial crisis, prudential policies (which were mainly micro in nature) were in most part unresponsive. This reflected several factors.

First, with the adoption of inflation targeting regimes, monetary policy in most advanced economies and several emerging markets had increasingly focused on the policy rate and paid little attention to monetary and credit aggregates. The few exceptions, such as the ECB's "two-pillar" policy, were regarded as vestiges from the past (and played a debatable role in actual policy setting). Even in the case of the ECB, the second pillar was not considered a financial stability pillar, but monetary aggregates were considered, for the medium and long run, key determinants of inflation.[1] As pointed out by Adrian and Shin (2010), the crisis reminded us that quantities convey crucial information about the behavior of individual financial intermediaries and, importantly, about the financial system as a whole; something that is not contained in prices. Credit, leverage, and monetary quantities and also gross and net cross-border financial positions reflect systemic risk exposures, which affect financial stability.

Second, existing bank regulation focused on individual institutions. It largely ignored the externalities within the financial sector and to the real sector along the macroeconomic cycle and, therefore, was ill-equipped to respond to aggregate dynamics. And, by and large, as for asset price bubbles, a benign neglect notion that it was better to deal with the bust rather than trying to prevent the boom prevailed. All this implied that the excessive risks and buildup of endogenous financial imbalances created in booms were in great part ignored. Again, there were exceptions. Spain introduced "dynamic provisioning" based on the rationale that it is during expansions that bad credits (high risks in general) are accumulated. Australia and Sweden adjusted monetary policy in response to asset price and credit developments and communicated the reason explicitly in central bank statements.[2] As we will see in this chapter, a few emerging markets experimented with applying prudential rules in a countercyclical way or in response to developments in credit and asset markets. But these exceptions formed a minority. Moreover the measures taken were often small in scale and, therefore, did not always have their desired effect. For example, in the case of Spain, these provision buffers reached the maximum value of 1 percent over total credit in the system.

Third, financial liberalization massively increased cross-border banking activities (including securitization) and financial globalization limited the effectiveness of (domestic) policy actions. In countries with de jure or de facto fixed-exchange-rate regimes, capital flows hindered the impact of monetary policy on credit aggregates. For example, Turkey could only decrease its massive credit growth with a strong tightening of macroprudential policy as domestic monetary policy was in great part ineffective due to global inflows. Moreover prudential measures were subject to regulatory arbitrage, especially in countries with developed financial markets and a widespread presence of global banks. For example, in the United States, the expansion of the shadow banking system and securitization was largely due to arbitraging prudential regulation (mainly bank capital requirements) as credit risk computes for capital requirements but not liquidity risk, and foreign liquidity (e.g., as in Germany and China) was crucial to absorb the securitized assets. More generally, it is almost impossible to have large credit booms and asset price bubbles, such as the ones observed in Spain and Ireland before the crisis, without cross-border liquidity.[3]

Finally, monetary policy and political economy considerations will also impact prudential policy, but we specifically analyze these issues in the next two chapters. In this chapter we define and offer a rationale for macroprudential regulation, drawing on the theoretical framework in chapter 3 (and chapter 4 to 7); give an overview of possible macroprudential tools; discuss the trade-offs involved in choosing an optimal policy mix (including the interaction with existing regulation) and the practical considerations when implementing these tools; give an overview of country experience to date in implementing macroprudential policies; present a critical review of the relevant elements of the new Basel III regulatory framework as well as the latest EU and US financial regulations in dealing with systemic risk; describe the boundaries, limits, and limitations of macroprudential regulation; and describe the challenges in building a macroprudential framework that supports and is consistent with monetary policy frameworks. The chapter proceeds as follows: Section 9.1 starts with a description of the limits of microprudential regulation. Section 9.2 offers the rationale for macroprudential regulation. Section 9.3 presents the range of macroprudential tools that can be used to manage systemic risk. Section 9.4 presents evidence to date on the effectiveness of macroprudential policies. And section 9.5 discusses the limits and boundaries of macroprudential regulation.

9.1 The Limits of Microprudential Regulation

The main problem with the regulatory framework for banks and other financial intermediaries prior to the crisis was that financial regulation had been too much focused on the risk of *individual* financial institutions rather than the financial system as a whole. Therefore prudential regulation had been too much micro-focused. The 2008 global financial crisis has clearly shown that financial regulation has to become more macro-focused, focusing on the risks of the financial system as a whole, both the buildup of financial imbalances, and the externalities within the financial sector and from the financial to the real sector. In other words, going forward prudential regulation should also focus on systemic risk.

Effective microprudential policy could lead to low systemic risk because if each financial institution in the financial system is sound, the financial system should in principle be more resilient. Yet, unfortunately, this does not necessarily need to be the case. The main tool that regulators have used to prevent bank failures since the 1980s has been bank capital regulation in the form of minimum capital requirements. However, the crisis has shown that this approach is insufficient to prevent costly financial crises. Under current capital regulations, capital adequacy levels are set on the implicit assumption that by creating buffers to absorb unexpected shocks at individual banks, the system as a whole is safer. However, by responding to capital regulations with only their own interest in mind, banks and other intermediaries can potentially behave in ways that collectively undermine the system as a whole.[4]

For example, banks can increase their capital to asset ratio by selling financial assets at fire sales and reducing their supply of credit, thereby causing strong negative externalities to other financial intermediaries and the real sector in terms of fire sales and credit crunches. Or, for example, in a crisis, banks can hoard liquidity to boost their liquidity ratios but cause a freeze in the wholesale markets, hampering the distribution of liquidity among financial intermediaries. In both cases, what seem optimal actions from the perspective of an individual bank can increase systemic risk at the banking system level, and therefore be suboptimal from the perspective of the system as a whole.

Moreover there are systemic financial institutions that should have higher capital requirements because their failures cause even stronger negative externalities to the financial and real sector as these systemic institutions are very large or too connected with other financial institutions and the real sector. Microprudential policy also ignores this *cross-sectional* dimension of systemic risk.

A related problem with the current regulatory framework for banks is its excessive pro-cyclical nature, the time dimension of systemic risk. During boom episodes, when risk appetite is large and asset values rise, banks appear overcapitalized and respond by expanding their business and increasing leverage. In the words of former Citigroup chairman Chuck Prince "as long as the music is playing, you've got to get up and dance." By contrast, during busts when asset prices collapse and measured risk rises, banks try to maintain capital adequacy ratios by shrinking their balance sheets, as capital has become scarce and expensive, thereby reducing access to finance for firms and households. As a consequence bank credit cycles tend to closely follow economic cycles. Basel II, which was microprudential in nature, even aggravated this problem. As risk is high in crises, capital requirements were higher during the crisis, thus even amplifying credit cycles and excessive pro-cyclicality in the bank sector. Basel III tries to be more macroprudential and has capital requirements (at least part of them) that are pro-cyclical—meaning higher requirements in good times and/or lower requirements in bad times, which implies that once a crisis hits, banks will have higher buffers than required by regulators, thus have a countercyclical capital buffer.

As credit should follow economic fundamentals (demand), credit cycles are not necessarily negative for systemic risk. However, there is evidence that excessive risk-taking (including lending) is taken in the boom, and banks may lend into negative net present value loans or engage in asset price bubbles because of, for example, the explicit and implicit executive compensation contracts and government subsidies (Rajan 1994, 2005). In fact the externalities are key in the boom as explained in chapter 4. Throughout the financial system, financial intermediaries are rewarded for beating imperfect risk benchmarks, and given the compensation structure, it is optimal for managers to herd with other managers on credit and investment choices as herding provides insurance that the manager will not underperform his peers. Moreover, given the short-term nature of their contracts, they can take on long-term risks via exposure to tail risks. However, herd behavior can move asset prices away from fundamentals. Tail risks and herd behavior can reinforce each other during an asset price boom, when investment managers are willing to bear the low probability "tail" risk that asset prices will revert to fundamentals abruptly, and even write guarantees against it, while the knowledge that many of their peers are herding on this risk gives them comfort that they will not underperform significantly if boom turns to bust. Worse, if a crisis comes, there may be too many to fail and government insurance via bailouts and lender of last resort makes more optimal the ex ante excessive (systemic) risk-taking.

During crisis times, negative externalities are even clearer. In a crisis, investment and consumption needs are lower, and this implies a demand-side induced lower provision of credit. Additionally banks with a shortage of capital in a crisis may be prompted to restore their capital and liquidity levels, and reduce credit even to firms and household with positive NPV, thus creating a credit crunch in the economy. Moreover, with public debt increasing during systemic crises (as a result of lower growth, accommodative fiscal policy, and/or public interventions in ailing financial institutions), banks and other financial intermediaries may engage more in lending to the sovereign, thereby crowding out real investment through a reduction of the supply of credit for private consumption and investment.

By seeking to align capital levels at individual banks with a bank's own risk exposures, microprudential regulation has done too little to restrain bank expansion and the buildup of systemic risk in the upswing, nor has it been able to provide much support against the downfall of the system as a whole. Basel II has been too procyclical thus magnifying economic fluctuations: as risks are "apparently" low in good times and too high in bad times, bank capital ratios were procylical, thus making the financial sector even more procyclical, thereby increasing systemic risk. During the recent crisis, it became clear that a changing paradigm for the regulatory framework is needed to dampen the pro-cyclical nature of the financial system, targeting this *time* dimension of systemic risk. The countercyclical capital buffers under Basel III go a long way to addressing the time dimension of systemic risk, although there remain questions about the appropriate levels of such capital buffers and the appropriate conditions that trigger their implementation.

9.2 Macroprudential Regulation, Oversight and Policies

The purpose of macroprudential regulation is to protect the financial system as a whole, by limiting both the likelihood of systemic crises from occurring and, conditioning on crises, the strong costs for the real sector of an impairment of the overall financial system. This is in stark contrast to microprudential regulation which purpose is to protect small depositors, by limiting the frequency and cost of individual bank failures (Bhattacharya and Thakor 1993; Freixas and Rochet 2008).

Macroprudential regulation is justified by the market's failure to deal with aggregate risks and financial stability (Rochet 2004). An important externality is that each bank free-rides on the willingness of others to pay for the public good of financial stability (e.g., lower individual bank profits by holding higher liquid assets). The existence of externalities that operate between financial institutions and that either contribute to the accumulation of vulnerabilities during boom periods or to the amplification of the negative shocks during busts provide the two main rationales for macroprudential regulation, along with the externalities from the impairment of the financial sector to the real sector.

While microprudential regulation can in principle be dealt with at a purely private level, macroprudential regulation has an intrinsically public good component. Nevertheless, governments have traditionally controlled both dimensions of regulation through official oversight. This approach has been the source of serious time inconsistency problems, associated with political pressure on supervisors, regulatory forbearance, too big to fail policies, and mismanagement of banking crises (Rochet 2008). These time inconsistency problems arise because democratically elected governments cannot precommit to limit liquidity assistance to insolvent banks once a crisis erupts. For example, central banks will face political pressures to overextend liquidity to ailing banks when it is in the interest of the public at large to maintain the momentum of a credit boom. Similarly regulators will face political pressures to forbear on capital regulation during a crisis, even when prompt corrective action regulations are in place, because democratically elected governments can pass the bill on to future generations.

And regulators also have self-interests, such as career concerns, that may prevent them from closing ailing institutions early on (Boot and Thakor 1992). As a result of these political pressures, there are too few bank closures and too many government interventions. Importantly, banks take excessive systemic risks in anticipation of such interventions and regulatory forbearance.

A macroprudential perspective would balance these distortions and moral hazard considerations against the benefit from preventing costly bank runs (and runs on other financial intermediaries) through government interventions. This is a delicate balancing act, as illustrated by crises of Lehman Brothers and Northern Rock. The absence of timely government intervention (i.e., capital support by the US Treasury in the case of Lehman Brothers and liquidity support by the Bank of England in the case of Northern Rock), in part motivated by moral hazard considerations not to create examples of excessive government intervention, together with media coverage about liquidity problems at Northern Rock, contributed to costly bank runs in both cases. At the same time much of the inaction can also be explained by the lack of an efficient resolution framework for failing financial institutions. Moreover the same political economy problems that plague the effectiveness of microprudential regulation also undermine macroprudential regulatory frameworks. Even with resolution frameworks in place, there will be political pressure on regulators and central banks not to enforce such regulations during a systemic crisis ex post. And countercyclical capital requirements or dynamic provisioning rules are bound to face stiff pressures from politicians to be relaxed during boom periods (e.g., in Spain), thereby softening budget constraints on banks and preventing a buildup of adequate buffers to face crisis times.

Even though excessive risks are taken prior to crises (during booms and in the buildup of financial imbalances) and are partly a result of policy (e.g., potential bailouts, lender of last resort policies, and other government subsidies), it is clear that ex post crisis management policies are very important as well. Not providing liquidity to the financial system or increasing capital and liquidity ratios during a financial crisis can greatly exacerbate (systemic) costs to the real sector once a banking crisis occurs. Macroprudential policy has also an ex post element in terms of curing the illness. However, given that this creates moral hazard problems and that risks are mainly taken in good times, the preventive role of macroprudential policy (both regulation and oversight) should be particularly strong to limit the likelihood of systemic (strong) financial crises. Moreover political economy considerations make it very hard to tighten macroprudential policies during a crisis.

Macroprudential policies are policies to limit systemwide risks in the financial system. In a strict sense, they include prudential tools and regulations to address externalities within the financial system and from the financial to the real sector (BIS 2011; IMF 2011a). In a broader sense, however, the objective of macroprudential policies is to smooth excessive financial and credit cycles in order to prevent systemic crises and to provide buffers against their adverse systemic costs once the crises occur.

Macroprudential policy seeks to address two specific dimensions of systemic risk: the time dimension and the cross-sectional dimension (Borio 2009; Bank of England 2012). The time dimension reflects the procyclicality of the financial system, which is the tendency to increase risk exposures during the boom phase of a financial cycle and to become overly risk averse during the bust phase. Procyclicality manifests itself in credit, liquidity and asset price cycles and the buildup of aggregate risk during boom periods, making the system more vulnerable to shocks, thereby increasing both the likelihood of financial crises and the systemic costs once the crisis arrives. It is important to note, as we did in previous chapters, that the nature of the excessive risks are endogenous, not exogenous; therefore a buildup of endogenous risks may arise due to explicit and implicit incentives from private contracts (e.g., executive compensation) and public policy (e.g., prudential and monetary).

The cross-sectional dimension reflects the distribution of risk in the financial system at a given point of time, which could give rise to contagion, fire sales and other spillover effects. This distribution of risk is a function of the size of institutions, their leverage, concentration of their activities, and their interconnectedness (IMF 2011b). Linkages could arise due to inter-institution direct exposures or their vulnerability to common shocks (e.g., due to indirect but correlated exposures), creating channels of contagion through spillovers between institutions. These direct and indirect linkages expose all financial intermediaries to cascading effects arising from the failure of individual financial institutions, with the potential to grow into systemwide depositor runs and fire sales.

The cross-sectional dimension of systemic risk is not independent of the time dimension. As shown by Iyer and Peydró (2011), contagion effects in interbank markets are stronger when the fundamentals of the system as a whole are worse. Put differently, spillovers are less important when the liquidity and capital of the financial system is stronger. This implies that transmission of idiosyncratic shocks and similar reactions to common aggregated shocks reinforce each other in increasing systemic risk. Finally, it is important to note that it is difficult to disentangle which part of systemic risk is due to pure contagion effects and which part is due to common risk exposures. In hindsight, the Lehman failure can be seen as having created not only a pecuniary contagion effect from a large connected financial institution to the rest of the financial system in a narrow sense but, more important, also as a signal of common vulnerabilities within the financial system (due to buildup of excessive systemic risk in the good times).

The other key aspect of macroprudential policy is its systemwide perspective. This is because of the "fallacy of composition" of microprudential policy: actions that are appropriate for individual firms may collectively lead to, or exacerbate, systemwide financial stability problems. Examples include, as discussed earlier, increasing microprudential capital and liquidity ratios during a crisis, or the countercyclicality of capital requirements over the cycle. Moreover "the complexity of processes that can generate systemic risk, and the ease at which risk can migrate across the financial system, call for a broad focus on the whole range of financial institutions (banks and nonbanks alike), instruments, markets, and infrastructure" (IMF 2011b). Such systemic risk came in many forms and disguises, and a broad range of institutions played a key role in the buildup and transmission of systemic risk. For example, not only US but also European banks played a key role in the functioning of the US shadow banking sector, US money market funds were key for the liquidity of European banks, insurance firms like AIG played a crucial role in the CDO market, creating systemic risk by generating counterparty risk exposures to banks, the lack of appropriate infrastructure for over the counter derivatives also contributed to systemic risk, and there are important interlinkages between sovereign and bank risk.

Table 9.1 summarizes the main differences between microprudential and macroprudential regulation explained above (and in earlier chapters of this book). Microprudential takes into consideration a single financial intermediary, a partial equilibrium analysis, while the macroprudential policy takes into consideration the linkages of a financial institution with the rest of financial institutions and the market, and

Table 9.1
Microprudential and macroprudential regulation compared

	Microprudential:	Macroprudential:
View	Partial equilibrium	General equilibrium
Risk	Risk in isolation (VaR)	Risk of system (CoVar)
Distortions	Socialization of losses	Externalities/spillovers
		Amplification/endogenous risk
		Financial cycle/procyclicality
Results	Excessive risk-taking	Excessive systemic risk
	Hide risk in tail	Herding/irrational fashions
	Gambling for resurrection	Create tails
	Diversification	Diversity
Fallacy of composition	Fire sale of assets is microprudent	Fire sale not prudent in aggregate
	Deleveraging to meet capital or liquidity requirements is microprudent	Need to raise equity, not sell assets or not renew loans
	Individual bank run	Credit crunch and aggregate liquidity dry up

Source: Brunnermeier (2013) and authors

also with the real economy. That is, as explained in chapter 3, a general equilibrium perspective with both a real and financial sector, where the financial sector is not a representative institution, but a set of heterogeneous financial intermediaries.

The measure of risk in the micro setting is the value at risk (VaR) of a single financial institution, independently of both how it obtains the capital and liquidity and the potential externalities to others, whereas in a macro view it is measured by systemic risk, such as CoVaR or SRISK. As explained in chapter 7, measurement of systemic risk is more difficult than the measurement of insolvency at the individual bank level. Diversification within the banking sector could help to reduce systemic risk, but it is not necessarily the case. While diversification at the institution level can be optimal to reduce insolvency risk, it can cause higher systemic risk at the financial system level as it connects more all the parts of the financial system (or more complete markets, as in Allen and Gale's 2000a terminology). Moreover, as explained by Shin (2009), diversification (e.g., through securitization) can increase endogenously the correlated risks in the financial system, thus increasing systemic risk.

As micro takes into account the individual failure and externalities to retail depositors of the bank, it can introduce as a distortion the socialization of losses of the individual failure. In the case of macroprudential, externalities within the financial sector and to the real sector, endogenous risks in the buildup of financial imbalances and excessive procyclicality are the main distortions. Of course, the micro and macro dimension of prudential policy can be related. As small banks may not receive a bailout, the main distortion at the individual level can come from taken correlated risks with other banks (by being exposed to a credit boom and asset price bubble), thus also increasing the systemic risk in the system. Hence the differences between micro and macroprudential are sometimes blurred.

The excessive risk-taking at the individual level can cause the individual failure (e.g., in gambling for resurrection when bank capital is too low), but it does not affect financial stability unless the risk-taking is systemic in nature—either with correlated risks (herding) or with transmission of idiosyncratic risks of a large connected financial institution to the rest of the financial system. Moreover herding and tail risks reinforce each other incentives to risk-taking as potential bailouts and LoLR will benefit all institutions. Finally, from a macroprudential perspective (as opposed to a microprudential one) it is not desirable, especially during a systemic crisis, to hoard liquid assets (e.g., by pulling out of wholesale markets), increase capital to asset ratios by selling financial assets at fire sales or, importantly, to reduce lending to firms and households, thereby creating a credit crunch, because each of these actions jeopardize financial stability and create large costs for the economy at large.

All in all, the key question for macroprudential policy is why there is systemic risk (what are the externalities to regulate), when is systemic risk increased (time dimension) and by whom (the cross-sectional dimension of systemic risk). In general, excessive systemic risk is taken more in good times, but maybe without ex post crisis management policies, systemic risk could be taken massively in crises, for example, as correlated gambles for resurrection—that is, incentives can change in the future. Therefore it is crucial to continuously monitor systemic risk, understanding how policy and structural changes can affect the incentives for systemic risk-taking. This is even more important given regulatory arbitrage practices. In this sense, the oversight of macroprudential policy could play a key complementary role by increasing its intensity when the incentives for systemic risk are higher.

Table 9.2
Macroprudential instruments

Time dimension	Cross-sectional dimension
Countercyclical capital buffers	Systemic capital surcharges
Time-varying systemic liquidity surcharges	Systemic liquidity surcharges
Countercyclical change in risk weights for exposure to certain sectors	Levy on non-core liabilities
Through the cycle valuation of margins or haircuts for repos	Higher capital charges for trades not cleared through central counterparty (CCP) clearinghouses
Time-varying LTV, debt to income (DTI) and loan to income (LTI) caps	Powers to break up financial firms on systemic risk concerns
Time-varying limits on currency mismatch or asset exposures	Capital charge on derivative payables
Time-varying limits on aggregate credit, credit growth, and loan to deposit ratios	Deposit insurance risk premiums sensitive to systemic risk
Time-varying limits on aggregate credit, credit growth, and loan to deposit ratios	Deposit insurance risk premiums sensitive to systemic risk
Dynamic provisioning rules	Restrictions on permissible activities (e.g., ban on proprietary trading for systemically important banks)

Source: IMF (2011b)

9.3   Macroprudential Tools

Macroprudential tools can be grouped in two categories: (1) instruments tailored to mitigate the time-varying dimension of systemic risk and (2) instruments tailored to mitigate the cross-sectional dimension of systemic risk. Table 9.2 shows the groups that have used these macroprudential tools.

It is clear from this table that the core instruments of macroprudential policy that have been put forward are traditional prudential instruments (as detailed in chapter 8), calibrated and used to deal specifically with systemic risk (e.g., by making them time-varying to reduce the excessive procyclicality of the financial system or by applying them to systemically important institutions with higher impact), and applied with a broader financial system perspective (e.g., to reduce financial connections in the financial system or to apply them to derivatives, for example).

For instance, a number of countries have recalibrated existing prudential instruments to address procyclicality of the financial system.

Specifically, some countries have included countercyclical changes in risk weights on banks' exposures to certain instruments, sectors, or markets to dampen the excessive build up of credit risk during periods of high credit growth and asset price movements. A rule-based dynamic provisioning framework has been implemented in Spain since 2000, requiring banks to build up buffers of general provisions, which can be drawn down in a recession, to avoid the commonly observed very low provisions in good times and very high in bad times around the world (Laeven and Majnoni 2004). In practice, a clear delineation of microprudential and macroprudential instruments is often difficult, as the same instruments may serve multiple objectives depending on how they are used. For example, the Spanish dynamic provisions could be seen as a microprudential policy to buildup buffers for expected losses at the individual bank level. However, its time-varying dimension and its purpose to smooth the credit cycle makes it mainly macroprudential.

Another way of grouping macroprudential tools is not by which type of risk they target but by *how* they alter the behavior or limit the ability of financial institutions to contribute to and manage systemic risk. Following this approach, the most commonly used macroprudential tools can be grouped into three categories (Dell'Ariccia et al. 2012):

First, measures that affect the cost or composition of the liabilities of financial institutions by increasing their capital and liquidity buffers. This group consists primarily of capital and liquidity requirements. For instance, countercyclical capital requirements may increase the overall cost of finance for banks capital and thus potentially reduce excessive credit growth (though some argue against the cost of bank capital; see for example Admati and Hellwig 2013). Dynamic loan loss provisioning rules, which also affect the bank's liability structure allow a bank to enter into a crisis with higher capital buffers, at a moment when it is very costly to issue equity and bank profits are low or negative, thus reducing the overall cost over the credit cycle. However, regulation is needed as bankers would not do it fully on their own as it may reduce bank profits in good times, when bankers want to maximize their bonuses.

Liquidity requirements also fall in this first category of measures, if they reduce short-term wholesale finance for banks and other financial intermediaries as the shadow banking sector. These measures may be costly in good times as wholesale short-term finance is the cheapest source of finance for banks (after retail deposits) as explained in Calomiris and Kahn (1991) and Diamond and Rajan (2001). However, an increase in long-term finance for banks would reduce the refinancing risk and contagion in crises, and therefore would decrease systemic risk.

Notice that capital and liquidity requirements can therefore be countercyclical to smooth the credit cycle, but they can also include surcharges for systemically important financial institutions to limit the buildup of risk of systemic institutions and to reduce their strong negative externalities in crises.[5]

Second, measures that alter the composition and risk profile of the assets of financial institutions. This group consists primarily of asset concentration and asset growth limits. Examples include speed limits on credit expansion, limits on foreign currency exposure, limits on liquid assets, and limits on sectoral concentration of loan portfolios. Sectoral exposure limits aim to preserve loan portfolio diversification, thereby altering the composition of financial firms' assets. This group of measures is particularly important because excessive credit and asset expansion have been among the main drivers of bank failures in history (Lindgren, Garcia, and Saal 1996). In the last round of banking crises, this was the case, for example, in Washington Mutual in United States, Anglo Irish in Ireland, the biggest banks in Iceland and Cyprus, and Bankia in Spain. Other banks, such as Northern Rock in the United Kingdom, combined strong expansion on the asset side with short-term wholesale funding on the liability side, the worst possible cocktail. Sectoral measures can also play a crucial role. For example, in the case of Spain, a saving bank had more than 90% of its assets in credit to the real estate sector. One of the weakest elements of the Basel I and II frameworks was that concentration risk in a sector and interconnectedness to other financial institutions were not sufficiently penalized, and therefore banks were not discouraged to be exposed to a bubble, a key source of systemic risk.

Third, measures that improve the average quality of borrowers are another type of macroprudential tools. This group consists primarily of loan eligibility criteria that limit the pool of borrowers that have access to finance. Examples include loan-to-value (LTV) and debt-to-income (DTI) limits. These limits seek to leave the "marginal" borrowers out of the pool. Eligibility criteria can be tailored to fit a loan portfolio's risk profile. For example, LTV limits can be set based on local house price dynamics or be differentiated based on whether loans are made in foreign currency to unhedged households or not.

All the previous measures could have some costs for the system, especially in good times, but clearly this last group of measures can have negative implications in terms of equality and welfare, by excluding for example students from loans, low-income families or new start-ups with intangibles. We emphasize the real effects for the economy at large. These come not only in the form of aggregate output losses and fiscal costs, but also increased inequality, for example coming from lower access to finance or from unemployment in systemic crises. Rajan (2010) argues that inequality has implied a higher likelihood of financial crises as (1) inequality increased before the Great Depression of 1930 and the Great Recession of 2008 and (2) excessive credit supply can be a way to allow consumption despite increasing income inequality.[6] However, as we saw in chapter 4, the general evidence on crises yields that ex ante credit booms rather than income inequality is the main driver of systemic risk. In any case, another issue regarding inequality is that policies to boost asset prices during systemic crises normally help rich people (the owners of these assets, e.g., bankers). Therefore the distributional consequences of macroprudential policy and its impact on inequality, both ex ante and ex post, is an important issue for systemic risk.

There are also costs associated with excessive regulation. One direct cost of regulation is that the regulation measure hurts the real economy. For example, measures that limit credit booms associated with strong fundamentals will be negative for aggregate output, employment and welfare. Other regulatory measures may reduce systemic risk but increase the cost of financial intermediation and even hurt financial stability. For example, limits on the ratio of credit to deposits that limit the risks associated with the financing of loans with short-term wholesale funding are likely to induce a higher competition for retail deposits, resulting in lower bank margins and deterioration in bank solvency, with negative consequences for financial stability. And there is a risk that regulatory measures, by limiting systemic risk in one segment of the market, increase systemic risk for the market as a whole when these measures displace activity to less tightly regulated segments of the market. Furthermore suggestive evidence by Jiménez et al. (2013) and Dassatti and Peydró (2013) shows that a tightening of prudential measures will induce a reduction in credit supply, with banks compensating for the loss in profits by taking on higher risk (in search for a higher yield), with negative implications for financial stability. Regarding credit supply reduction, an optimal financial system could have not only banks as powerful intermediaries but also venture capitalists and private equity which could target firms with little collateral but strong investment opportunities. To curtail higher risk-taking and search for yield due to tighter macroprudential measures, the intensity of supervision should be increased and regulatory policies should be adjusted to take into account the incentives of the financial intermediaries that are being regulated.

Other instruments can be modified to become part of the macroprudential toolkit provided that they target systemic risk explicitly and are placed at the disposal of an authority with a macroprudential mandate. Indeed, 2010 IMF survey responses, summarized in figure 9.1, suggest that countries have used a variety of other tools—including monetary, exchange rate, fiscal, and competition policies—for the purpose of constraining systemic risk. Those instruments would typically not be considered macroprudential, unless they are modified to target systemic risk explicitly. For instance, some countries have also used direct monetary policy instruments to constrain credit supply during booms, such as limits on the level or growth rate of aggregate credit or specific exposures, and marginal reserve requirements, as well as fiscal policy tools, such as stamp duties on property holding to tame speculation in real estate markets. Capital controls, which are motivated by both macroeconomic and financial considerations, are not typically macroprudential instruments, although they could be, if they specifically target systemic risk. For example, in 2008 Uruguay increased the reserve requirements for foreign-currency deposits of nonresidents, including foreign banks, to limit risks of sudden stops and bank fragility (Dassati and Peydró 2013).

The main macroprudential policy tools that have been used in the past and that have been proposed by the major international organizations and central banks are basically traditional prudential instruments that have been calibrated and used to deal specifically with systemic risk, both its cross-sectional and its time dimension. But there are potentially other policy tools, designed specifically with systemic risk in mind.

As we have noted before, systemically important financial crises tend to be preceded by strong credit growth, affecting both the likelihood of the crisis and the costs for the economy at large once the crisis occurs. Therefore excessive credit (in the form of leverage and debt) cycles are a key source of systemic risk.

The market failure of credit booms in good times comes from excessive credit supply (e.g., in taking correlated risks and the financing of a real estate bubble) and in the bad times arises because debt is *not* state

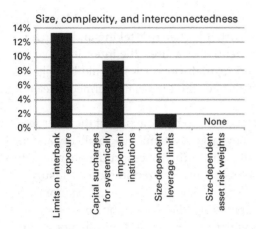

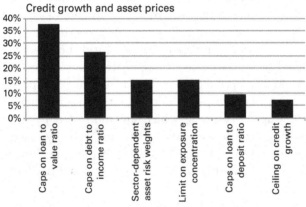

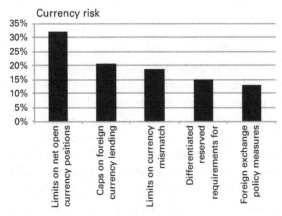

■ Percentage of countries

Figure 9.1
Use of macroprudentials tools around the world, end-2010. Source: Data from IMF Macroprudential Survey, December 2010, 53 countries in total

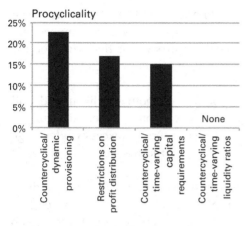

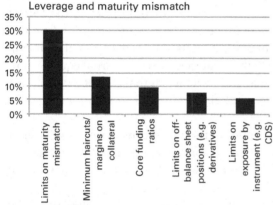

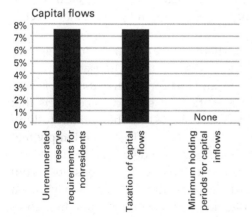

■ Percentage of countries

Figure 9.1 (continued)

contingent and there are also coordination problems. Moreover, given that the economy would enter into the crisis with too much debt built-up in the good times, there will be strong negative effects on the real economy arising from debt overhang, deleveraging, deposits runs and/or credit crunches.

Therefore a policy tool that could limit both the likelihood and the cost of systemic crises would be welcome, especially policies that automatically limit *both* the attractiveness of (excessive) leverage in the booms and the negative effects for the real sector in systemic crises.

Suppose there is only one part of the economy that can take debt. Then if creditors were to lose part of this debt in a crisis, as in a bail-in, then this would reduce the negative consequences associated with too much debt during the crisis, and creditors would price in the loss of attractiveness of debt already in the good times, thus limiting leverage ex ante also in the boom. In many models, debt is the optimal financing claim, but what we argue here is that these (mostly partial equilibrium) models abstract from the many important externalities (both within the financial sector and between the financial and real sectors) that drive systemic risk.

Of course, many complications arise when considering how to limit the attractiveness of debt in the economy, both because different sectors can take on excessive debt, and because there are different ways to implement this policy.

In the United States, for example, the excessive leverage during the recent global financial crisis occurred mainly in the household sector, whereas in Spain it was in the banks and firms (see Upper et al. 2013), and subsequently the sovereign. Therefore the cost in the crisis depends on which sector experiences debt overhang: firms, households, financial intermediaries, and sovereign, and on how much of the debt is held by foreigners. For example, automatic clauses in debt contracts that convert debt into equity (debt–equity swaps) can be optimal to limit problems in firms and financial intermediaries. This would imply that the value of debt in good times and the level of debt in bad times would be reduced. Another policy could be to "bail-in" (i.e., impose losses on) the debt of senior and subordinated debtholders. Some have even argued for the bail in of wholesale short-term depositors, though in this case there could be a massive wholesale run before the automatic clause kicks in (therefore, for banks, limiting short-term wholesale deposits is also necessary). Other measures that protect the creditor, such as loans with full recourse, may generate too much debt overhang in a crisis, and may not limit the debt in the good times if borrowers (households) have less information and sophistication than lenders (banks).

Measures that impose losses on foreigners, while appealing for individual countries with large amounts of external debt, constitute beggar thy neighbor policies that can have damaging contagion effects, especially when much of the debt is held by (highly leveraged) financial intermediaries. Such policies need to be coordinated and as a rule are better avoided through the ex ante prevention of excessive external debt. From this perspective, the painful experience of Ireland, where the taxpayer subsumed the large losses and debt of Irish banks with excessive external debt, shows that countries should take preventive measures to prevent the financial liabilities of their financial systems from growing to multiples of gross domestic product. Such measures could come in the form of higher capital requirements, and while such measures may hurt growth (even though they would push the economy to look for comparative advantages outside of the financial sector), they would benefit financial stability.

It is important to be mindful that the objective of reducing debt in the economy could be partially accomplished with monetary policy (as we will see in detail in the next chapter on monetary policy). Expansive monetary policy in the bad times favors the debtors, especially short-term ones, over the creditors, thus reducing the fragility of highly indebted borrowers (banks, firms, and sovereigns); and contractive monetary policy in the good times limits the buildup of credit. However, the previous macroprudential policies can target more specifically some strategic sectors, and there are political difficulties in raising monetary rates in good times if there are no inflation problems.

Banking competition also affects financial stability, as explained in chapter 4. Moreover there has been an explicit reduction in banking competition in, for example, Spain and Portugal during the recent crisis by introducing caps on bank deposits. There is an incentive by weak banks with difficult access to the wholesale market to increase deposit rates, and if deposit insurance is credible, there is an incentive for retail depositors to move their deposits from strong to weak banks. Both the increase in deposit rates (and decrease in lending margins) during a crisis and an increase of funds from good to worse banks (the opposite of market discipline) increase systemic risk. To limit these externalities within the financial system, Spain introduced limits on deposit rates in

2011 and 2013 (Mencia et al. 2013). Portugal introduced limits on loans to deposits, which banks can meet either through a reduction of loans or an increase in deposits. This has led to high competition for deposits, forcing Portugal to limit the competition with deposit rate caps (Lopes et al., 2014).

As Freixas and Dewatripont (2010) show, bank mergers and acquisitions are facilitated in crisis times. This may benefit financial stability in a microprudential sense because strong banks take over badly managed banks and because the resulting consolidation will reduce competition, thus increasing bank profits and bank capital. However, these policies may increase the too-big-to-fail problem, by increasing the size of large banks, and worsen the cross-sectional dimension of systemic risk because it becomes even harder not to bail out these banks. Therefore the interactions between competition policy and microprudential and macroprudential policies require coordination.

In general, there has been an increase in the use of macroprudential tools since the 2008 global financial crisis, as shown in figure 9.2, which contrasts responses from the 2010 IMF survey on the use of macroprudential tools with those from a more recent 2013 IMF survey. Limits on interbank exposures, loan-to-value ratios, and exposure concentration have particularly become more common, with loan-to-value limits now in place in over half the countries surveyed.

9.4 Implementation of Macroprudential Policy

9.4.1 Macroprudential Regulation under Basel III
The Basel III set of regulations, together with national legislative reforms such as the Dodd–Frank Act in the United States, are proposing the implementation of macroprudential policy, drawing on the tools presented in table 9.2, to contain systemic risks. These policies center on increasing capital buffers for systemically important financial institutions (SIFIs) and on managing counterparty exposures and interlinkages in the financial system (IMF 2011b). The new Basel capital and liquidity standards, known as Basel III, not only have microprudential implications (as discussed in the previous chapter) but also macroprudential ones. Requiring financial institutions to hold higher capital buffers could reduce their risk-taking, thereby reducing their default probability and the spillover effects that would result from a failure. Thus higher capital and liquidity requirements, by making each bank safer, also make the entire banking system safer. First, some theories

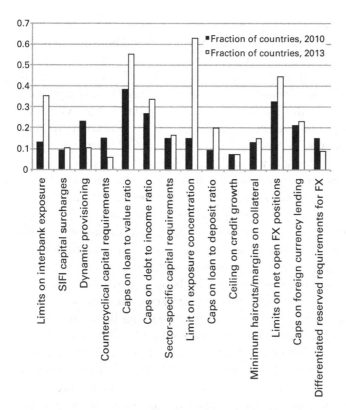

Figure 9.2
Use of macroprudential tools around the world, 2010 and 2013 compared. Source: Data from IMF Macroprudential Survey, December 2010, and IMF Macroprudential Survey, December 2013

argue that banks will take lower ex ante excessive risks as shareholders will have more money at stake to lose (Holmstrom and Tirole 1997), although as we saw in chapter 4, some excessive risks are systemic as in asset price bubbles financed with credit.[7] Second, once a crisis occurs, a bank with higher capital and liquidity buffers will generate less negative externalities to other financial intermediaries and to the real sector as the bank will need to sell less assets and reduce credit less (so it will need to deleverage less) and can even provide more liquidity to other financial intermediaries.[8]

Capital requirements under Basel III will be increased both in terms of quantity and quality. The minimum common equity tier 1 (CET1) capital ratio will be raised from 2 to 4.5 percent. On top of this, there will be a mandatory capital conservation buffer of another 2.5 percent.

The conservation buffer requires banks to maintain adequate buffers during crises by restricting dividend distribution and bonuses. In addition there will be a discretionary countercyclical buffer, which would allow national regulators to require up to another 2.5 percent of capital on a discretionary and bank-specific basis, for instance, during periods of high credit growth. The countercyclical capital buffer will vary across banks and time and thus introduce a pro-cyclical component of capital requirements. Beyond this, there will be 1 to 2.5 percent capital surcharges for systemically important financial institutions (SIFIs) above the minimum capital level, capital conservation and countercyclical buffer requirements introduced under Basel III. This additional loss absorption capacity is to be met with common equity.

Pro-cyclical capital requirements provide a measure to reduce the time dimension of systemic risk. Introducing countercyclical bank capital buffers aims to achieve two macroprudential objectives at once. First, boosting equity requirements in booms provides additional buffers in downturns that help mitigate credit crunches and deleveraging with fire sales. Second, higher requirements on bank own funds can cool credit-led booms, either because banks internalize more of the potential social costs of credit defaults (through a reduction in moral hazard by having more "skin in the game") or charge a higher loan rate due to the higher cost of bank capital. Pro-cyclical capital requirements (i.e., countercyclical bank capital buffers) could therefore lessen the excessive procyclicality of credit, namely those credit supply cycles that find their root causes in banks' agency frictions. Smoothing bank credit supply cycles will moreover generate positive firm-level real effects if bank-firm relationships are valuable and credit substitution for firms is difficult in bad times.

Finally, higher capital requirements for SIFIs tries to reduce the cross-sectional dimension of systemic risks by making the largest, more connected, banks hold higher buffers, which can reduce both the likelihood of systemic crises, and the ex post strong negative effects once a crisis occurs.

In terms of liquidity requirements, Basel III introduces two new requirements. The liquid coverage ratio (LCR) requires high-quality liquid assets to cover a bank's total net cash outflows over thirty days. This measure has already been agreed upon and will be introduced gradually. This measure is to help banks resist liquidity shocks when a crisis or panic occurs. The net stable funding ratio (NSFR), which is still being developed, is to require the available amount of stable funding to exceed the required amount of stable funding over some period of extended stress. This measure aims to reduce the likelihood of a liquidity crisis.

The Basel liquidity requirements penalize short-term financial connections among banks, as for example overnight unsecured interbank loans. This will reduce the level and complexity of asset and liability connections among financial intermediaries. This may reduce systemic risk as contagion effects in principle will be reduced. Moreover some of the negative effects of ex post pulling out financial linkages in the wholesale market will also be reduced, as banks will have higher ex ante liquidity buffers. Furthermore, as banks are key providers of funding for the shadow banking sector (e.g., providing liquidity puts to SPVs or primer brokers for hedge funds), the new liquidity requirements may also reduce systemic risk stemming from the less-regulated financial sector, as banks will also be regulated on this part of their claims (e.g., contingent off balance sheet liquidity claims).

A number of instruments are still being developed, specifically those associated with liquidity requirements and interconnectedness in the financial system. Moreover most requirements are being phased in gradually over time, and for some the date of introduction is still to be agreed. For example, the net stable funding ratio (NSFR) is still being developed and has no date so far.[9]

Taken together, the Basel III capital surcharges for systemically important financial institutions and the supplementary countercyclical capital buffers that would apply only to large and internationally active banking organizations go a long way to addressing systemic risks, although there remain questions about the appropriate levels of such capital requirements.

9.4.2 Other Macroprudential Regulatory Proposals

One of the problems that surfaced in the recent crisis is that neither financial market participants nor their regulators had a good overview of the counterparty risk associated with financial transactions. Many transactions between parties had taken place over the counter, with neither party knowing much about other transactions that either party had outstanding with third parties. And the settlement of payments or exchange of securities often occurred with delays, which was not a problem during normal times, but created significant hold-up problems during the crisis. Proposals to mitigate systemic spillovers arising out of counterparty exposures and balance sheet interlinkages focus on building a robust market infrastructure, including the design and over-sight of payment, settlement, and clearing systems, such as to reduce the buildup of counterparty exposures in these systems and the potential for spillovers from a failure of system participants. Examples in this area are the generalization of real time gross settlement (RTGS) and delivery versus payment (DvP) for national payment and settlement systems, the introduction of payment versus payment (PvP) in the settlement of foreign exchange transactions via continuous linked settlement (CLS), and the establishment of central counterparty (CCP) clearinghouses for the majority of trades in the over the counter (OTC) derivatives market (IMF 2011b).

Some countries are considering structural measures to limit risk concentrations and interconnectedness in the financial system directly. Legal restrictions on permissible activities have been in place at different times in different countries, although not necessarily with a view to addressing systemic risk. Examples include the Glass–Steagall Act in the United States, established in 1933 and repealed in 1999, which placed constraints on commercial banks to engage in securities transactions and limited affiliations between commercial banks and securities firms.

Recent policy initiatives falling under this category include the "Volcker rule" under the Dodd–Frank Act, which limits proprietary trading for systemically important US banks, the Vickers report in the United Kingdom, and the Liikanen report and the proposed new rules for structural banking reform in the European Union. As we explained earlier, banks have incentives to take excessive risks (e.g., through herding). Though excessive risks can be taken with simple lending as in the Spanish crisis (loans to real estate firms), derivatives and proprietary trading allow banks to expand the set of investments to take on excessive risks. Moreover deposit insurance, bailouts, and LoLR that generate moral hazard ex ante, as shown by Farhi and Tirole (2012a), can be justified to avoid negative externalities from bank failures on credit crunches for the economy at large, but these policy measures are not justified for the investment part of universal banks.

Put differently, it is not only that banks are too big, but that their access to derivatives makes them excessively complex. Their combination of activities creates conflicts of values, of interests and of objectives. A culture of investment banking that is dominated by trading may be incompatible with the requirements of reliable retail banking. Central banks and governments have flooded banks with funds to support domestic lending, but the balance sheets of these banks remain dominated by transactions with other financial institutions.

Still, it is very difficult for a regulator to know when a bank is using a derivative position (e.g., a CDS) to hedge (to limit some risks) or to speculate engaging in excessive risks. Moreover, in some financial systems, banks concentrate many functions (think about universal banks in Germany) and it would be very costly for the economy to impose these restrictions on banks' activities.

Finally, in some countries prudential policies have gone even further. For example, the UK Parliamentary Commission on Banking Standards has proposed criminal sanctions for those who recklessly pursue their own interests ahead of those of the banks they control.[10] As Alistair Darling, former Chancellor of the Exchequer, said: "Frankly there needs to be something more than just losing a knighthood [in reference to the RBS former CEO]." The new laws discussed would involve potential jail sentences. These points are important as all the models based on agency problems discussed in this book on why financial intermediaries take excessive (systemic and not systemic) risks are based on limited liability and leverage. Therefore limits to limited liability can reduce systemic risk. For example, previously, the ring-fencing of risky activities—such as trading bonds or shares—into entities in which there was individual and collective almost unlimited personal liability for one's own company's losses but also ultimately for those of others in the same line of business, constrained the excessive risk-taking (Esty 1998).

9.4.3 Practical Considerations for the Implementation of Macroprudential Tools

The ability to identify and measure systemic risks and vulnerabilities is a key factor for successfully implementing macroprudential policy. Imprecise timing of macroprudential policy can result in overshooting or undershooting of macroprudential objectives. This is particularly problematic because the costs of a mistimed activation are likely to be asymmetric, as delayed action is generally more costly than a premature intervention. Delayed activation may render macroprudential policy ineffective, as there is insufficient time for policy instruments to gain traction, or it may even trigger a crisis by initiating the disorderly unwinding of imbalances. Implementing macroprudential policy too early, in contrast, is likely to incur unnecessary regulatory costs and may weaken the impact of the chosen instrument, as market participants will have more time to develop strategies to avoid and arbitrage them. Reversing macroprudential policy is problematic as well. Deactivating macroprudential policy too early may give market participants a wrong signal and prolong the crisis, while deactivating them too late may amplify procyclical effects by forcing banks to deliver more than is needed to satisfy additional macroprudential buffers.

The Committee on the Global Financial System (CGFS) established a Working Group, chaired by José-Manuel González-Páramo (then Board member at the European Central Bank), to provide practical guidance for policy makers on how macroprudential instruments should be chosen, combined and applied (see CGFS 2012). Specifically, the excellent CGFS's report provides guidance on how to assess three high-level criteria that are key in determining the selection and application of macroprudential instruments from a practical perspective: (1) the ability to determine the appropriate timing for the activation or deactivation of the instrument, (2) the effectiveness of the instrument in achieving the stated policy objective, and (3) the efficiency of the instrument in terms of a cost–benefit assessment, conditional on the impact of other regulatory measures.

In trying to operationalize these criteria, the report proposes a number of practical tools. First, to help policy makers determine the appropriate timing for the activation and deactivation of their policy tools, the report lays out stylized scenarios in which macroprudential instrument settings may be tightened or released. The identification of these states is facilitated by two alternative approaches (top-down and bottom-up) that seek to link systemic risk analysis and instrument selection. To determine the optimal timing of the release of macroprudential policy, it is important to condition on whether the downturn of the financial cycle coincides with a financial crisis or not. In a crisis context, macroprudential policy may need to be relaxed to avoid excessive deleveraging. However, this may need to be combined with an increase in the overall level of capital and liquidity in the system to restore market confidence. When the downturn in the financial cycle does not coincide with a crisis, relaxing the macroprudential policy stance may be warranted to soften the impact of the downturn and avoid unnecessary deleveraging. Finally, when the economy is booming but the financial cycle is turning, policy makers face a trade-off. In such situations, a relaxation of macroprudential policy may help absorb part of the impact of the turning financial cycle at the risk of delaying appropriate responses by banks to boost capital and liquidity.

Second, to support the evaluation of the effectiveness and efficiency of macroprudential tools for a range of macroprudential instruments, the report proposes "transmission maps"—stylized presentations of how changes in individual instruments are transmitted and expected to contribute to the objectives of macroprudential policy. For example, on capital requirements, the report concludes that "Empirical evidence...indicates that capital-based macroprudential policy instruments are effective in affecting (i) the price and (ii) the quantity of credit, even though the uncertainty about precise magnitudes is relatively large."

Third, the report discusses the interaction between macroprudential instruments as well as between macroprudential policy and other policies, such as monetary, fiscal, and regulatory policy (as we do in section 10.5). Macroprudential policy instruments will tend to be complements that can be used to address different aspects of systemic risk at the level of individual vulnerabilities. For example, excessive leverage can be curtailed both through raising capital requirements and a tightening of LTV ratios.

In addition, there are potential interactions between macroprudential tools. For example, a tightening of capital-based instruments may reduce house prices, which in turn affects the tightness of LTV policies. Equally, in response to tighter LTV ratios, banks may change their asset holdings, thus impacting on capital requirements. This suggests that combinations of tools should be considered when implementing macroprudential policies in practice.

The optimal policy mix is likely to be highly country specific and depend on the state of the economic and financial cycles. During boom periods with excessive buildup of leverage, for example, it may be most prudent to not only constrain the buildup of leverage with capital-based tools, but also target borrowers directly by tightening limits on LTV or DTI ratios.

To implement such a policy mix, policy makers need to have legal powers over a range of policy tools that can address the main sources of systemic risk, in both the time series and cross-sectional dimension. However, the range of tools over which these powers can be used needs to be limited because there is a risk that tools interact in unanticipated ways. This is especially the case for policies such as countercyclical liquidity requirements, where evidence to date on their effectiveness and impact is rather limited.

9.5   Effectiveness of Macroprudential Policies: Evidence to Date

The empirical evidence to date on the effectiveness of macroprudential tools is mixed to somewhat positive, in part because of limited experience of countries using these tools. An exception is Lim et al. (2011) who show, on the basis of IMF survey results, that for a sample of forty-nine countries from 2000 to 2010 a number of macroprudential instruments proved to be effective in reducing the procyclicality of credit and leverage.

Moreover the adoption of macroprudential tools frequently occurs in response to signs of growing risks and imbalances in the financial system, making it hard to (empirically) identify the impact of the macroprudential tool—namely to create a counterfactual on how the buildup of the imbalances would be without the tool. In addition macroprudential tools happen in combination with traditional macroeconomic policies, making it difficult to disentangle the independent effect of macroprudential policy on managing systemic risk. Nevertheless, macroprudential tools have been met with some success in a number of countries, although they have tended to perform better in reducing excessive costs during boom-bust cycles rather than in preventing them altogether (Dell' Ariccia et al. 2012).

Country experience with the most common macroprudential tools can be summarized as follows. Instruments to build capital and liquidity buffers, such as capital surcharges and time-varying capital requirements, have been broadly successful in building up buffers to reduce the ex post adverse consequences from a financial crisis for financial stability and the supply of credit to the real economy. With some exceptions they have also been less successful in curtailing the ex ante incidence and duration of credit booms. Where reserve requirements were increased substantially during boom years, banks were forced to keep a high share of liquid assets, which proved very useful when funding dried up during the bust. Similarly, where capital and/or provisioning requirements were made stricter, banking systems had a better capacity subsequently to absorb loan losses.

For example, in Poland, capital requirements were raised in reaction to buoyant activity in credit markets through a recommendation of a quasi-regulatory nature in 2006. This move is seen as having been effective in curbing the growth of foreign currency denominated loans to households and in keeping the banking system resilient during the global financial crisis in 2007 to 2008 (Kruszka and Kowalczyk 2011).

Similarly tight capital and reserve requirements in Croatia are viewed as having been effective in increasing the banks' liquidity and capital buffers, helping Croatian banks weather the global financial crisis, but as less effective in slowing credit growth and capital inflows (Kraft and Galac 2011).

A very interesting case are the dynamic loan loss provisioning rules introduced in Spain in 2000 as these are countercyclical capital requirements, there has been a full credit cycle to observe (2000–2013), Bank of Spain has excellent data to disentangle credit demand and supply boom and bust, and there were several changes to the policy. Jiménez et al. (2013) empirically analyze the impact of these provisions on credit supply and associated real effects (the externalities to the real sector). Dynamic provisions are not related to bank-specific losses, are forward-looking provisions, which build up a buffer before any credit loss is recognized on an individual loan (i.e., the dynamic provision fund) from retained profits in good times that can then be used to cover the realized losses in bad times (i.e., those times when specific provisions surpass the average specific provisions over the credit cycle). The buffer is therefore countercyclical. The required provisioning in good times is over and above specific average loan loss provisions and there is a regulatory reduction of this provisioning (to cover specific provision needs) in bad times, when bank profits are low and new shareholders' funds through, for example, equity injections are costly. Dynamic provisioning has been discussed extensively by policy makers and academics alike, and dynamic provision funds are now considered to be tier 2 regulatory capital.[11]

The authors analyze its introduction in 2000, a modification in 2005 still during good times, its amendment and reaction in 2008 when a severe crisis shock struck causing bad times. The policy changes coupled with comprehensive bank-level, firm-level, loan-loan, and loan-application-level data provide for an almost ideal setting for identification to understand well the workings of a macroprudential policy. To identify the availability of credit the authors employ a comprehensive credit register that comprises loan (i.e., bank-firm) data on *all* outstanding business loan contracts, loan applications for noncurrent borrowers, and balance sheets of all banks collected by the supervisor. They calculate the total credit exposures by each bank to each firm in each quarter, from 1999:Q1 to 2010:Q4. Hence the sample period includes six quarters before the first policy experiment (essential to run placebo tests) and more than two years of the financial crisis. They analyze changes in committed credit volume, on both the intensive and extensive margins, and also credit drawn, maturity, collateral and cost. By matching with firm balance sheets and the register for firm deaths, they can also assess the effects on firm-level total assets, employment, and survival.

Their estimates show that countercyclical dynamic provisioning can smooth cycles in the supply of credit and in bad times upholds firm financing and performance. Effects are strongest in crisis times. Firms with banks with a 1 percentage point higher dynamic provision funds (over loans) prior to the crisis get a 6 percentage points higher credit *availability* growth, a 2.5 percentage points higher asset growth, a 2.7 percentage points higher employment growth, and a 1 percentage point higher likelihood of survival.

Aiyar, Calomiris, and Wieladek (2014) examine micro evidence on UK bank capital regulation and credit. In the United Kingdom, regulators have imposed time-varying, bank-specific minimum capital requirements since Basel I. Capital requirements increase in good times, so the regulation could be seen as macroprudential. Over the 1998 to 2007 period, the authors find that UK regulated banks reduced lending in response to tighter capital requirements. But non–UK regulated banks (resident foreign branches) increased lending in response to tighter capital requirements on a relevant reference group of regulated banks. This "leakage" was material although only partial: it offset by about one third the initial impulse from the regulatory change. These results suggest that, on balance, changes in capital requirements can have a substantial impact on aggregate credit supply by UK resident banks. But they also affirm the importance of cross-country cooperation on macroprudential policies as macroprudential policies can be partly arbitraged (in this case by foreign bank branches). Such a substitution of domestic loans by foreign ones could be efficient, as it reduces credit crunch, if foreign banks do not bear the same risks and their activity does not support the bubble; it could be inefficient if foreign banks benefit from an unfair, regulatory driven, competitive advantage while facing the same risks.

In an interesting case targeting a specific class of assets, in December 2010, the Brazilian authorities raised the risk weight on high-LTV car loans, thereby raising capital requirements for such loans, to restrain the rapid growth in this segment. Preliminary evidence suggests that this move has had its intended effect of raising interest rates on car loans and slowing down the supply of such credit.

Measures to limit asset concentration and credit growth have been met with some success in slowing down the pace of credit, although often at the expense of building up concentrations of risk elsewhere in the system. For example, while credit growth in Romania remained strong despite a wave of measures, strict foreign exchange exposure limits introduced between September 2005 and January 2007 managed to curb foreign currency denominated loan growth somewhat. In Croatia, speed limits on credit growth by banks introduced in 2003 (limiting the annual growth of banks' domestic credits to 16 percent), combined with a penalty in the form of minimum retained earnings if credit growth exceeded this limit, were met with some success in reducing the growth rate of bank credit (which fell from 28.7 percent in 2002 to 11.8 percent in 2003) as the penalty for breaching the rule was high. However, the growth of total domestic credit (including credit from nonbanks) barely declined as banks circumvented the rule by booking loans directly on their foreign parent banks and by lending to the private sector through their nonbank (e.g., leasing company) subsidiaries (Kraft and Galac 2011). This contributed to the buildup of systemic risk in the nonbank financial sector.

Experience with the introduction of loan eligibility criteria is limited, but where they have been used, they seem to have been effective in curbing the deterioration in lending standards typically associated with credit booms (Dell'Ariccia et al. 2008). For example, the resilience of the banking system in Hong Kong during the Asian financial crisis in 1998 has been attributed to the introduction of actively managed LTV and DTI restrictions (Wong et al. 2011). Similarly, in Korea, LTV and DTI limits seem to have discouraged speculation in housing markets (Igan and Kang 2011). In Poland, loan eligibility requirements on foreign currency denominated mortgage loans are being credited for keeping default rates during the global financial crisis low, despite the zloty's significant depreciation against the currencies (euro and Swiss franc) in which these loans were denominated.

Quantitative evidence on the strength of transmission channels for liquidity-based measures is hardly addressed in the literature, due to the fact that most of the tools are not yet implemented. However, some inference can be drawn from studies looking at the potential effects of Basel III liquidity requirements or reserve requirements, both the impact on resilience, the impact on the credit cycle, and the impact on output.

Van den End and Kruidhof (2012) analyze the systemic implications of a cyclical application of the liquidity coverage ratio (LCR) in a liquidity stress-testing model, which takes into account the endogeneity stemming from bank reactions and second-round feedback effects (see CGFS 2012 for an exhaustive review of this and other empirical results). The authors show that a flexible approach of the LCR, in particular one that recognizes less liquid assets in the buffer in times of stress, is a useful macroprudential instrument to mitigate its adverse side effects during times of stress. Lowering the minimum level of the LCR in times of stress postpones banks from breaching the LCR requirement and thus the development of negative feedback spirals. Hence a cyclical application of the LCR increases resilience.

Given the experience in Latin America on liquidity requirements, there is evidence that reserve requirements on insured and uninsured deposits decrease credit supply. For instance, Gelos (2009) finds that increasing reserve requirements on demand deposits by 10 percentage points increases net interest margins by around 0.4 to 0.7 percentage points. For Brazil, there seems to be evidence that reserve requirements can affect bank interest rates on loans with little impact on loan default rates, while there also seem to be implications for banks' and nonfinancial companies' stock returns (Carvalho and Azevedo 2008). In another study on Brazil, Evandro, and Takeda (2011) conclude that reserve requirements lead to a contraction in credit for households, especially from smaller banks. Using the credit register in Uruguay, Dassati and Peydró (2013) find that reserve requirements for short-term foreign deposits, including interbank deposits, reduce the credit supply with negative effects at the firm-level.

As a whole, macroprudential tools show some promise in dealing with the buildup of systemic risk to prevent systemic crises, especially given their more targeted nature as compared to traditional macroeconomic policies, and especially the tools are important in reducing the systemic costs once a crisis occurs. However, more time and more empirical and conceptual analysis are needed for a full assessment of their effectiveness. In fact some experimenting in policies could be useful to understand better macroprudential policies; however, these policies are too important for policy makers to learn by experimenting.[12] Moreover a potential problem with the more targeted nature of macroprudential instruments is that it makes them more susceptible to circumvention, arbitrage, and political influence as compared to monetary policy (see chapter 10).

9.6 Boundaries and Limits of Macroprudential Regulation

Although macroprudential regulation serves to reduce systemic risk, its introduction can have undesirable consequences due to regulatory arbitrage. Regulatory arbitrage—the transfer of activity from a regulated sector to a less regulated or unregulated sector—can displace and thus restore systemic risk. For example, by imposing stricter and more costly regulation on the banking sector in order to reduce systemic risks, activity could flow to other sectors such as the insurance industry. Thus systemic risk will migrate from one heavily regulated sector to another more lightly regulated sector. Regulatory arbitrage may end up masking or increasing systemic risks rather than decreasing them by shifting credit activity into less-regulated intermediaries or to riskier loan types (Kane 1977; Borio 2003, 2009). Such regulatory arbitrage complicates the control of systemic risk and raises the question about the boundary of regulation.

A key segment of the market that so far has gone largely unregulated is the shadow banking system (except for the shadow banking activity carried about by already regulated financial entities, e.g., commercial banks, broker-dealers, and insurance companies). Under the right conditions, the existence of shadow banking which is less tightly regulated than the formal banking system can be efficient (as explained earlier in section 8.5). Specifically, for shadow banking to be efficient, two conditions need to be met. First, the transfer of risks to the shadow banking sector should not distort in any way the risks taken by the originating banks. Second, the ultimate risk should be borne by well-diversified institutions that either cannot go bankrupt or whose bankruptcy has no social cost, because it does not affect financial stability, does not cause contagion or an increase in overall macrofragility. Clearly, these two conditions are not met in the real world, as evidenced by the financial instability and real effects caused by the collapse of the US shadow banking system in 2008, including the freeze in wholesale funding markets, the decline in securitization, and the collapse of ABCP vehicles. Thus there is a strong argument in favor of extending the boundary of financial regulation into shadow banking.

To be effective, macroprudential regulations should apply comprehensively to all levered institutions, so that heavily regulated banks do not have an incentive to shift activities to lightly regulated institutions during an economic boom. This raises the issue of the boundary of financial regulation.

For example, countercyclical capital requirements—raising bank capital requirements significantly in good times, while allowing them to fall somewhat in bad times—have been proposed by many as a form of "cycle-proof" regulation (e.g., Brunnermeier et al. 2009), and such form of macroprudential regulation has already been included as part of the new Basel III framework.

Yet the effectiveness of countercyclical capital requirements is not without doubts. By forcing banks to hold more capital during booms than the market demands, they will shift activity to unregulated intermediaries. Similarly forcing banks to hold less capital than the market demands during crisis times is bound to fail "as the will of the market will naturally prevail" (Rajan 2009). Such unintended consequences need to be taken into account when crafting new regulations.

Identifying the boundary of regulation is a challenging task, because the regulatory perimeter will naturally shift as banks respond to new regulations by shifting activity to lightly regulated or unregulated parts of the financial sector. The intensity and span of regulation should be guided by a financial institution's size, leverage, and interconnectivity with the rest of the financial system, and be balanced against the desire not to distort the allocation of private capital.

In the United States the setting up of the Financial Stability Oversight Council under the Dodd–Frank Act has been an important step toward reducing the buildup of systemic risk, by giving the Federal Reserve the flexibility to bring nonbank holding companies that it deems systemically important under its regulatory wings. Yet there remain important uncertainties surrounding the implementation of these new powers, including how to determine which nonbank institutions are systemically important and how wide to set the regulatory perimeter given the costs of excessive regulation.

To the extent that banks are central to the functioning of nonregulated entities or have important relationships with other financial intermediaries (and regulators have access to such information), one can indirectly regulate parts of the financial system through banks. This is the case for the US shadow banking system where banks are the primary brokers of hedge funds. Moreover, if banks engage in many nonbanking activities, say through subsidiaries, regulators already have direct oversight over parts of the nonbanking financial system. This is the case for US bank holding companies, which have nonbank subsidiaries that play an important role in securitization markets (see Cetorelli and Peristiani 2012) and which are already subject to regulatory oversight. Thus, by regulating parts of the financial system through banks (or other entities that fall within the regulatory perimeter) regulators can accomplish a more far-reaching span and intensity of oversight than would be implied by the simple boundaries set by regulation.

Another difficulty in delineating the boundaries of macroprudential policy is that other public policies also affect financial stability. While primary responsibility for ensuring the stability of the financial system needs to rest with macroprudential policy, other policies (e.g., monetary and competition policy) should be able to complement it. No matter how different policy mandates are structured, addressing financial stability and systemic risk is a common responsibility (IMF 2011b).

Even countercyclical and other macroprudential regulations themselves may not be immune to the cycle. At the height of a crisis a popular call for tougher regulations is counterproductive to the desire to implement countercyclical regulations. And in good times, once memories of the current crisis abate, the political pressure to relax regulations or their enforcement will increase.

Moreover, since the losers and winners of a particular measure are more clear-cut than in the case of ex ante macroeconomic policies, it might be easier to gather and organize public opposition to the implementation of certain measures. There is then a tension between a rule-based approach to the application of these measures to minimize political interference and a discretionary one that could better deal with regulatory arbitrage. In comparison, it was relatively easy to give monetary independence to central banks as they have basically one or two instruments and one clear and easily measurable objective. On the contrary, macroprudential policy has an objective which is not easily measurable and has many potential instruments.

The current regulatory framework has very much relied on the market giving a helping hand to the regulators to keep banks in check and safeguard financial stability. Unfortunately, not only the regulator but also the market was unable to act preventively and in the interest of the public.

In principle, shareholders and debtholders of banks are supposed to discipline the manager from taking risks that are not in their own interest. This is known as market discipline. Given that shareholders only stand to gain when the bank does well and their losses are limited, they will encourage bank managers to take more risk than is socially optimal.[13] Moreover these risk-taking incentives from shareholders are higher with higher leverage, and some banks were even leveraged to more than 30 to 1. It is therefore up to debtholders who stand to lose the most from a bank failure to ensure that the bank takes prudent risk. However, with depositors enjoying protection of their investment in the form of government deposit insurance and uninsured debtholders enjoying implicit government protection from government bailouts, banking regulation has largely displaced debtholder discipline.[14] In fact ex post, with an increase in deposit insurance and in some cases guarantees for wholesale deposits and even senior debt, it was rational to some debtholders neither to monitor nor to discipline banks.

Market discipline of banks is also difficult because bank risk is hard to assess by outsiders. Banks are opaque and engage in complex financial transactions. This makes it difficult to assess the risk that banks take, including for the banks' shareholders and debtholders that are supposed to discipline bank managers from taking excessive risks. For example, Huizinga and Laeven (2011) show that shareholders were able to distinguish between good and bad banks only during the onset of the crisis, in other words, too late into the game, and that accounting information of banks during the crisis had deteriorated to the point of becoming a misleading guide for investors.[15]

Moreover market discipline has been little defense against the macroprudential risks that come with the economy cycle. Markets too are complacent while the music plays. In the boom, almost all financial institutions look good, and differentiation among banks is poor. Market discipline is therefore generally too lax during good times when asset prices explode. This is in part due to behavioral biases as for example limited memory by neglecting tail risks in good times, but also because of agency problems as the wholesale market is composed of financial intermediaries who invest money from others and who benefit from short-term profits. So the marginal provider of finance to a bank is another bank or financial intermediary with also high incentives for risk-taking.

Santos (2009) finds that credit spreads (over treasuries) in the primary market of bonds issued by banks are lower during booms than during recessions, even when compared to credit spreads for nonfinancial firms, implying that investors in bank debt demand lower risk premiums during booms. As Warren Buffett, the world's most famous investor, remarked: "you see who is swimming naked only when the tide runs out." During busts, when asset prices implode, the market often punishes banks too severely, as illiquidity problems and asset fire sales result in an overreaction by the market. It would therefore be unwise to rely exclusively on market discipline to deal with systemic risks.

Determining optimal macroprudential policy is also complicated by the lack of a generally accepted framework for quantifying the trade-offs involved in implementing macroprudential policy. Surely there are powerful macroprudential tools at authorities' disposal, even while new tools are being developed and added to the existing arsenal. These include capital controls, credit speed limits, reserve requirements, etc. However, many of these are blunt tools and while correcting imbalances that they target they may generate other distortions or be detrimental to economic growth and welfare.

For example, from Dell'Ariccia et al. (2012) we know that only one in three credit booms end up in crises. While surely there are powerful tools, such as credit speed limits, that, if effectively applied, can stop credit booms, such tools could also kill good credit booms that result in sustainable financial deepening and economic growth. Factoring in the counterfactual is difficult and distinguishing credit demand (fundamentals) driven booms from those based on excessive risk-taking is only possible with very detailed microdata from credit registers.

9.7 Conclusions

In this chapter we discussed the limits of microprudential regulation and the rationale for macroprudential regulation. We classified macroprudential tools into two categories: those that deal with the time dimension and those that deal with the cross-sectional dimension of systemic risk. We considered the strengths and weaknesses of these tools and the trade-offs involved in choosing an optimal policy mix. We emphasized the preventive role of macroprudential policy in limiting the possibility and impact of financial crises, and concluded that the macroprudential policy mix needs to be chosen such that it includes both the time dimension and the cross-sectional dimension of systemic risk. Macroprudential policy needs strong oversight to prevent the buildup of systemic risk through correlated risk exposures and risk-taking by systemically important financial intermediaries.

10 Monetary Policy and Systemic Risk

The 2008 global economic and financial crisis shook the consensus on how to conduct macroeconomic policy, notably monetary policy, and also showed the importance of financial intermediaries for the macroeconomy and monetary policy. Before the crisis, the common view was that monetary policy should only target inflation, not "lean against" credit and asset price bubbles; instead, monetary policy should be used to clean up the mess arising from the bursting of the bubble, if anything (e.g., the Bernanke–Svensson–Greenspan view).[1]

The large economic costs associated with credit and asset price busts and doubts about the effectiveness of new prudential regulatory tools reopened the "lean versus clean" debate on how to deal with credit and asset price bubbles. On prudential policy, for example, an important source of the crisis was capital regulatory arbitrage through the shadow banking sector. Hence new prudential measures, apart from being largely untested, can also be partially arbitraged and thus evaded. Moreover we now understand better the process of the ex ante buildup of financial imbalances—credit booms are central for the worst asset price bubbles—and monetary policy can have an ex ante preventive role as it affects credit developments, both in terms of volume and risk composition.

The critical role of monetary policy in managing this recent crisis has moreover shown the relevance of monetary policy as a means to reduce systemic costs ex post. However, this role for central banks is not new. Financial stability has long been a key objective for central banks, going back to the first central bank, the Bank of Sweden, which was established in 1668 (followed soon after by the Bank of England).[2] Toward the end of the nineteenth century, following a number of banking panics in the United Kingdom, the modern lender of last resort function was created, whereby the central bank, as argued by Bagehot

(1873), would lend freely, but at a high rate of interest relative to the pre-crisis period and only to borrowers with good collateral (with assets valued at between panic and pre-panic prices).[3] However, as originally designed for a financial system in which intermediation was almost entirely through banks, the lender of last resort function only applied to deposit-taking banks. This proved to be a shortcoming during the recent financial crisis, which also affected other financial intermediaries. The last crisis has shown that to preserve financial stability, central banks acting in their function as lenders of last resort need to cover other financial intermediaries to ensure the liquidity of the financial system as a whole. Central banks have flexibly increased their traditional lender of last resort function both in scale and scope, notably through long-term liquidity to banks and non–deposit-taking institutions, change in collateral rules to access liquidity, and the extension of liquidity to specific market segments and (indirectly) sovereigns.[4] Apart from unconventional monetary measures to support the banking system, the zero lower bound on monetary rates has implied a move to forward guidance in policy to affect medium- and long-term rates. Moreover, given the financial globalization experienced in the last decades, a key policy during the recent crisis has been the establishment of liquidity swap lines among central banks, for example, to provide dollar funding to European banks. Central banks have even bought financial securities (e.g., private and public debt), expanding substantially their balance sheets, the so-called quantitative easing.

There is therefore a potential direct role for monetary policy both in terms of preventing the buildup of systemic risk and in terms of managing such systemic risk when it arises. In the previous chapters we have seen that systemic crises are generally preceded by credit booms, and hence this is not unique to the last global financial crisis; in fact, historically, credit booms have proved to be the strongest predictor of financial crises. However, credit booms triggered by strong economic fundamentals (credit demand) are generally not dangerous for systemic risk. In fact only one-third of credit booms are followed by financial crises.[5] It is the buildup of financial imbalances, through leverage and excessive risk-taking by financial intermediaries, that is the most dangerous source of systemic risk associated with credit booms. Historical evidence indeed suggests that the worst credit booms are accompanied by strong asset price bubbles and monetary expansions (Brunnermeier and Schnabel 2014; Jordà et al. 2014).

Once the financial crisis arrives, the central transmission channel for systemic risk is the reduction of the credit supply, which gives rise to a credit crunch with strong negative externalities from the financial to the real sector. The capital and liquidity problems in financial intermediaries and the weak balance sheets and debt overhang problems of firms and households lower the availability of credit for households and firms, in turn causing a reduction in aggregate output, employment, and welfare. A related channel operates through a reduction in asset prices, leading to fire sales in asset prices, and this also reduces aggregate output, employment, and welfare.

Credit cycles (especially when supply-driven) therefore can induce systemic risk, especially when credit finances asset price bubbles. As monetary policy influences credit supply and demand, it is a natural policy tool to reduce systemic risk, both from an ex ante (preventive) perspective, in the boom before the crisis arrives, and from an ex post (crisis management) perspective to minimize the systemic costs of credit crunches and of illiquidity problems in financial institutions. Moreover, not only can monetary policy be important for the *time* perspective of systemic risk (the credit and asset price cycle) but also for the *cross-sectional* dimension, since monetary policy can be extended to *all* financial intermediaries to reduce regulatory arbitrage, with the highest impact for the financial intermediaries with the highest short-term leverage—that is, the most financially fragile institutions.

An important backward-looking motivation for this chapter is that many commentators have suggested that low levels of monetary policy rates in United States and Europe induced an excessive softening of lending standards, notably on real estate, in the run-up to the 2008 global financial crisis.[6] For instance, Rajan (2005), in his famous speech in Jackson Hole as IMF Chief Economist, pointed out that a low short-term interest rate may make riskless assets less attractive and may lead to a search for yield by financial intermediaries with short-term time horizons.[7] Many others have played down the monetary policy link and argue instead that the low levels of long-term interest rates (as a consequence of the saving glut and global imbalances) were the key contributing macro factors (Bernanke 2010).

Looking at the developments during the crisis, it is clear that monetary policy has been the critical tool used to reduce the systemic costs of the crisis, both through a massive reduction of policy rates and the use of nonstandard monetary measures. However, these measures have come at the expense of increased expectations of future bailouts and thus increased excessive risk (moral hazard). Moreover there are a number of concerns surrounding the exit from these unconventional monetary policies, notably as a significant part of the Western financial system has become addicted to the massive liquidity provided by central banks, and there has been a period of large international capital flows to emerging markets. A key concern for systemic risk is the normalization of interest rates by raising monetary policy rates from the historically low levels seen today to their normal levels. A rapid increase in interest rates can increase credit risk of banks' loan portfolios and lead to losses from a repricing of (long-term) debt instruments, yet maintaining interest rates at low levels for too long a period can also be detrimental to systemic risk by encouraging leverage and excessive risk-taking by banks. Striking the right balance is a fine balancing act for central banks.

Moreover there are concerns associated with a reversal of capital flows to emerging markets when the policy rates increase to normal levels from their low levels today. This risk already materialized during the "tapering talk" in the United States, which triggered some capital outflows from emerging markets in late 2013. For emerging markets, the tightening of monetary policy in the United States could imply a "sudden stop" of capital flows, especially for countries with weaker fundamentals that received strong capital inflows during the boom.

Looking forward, the new responsibilities for the major central banks (e.g., the Federal Reserve, the European Central Bank, and the Bank of England) in the area of financial stability imply that a key question is the relationship between monetary policy and macroprudential policy. This is not a new role per se. Historically the foremost concern of central bankers has been financial stability. Endeavors to ensure their financial stability should have consequences for the organization, accountability, and independence of central banks.

This chapter shows that monetary policy influences credit and asset price booms and excessive risk-taking by financial intermediaries. Monetary policy influences real term premiums (including at longer maturities) and the composition of the supply of credit due to "search for yield" and risk-shifting incentives in financial intermediaries (i.e., the risk-taking channel) arising from limited liability and leverage (Allen and Gale 2003; Rajan 2005; Borio and Zhu 2012; Adrian and Shin 2011; Dell'Ariccia et al. 2014; Jiménez et al. 2014a). This finding is at odds with standard New Keynesian macro models, in which the central bank's ability to influence real variables stems from goods' prices that are sticky in nominal terms; in such models, a change in monetary policy should have no effect on forward real rates at a horizon longer than that over which all prices can adjust, and it seems implausible that this horizon could be in the order of ten years (Stein 2013b).[8]

Macroprudential tools can provide a new policy lever to curb dangerous booms and contain imbalances. However evidence about their effectiveness is mixed, not in the least because macroprudential policies can often be arbitraged away, and our understanding of how best to implement macroprudential policy is still in its infancy. Therefore for the time being monetary policy may need to "lean against the wind" (i.e., be less accommodative) to reduce the buildup of financial imbalances and fragility, even if as a policy it may be less targeted than macroprudential policy. Over time, the implementation of a macroprudential approach will reduce the need for monetary policy to focus on financial stability issues. Using monetary stimulus during financial crises to boost demand and ease the interest rate burden on highly indebted borrowers remains an appropriate policy tool to manage the fallout of financial crises on the economy. However, these actions need to be traded off against the risks of generating moral hazard and search for yield behavior, with the possibility of seeding the next crisis. Moreover, using central bank liquidity to support insolvent banks comes at the risk of delaying the financial restructuring process, giving time to distressed banks to gamble for resurrection, and delaying an economic recovery. Additionally international spillovers of unconventional monetary policy (e.g., quantitative easing and tapering talk in the United States) can pose significant risks to global financial stability, especially in emerging markets (an issue we take up in more detail in chapter 11). Importantly, evidence shows that ex ante macroprudential policy can diminish the need for ex post expansive monetary policy through the buildup of higher capital and liquidity buffers that can be tapped into during the crisis and by installing less dependence of short-term wholesale liquidity (which is very fragile).

All in all, we show that there is a role for monetary policy to combat systemic risk, but that part of this role will be reduced once macroprudential policy frameworks have been credibly established and are fully operational.

The objective of financial stability exists alongside central banks' main objective of price stability. The two objectives are complementary in the sense that price stability is a precondition for financial stability. But the two objectives can also be conflicting—such as when debt overhang problems and associated financial stability concerns demand a higher inflation than price stability considerations alone would suggest (to reduce debt written in nominal terms)—and therefore additional macroprudential instruments alongside monetary policy are needed. As the recent crisis has made clear, central banks cannot ignore asset prices and credit conditions when setting monetary policy.

The remaining parts of this chapter are divided in the following subsections: First, we analyze the pre-crisis view of monetary policy and systemic risk. Second, we analyze how monetary policy influences credit cycles. Third, we analyze the risk-taking channel of monetary policy and credit and asset bubbles. Fourth, we analyze the ex post crisis management role of monetary policy for systemic risk. Fifth, we analyze the interrelations between macroprudential and monetary policy. Finally, we offer some concluding remarks on the topic of monetary policy and systemic risk.

10.1   The Limits of the Pre-crisis View of Monetary Policy and Systemic Risk

The prevailing view before the 2008 global financial crisis was that monetary policy is best used to prevent inflation and not to control financial imbalances in the economy such as credit booms and asset price bubbles.[9] One of the arguments for central banks' special attention to inflation was the so-called divine coincidence. This is the view of central banks that by maintaining price stability, monetary policy could keep output close to its potential. And even though "no central bank believed that the divine coincidence held exactly, it looked like a sufficiently good approximation to justify a primary focus on inflation and to pursue inflation targeting" (Blanchard et al. 2013, p. 5).

Inflation (in consumer prices) and output and inflation volatility were low before the crisis—the so-called great moderation—thus there were no warning signs of the buildup of excessive risk-taking leading up to the Great Recession. Major central banks such as the US Federal Reserve, the European Central Bank, and the Bank of England had helped deliver an unprecedented period of low and stable inflation in line with its mandate since the 1980s. But this meant that monetary short-term interest rates were low by historical standards.

Some central banks moreover reduced policy rates significantly during the 2002 to 2005 period. For example, the Fed kept rates at 1 percent until 2004 to clean up the burst of the 2000 dot-com bubble and the ECB kept rates at 2 percent for a prolonged period of time given both the economic problems in Germany and the low levels of US interest rates. Nominal rates were the lowest in several decades and below the Taylor rule implied rate in many countries, and even real rates were negative in some countries such as Ireland and Spain (Taylor 2007). Some have argued that policy rates were not unusually low when compared to the Taylor rule, since there were some (not realized) expectations of deflation (Bernanke 2010). But, all in all, the period leading up to the 2008 global financial crisis was characterized by low monetary policy rates and low inflation in consumer prices. However, there were some signs of credit booms and asset price bubbles, notably in real estate but also in sovereign debt markets (especially in peripheral Europe as compared to core euro area countries) and in risky firm, household, and bank assets.

Though the view before the crisis was that monetary policy should not target credit and asset price bubbles, it was also generally thought that price stability was a crucial condition for financial stability. Therefore, to manage output, employment, and systemic risk, the view was that central banks should target price stability. However, the financial crisis which occurred following the period of "great moderation" has challenged the view that price stability is sufficient for macroeconomic stability. During the pre-crisis period, excessive financial risks were built up that eventually led to the crisis. The severity of the recession that followed has questioned the benign neglect view to managing credit and asset price bubbles that existed prior to this crisis (Blanchard, Dell'Ariccia, and Mauro 2013). Given the high economic cost of the crisis, the issue of whether monetary policy should include financial stability among its targets has been high on the policy agenda since the start of the crisis.[10]

According to Blanchard et al. (2013), the monetary policy rate is not the best tool for dealing with the ex ante financial imbalances and excessive risk-taking by financial intermediaries that led to the crisis: "[i]ts reach is too broad to be cost effective" because higher monetary policy rates (not supported by higher inflation expectations) may reduce aggregate output and employment and not *all* the sectors suffer the buildup of financial imbalances. In addition some research suggests that monetary policy has limited power in affecting credit supply (Romer and Romer 1990) and some academics point out that lower monetary policy rates may actually reduce asset price bubbles, not create and increase them (Galí 2014).[11]

Instead, a consensus is emerging that more targeted macroprudential regulation should be used for dealing with systemic risk, which is the subject of this book. However, macroprudential tools are not a panacea and its implementation is not without challenges, as we explain in chapters 9 and 11. They are relatively new and their effectiveness is not without doubt. For example, they can partly be arbitraged away because, by their very nature, they target some sectors, thus leaving other parts of the financial system less regulated. Moreover, they may be subject to problematic political economy constraints (see the last chapter of the book). Given all these limitations, and given that we have a better understanding of the impact of low monetary rates on excessive credit and risk-taking, the debate on whether central banks should use the policy rate to lean against bubbles has been reignited.

A limitation of central banks choosing to lean against bubbles is that "bubbles are rarely identifiable with certainty in real time" (Bernanke and Gertler 2003; Blanchard et al. 2013, pp. 6–7). For instance, Greenspan (2002) has argued that while the Federal Reserve cannot recognize or prevent asset price booms, it can "mitigate the fallout when it occurs and, hopefully, ease the transition to the next expansion." The uncertainty about a bubble suggests that "central banks may have to react to large movements in some asset prices, without knowing whether such movements reflect strong fundamentals or [just] bubbles" (Blanchard, Dell'Ariccia, and Mauro 2013, p. 7). Given the huge economic costs associated with financial crises, "higher type I errors (assuming that it is a bubble and acting accordingly, when in fact the increase reflects fundamentals) in exchange for lower type II errors (assuming the increase reflects fundamentals, when in fact it is a bubble) may well be justified" (Blanchard et al. 2013, p. 7). This may be especially the case for certain asset price booms, such as those funded through bank credit, which have proved particularly dangerous in many financial crises throughout history (see Kindleberger 1978; Brunnermeier and Schnabel 2014; Jordà et al. 2014).

Moreover, as we discuss in chapters 4 and 7, there are potential real time indicators of excessive credit supply and risk-taking that can be used to identify credit bubbles in real time. For example, in United States, the credit bubble could have been identified in real time from the available data, which showed that there was a credit boom due to securitization (sold to third parties) well in advance of the first failures of subprime lenders in 2007, especially to subprime borrowers, even when the differential of income of prime over subprime borrowers was increasing, and even in areas in which real estate prices were not increasing (Mian and Sufi 2009). Or, in the case of Spain, where there is a comprehensive credit register, there were real time indicators that could have been used to identify that there was a credit boom mainly driven by banks that were lowly capitalized, depended more on securitization (both covered bonds and ABS) and wholesale funding markets (Jiménez et al. 2012, 2014a, b). So, especially for credit booms (and asset price bubble financed with credit), one can significantly decrease type I errors and, therefore, act preventively.

Finally, it is fair to say that financial intermediaries and financial imbalances (e.g., credit booms and market and funding illiquidity) were not considered to be very important by most macroeconomists before the crisis. Therefore it is not a surprise that the generally accepted view about monetary policy at the time was that the focus should be on inflation targeting rather than financial stability, and that macroprudential policy was largely an unknown area to macroeconomists. However, it was clear that there was a credit boom in several countries, and that credit booms were an important ex ante correlate of financial crises, with strong negative aggregate real effects (Kindleberger 1978).

10.2   Credit Cycles, Systemic Risk, and Monetary Policy

Credit cycles are crucial for systemic risk, as discussed in chapter 4, as they increase the likelihood of a systemic financial crisis, and conditional on the existence of a financial crisis, they increase real costs for the economy at large. Therefore an important use of monetary policy in limiting systemic risk may be via limiting credit growth. But does monetary policy affect credit cycles? And, if so, how?

The answer to these questions is very important for using monetary policy to limit ex ante and ex post systemic risk, but research was not conclusive on these issues. In the last issue of the *Handbook of Monetary Economics* (2011), Boivin, Kiley, and Mishkin (p. 415) state that "... one of the extremely important outstanding questions for research is the ... role of the credit channel in our understanding of economic fluctuations and monetary policy. The literature in this area remains thin, and this thinness reflects difficulty in specifying the relevant mechanisms and finding the supporting empirical evidence."

The so-called bank lending channel of monetary transmission states that central banks can shift banks' supply of credit. For example, according to the lending channel, an increase in reserve requirements leads banks to reduce loan supply, thereby raising the cost of capital to bank-dependent borrowers (see Kashyap and Stein 2000). Another way by which contractionary monetary policy reduces credit supply is through increasing short-term interest rates. Central banks by increasing monetary rates reduce the net worth of banks (as they are mainly financed with short-term debt claims), thus reducing their liquidity, and thereby causing a negative impact for their supply of credit to households and firms (see Bernanke 2007; Bernanke and Gertler 1995).

The bank lending channel is centered on the failure for banks of the frictionless world of Modigliani–Miller (MM) (1958; see also Kashyap and Stein 2000; Stein 1998, 2012). For example, when the Fed drains reserves from the system, it worsens banks' ability to raise reservable forms of finance (e.g., insured retail deposits), but it cannot constrain banks' use of nonreservable liabilities (the wholesale market—e.g., large-denomination CDs, covered bonds, or interbank deposits). In an MM world, banks are indifferent at the margin between issuing retail deposits and wholesale deposits because they would carry the same cost, so shocks to the former do not affect their lending decisions.

Hence, if there is an active bank lending channel of monetary policy, it must be that banks cannot without frictions obtain uninsured sources of funds to make up for a central bank-induced shortfall in insured deposits. As there are several key classes of bank liabilities not covered by deposit insurance that escape reserve requirements, they are potentially subject to adverse-selection problems and credit-rationing (both were crucial during the 2008 global financial crisis). In other words, if there is adverse selection in the market for wholesale finance, a bank that loses a dollar of insured deposits will not raise a full dollar of new wholesale financing to offset this loss.

Moreover the lending channel requires MM not to hold for firms; in particular, some borrowers (e.g., small and medium enterprises) cannot find perfect substitutes for bank loans. As banks can monitor and screen opaque borrowers, these may prefer bank loans as compared to market finance. Therefore a change in bank credit supply due to monetary policy has significant effects for firms.

The bank balance sheet channel of monetary policy implies that an increase in short-term rates negatively impacts bank lending by lowering bank net worth and reducing funding liquidity (see Bernanke 2007). Bernanke and Blinder (1988, 1992) showed that changes in the stance of monetary policy are followed by significant movements in aggregate bank lending volumes, consistent with changes in credit supply but also with credit demand because activity is being depressed via standard interest rate effects. Kashyap, Stein, and Wilcox (1993) show that while a monetary contraction reduces bank lending, it also increases commercial paper volumes. This suggests an inward shift in bank loan supply, rather than an inward shift in loan demand. However, other papers have questioned this interpretation: it is possible that in recessions there is a compositional shift, with large firms performing better than small ones, and actually demanding more credit; since most commercial paper is issued by large firms, this could explain the previous results (Oliner and Rudebusch 1996). However, Kashyap, Stein, and Wilcox (1996) note that even within the class of the largest firms, commercial paper rises relative to bank lending after a monetary contraction. Recent evidence by Becker and Ivashina (2013) and Adrian, Colla, and Shin (2012) provide recent firm-level micro evidence on this substitution between market debt and bank loans.

Several papers find that contractions in monetary policy intensify liquidity constraints in the inventory and investment decisions of small firms. While this is consistent with the bank lending channel, it is also consistent with what Bernanke and Gertler (1995) call a (nonfinancial borrower) "balance sheet channel," whereby tight monetary policy weakens the creditworthiness of small firms, and hence reduces their ability to raise funds from any external provider, not just banks. This channel may also be important for systemic risk in the sense that lower monetary policy rates—by increasing the net worth and collateral value (e.g., real estate) of firms and households—may amplify the credit cycle (e.g., see Kiyotaki and Moore 1997; Gertler and Gilchrist 1994). For example, asset price bubbles in real estate may support too much credit based on overvalued housing collateral, thus leading to debt overhang in correlated risky exposures once real estate prices collapse, generating large credit cycles with huge economic costs. Yet overvalued housing collateral can have positive effects by increasing economic output through alleviating credit restrictions of smaller firms (Martin and Ventura 2012).

Kashyap and Stein (2000) use bank level data to make progress in the identification of credit supply, as some banks should be more affected than others. With a twenty-year panel that includes quarterly data on every insured commercial bank in the United States (approximately one million bank quarters in all), they analyze whether there are important cross-sectional differences in the way that the lending of banks with varying characteristics responds to monetary policy shocks. In particular, they ask whether the impact of monetary policy on lending behavior is stronger for banks with less liquid balance sheets, where liquidity is measured by the ratio of securities to assets. The answer is a resounding "yes." Moreover their result is largely driven by the smaller banks—those in the bottom 95 percent of the size distribution.[12]

There are two crucial problems with the previous empirical identification. First, banks of different liquidity and size could face different borrowers (demand), and therefore it is not possible to identify credit supply without loan applications from the same borrower to different banks at the same time. Second, some (more affected) banks may reject more borrowers when monetary policy is tightened, but less affected banks could provide more finance (to the rationed firms), thereby neutralizing the aggregate effects of credit supply restrictions. Jiménez et al. (2012) address these two problems and, therefore, identify the impact of monetary policy on the supply of bank credit. They analyze a novel, supervisory dataset with loan applications from Spain.

Accounting for time-varying firm heterogeneity in loan demand, they find that tighter monetary policy substantially reduces loan granting, especially from banks with lower capital or liquidity ratios (banks with weak balance sheets).[13] Moreover firms cannot offset the resultant credit restriction by applying to other banks. All in all, monetary policy affects bank credit supply and the effects are binding. The estimated effects are also economically relevant. A 100 basis point increase in the interest rate reduces loan granting by weak banks by 11 percent more than by strong banks.[14]

Landier, Sraer, and Thesmar (2013) uncover another credit channel of monetary policy. They show empirically that banks' exposure to interest rate risk, or income gap, plays a crucial role in monetary policy transmission. When a bank borrows short term but lends long term at fixed rates, any increase in the short rate reduces its cash flows, which may prompt a need to raise additional capital. Since issuing equity is expensive, the bank has to reduce lending in order to prevent leverage from rising. This channel rests on three elements. First, commercial banks tend to operate with constant leverage targets (Adrian and Shin 2010). Second, banks are exposed to interest rate risk (Flannery and James 1984; Begeneau et al. 2012). Third, there is a failure of the Modigliani–Miller proposition, which prevents banks from issuing equity easily in the short run (see Kashyap and Stein 2000).

As pointed out by Kashyap and Stein (2000), the micro identification does not analyze the total effect of a monetary policy shock on real activity (how much GDP changes with a change of monetary policy through the different credit channels), but only a difference in difference effect by comparing banks (e.g., see Kashyap and Stein 2000) or nonfinancial borrowers (e.g., see Gertler and Gilchrist 1994) with different sensitivity to monetary policy. Ciccarelli, Maddaloni, and Peydró (2013, 2014) use the Bernanke and Blinder (1992) macro-type model and tackle the problem of unobserved credit channels by using the detailed answers of the confidential Bank Lending Survey (BLS) for the euro area and of the Senior Loan Officer Survey (SLOS) for the United States, which contain quarterly information on the lending standards that banks apply and on the loan demand that banks receive from firms and households. The information refers to the actual lending standards that banks apply to the whole pool of borrowers (not only to accepted loans).[15]

Ciccarelli, Maddaloni, and Peydró find that the credit channel amplifies a shock of monetary policy on GDP and inflation, through the balance sheets of households, firms, and banks. In the euro area all balance sheet channels are important in transmitting monetary policy shocks to GDP and inflation, with the bank lending and the demand channel being the most important channels for corporate and mortgage loans, respectively. Counterfactual experiments suggest that if they shut down the bank lending channel, the median effect on GDP growth of a monetary policy shock would be reduced at the peak by about 35 percent for both GDP and inflation. Further analysis based on disaggregated data suggests that heterogeneity of firms and banks may matter for the credit channel of monetary policy, with differences depending on the financial structure and on the borrower's category. Monetary policy has more impact on GDP through the credit granted to both large and small firms in the euro area, and to small firms only in the United States. In addition all channels in the euro area (demand, bank-lending, and borrower's balance sheet) are significant for both small and large banks.

All in all, monetary cycles do affect credit cycles—in particular, access to credit through the bank lending channel, and the firm and household balance sheet channel. Economic effects overall are important, but the importance of the different sub-channels depends on country circumstances. For example, the credit channel of monetary policy is likely more potent in economies dominated by banks (e.g., the euro area) than in economies where financing is provided to a large extent by nonbank financial intermediaries and markets (e.g., the United States); see Mihov 2001 and ECB (2009). [16]

10.3   The Risk-Taking Channel of Monetary Policy and Bubbles

So far we have seen that monetary policy affects credit supply by increasing liquidity to banks and improving the net worth and collateral value of banks, firms, and households. However, as we have seen throughout the book, banks face strong agency problems due to implicit and explicit government subsidies, high (short-term) leverage, little market discipline and deficient corporate governance. So, is there also an impact of monetary policy on banks' risk-taking? Do financial intermediaries have incentives to take excessive risks by searching for yield when monetary rates are low?

Adrian and Shin (2011) in the latest *Handbook of Monetary Economics* discuss the risk-taking channel of monetary policy arguing that monetary policy actions affect the risk-taking capacity of the banks, due to banks' moral hazard problems, and this leads to shifts in the supply of credit, both in aggregate volume and in the composition with respect to risk. Borio and Zhu (2012) have coined the term "risk-taking channel" of monetary policy to describe this set of effects working through the risk appetite of financial intermediaries. For these reasons, short-term interest rates matter directly for financial stability. They argue that this perspective on the importance of the short rate as a price variable is in contrast to previous monetary thinking, where short term rates matter only to the extent that they determine long-term interest rates, which are seen as being risk-adjusted expectations of future short rates.

Recent theory shows that expansive monetary policy through the increase in funding provided by households and other agents to banks may cause an increase in risk-shifting in lending, as banks face strong moral hazard problems—especially banks with lower capital amounts at stake that do not fully internalize loan defaults.[17]

Consistent with these theories, several central bankers and commentators are warning against the systemic risk consequences of the current environment of prolonged, extremely low policy rates, which provides incentives to reach for yield (i.e., investing in higher yielding but riskier securities) and may plant the seeds for the next credit and asset price bubbles (e.g., see speeches by Fed governor Jeremy Stein 2013 and the most recent BIS Annual Report 2014). They are calling for a tightening of monetary conditions, arguing that low rates are threatening financial stability by encouraging excessive leverage and risk-taking.

However, there is not a broad consensus on the relevance of the risk-taking channel of monetary policy, reflecting ambiguous theoretical predictions and different views about the relative importance of the underlying channels. Some central bankers play down the risk-taking channel (Svensson 2013) or even claim that an increase in risk-taking is desirable during an economic slowdown (e.g., Yellen 2014). They posit that monetary accommodation remains appropriate given persistent unemployment and argue that a monetary tightening can actually impair financial stability by weakening the economy, increasing the interest rate burden, and lowering asset values. The empirical evidence we discussed in the previous section shows that expansive monetary policy can increase credit supply and economic output in crisis times, and thus may be beneficial also for systemic risk by reducing the real costs of financial crises.

The idea that the liquidity provided by central banks is important in driving excessive risk-taking is, however, *not* new: as Kindleberger (1978) explains, "speculative manias gather speed through expansion of money and credit or perhaps, in some cases, get started because of an initial expansion of money and credit" (Kindleberger 1978, p. 54).

The initial models analyzing the impact of monetary policy on excessive risk-taking in lending are by Allen and Gale (2000c, 2003, 2007) and by Diamond and Rajan (2012)—for a summary of these models, see Allen and Rogoff (2011). The Allen and Gale models show the link between monetary policy, credit and asset price bubbles, and the model by Diamond and Rajan (2012) show the link between monetary policy and excessive risk-taking in lending due to bank moral hazard problems.

As Allen and Gale (2000, 2003, 2007) have argued, asset price bubbles are also caused by growth in credit due to bank agency problems. They show how a risk shifting problem in the banking system can lead to asset price bubbles. Their model is particularly applicable to real estate. Banks can buy assets at prices higher than fundamentals, thus entering into negative net present value investments, as they are financed with high short-term leverage. This risk-shifting is rational for bank shareholders as it yields positive expected payoffs for bank shareholders at the expense of bank depositors and debtholders (and taxpayers).

Credit expansion (financed through expansive monetary policy) encourages investors to fund risky investments today, and thus credit expansion has a contemporaneous effect on asset prices. However, the anticipation of future credit expansion can also increase the current price of assets and this can have an effect on the likelihood of a future crisis.

The Allen and Gale models explain how a bubble can arise but cannot explain why many countries operate without bubbles for long periods of time. An important extension, as explained by Allen and Rogoff (2011), would be to understand why there appear to be two regimes, one where fundamentals drive asset prices and one where there is a bubble. They argue that one of the important inputs into these two regimes is likely to be interest rates that are perceived to be temporarily low.[18] Thus by creating a very favorable environment for investment in real estate and other financial assets it is possible to depart from normal times and set off a bubble.[19]

This kind of theory of asset price bubbles can provide a justification for the need for monetary policy to lean against the wind: by maintaining a less accommodative monetary policy it may be possible to prevent the start of a bubble and by maintaining interest rates at relatively high levels and restricting credit it may be possible to cool off bubbles and prevent asset prices from reaching dangerously high levels. This will also reduce the severity of any subsequent collapse and possible crisis that will follow. Additionally this theory suggests that discretionary macroprudential policies that make it more expensive to finance real estate transactions could have an important role to play in limiting bubbles and subsequent financial crises (Allen and Rogoff 2011). Therefore stronger and better macroprudential policy implies less need for monetary policy to target systemic risk.

Diamond and Rajan (2012) provide another explanation for leaning against the wind in monetary policy due to banks' excessive risk-taking. They study the impact of monetary policy-induced changes in interest rates in an economy where banks invest in long-term illiquid projects and are financed by short-term debt in the form of demandable deposit claims from risk-averse households.[20] In case of widespread funding withdrawals (resulting in higher interest rates) that can trigger bank insolvencies, untargeted lending at penalty rates by the central bank to any solvent bank can reduce the possibility of a crisis. Such liquidity interventions by the central bank constitute a bailout.[21]

However, the central bank's willingness to lend ex post can result in more (excessive) bank risk-taking ex ante (a point also made by Farhi and Tirole 2012a).[22] The ex post central bank liquidity intervention implies a lower penalty on highly leveraged banks with low liquidity.

If banks expect that the central bank will reduce interest rates at times of financial stress, banks will take on more short-term leverage or make more risky and illiquid loans, thus increasing the likelihood of a crisis and bringing about the very need for intervention.

In such cases it may be better for the central bank to change banks' risk-taking incentives by altering its monetary policy. The central bank may want to indicate that it will raise interest rates in normal times above the market-determined level to preserve bank incentives to maintain low leverage and high liquidity. Stability-focused central banks should also be reluctant to create expectations that real rates will be low for an extended period for fear that bank responses will make the system more fragile and force the central bank to continue keeping rates low. While central banks have become more credible in fighting inflation by binding themselves to inflation targets, they may now have to build credibility in a new direction so as to enhance financial stability.[23]

Acharya and Naqvi (2012) also examine how the banking sector may ignite the formation of asset price bubbles when there is access to abundant bank liquidity and discuss the optimality of monetary policy to lean against the wind. They show that access to abundant liquidity aggravates bank risk-taking (moral hazard), giving rise to excessive lending and asset price bubbles. As banks become flush with liquidity they relax lending standards fueling credit booms and asset price bubbles and sowing seeds of the next crisis. Their model suggests that a central bank should follow a "leaning against liquidity" approach, adopting a contractionary monetary policy at times when banks are awash with liquidity.

Low interest rates can also increase risk-taking by increasing bank leverage. A decline in the safe interest rate reduces funding costs. For banks operating under limited liability, the decline in funding costs will increase leverage (Dell'Ariccia et al. 2014). The same may be true when a decline in interest rates reduces the cost of holding collateral or required reserves and banks face binding collateral constraints or reserve requirements (Stein 2012). The increase in leverage may in turn be associated with an increase in risk-taking since financial intermediaries that are protected on the downside by limited liability are less cautious in their portfolio allocation once they have less capital at stake. Similarly Adrian and Shin (2011) argue that a lower monetary policy rate increases risk-taking in bank lending by relaxing the bank capital constraint that is present due to bank moral hazard problems. Lower monetary rates reduce the credit risk of existing loans, thus softening the bank capital constraint, and thereby allowing banks to increase their supply of credit to marginal borrowers, which tend to have higher credit risk.

Low interest rates have a greater potential to increase risk-taking in those financial intermediaries that face rigidities on the liability of their balance sheets. For example, life insurance companies or private defined-benefit pension funds that are financed with predominantly long-term liabilities might "search for yield" when interest rates are low by investing in risky securities to generate sufficiently high returns to pay their liabilities (Rajan 2005). Money market funds are also prone to reach for yield in an attempt to cover administrative costs without increasing fees (Chodorow-Reich 2014b).

Yet other theories posit that monetary policy has ambiguous effects on risk-taking. Chodorow-Reich (2014b) argues that lower interest rates not only increase risk-taking by reallocating wealth from safe assets to risky projects but also affect the composition of the risk portfolio. In particular, a lower risk-free rate raises the hurdle rate for investment and induces risk-neutral agents to choose risky projects that have a lower risk profile (i.e., lower returns but lower risk). The impact on the riskiness of the risky investment portfolio is then shown to be ambiguous. The portfolio variance declines if the marginal projects that are financed have lower returns but lower risk, while it increases if they have higher returns but higher risk. Therefore it is possible that a reduction in interest rates leads to a reduction in overall risk-taking by decreasing the riskiness of risky assets, even though it increases the share allocated to risky assets.

Dell'Ariccia, Laeven, and Marquez (2014) also obtain ambiguous effects of monetary policy on risk-taking in a model of financial intermediation with asymmetric information. They show that the overall effect depends heavily on the endogenous response of the bank's leverage to a reduction in funding costs arising from a decline in interest rates. On the one hand, financial intermediaries tend to increase leverage in response to a reduction in funding costs, increasing the fraction of risky assets in their portfolio. On the other hand, the reduction in funding costs will reduce the risk shifting by banks that are protected by limited liability in case of insolvency, with the effect being the strongest for highly leveraged banks (as in Hellmann et al. 2000). The net effect is ambiguous and depends on the sensitivity of leverage to changes in interest rates.

More generally, there are important general equilibrium effects that these partial equilibrium models of risk-taking do not capture, and that may attenuate the risk-taking channel. For example, a reduction in interest rates will boost aggregate demand, raising corporate profits and lowering unemployment. This in turn will translate into lower loan delinquency rates especially if borrowers' balance sheets are distressed to begin with, to the benefit of financial intermediaries. Lower interest rates also tend to boost asset prices, further relaxing collateral constraints and strengthening the balance sheets of households and firms, and reducing credit risk of financial intermediaries.

Lower interest rates also increase the value of legacy assets held by financial intermediaries, a phenomenon Brunnermeier and Sannikov (2012) have dubbed "stealth recapitalization." The resulting increase in net worth will discourage any risk-shifting behavior of these financial intermediaries.

Consistent with these theories, several papers find evidence in support of the existence of a risk-taking channel of monetary policy across different countries and time periods, although studies provide conflicting evidence on the magnitude of the effect. Maddaloni and Peydró (2011, 2013) analyze the surveys on the euro area and the US bank lending standards to analyze some of the previous testable hypotheses. The euro area is very useful to exploit some unique features of the Monetary Union. First, the euro area represents a unique institutional setting with a common monetary policy but with important differences in the business and credit cycle and also in prudential supervision. Second, in the euro area, funding to the corporate sector largely comes from banks and, therefore, a crisis affecting the banking sector has dramatic consequences for the real economy through the reduced credit provision. Finally, the authors take advantage of a unique dataset on lending conditions for the euro area (the Bank Lending Survey, BLS), where they know whether and why loan conditions change for the pool of all borrowers, including the rejected applications.

They find that low (monetary policy) short-term interest rates soften conditions, for household and corporate loans. Low monetary policy interest rates soften lending conditions unrelated to borrowers' risk in the period prior to the crisis, and there is some suggestive evidence of excessive risk-taking due to low interest rates for mortgage loans. Moreover the softening in lending conditions is amplified—especially for mortgages—by securitization activity and by holding monetary policy rates too low for too long. Conversely, they find that low long-term interest rates do not soften lending standards. Finally, countries with softer lending standards before the crisis related to negative Taylor rule residuals experienced a worse economic performance afterwards.

Using loan application level data from the Spanish credit register, Jiménez et al. (2014a) analyze changes in credit risk-taking by banks following changes in monetary policy rates. They separate the changes in the composition of the supply of credit from the concurrent changes in the volume of supply and quality and volume of demand. They employ a two-stage model that analyzes the granting of loan applications in the first stage and loan outcomes for the applications granted in the second stage, and that controls for both observed and unobserved, time-varying, firm and bank heterogeneity through time × firm and time × bank fixed effects.[24]

They find that a lower overnight interest rate induces lowly capitalized banks to grant more loan applications to ex ante risky firms and to commit larger loan volumes with fewer collateral requirements to these firms, yet loans to these firms have a higher ex post likelihood of default.[25] All findings are statistically significant and economically relevant. A decrease of one percentage point in the overnight rate, for example, increases the probability that a loan will be granted by a lowly versus a highly capitalized bank (with a difference of one standard deviation between them) to a firm with a bad credit history by 8 percent, the resultant committed amount of credit increases by 18 percent, while the future likelihood of loan default of these loans increases by 5 percent, and the required collateral decreases by 7 percent. A lower long-term interest rate and other key aggregate bank and macro variables, such as more securitization or higher current account deficits, have no such effects. Importantly, when the overnight rate is lower, virtually all banks grant more credit to firms with higher risk (by around 19 percent for the average bank).

The estimates suggest that a lower monetary policy rate spurs bank risk-taking and hence that monetary policy affects the composition of the supply of credit beyond the well-documented effects of both the bank- and firm balance-sheet channels. Consistent with "excessive" risk-taking are the findings that especially banks with less capital "in the game," namely those afflicted more by agency problems, grant more loan applications and resultant credit to ex ante risky firms, that these banks require less collateral from these firms, and that these banks face more default on their granted loans in the future—all bank actions accordant with risk-shifting.[26]

Dell'Ariccia, Laeven, and Suarez (2013) present evidence of a risk-taking channel of monetary policy for the US banking system. Their analysis uses information on risk-taking at the loan level, and therefore complements the analysis in Jiménez et al. (2014a) who construct a measure of risk-taking at the firm level. Specifically, they use confidential data on the internal ratings of US banks on loans to businesses over the period 1997 to 2011 from the Federal Reserve's survey on the terms of business lending to show that ex ante risk-taking by banks (as measured by the risk-rating of the bank's loan portfolio) is negatively associated with increases in real policy rates, and that this relationship is less pronounced for banks with relatively low capital or during periods when banks' capital erodes, such episodes of financial and economic distress. However, the quantitative effects of these results are relatively small, consistent with the countervailing forces in the model by Dell'Ariccia, Laeven, and Marquez (2014).

Altunbas, Gambacorta, and Marquez-Ibañez (2014), using rating agency estimates of default probabilities as a proxy for risk-taking, find that decreases in interest rates and negative Taylor rule residuals (expansive monetary policy) are positively associated with default risk measures. A paper by Paligorova and Santos (2012) studies syndicated loan pricing for US corporates together with data from the Federal Reserve's Senior Loan Officer Opinion Survey results on bank lending standards and finds that loan pricing of riskier borrowers is more favorable (relative to safer borrowers) during periods of loose monetary policy, and that this effect is more pronounced for banks with greater risk appetite.

Jiménez et al. (2014b) examine all Spanish business loans through the detailed information contained in the loan register and show that a lower short-term interest rate lowers the hazard rate of default on existing loans (i.e., it favors legacy assets). In addition they show that the hazard rate of default for new loans increases after the cut in short-term rates. These findings are consistent with the leverage channel in the model of Adrian and Shin (2011), where a lowering of short-term interest rates leads to increased balance sheet capacity and hence the taking on of lower quality projects that previously did not meet the standards of the bank before the interest rate cut.

The same combination of a lowering of a hazard rate of default on existing loans and an increase in the hazard rate of default on new loans is also observed in Ioannidou, Ongena, and Peydró (2014). In this study the authors examine the effects of monetary policy on bank risk-taking in lending by Bolivian banks. To get exogenous variation of monetary policy, the authors exploit shifts in the US Federal Funds rate as the Bolivian banking system is close to being dollarized. As the US Federal Funds rate is determined independently of the events in Bolivia, it can be used as a proxy for exogenous changes in Bolivian short-term rates to analyze the impact of short-term interest rate movements on bank asset quality. The results reveal that a cut in the US Fed Funds rate leads to an improvement in the quality of existing assets, but new assets are of a lower quality.

There is also evidence in the literature suggesting a correlation between the monetary policy rate and risk-taking outside of banks. Bernanke and Kuttner (2005) find that higher interest rates reduce equity prices, interpreting that tight money may reduce the willingness of stock investors to bear risk.[27]

In related work, Hanson and Stein (2015) uncover an interesting effect of conventional monetary policy: changes in the stance of policy have surprisingly strong effects on long-term forward real interest rates. Over the period 1999 to 2012, a 100 basis point increase in the two-year nominal yield on FOMC announcement day, which they take as a proxy for a change in the expected path of the federal funds rate over the following several quarters, is associated with a 42 basis point increase in the ten-year forward overnight real rate, extracted from the yield curve for Treasury inflation-protected securities (TIPS).[28]

Stein (2013b) argues that this finding is at odds with standard New Keynesian macro models, in which monetary policy's ability to influence real variables stems from goods prices that are sticky in nominal terms. In these models, a change in monetary policy should have no significant effect on forward real rates at ten-year horizons as consumer prices adjust faster than that. Moreover Stein (2013b) argues that the result suggests that monetary policy could have a stronger impact than is implied by the standard model, precisely because long-term real rates are the ones that are most likely to matter for investment decisions.

Stein argues that the movements in long-term forward real rates reflect changes in term premiums, as opposed to changes in expectations about short-term real rates far into the future. Put differently, if the central bank eases policy today and yields on long-term TIPS go down, this does not mean that the real short rate is expected to be lower ten years from now, but rather that TIPS have gotten more expensive relative to the expected future path of short rates.

Why would monetary policy be able to influence real term premiums? Hanson and Stein (2015) argue that low nominal interest rates can create incentives for certain types of investors to take added risk in an effort to "reach for yield," as initially suggested by Rajan (2005). While the body of empirical research previously summarized in this subsection investigates this hypothesis in the context of credit risk, documenting that banks tend to make riskier loans when rates are low, Hanson and Stein's (2015) focus is instead on the implications of the reach for yield mechanism on the pricing of interest rate risk (i.e., duration risk). They assume that "yield-oriented" investors allocate their portfolios between short- and long-term Treasury bonds and, in doing so, put some weight not just on expected holding-period returns, but also on current income. This preference for current yield could be due to agency or accounting considerations that lead these investors to care about short-term measures of reported performance. Therefore a reduction in short-term nominal rates leads investors to rebalance their portfolios toward longer-term bonds in an effort to keep their overall yield from declining too much. This in turn creates buying pressure that raises the price of the long-term bonds and hence lowers long-term yields and forward rates.

Becker and Ivashina (2013) analyze the US insurance industry to estimate the reaching for yield for nonbanks. Identifying excessive risk-taking behavior among financial institutions is challenging as search for yield is only a concern if it leads to more risk-taking by financial institutions than their shareholders or other stakeholders desire. Insurance companies' risk-taking is closely related to their capital requirements. To determine the credit-risk component of capital requirements for US insurers, Becker and Ivashina (2013) sort corporate bonds held by insurance companies into six categories based on their credit ratings. However, different bonds with the same credit rating's risk category can have significantly different credit and liquidity risk profiles. An insurance company can therefore easily alter the risk exposure and the yield of its bond portfolio without affecting capital requirements at all. Such search for yield can become an important factor because insurance companies invest most of their securities holdings in fixed income.

Becker and Ivashina (2013) find a notable reaching for yield by US insurance companies. Among investment-grade bonds, insurance companies hold 88 percent of their bond portfolio in the highest yield-spread quartile.[29] These bonds are riskier, and insurance firms' bond holdings have higher systematic risk than those of many other investors. The authors find that this risk-taking behavior disappeared completely in the financial crisis, and that it returned when credit markets (and insurance companies' capital positions) recovered.[30] Moreover they show that times of pronounced reaching for yield by insurance firms coincide with periods of unusually high issuance activity by riskier firms. Therefore the authors conclude that changes in risk-taking affect the supply of credit in the economy.

Chodorow-Reich (2014b) similarly find evidence in support of reach for yield by private defined-benefit pension funds and money market funds during the period 2009 to 2011, which was characterized by unconventional monetary policy in the form of large scale asset purchases by the Federal Reserve. A combination of low nominal interest rates and high administrative costs forces money market funds to waive fees, providing an incentive to reach for yield to reduce waivers. Chodorow-Reich finds that especially money market funds with higher costs reached for higher returns on their investments during the period 2009 to 2011.

Like financial regulators, investors who delegate portfolio decisions need to rely on noisy (sometimes biased) measures, such as credit ratings. Financial intermediaries are, in general, rewarded for beating imperfect risk benchmarks that do not take into account excessive risk via reaching for yield, for example, as with exposing to tail risks and long-term lending (Rajan 2005; Stein 2013a). Moreover, given the compensation structure, it is optimal for managers to herd with other investment managers on investment choices because herding provides insurance that the manager will not underperform his peers. However, herd behavior can move asset prices away from fundamentals, and thus tail risks and herd behavior reinforce each other during an asset price boom: investment managers are willing to bear the low probability tail risk that asset prices will drop sharply, and as many of their peers are herding on this risk, they will not underperform in case a sharp drop in prices occurs.

These risk-taking behaviors can be compounded in an environment of low interest rates as some investment managers have fixed rate obligations that force them to take on more risk as rates fall. For instance, Feroli et al. (2014) and Morris and Shin (2014) argue that due to concerns about their relative performance rankings, assets managers of fixed-income mutual funds may respond to low policy rates by shifting their portfolios toward high return but riskier investments. Thus not only do the incentives of some participants to reach for yield increase in a low interest rate environment but also asset prices can significantly go upward, thus increasing systemic risk.

Monetary policy can also influence risk-taking by affecting uncertainty and risk aversion in financial markets and, through it, impact global financial conditions, with implications especially for emerging markets. Bekaert, Hoerova, and Lo Duca (2013) find that the VIX index, the option-based implied stock market volatility, strongly co-moves with measures of the monetary policy stance. When decomposing the VIX into two components, a proxy for risk aversion and expected stock market volatility (uncertainty), they find that a lax monetary policy decreases both risk aversion and uncertainty, with the former effect being stronger. Moreover Rey (2013) shows that there is a global financial cycle in capital flows, asset prices, and credit growth that co-moves with the VIX. Moreover asset markets in countries with more credit inflows are more sensitive to the global cycle. She shows that one of the determinants of the global financial cycle is monetary policy in the center country, which affects the leverage of global banks, capital flows, and credit growth in the international financial system. Importantly, whenever capital is freely mobile, the global financial cycle constrains national monetary policies regardless of the exchange rate regime. These results may explain why US monetary policy over the period 2010 to 2014 has been so powerful for emerging markets.

Taken together, these results point to the existence of a risk-taking channel of monetary policy. They suggest that low short-term interest rates lead to an increase in bank risk-taking, leading to an increase in leverage and a buildup of credit and asset price bubbles. Moreover low interest rates lead to a search for yield especially among financial institutions with rigid or long-term liabilities, such as insurance companies and pension funds. Therefore accommodative monetary policy for a prolonged period of time can lead to an increase in systemic risk and financial instability.

However, the magnitude of the risk-taking effect is more difficult to establish, reflecting opposing forces from endogenous leverage and general equilibrium effects. It depends on the degree of asset substitution among risky assets and the sensitivity of leverage and funding costs to changes in interest rates.

10.4   Monetary Policy during Systemic Crises

The realization of systemic risk implies strong negative externalities within the financial sector and from the financial sector to the real sector. Among the first type of externalities, contagion and illiquidity may be the most important source (as explained in chapter 5) and, among the second type of externalities, a reduction of credit supply to firms and households is likely the main source of real effects (as explained in chapter 6).

Central banks, through their conduct of monetary policy (interest rate policy, open market operations, and nonstandard measures) and as lender of last resort, can play an important role in reducing both externalities by providing liquidity to financial markets and institutions and through the credit channel of monetary policy. Moreover, if externalities within the financial sector are contained, the externalities to the real sector will in principle be reduced as well, because liquidity and solvency problems will be reduced for financial intermediaries. However, as financial crises tend to follow strong credit booms, debt overhang problems in the household and nonfinancial corporate sectors can still imply strong negative aggregate output and employment effects for the economy as a whole, even if acute problems at financial intermediaries are contained.

Finally, as public debt may substantially increase during financial crises due to financial sector support and a recession-induced decline in government revenues policies, monetary policy may play a role via nonstandard measures, as in the case of the US Federal Reserve's quantitative easing policies or the ECB's Outright Monetary Transactions (OMT) and Asset Purchase programs. Otherwise, high public debt may crowd out private investment, for example, through banks lending to the public sector instead of the private sector.

10.4.1   Externalities within the Financial Sector

Once the crisis arrives, financial intermediaries are forced to sell assets. As we have argued throughout the book, financial intermediaries have an incentive in booms to invest in information-sensitive, illiquid assets that have high returns (e.g., OTC derivatives and mortgage-backed securities). Once financial intermediaries are forced to sell these assets in a crisis, other investors may not have the specialized asset-specific knowledge needed to assess whether the lack of demand comes from excessive risk of the assets or from the unavailability of the typical buyers to buy the asset. Due to this adverse selection problem, outsiders may then decide to stay out of the market or price the asset with strong discounts to avoid a "winners' curse" problem (i.e., getting the asset may imply that the price paid was too high given other bids being lower or missing).[31] When this happens, market prices may collapse (with market illiquidity generating fire sales), and some financial intermediaries may lose funding liquidity, especially if based on short-term debt contracts.

Market illiquidity therefore dries up funding liquidity, leading to an increased sale of assets (Brunnermeier and Petersen 2009) and a vicious liquidity cycle between market and funding illiquidity and sales of financial assets. Illiquidity may then lead to insolvency. Multiple equilibria may also arise, with the expectation of insolvency leading to high interest rates and becoming self-fulfilling. Even in models of unique equilibria, solvent but illiquid banks may fail due to coordination problems among (wholesale) depositors with short-term contracts, as shown by Rochet and Vives's (2004) and Goldstein and Pauzner's (2005) extensions to the banking sector of the Morris and Shin (1998) global games' models applied to currency crises.

Liquidity dry-ups due to short-term debt problems were not only crucial in the last financial crisis, but also historically. For example, financial crises in the United States during the nineteenth century as well as the Great Depression were mainly runs on bank deposits (Bernanke 1983; Gorton 1988). The Penn Central financial crisis of 1970 was a liquidity dry-up in the commercial paper market (Calomiris 1994). The Asian financial crisis of 1997 was a liquidity dry-up of the foreign-currency denominated short-term debt of Asian banks (Diamond and Rajan 2001), while other international crises including the Mexican crisis of 1994 were on the short-term liabilities of the government (Cole and Kehoe 1996).

Therefore there is an ex post role for monetary policy and other public policy instruments related to liquidity, notably deposit insurance, for alleviating these funding and market illiquidity in crises that are compounded both by the presence of short-term debt (especially among dispersed debtholders with coordination problems) and by information-sensitive assets. For example, the introduction of deposit insurance with the creation of the Federal Deposit Insurance

Corporation (FDIC) in 1934 was a direct response to the retail runs on depository institutions in the United States, and the LoLR function of central banks was used already in the nineteenth century in the United Kingdom to combat banking crises (Bagehot 1873).

In the recent crisis, deposit insurance also played an important role to prevent runs by retail depositors. Its coverage limit was increased in most developed economies in October 2008 to reduce retail runs and boost confidence in the banking system. However, the crisis was mainly felt in the wholesale market, which had grown significantly in size. There were runs not only in interbank markets but, for example, also in the asset backed commercial paper (ABCP) market and money market funds.[32]

Moreover the euro area crisis showed that liquidity dry-ups could also extend to sovereigns in developed economies. Sovereigns are even more exposed than financial intermediaries to liquidity problems as their assets consist mostly of future tax revenues, which are hard to collateralize, though their liability is less short-term oriented than most financial intermediaries (Blanchard et al. 2013; Morris and Shin 2014). As banks invest in public debt, and sovereigns may bail out banks, there were substantial feedback effects between sovereign and bank insolvency risk, especially in the euro area where the debt is written in a common currency that cannot be printed by national central banks (in contrast to the United Kingdom and United States, which have independent monetary policies).

In fact several peripheral euro area countries experienced a slow run (on banks, firms, and sovereigns), in which foreign investors did not roll over their positions and some domestic investors moved their money abroad. For example, during the period 2011 to 2012 the external net asset position of Spain was reduced by 400 billion euros (or 40 percent of GDP). These runs were not a sudden stop (as in the emerging market crises of the 1980s and 1990s) because they did not lead to a currency crisis, but nevertheless inflicted significant financial and economic pain, albeit at a slower pace.

The liquidity that was made available by the major central banks in developed economies was crucial in the last crisis to avoid stronger negative externalities in financial intermediaries and markets. Through interest rate policy, LoLR, and nonstandard monetary measures, central banks provided liquidity to banks, other financial institutions, and sovereigns. In all cases this expansive monetary policy provided liquidity to the financial system, thus reducing illiquidity and insolvency and restoring the functioning of financial institutions and markets.

Are these ex post monetary policy actions always good for systemic risk? First, public policy could save insolvent (zombie) banks (or other institutions) that should fail, thus reducing the speed of adjustment to crises. It is often not possible to distinguish in real time between illiquidity and insolvency problems. In the case of the euro area, the ECB was lending to banks without detailed supervisory information on the borrowers and their collateral (only the national central bank had this information).[33] Moreover, for unregulated financial institutions, this problem is even worse. Second, the bailout of financial institutions using monetary policy interventions raises moral hazard by increasing the expectation of future bailouts. The expectation of liquidity provision will induce the accumulation of too risky correlated exposures (including more liquidity risk), thereby increasing the risk of a financial crisis (Farhi and Tirole 2012a; Diamond and Rajan 2012). This problem worsens further when using monetary policy for government financing to support the sovereign, as it is more difficult to limit a sovereign's ex ante actions relative to those of regulated and supervised banks. Haircuts (for discount window access by banks) and conditionality (for direct purchases of government bonds) can partly alleviate these moral hazard problems (Blanchard et al. 2013).

Despite these negative effects, we believe the overall evidence shows that there is an important role for ex post monetary policy to contain systemic risk, not only through liquidity provision and nonstandard measures, but also using interest rate policy. Two recent papers emphasize that there is a case for the central bank to lower interest rates during a crisis. First, Allen, Carletti, and Gale (2009) show that in the absence of such intervention, fire sales will lead to an excessive volatility of interest rates. Otherwise, to cope with liquidity shocks banks would resort to selling their long-term assets, thus creating excessive and unnecessary inefficiencies and costs.

Second, Freixas, Martin, and Skeie (2011) focus on the unsecured segment of the interbank market and consider the implications of the inelasticity of the supply and demand for short-term liquidity. They show that multiple equilibria exist and that these equilibria are not equivalent in their properties. Considering a Diamond–Dybvig (1983) framework, they show that in times of liquidity turmoil the central bank can allow agents to coordinate and reach the optimal allocation. This result is quite in line with the real effect of "open mouth operations," as seen in monetary policy actions by major central banks in the last crisis, where the announcement by the central bank is more important than the volume of the intervention (as evidenced in the positive impact of the "whatever it takes" speech by Mario Draghi in July 2012). Nevertheless, the lowering of interest rates during a crisis implies a corresponding increase during good times, so as to lead the banks to take the right ex ante decisions (as noted by Diamond and Rajan 2012).

10.4.2 Externalities to the Real Sector and the Credit Crunch

Not only do financial intermediaries (and sovereigns) face funding problems during a crisis but so do nonfinancial firms and households. Effects could be even worse to nonfinancial borrowers as their contracts have even higher illiquidity and information sensitivity, and less access to financial markets. These funding problems can lead to a reduction in aggregate private investment and consumption, and thus a fall in aggregate output and employment (as we also saw in chapter 6). Monetary policy by the nonfinancial (firm and household) and bank balance sheet channels can significantly reduce these costs. Therefore a key question is whether monetary policy affects output through these credit channels, and whether the effects are stronger in weaker (crisis) times and for weaker borrowers (firms and households but also banks and sovereigns).

The analysis of section 10.2 suggests that the effect of the bank lending channel of monetary policy has been partly mitigated especially in 2010 to 2012 by central bank policy actions. By providing ample liquidity through the full allotment policy and the longer term refinancing operations (LTROs), the ECB was able to reduce the costs arising to banks from the restrictions to private liquidity funding. These operations effectively substitute for the interbank market, which was not working properly, thereby inducing a softening of very tight lending conditions. As a result credit availability restrictions due to bank liquidity problems were reduced.

At the same time these policy actions seem not to have been very successful in alleviating credit availability problems for households and firms stemming from deteriorated net worth and a decline in aggregate demand, especially in peripheral countries. In other words, while ECB actions had gone a long way to repair the bank lending channel, the nonfinancial balance sheet channel of monetary policy was still greatly impaired.

The analysis therefore supports the adoption of complementary public policy actions that have been put in place successively, and in particular those specifically targeted at increasing credit to small firms to reduce their external finance premia and credit-rationing (e.g., the 2014 targeted LTRO program of the ECB). In fact the decision to enlarge the collateral framework of the eurosystem—in particular, by accepting loans to SMEs as eligible collateral—had the explicit objective of meeting the demand for liquidity from banks in order to support lending to all type of firms, notably SMEs. Empirical evidence indicates that these actions had positive effects on the availability of credit to SMEs.

Other alternatives can also be useful, such as the lending programs introduced in Japan and the United Kingdom by the government, although past experience shows that government interference in the allocation of credit (either directly or through guarantees) can be massively distortionary (e.g., Sapienza 2004 for the case of Italy). The Bank of Japan (BoJ) introduced in June 2010 a program to boost economic growth by providing funds to banks that are lending for or investing in growth areas. The program was extended in duration and size in March 2012. The BoJ also set up another lending facility in June 2011 specifically geared toward promoting equity investments and asset-backed lending, which the BoJ believes will allow small businesses and startups to seek loans and investments from financial institutions without real estate collateral or guarantees.

In July 2012 the Bank of England (BoE) and HM Treasury announced the launch of the Funding for Lending Scheme (FLS). Under the FLS, banks are able to borrow UK Treasury bills from the BoE for a period of up to four years against eligible collateral (including loans to households and businesses and other assets) for a fee. The provision of T-bills (rather than liquidity) is meant to stress that the operation should be seen as distinct from the regular monetary policy operations of the BoE. The BoE borrows the T-bills from the UK government debt management office and the scheme does not lead to an increase in the government debt outstanding. The FLS promotes lending to risky borrowers such as SMEs because under the FLS banks can use such loans to obtain better collateral in the form of T-bills, which also are the preferred instrument in the banks' repo operations.

In Ireland and Spain, there was a huge credit boom in the nonfinancial corporate sector (particularly in the real estate and construction sectors) prior to the crisis, and in the case of Ireland also in the household sector. In these cases liquidity provision by the central banks in its capacity of LoLR does not fully resolve the funding problems of banks, because the debt overhang problems in these nonfinancial sectors depresses economic growth (Myers 1977). The stress in peripheral European sovereign debt markets puts additional pressure on the balance sheets of banks, both through the negative valuation effects on the holdings of such assets and because the government provision of the banks' financial safety net in these countries is called into question.

To deal with a massive real sector debt overhang, a restructuring may be needed. One way is through the conversion of debt into equity. However, households may have more problems than firms in finding solutions. This is because many countries do not have a personal bankruptcy regime and mortgage loans tend to be with full recourse, meaning that the bank can go after the borrower's personal assets if the sale of the property (the collateral) is insufficient to cover the value of the mortgage. Achieving a resolution between banks and households through loan workouts is moreover complicated by the overwhelming number of households that may face distress, making a case by case approach to household debt restructuring a costly affair. For these reasons, households and banks may prefer to hold out, in the hope that better times will return and asset prices will rise, and thus they will prolong the debt overhang.

A potential solution to large-scale private sector debt distress involves a government-supported debt restructuring program that would allow for the partial write-down of debts together with a recapitalization of the banking sector if needed (Calomiris, Klingebiel, and Laeven 2003). To the extent that a reduction in debt overhang increases the value of the debt, it could benefit both the borrower and the lender, and the amount of recapitalization needs will be less. In most cases, however, a large-scale restructuring will have large adverse implications for the cash flow of banks, and require a sizable upfront recapitalization to safeguard financial stability.

Debt reduction of both the private and public sectors can also be done through debt forgiveness or debt moratoria. For example, Kroszner (1998) finds that large-scale debt relief related to repudiation of gold-indexation in debt contracts benefited both equity and debtholders of firms. Moreover countries that left the gold standard earlier in the Great Depression—which resulted in inflation and reduced debt burdens for nominal debt contracts—performed better ex post (Eichengreen and Temin 2000).

Another way to reduce debt overhang problems is through allowing higher overall prices in the economy. Such inflation will reduce the real value of debt as debt contracts are generally written in nominal terms. However, this measure could come at the expense of the central bank losing its reputation on price stability. Moreover all these policies, including inflation, have distributional consequences, favoring borrowers over savers, with political implications (as in the euro area today between debtor and creditor countries).[34] Indeed central banks are significant holders of government debt, and have a senior creditor status in any restructuring, which can crowd out private investment because the value of any additional private investments will be diluted. This raises the issue of whether central bank holdings of public debt should be *pari passu* with those of the private sector, to avoid such crowding out effects.

The debt overhang problems in the United States and Europe could increase systemic risk when there is a premature exit from unconventional monetary policies by the central banks in these countries. A key concern for systemic risk is the normalization of interest rates by raising monetary policy rates from the historically low levels seen today to their normal levels. A strong, rapid increase in monetary rates from very low rate levels can increase credit risk of banks' loan portfolios and losses from a repricing of (long-term) debt instruments (as discussed in section 10.3), yet maintaining interest rates at low levels for too long a period can also be detrimental to systemic risk by encouraging excessive risk-taking by banks and other financial intermediaries. Striking the right balance is a fine balancing act for central banks.

10.5   Interaction of Monetary and Macroprudential Policies

During a financial crisis, accommodative monetary policy will help provide the needed economic stimulus and liquidity support to the financial sector. However, as we mentioned in section 10.3, loose monetary policy can also encourage risk-taking by financial intermediaries, presenting a potential conflict between the macroprudential objectives of monetary policy and financial stability. This conflict can be illustrated using a simple diagram (figure 10.1). The bottom-right quadrant denotes the area where policy makers face a trade-off between monetary stimulus and financial stability. In such an event monetary accommodation is appropriate and macroprudential regulation should be the first line of defense to safeguard financial stability.[35]

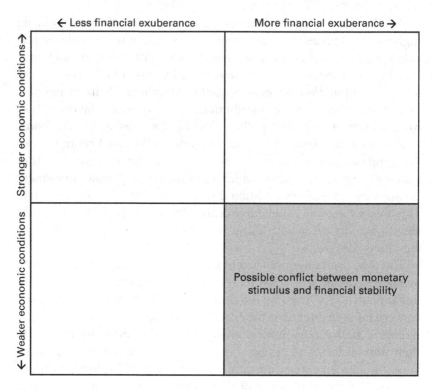

Figure 10.1
Trade-off between monetary policy and financial stability

If prudential policies were perfectly successful, then there should be no need for monetary policy to lean against the wind during boom times. Monetary and macroprudential policies could work perfectly together to achieve price and financial stability, with price stability the responsibility of the central bank, and financial stability the responsibility of the macroprudential authority (i.e., we would be in a one policy–one instrument world). For example, if an easing in the monetary policy stance would lead to an excessive increase in risk-taking, macroprudential tools could be tightened accordingly.

However, as discussed before, the effectiveness of most macroprudential policies is yet to be determined, and in practice, these policies can often be circumvented. Therefore, because both monetary and macroprudential policies work far from perfectly, each policy cannot ignore the limitations of the other policy. Monetary policy should take financial stability considerations into account and play both a preventive and crisis management role. Similarly, when monetary policy is constrained or unavailable to manage a country's economic cycle (as under a currency union or an exchange rate peg), macroprudential tools can play an important role.

Maddaloni and Peydró (2013) analyze whether more stringent prudential supervision and regulation for banks affect the impact of monetary policy on lending standards. They use two cross-country measures of prudential banking policy. The first is a measure originally developed by Barth, Caprio, and Levine (2001) at the World Bank on the stringency of bank capital supervision, concerning how strict capital requirements are applied to the banking sector in each country. The other measure, more related to macroprudential policy, is based on limits on loan to value (LTV) ratios for mortgage loans applied in different countries.[36]

Maddaloni and Peydró (2013) find that the impact of low monetary policy rates on the softening of lending standards is reduced by more stringent prudential policy on either bank capital or LTV—in other words, they find a heterogeneous impact of monetary rates on lending standards depending on the stringency of prudential policy. For the crisis period, they also find that banks entering the crisis with a better capital position can provide higher supply of credit than banks that are more capital constrained. All in all, their results suggest that the stronger prudential policy, the less there is a need for monetary policy to target financial stability and systemic risk.

In chapter 9 on macroprudential policy, we saw that the Spanish dynamic provisions were successful in reducing the credit crunch during the crisis due to the buildup of capital buffers in the good times that were used in the crisis times, but they were not as successful in curbing the pre-crisis credit supply boom (Jiménez et al. 2013). This implies that the need for expansive monetary policy was reduced in the crisis times (as compared to the case without capital buffers), but it would have been better to have had a less accommodating monetary policy in the good times. However, Spain is in a monetary union with important sources of country heterogeneity, which makes the coordination of monetary and macroprudential policies more challenging.[37]

Another problem is that in some countries, such as emerging markets and small open economies, an increase in monetary policy rates to lean against the wind can have the adverse consequence of a sudden increase in foreign capital inflows that can result in domestic credit and asset price bubbles, thus worsening systemic risk. In this case macroprudential tools are especially critical, and in some countries, some restrictions on foreign funding may be optimal (including capital controls), as in the recent cases of Uruguay and Brazil (see Ostry et al. 2011).

How should macroprudential and monetary policy formally coordinate? Should both be housed within the central bank? As explained by Blanchard et al. (2013), separate authorities independently setting monetary and macroprudential policy will in general not obtain the first-best solution as conflicts between price stability and financial stability can easily arise. For example, when aggregate demand is low, the central bank may loosen monetary policy by lowering interest rates to stimulate demand, while the macroprudential authority may respond by tightening macroprudential regulation as low interest rates may promote risk-taking in the financial sector. The outcome will be "a policy mix with interest rates that are too low and macroprudential measures that are too tight relative to what a coordinated solution would deliver" (Blanchard et al. 2013, p. 21).

Before the crisis, when macroprudential policy was not generally considered, the conventional wisdom was that separation of prudential and monetary authorities was the preferred setup. Indeed Goodhart and Schoenmaker (1993, 1995) show that central banks that have supervisory responsibilities experience higher inflation rates. Yet information from bank supervision helps the central bank to conduct monetary policy more effectively (Peek, Rosengren, and Tootell 1999). So the view before the crisis was that the most efficient structure was separation of responsibilities but with information exchange.

The consensus after the crisis is more in favor of consolidation of monetary and macroprudential policies under the central bank. However, giving the central bank responsibilities over the conduct of macroprudential policy, in addition to monetary policy, is not without costs.[38]

First, when macroprudential tools do not work effectively, a central bank with a dual mandate will find it more difficult to convince the public that it will contain inflation if and when this conflicts with its financial stability objective. For example, during a crisis the public may be convinced that the central bank will loosen monetary policy too much in support of financial stability. Second, central bank independence may be less acceptable politically under a dual mandate. Giving central banks the independence over monetary policy was facilitated by a clear objective (inflation targets) and by relatively simple operational tools (a policy rate). "The measurable nature of the objective allowed for easy accountability, which, in turn, made operational independence politically acceptable" (Blanchard et al. 2013, p. 22). The objectives of macroprudential policy are multifaceted (credit growth, leverage, asset price growth, etc.) and more difficult to measure, as we saw in chapter 7.

Third, the targeted nature of macroprudential tools may encounter strong political opposition. For example, households might object to tight limits on LTV ratios as it could prevent them from buying a house. Political interference with macroprudential policy could not only jeopardize the independence of macroprudential policy but also undermine the independence of monetary policy.

Taken together, our view is that combining macroprudential and monetary policies within the central bank, with appropriate safeguards, is the preferable approach. The United Kingdom may be showing the way forward, by having a monetary stability and a financial stability committee, both within the Bank of England. However, we believe that micro- and macroprudential need to be separated, as micro supervisors do focus too much on the stability of the financial sector alone, and macroprudential supervisors do pay more attention to the negative externalities to the broad economy. From this perspective, it would be best for macroprudential policy to be set within central banks, with full access to supervisory information, and to be physically separated from microprudential regulation.

It is clear that monetary policy during the crisis has been crucial to reduce systemic risk and avoid another Great Depression, not only in the United States but especially in the euro area. Governments were able to gain time to pursue structural reforms, such as the creation of a banking union in Europe. Still monetary policy needs to coordinate not only with macroprudential policy but also with other public policies.

10.6 Conclusions

This chapter shows that monetary policy influences ex ante credit and asset price booms and excessive risk-taking by financial intermediaries. Some of the conclusions of this book are that macroprudential tools are necessary and provide a new policy lever to curb dangerous booms and contain imbalances. But evidence about their effectiveness is mixed. Evidence also suggests that the more effective prudential regulation is, the less need there is for monetary policy to lean against the wind. So we envision that this strong preventive role of monetary policy does not need to be maintained in the long term once the prudential framework has been strengthened.

The crisis management role of monetary policy is also necessary to reduce systemic costs, as was evident during the recent global financial crisis. However, one dangerous part of accommodative monetary policy during financial crises is the moral hazard cost that comes from the generous provision of liquidity support and that can make systemic crises more likely going forward. Evidence also shows that macroprudential policy can diminish the need for ex post expansive monetary policy by requiring banks to hold higher capital and liquidity buffers prior to entering a crisis and to be less dependent on short-term wholesale funding liquidity.

All in all, we show that there is a role for monetary policy to combat ex ante and ex post systemic risk, but we believe that this need will be reduced once macroprudential policy is operational and effective. Macroprudential policy does have a clear advantage over monetary policy by being able to target those sectors that contribute to systemic risk. In contrast, monetary policy, by affecting all sectors, is more difficult to circumvent and arbitrage ("it gets into all the cracks") compared to macroprudential policy. Yet, we believe, there will continue to be a (potentially small) role for monetary policy in controlling systemic risk.

11 New Challenges for Regulatory Policy

We conclude the book with remaining challenges for creating an effective macroprudential regulatory framework and with financial regulatory reform more broadly. The problem with the pre-2007 regulatory framework for the financial system, notably banks, was at least sixfold.

First, financial regulation had been focused too much on the risk of individual financial institutions rather than the system as a whole. Prudential policy had been too micro-focused and insufficiently macroprudential. Moreover, even though financial crises mainly originate from endogenous rather than exogenous risks, regulation had focused too little on the endogenous buildup of financial imbalances over time. Supervision also focused too much on banks and too little on the risks emerging from the shadow banking system, nonbank financial institutions, and financial markets.

Second, financial regulation had displaced market discipline of banks as deposit insurance and bailouts reduced incentives for market disciplining. Such a lack of market discipline makes banks different from nonfinancial firms where bad performance results in failure due to competition, as consumers and suppliers vote with their feet by turning to other firms. Recent regulation for bail-ins, living wills, and resolution mechanisms will improve market discipline. Moreover corporate governance—especially in banks—encourages excessive risk-taking, including lack of proper risk management, as maximizing only shareholder value of a highly leveraged institution creates substantial inefficiencies. Excessive risk-taking is even higher when competition is high, as implicit bank capital (charter value) is eroded. We believe that reducing competition, and allowing even substantially larger TBTF banks, is *not* the solution, but an improvement should come from substantially higher capital requirements in good times, and better corporate governance where not only the interests of shareholders but also those of debtholders (including depositors) and taxpayers are taken into account.

Third, the regulatory framework suffered from the lack of a credible mechanism to intervene early on in failing banks and other intermediaries. To restore some form of market discipline we therefore need resolution mechanisms to allow the failure of the weak parts of the financial system without causing significant negative externalities to the economy. The lack of a credible mechanism is partly because regulators have not had adequate tools to intervene in banks and minimize losses for taxpayers. This problem is particularly pronounced for large banks that are deemed too big, connected, or complex to fail, in turn increasing ex ante pre-crisis moral hazard and excessive risk. Moreover competition policy has been especially lax in the recent crisis (as in previous crises) allowing many banks to expand through mergers or acquisitions, and therefore the too big to fail problem could be even worse in the next systemic financial crisis. Additionally, during the recent crisis, moral hazard problems have been exacerbated by central banks' massive liquidity assistance and low rates.

Fourth, regulatory failures and weak supervision created opportunities for regulatory arbitrage, partly because financial participants have incentives for finding loopholes and partly because regulators can be captured through practices such as revolving doors and lobbying, and through the political influence of very large banks. The existence of a resolution mechanism can empower supervisors to intervene early on in failing banks but its credibility and effectiveness ultimately depends on the strength and will of the supervisors. The need for more intense and effective supervision should therefore be a priority in financial regulatory reform.

Fifth, prudential regulation has paid insufficient attention to international issues such as gaps in the supervision of cross-border banks and risks from international cross-border flows. Prudential regulation has largely been a national affair even though banks operate at a global level and global capital flows have grown rapidly over the past decades. Contributing to most crises are international financial flows, particularly short-term flows in foreign currency. Moreover the regulation of internationally active banks has seen gaps arising from home-host country supervision rules or from limited access to information on foreign activities by national supervisors. The new macroprudential framework will have to look beyond national borders, notably at systemic risks from international linkages and exposures.

Finally, when emerging from a major financial crisis, such as the one experienced in recent years, it is tempting to overregulate the financial system to prevent financial crises from ever happening again. However, there is a crucial trade-off between financial stability and economic growth. The new regulatory framework should strike a balance between these two objectives, without imposing excessive costs on the regulated, including by ensuring a level playing field between the regulated and unregulated parts of the financial system. For example, an increase of capital requirements in *bad times* has important costs in terms of reduced extension of credit to the real economy.

Ultimately, the difficulties in creating an effective macroprudential framework can be attributed to economic agents' incentives. Deviations between social welfare maximizing behavior and individual benefits concern the regulatory agencies as well as the bank managers. Regulators' incentives could, of course, derive from personal objectives that diverge from social welfare maximization, as in the private benefit or regulatory capture theory view of regulation. The objective function of the regulator could also be biased if the regulator is more concerned about his or her reputation than about social welfare (Boot and Thakor 1993; Morrison and White 2013). Then again, the regulator may not be absolutely independent from the political power, whether government or parliament, leading to inefficient political economy equilibria in the absence of the equivalent of Calvin's adequate system of checks and balances. If the issue of political interference is already worrisome in a one-country framework, it becomes inextricable when considered from an international perspective.

Nevertheless, some caution is needed to find the adequate level of regulation in the aftermath of a crisis. The intensity and span of regulation should be guided by a financial institution's size, leverage, and interconnectivity with the rest of the financial system, and be balanced against the desire not to distort the allocation of private capital. There is a tendency to overregulate at the height of a crisis, and we should be fully aware that an inefficient regulation might be corrected in good times, thus leading to insufficient regulation and planting the seeds of the next crisis.

Much progress has been made in building a regulatory framework that is more robust and capable of dealing with systemic risk but a number of challenges and open ended questions remain. These relate to the political economy dimension of regulation, microprudential challenges (including market discipline, improved supervision, improved resolution, boundaries of regulation, and corporate governance) and macroprudential challenges (including implementation, data collection and information sharing, systemic risk measurement, and international issues). In particular, we will discuss the challenges in strengthening supervision, and the need for more comprehensive and detailed data, improved models, and practical measures of systemic risk. Consideration will also be given to the institutional setup and organization of macroprudential policy, including the existing toolkit, the regulatory challenges arising from the multiplicity of regulatory bodies in the United States, the creation of a banking union in the European Union, the supervision and resolution of cross-border financial institutions. Finally, we will discuss challenges arising from international policy spillovers, including the impact of monetary policy in advanced economies on capital flows and the buildup of asset and credit bubbles in emerging market economies, and the role of macroprudential policy in managing capital flows in emerging markets.

At the present stage of the analysis, it may well be the case that this chapter provides more questions than answers. Our only line of defense against such criticism is that providing answers would be purely speculative and not yet substantiated by strong theoretical and empirical work. It is our belief that it would be injudicious and confusing to report speculative opinions on how to answer all of the current challenges in a book whose intent is to cover rigorous research providing a strong foundation for both future research and policy implementation.

11.1   The Political Economy Dimension

Political economy forces exert a large influence on regulatory policy. While regulators will claim that regulations serve the public interest, there is much evidence in support of the private interest view of regulation, where regulators serve their own interests and respond to the interests of the financial services industry (e.g., see Kroszner and Stratmann 1998).

11.1.1   Regulatory Cycles
According to the private interest view of regulation, regulatory authorities act in the interest of the regulated industry either to improve their career opportunities or because of private, possibly nonpecuniary, benefits, equivalent to a side payment or a bribe. However, the most

common mistake of financial regulators seems to be the lack of independence from political pressure and forbearance.

This lack of independence of regulators leads to waves of underregulation and overregulation as well as to time inconsistencies. In the immediate aftermath of a crisis, changes in the regulatory framework are immense, and given a completely new set of rules, it should be impossible for the previous crisis to repeat itself. This situation can lead to both overregulation and complacency. Indeed, with the myriad of regulations being proposed to correct regulatory failures and improve the regulation of the financial system, there is a risk of overregulation, which could impose excessive costs on the regulated financial industry and stymie growth.

Yet, overregulation and complacency have in themselves the seeds of deregulation. As the boom succeeds the crisis, financial markets prosper and financial innovations blossom with the impression of a perfectly functioning arrangement, supported by the fact that under current regulation the previous crisis will not be possible. As emphasized by Borio (2013), it is precisely when the economy is at the top and most indicators are favorable—when in fact asset bubbles may be flourishing—that regulators should worry.

Even countercyclical and other macroprudential regulations may not be immune to the cycle because of the popular call for tougher regulations in bad times and relaxed regulations in good times. This is why macroprudential regulation would be better at reducing the excessive cost of a systemic crisis than at preventing its occurrence.

The title of Reinhart and Rogoff's book on the history of financial crises, *This Time Is Different*, illustrates perfectly the overconfidence that is generated by having adequately put in place the mechanisms that make the repetition of the previous crisis impossible. Nevertheless, the next crisis will not be an exact repetition of the previous one. Still, at a general level we must acknowledge that research has identified a number of characteristics of financial fragility that are repeatedly observed before a systemic crisis—notably the presence of asset bubbles, excessive leverage, and regulatory arbitrage—even if their power as early warnings is limited. So the next crisis will be different, as history does not repeat itself exactly even though the major driving forces of the crisis will remain unchanged. The next crisis will again come as a surprise to most, as the trigger will come from a different part of the financial system following a period of overconfidence; but with hindsight everyone will agree that the ingredients were there, only waiting for the spark to ignite the fuel mixture.

11.1.2 Rules versus Discretion

As the analysis of the political economy of prudential regulation shows, although supervisors have plenty of discretion to intervene in banks, they find it hard to use these powers because of the politics of economic booms. All economic agents want a boom to last, as everyone benefits from economic growth: consumers and politicians because of the availability of cheap credit; regulators because banks appear stable; shareholders because banks are profitable; and bank managers and loan officers because their options are in the money. As a consequence regulatory discipline is often weak during a boom, especially for large banks.

The implication is that bank regulation should therefore become more rules based rather than left to discretion, both in booms and busts. Failure to conform to minimum rules would require prompt corrective action that could range from removal of management, suspension of dividends, and an order to find additional capital. Rules-based macroprudential tools, such as contingent capital, could give a helping hand to a regulatory agent and could give debtholders an incentive to discipline the bank in order to reduce the probability of failure. This is related to the creation of specific institutions with clearly defined responsibility and accountability, a point we examine hereafter in the context of macroprudential regulation. The example of the US FDICIA, which promoted the well-defined rule of "cost minimization" rather than the more ambiguous "welfare maximization," illustrates the trade-off. Less flexible and therefore less efficient rules might be optimal if the contingent efficient solutions are prone to manipulation and to political interference.

The choice is not "all or nothing" but that of finding the right balance of rules and discretion. Ex ante rules may be set that specify clearly what will occur if some events take place, for instance, if a bank is in distress, which liability holders will be penalized, what liquidity support will be provided to its counterparts and the like. This does not imply that there have to be rules that trigger the implementation of the countercyclical buffer without leaving any degree of discretion to the authorities in charge.

11.1.3 Accountability and Targets

The threatening lack of independence of regulators is in part due to their mandate being to protect the financial stability in their own country, and consequently regulators may give in to industry pressures to support domestic financial institutions.

Yet another dimension of the lack of accountability, especially as regards macroprudential policy, is whether the regulatory authorities are responsible for a well-defined task. Because the impact of regulation on financial stability is difficult to measure, accountability of regulatory agencies is limited, which makes them vulnerable to political pressures.

The lack of a measure of success or complete failure of the regulatory agency is particularly clear when it comes to systemic risk. Indeed, while it is difficult to measure systemic risk as a systemic crisis appears to be lurking, it is just as difficult to choose the right instrument, whether aggregate as in countercyclical buffers or targeted as in loan to value ratios, and to ascertain its effectiveness. This is all the more complex because financial institutions will game the regulatory system by engaging in regulatory arbitrage.

11.2   The Microprudential Challenges

It is clear that the new regulatory framework constitutes an improvement over the pre-2007 one, as it has benefited from the additional knowledge provided by the current crisis. Nevertheless, there are several reasons for concern. First, the next crisis may be substantially different, but the new regulation is designed to cope with a crisis similar to the previous one. Second, the new regulatory framework remains subject to political economy forces that cater to private interests and continues to be an equilibrium outcome of the regulatory game between the regulator and the regulated, casting doubt on whether supervision will be strong and independent especially in the case of what are deemed to be too big to fail financial institutions. In what follows our use of the term "challenge" reflects a lack of a sound theoretical and empirical foundation for the regulatory rule, and thus a possible divorce between the justification of the regulatory rule and its possible consequences in a crisis that does not replicate the 2008 crisis.

11.2.1   Reestablishing Market Discipline

Banks are opaque, engage in complex risky operations, and consequently their risk is hard to assess by outsiders. A capital increase, as proposed by Admati et al. (2013) would obviously lead to better align the interests of bank managers with those of debtholders and taxpayers as banks will then internalize a larger part of the cost of bank failures. This in turn would reduce systemic risk both by reducing the probability of a meltdown of the banking system and by increasing buffers should such a meltdown occur. Yet, in a capital market characterized by financial imperfections where equity is costly, this would increase the cost of bank capital and reduce banking activity, which may not be socially optimal. On balance we see higher capital requirements as desirable but caution against raising them too much.

The ideal solution would be to improve debtholder discipline. However, depositors are unlikely to exert effort to monitor bank managers as long as their investments are protected by government deposit insurance (see Demirguc-Kunt, Kane, and Laeven 2008). Moreover, reducing deposit insurance is not a political solution. The burden of disciplining bank managers therefore falls on the shoulders of uninsured debtholders. To give them an incentive to monitor bank management, we need to make sure that uninsured debtholders are no longer bailed out in case of bank failures, while insured deposits are fairly priced. A first step in that direction has already been taken in the majority of countries as deposit insurance premia generally are now usually risk based and should ideally be fairly priced, although from a theoretical standpoint the risk adjustment should be continuously revised. This way banks that take more risk pay a higher insurance premium to the deposit insurance company.

A better bank resolution regime, the issue we review next, constitutes a precondition for better market discipline, and recent changes in regulation go precisely in this direction. However, before we turn to resolution, we first briefly discuss the need to restore market discipline and improve the protection of consumer interests.

Concerns about Market Discipline   Reinforcing market discipline will be beneficial because it will allow closing down inefficient banks in good times, thus diminishing the cost of a banking crisis. Still, there are two serious concerns regarding the effectiveness of market discipline.

First, market discipline has been little defense against the macroprudential risks that come with the economy cycle. In the boom, the probability of a systemic crisis seems remote and all financial institutions look good, and differentiation among banks is poor. So, even if market discipline is improved in the banking industry, because it does not reflect systemic risk, it will generally be too lax during good times when asset prices explode. Market discipline cannot be based on market indicators that are likely to embody a bubble.

Second, one of the lessons of the current crisis is that market discipline does not help in a systemic crisis. Investors' flight to quality leads them to abandon all investment in the banking industry rather than keeping the good banks and getting rid of the bad ones (see Huizinga and Laeven 2011). From that perspective, market discipline could have a negative effect. Indeed, during a systemic crisis, better market discipline means more short-term investors and their indiscriminate flight to quality will generate a bank panic.

Consumer Protection   Interestingly enough, the Dodd–Frank Act emphasizes consumer protection by creating a special agency, the Bureau of Consumer Financial Protection to limit banks' abuse of investors' limited financial culture. This does not have an equivalent in Europe, so it is only natural to raise the question of whether consumer protection is an important part of banking regulation. We will argue that it is and, of course, the implicit implication is that Europe should improve its consumer protection programs.

There are many examples of banks misrepresenting financial services to uninformed investors. The mix of low interest rates with less visible fees, the selling of foreign currency denominated mortgages without informing of the currency depreciation risk, as it happened in Hungary, and the retail selling of highly risky preferred equity to retirees in Spain claiming the product was equivalent to a deposit are some of the better-known scandals.

In principle, it should be possible to separate consumer protection, which is usually the responsibility of one agency, from systemic risk, which is the responsibility of the macroprudential regulatory authorities. In practice, these are strongly linked. The selling of subprime mortgages to uninformed investors led to an excessive risk for banks engaging in this line of business, as the impossibility to repay the loan-triggered repossessions in turn led to additional downward pressure on real estate prices. Making the social cost of the crisis even more costly was the lack of consumer protection, and this created additional concerns as the reputations of the involved banks and confidence in the banking system eroded.

11.2.2   Improving Resolution of Banks

The social cost of bankruptcies is the main externality generated by banks' failures. Other distortions, such as governments' predisposition to bailout banks and banks' excessive risk-taking, and, more generally the distortion derived from the very existence of a safety net can be traced down to the absence of an efficient resolution procedure. Indeed existing resolution procedures have not presented a credible threat, leading authorities to resort to costly bailouts of banks.

The average banking crisis has cost the taxpayer a staggering 10.0 percent of GDP in terms of bailing out banks (Laeven and Valencia 2010), and this figure does not even include taxpayer money put at risk (but not used) to contain the crisis. This cost figure also does not take into account the accommodative macroeconomic policies in response to banking crises that typically imply a massive wealth transfer from the taxpayer to the banking sector. The huge cost of these crises can largely be attributed to inefficient bank resolution, namely the lack of a credible mechanism to intervene early on in failing banks to minimize the cost to taxpayers of bank failures. The absence of an efficient resolution mechanism that does not threaten financial stability appears as the main cause of regulatory forbearance. Yet, by allowing problems to linger and using a piecemeal approach to crisis management, the ultimate fiscal and economic costs associated with a banking crisis can be multiples higher (see Honohan and Laeven 2005). Even in countries where the bank bankruptcy rules are well defined, as in the United States, with the prompt corrective action, regulatory authorities cannot or dare not implement those rules when a systemic crisis develops for fear of the financial stability consequences, a recent occurrence being the systemically important US commercial bank Citigroup.

Regulators' forbearance is particularly pronounced for large banks that are deemed too big to fail and systemically important (too interconnected to fail). With banks growing ever larger and more complex, the too big to fail problem has become ever more pressing. Today's banks engage in complex financial transactions, which risk supervisors cannot assess. This may lead regulators to forbear as the safest strategy when confronted with a possible crisis that, of course, is denied by the bank.

The ongoing regulatory reforms are redefining banks' resolution procedures with a combination of contingent capital and bail-in mechanisms. These regulatory changes include the Dodd–Frank Act in the United States, which gives new powers to intervene and resolve the failures of systemically important financial institutions, the additional contingent capital requirements for large banks in Switzerland, and the good bank/bad bank separation structures that allow for bail-ins as in the Danish resolution framework provide the tools to reduce the social cost of banks' resolutions (see chapter 8). These changes, if duly implemented, will definitely increase the market discipline of banks and reduce some of the existing distortions in banks' risk-taking incentives.

However, do these regulatory reforms imply that bank resolution will be efficient and market discipline restored? Can we assert that, at least from the banks' resolution perspective "this time is different"? Again, there are serious reasons for concern.

In an ideal world, the forbearance problem as well as the too big to fail problem would be solved by appointing strong supervisors with a clearly defined mandate. However, such individuals are easy to find in a pure theoretical framework but not in a world confronted with lobbying and political pressures to promote credit expansion and economic growth.

In addition the issue of how to deal with cross-border banks still needs to be worked out. A private interest view or a political economy view of the equilibrium outcomes of current regulatory reform may curb our enthusiasm and predict that some level of forbearance will still prevail, thus raising the issue of how to cope with it.

11.2.3 The Boundaries of Regulation

It may be efficient to separate the "casino" and "utility" functions of financial institutions. We emphasize this because the lack of market discipline associated with the implicit or explicit guarantees on banks' liabilities incentivizes risk-taking and free-riding on debtholders and ultimately taxpayers.

Looking for Boundaries One of the lessons of the current crisis is the importance of a broad definition of the boundaries of the banking system, with a mandate for the supervision and regulation authorities to cover not only banks but systemically important financial institution (SIFIs). This concerns both shadow banking, and includes not only securitization but also CDS and OTC operations, financial conglomerates, and nonbanking financial institutions (e.g., AIG). In chapter 8 our discussion centered on three points:

First, allowing traditional banks to engage in nontraditional activities of the resort of investment banking would lead to free-ride on deposit insurance and on the implicit guarantees provided by the safety net. This, of course, means either a high insurance premium, which would be inefficient, or a high cost for the deposit insurance company and ultimately for taxpayers.

Second, if capital is costly and capital requirements are necessary to make up for risk-taking incentives caused by deposit insurance, it is efficient to have holding companies where commercial banks and non-banks are separate legally independent subsidiaries each with its limited liability, so that the bankruptcy of one does not affect the bankruptcy of the other.

Third, the empirical evidence, although somewhat mixed, indicates that more restrictions on banking activity lead to more risk-taking by banks.

Narrow Banking and Ring Fencing   Some current proposals go in the direction of limiting the range of activities banks can engage in or limiting their size. For example, the Volcker rule in the United States (part of the Dodd–Frank Act) prohibits banks from carrying out certain types of investment banking activities (notably proprietary trading) if they are to continue to seek deposit funding and to retain banking licenses. More extreme proposals advocate reverting back to a narrow banking model, in which deposit-funded banks would be converted into traditional payment function outfits with other financial services (notably lending and investment banking) being carried out by other financial institutions.

A more refined proposal is that of retail ring fencing in the United Kingdom—known as the Vickers rule proposed by the Vickers report—which would allow banks to continue providing both retail and wholesale banking services, but would force banks to organize their retail activities as separate legal entities and would prohibit these bank subsidiaries from undertaking other activities and risks, while establishing separate minimum capital and liquidity standards for these subsidiaries, thereby effectively limiting ("ring fencing") any capital or liquidity transfers from such retail subsidiaries to other parts of the banking group. This would allow a continuation of retail operations at such banking groups when other parts of the group are in distress.

In the European Union, the European Commission in January of 2014 came out with a legislative proposal on structural reform of EU banks that would apply to the largest and most complex EU banks with significant trading activities.[1] This proposal builds on the Liikanen report commissioned by the European Commission to propose a set of structural measures to enhance financial stability in the Union. The EC proposal consists of three core elements. First, much like the Volcker rule in the United States, it proposes to ban proprietary trading in financial instruments and commodities, namely trading on own account for the sole purpose of making profit for the bank. Second, it would grant supervisors the power and, in certain instances, the obligation to require the transfer of other high-risk trading activities (e.g., market-making, complex derivatives and securitization operations) to separate legal trading entities within the group ("subsidiarization"). The objective is to avoid the risk that banks would get around the ban on the prohibition of certain trading activities by engaging in hidden proprietary trading activities that become too significant or highly leveraged and potentially put the whole bank and wider financial system at risk. Third, it would provide rules on the economic, legal, governance, and operational links between the separated trading entity and the rest of the banking group.

Although these regulatory initiatives are all justly motivated by the desire to enhance financial stability, they raise several concerns.

First, the financial stability gains that could be accomplished from ring fencing should be carefully weighed against the loss in efficiency in terms of financial services provision, as this will undoubtedly shrink the size of the financial services industry, raise the cost of borrowing for households and firms, and depress economic growth. The Modigliani–Miller irrelevance argument cannot be invoked here, as banks emerge because of the existence of a financial market imperfection.

Second, as mentioned, even if from a theoretical perspective, it makes sense that banks internalize the social cost of their access to the safety net, this does not mean that ring fencing is the best way to force them to do so. As usual, externalities could be addressed through taxes, which in the present case imply a risk-weighted deposit insurance that take into account all risks.

Third, ring fencing may not be perfectly watertight. Private financial institutions will naturally try to avoid the cost of regulation through regulatory arbitrage. As a consequence risks may shift to unregulated parts of the financial system. Theoretically this is right because these parts of the financial system have better market discipline. Yet, if the unregulated part of a bank holding company becomes systemically important ring fencing is useless. So a prerequisite for ring fencing is that nonbanks' financial entities are not systemic and have a smooth bankruptcy procedure, so that their failure does not jeopardize financial stability. Given these challenges with calibrating and enforcing quantity restrictions such as ring fencing or broad-based Volcker type rules that would restrict trading activities, we think it is better to use capital-based instruments to improve banks' incentives to better manage the risks associated with these activities.

To sum up, identifying the boundary of regulation is a challenging task, because the regulatory perimeter will naturally shift as banks respond to new regulations by shifting activity to lightly regulated or unregulated parts of the financial sector.

11.2.4 Corporate Governance
Financial regulation has displaced market discipline, rendering corporate governance of banks to be weak. This has strengthened the position of bank managers who enjoy large private benefits.

Maximizing Shareholder Value When Market Discipline Is Missing
The current regulatory framework has largely relied on the market giving a helping hand to the regulators to keep banks in check and safeguard financial stability. Unfortunately, not only the regulator but also market discipline has been weak.

In a Modigliani–Miller world, where debt is duly priced, by maximizing the value of their shares, stockholders are also maximizing the value of the firm. Nevertheless, when debt is guaranteed or subsidized, and market discipline is insufficient, the price of banks' debt need not reflect the risk taken by the bank. Consequently shareholders only stand to gain when the bank does well and will encourage bank managers to take more risk than is socially optimal.

Implications for Corporate Governance   The recent crisis has raised questions about the sensibility of executive compensation packages at banks. The bonuses that Wall Street bankers received on top of their base salaries reached a staggering $200,000 per employee in 2007 (see Philippon and Reshef 2012). One popular view is that bank managers took too much risk because their stock options gave them steep incentives to invest in short-term risky strategies. Such strategies may have been in conflict with shareholders' objective of value maximization. More generally, the recent crisis has also reinvigorated a debate about whether banks are properly governed. Yet, by focusing on the agency problems between managers and shareholders that are related to compensation, the more important agency problem between shareholders, on one hand, and debtholders and taxpayers, on the other, has been underplayed.

This is directly related to the lack of market discipline and the fact that debt is implicitly or explicitly guaranteed, a point acknowledged by all. Unfortunately, its consequence, the existence of a wedge between asset value maximization and shareholders' value maximization, has not been taken to its ultimate conclusion, the behavior of the bank managers and the decisions of the board of directors. While for nonfinancial firms it is efficient for the board of directors to protect the interest of shareholders with a mandate of maximizing the shares value, financial firms will maximize the value of their shares sometimes at the expense of debtholders and taxpayers because of the wedge between share value and firm value maximization.

Research offers few insights into these pressing governance issues. Traditional models of banks and financial regulation assume benevolent regulators and no governance problems. Moreover little is known about how private governance mechanisms interact with national regulations to shape bank risk-taking. Rather, researchers and policy makers have focused on using regulations to induce sound banking, while largely ignoring how owners, managers, and debtholders interact to influence bank risk.

Laeven and Levine (2007, 2009) find that private governance mechanisms exert a powerful influence over bank risking—for example, banks with more powerful owners tend to take greater risks—and that the same regulation has different effects on bank risk-taking depending on the bank's governance structure. Since governance structures differ systematically across countries, this implies that bank regulations must be custom designed and adapted as financial governance systems evolve. Regulations should be geared toward creating sound incentives for owners, managers, and debtholders, not toward harmonizing national regulations across economies with very different governance structures.

The alignment in the objectives of shareholders and managers, which contradicts the thesis of a bad executive compensation package, is also one of the implications of Fahlenbrach and Stulz (2011) and Ellul and Yeralmilli (2010) work based on the post-crisis empirical evidence.

Prior to the crisis, this wedge between the objectives of shareholders and other stakeholders was not fully appreciated. For example, even though it is true that shareholders will lose the whole value of their claim, the empirical evidence shows that in the years before the crisis, boards of directors encouraged banks' risk-taking (Ellul and Yerramilli 2010).

The regulation of banks' corporate governance is based on a series of recommendations, and quite often followed the basic principles that were applied to nonfinancial firms, such as the nomination of independent directors. The current trend in banking corporate governance recommendations does not constitute a radical alteration in managers' and directors' incentives to choose the risk return combination that maximizes the value of the financial firm. It is therefore likely that board of directors will continue serving shareholders' interest and choose the combination that maximizes shareholders value at the expense of debtholders and taxpayers (except in countries where directors are given the explicit fiduciary mandate to maximize the value of all the banks' stakeholders).

While executive compensation has been seen as having a key role in generating the incentives for risk-taking, the shareholders' mandate to maximize shareholder value has seldom been criticized in the context of banking. This may be the reason why changes in regulation have focused on executives' compensation packages rather than on shareholders and board of directors' decisions. Still, the wedge between shareholders value maximization and firm value maximization implies that the bank's decision may lead to the extraction of debtholder rents. Their absence from the board of directors and their powerlessness to curb corporate governance decisions affecting them may lead to ex post litigation.

On the basis of empirical evidence, it would be quite simple to set minimal requirements for someone to become part of a board, particularly to require banking experience. Another option would be to require some representation of debtholders on the board of directors. Nevertheless, no such regulations have been put forward and banks' corporate governance rules are basically the same as for nonfinancial corporations, while the banks' board of directors environment and decisions are completely different, because banks differ in the market discipline they face as well as in the leverage they choose.

11.2.5 Simple versus Complex Rules

With Basel II internal models have reached unprecedented levels of sophistication. This was heralded as a key achievement in promoting "best practices" and enhancing banking efficiency. Nevertheless, it was also a way for banks to identify loopholes and use them to their benefit. This led to the securitization of assets in structured vehicles that issued short term asset-backed commercial paper secured by a liquidity line from the originator, so that in fact the securitization was incomplete and the originator had to repatriate the toxic assets at the worst possible point in time. Other anecdotic evidence includes here the use of the now-infamous "Repo 105" accounting practice by Lehman Brothers to improve their accounts, thus going much beyond the industry's standard practices for window dressing.

Whatever the rules it is clear that financial institutions' responsibility is to maximize the return on their capital and, consequently exploit all possible loopholes. This has led to concerns, because in a highly sophisticated system it is much more difficult for regulators to identify the possible loopholes financial institutions are taking advantage of.

As a consequence it has been argued that simple rules may have an advantage over more sophisticated ones. The point is particularly relevant in the context of models of asymmetric information, where the regulator is at an informational disadvantage. The natural assumption is that ex post verification is much more costly under complex than under simple rules. If this is the case, there is a trade-off between the two. Indeed the efficiency of complex rules under perfect information is of no use if, in practice, regulatory authorities are confronted with asymmetric information.

To some extent, this idea has already been acknowledged in the introduction of a leverage ratio in Basel III. If we take seriously the internal rating based regulation of Basel II, internal models as "best practices" should dominate any leverage ratio. The advantage of the leverage ratio is however its simplicity. That is to say, the simplicity of the leverage ratio would make it much more difficult to manipulate it without committing fraud, which is not the case for internal ratings. During the 2008 global financial crisis this characteristic of the leverage ratio made it a more valuable piece of information of bank solvency for the banks' claimholders and potential investors than the risk-weighted capital ratio. What was lost on the side of precision was compensated for by it being less subject to manipulation.

More generally, ex ante adequate incentives are based on ex post penalties for noncompliance, but if noncompliance is a fuzzy concept that courts will presumably not identify as such, then the ex ante incentives will collapse. Internal ratings models enter this category. It can be very difficult to prove fraud regarding the use of an internal ratings model, as probabilities can only be shown to be incorrect on the basis of a large number of observations, and in any case, an excessively low risk weight can always be attributed to a model's mistake, making fraud impossible to prove.

11.3   The Macroprudential Challenges

The macroprudential approach to banking regulation implies that, instead of considering bank risk as exogenously determined, the distribution of risks that banks are facing is endogenous as results from the interplay of individual banks' strategies. This affects the losses each bank will suffer when other banks are in distress. General equilibrium considerations, in particular, pecuniary externalities and feedback reinforcing effects lead indeed to a different risk distribution conditional on banks' financial distress. In terms of externalities, this means that there are three major externalities macroprudential policy can address: herding, fire sales, and contagion (De Nicolo, Favara, and Ratnovski 2012).

11.3.1   Implementing Macroprudential Policy

Setting Objectives   Putting in place a macroprudential regulation implies, first, setting an objective function for the institution in charge. Prima facie, the objective function is obvious, as the aim of macroprudential regulation is to preserve financial stability through the identification of systemic risks. Yet, in reality, this may prove to be more difficult than foreseen.

The comparison with monetary policy comes to mind. While it is easy to establish whether the monetary policy authorities have reached the inflation objective or have missed it and by how much, there is no equivalent for a binary event. The observation will be either of a crisis or of the absence of a crisis. Consequently it is difficult to identify the results of macroprudential regulation, because it relies on speculation regarding counterfactuals. What would have happened if the macroprudential policy instrument had not been applied? Would a crisis have emerged? What was the cost in terms of lost economic growth? The fact that answers to these questions can only be provided based on models makes it more difficult to define clear-cut accountability, and this can make it more difficult to establish the independence of the institution.

As a consequence the impossibility of measuring whether the objective has been reached makes it unrealistic to set financial stability as an objective. It is only possible to state whether the objective has not been reached, namely whether we observe a systemic crisis. The implication is that it is necessary to settle for a second-best solution, which will consist of establishing a number of economic indicators that are directly related to the risk of a systemic crisis.

The use of a vector of economic indicators opens up several additional problems. First, as we saw earlier, there is little agreement to date about how best to measure systemic risk. Financial crises being tail risk events make setting macroprudential policy inherently more difficult than policy-making that can rely on outcome variables that are directly observable, such as inflation rates in the case of monetary policy.

Second, most proposals for measuring systemic risk require detailed data on financial institutions and their exposures that are difficult and costly to assemble on a high frequency basis at a national level, let alone at a cross-border level, where constitutional and institutional constraints often limit the possibility of data exchange and cooperation. As a consequence the institution in charge of macroprudential regulation would have to follow economic variables with different frequency and different levels of significance in the prediction of systemic risk. Setting a vector of economic indicators moreover poses the problem of how to combine the indicators, by giving specific rules or delegating the decision to a financial stability committee, an issue we examine hereafter.

Finally, the design of a macroprudential framework faces important institutional challenges, including those related to the setting up of a macroprudential authority, its mandate and powers, and its interaction with the conduct of monetary policy. This requires a framework for macroprudential policy with a range of macroprudential tools and a clear division of tasks and responsibilities.

Macroprudential Policy Trade-Offs   As macroprudential policy has direct costs, including the potential reduction in growth and the possible distortions in the allocation of funds to firms and households, the institution responsible for the setting of macroprudential policy has to carefully weigh its decision. On the one hand, the macroprudential institution may fail to identify the potential systemic risk existing in the economy and miss the building up of a crisis (type I error). On the other hand, macroprudential policy may overestimate systemic risk and implements measures that are not needed (akin to a type II error). Clearly, it will be difficult to fine-tune the balance between acceptable type I and type II errors in an environment characterized by uncertainty rather than by risk—using Knight's distinction—and there is a concern regarding the independence of the institution in an environment characterized by uncertainty. Indeed, how to balance type I and type II errors is a political choice that society has to make. In a perfect world characterized by well-measured risk, the people's representatives should set the parameters in the objective function. However, in the real world, striking the balance between type I and type II errors should be left to the independent macroprudential institution, which means that the institution is not a pure instrument of implementing technical decisions but more of interpreting the society's will. There is no easy way out.

The choice of the correct macroprudential policy instrument is a complex one. Authorities should decide whether they want to intervene at the global level or at the specific industry, market, or product level. An intervention at the global level, such as the implementation of the countercyclical buffer or a leaning against the wind policy, will affect the overall rate of growth and expansion of the credit markets. Instead, a targeted intervention, such as imposing loan to value ratios or limiting construction and development loans, will affect only a fraction of the economic activity by restricting access to funds for some types of borrowers. Electing one or the other will depend foremost on the effectiveness of the intervention but also on the quality of information available to the macroprudential regulatory institution.

In either case regulatory intervention will be difficult. First, the scant number of cases that can be studied where both a financial crisis was likely and a correcting macroprudential instrument was implemented render it difficult to test the effectiveness of feasible macroprudential instruments and to calibrate their use. Second, accurate and relevant information may only be available with a time lag, limiting the availability of data at the time a decision needs to be made on the stance of macroprudential policy, further complicating policy decisions. Third, the probability of a crisis tends to be measured with a high level of imprecision, complicating the decision when it is time to take action. Fourth, the impact of the macroprudential instrument on the intermediate and final targets is uncertain (if not unpredictable), making it difficult to calibrate their use. These four drawbacks will make the implementation of a macroprudential policy particularly complicated and, as a consequence, the trade-offs between type I and type II errors as well as the resulting decision much more intricate.

Complementarity with Other Polices Obviously, if active and effective, macroprudential policy cannot ignore other policies in place, nor can these policies ignore the existence of a macroprudential policy. Five policies have a direct relationship with macroprudential policy:

- Microprudential policy
- Monetary policy
- Competition policy
- Consumer protection policy
- Fiscal policy

The most important to coordinate with macroprudential policy is microprudential policy. Macroprudential policy constitutes here a key input for microprudential policy. The raison d'être of macroprudential policies is the composition fallacy that each bank acting in isolation does not take into account the overall endogenous risk it potentially generates through herding, fire sales (in case of liquidity shortages), and contagion. As a consequence macroprudential authorities would have a more accurate assessment of potential risks, and this will be an invaluable ingredient in the role of microprudential authorities of supervising financial institutions' risk models and capital buffers policy. Also the coordination is necessary because some regulatory instruments, such as loan to value (LTV) or debt to income (DTI) ratios, are microprudential in nature but have clear macroprudential effects.

Monetary policy, given the notion that the combination of monetary policy and banking regulation provides an effective set of tools to deal simultaneously with price stability and financial stability, is the means by which monetary and regulatory authorities can coordinate their financial stability policy and make it operational. Should these be separate entities or should one agency have responsibility for both stability concerns? And, even if they are to be separated, what should be the degree of coordination between the two?

The increasing trend prior to the global financial crises of separating central banks and financial supervisory agencies may well have to be reversed. In the United Kingdom, the regulatory functions of the Bank of England and the newly created Financial Conduct Authority and Prudential Regulation Authority were restructured with the Financial Services Act, and the Financial Services Authority was abolished. When monetary policy affects banks' risk-taking, the separation of monetary policy from banking regulation may well be inefficient (Agur and Demertzis 2010). The empirical evidence also points out that the separation was in fact incomplete, at least in the United States. For example, Ioannidou (2005) points out that when the Federal Reserve increased the federal funds rate it became less strict in its role of bank supervisor. Of course, this does not tell us whether this coordination was efficient or not.

Central banks are obvious candidates to be in charge of macroprudential regulation, not only because in several countries they already regulate banks but also because their access to information and research capability ideally positions them to monitor macroeconomic developments. Moreover central banks are well positioned to deal with both the financial stability and real economy dimensions of systemic risk since in an implicit or explicit way they have always combined the objectives of price and financial stability with aggregate output and employment considerations. Communication challenges that need to be overcome with separate entities (as evident in the case of Northern Rock in the United Kingdom) also speak in favor of one agency. And the interactions among banking market conditions, monetary policy decisions, and bank risk-taking further favor the centralization of macroprudential responsibilities within the monetary authority (Blanchard et al. 2009). Against centralization, two arguments are commonly made, and tended to prevail in the past. The first is that centralization will increase the risk of the central bank taking a "soft" stance against inflation, since interest rate hikes would have a detrimental effect on bank balance sheets and thus on financial stability. The second is that the central bank would have a more complex mandate when it is also responsible for macroprudential regulation and thus be less accountable. Accountability is particularly a concern given that successful outcomes of macroprudential policy in terms of enhancing financial stability cannot be measured with precision (unlike inflation rates). Both arguments have merit and, at a minimum, imply a need for further transparency and a clear communication of policies if the central bank is given responsibility for macroprudential regulation (IMF 2011).

Macroprudential policy is also affected by competition policy for three reasons. First and foremost, competition policy may lead financial institutions to take more or less risks, as originally stated by Keeley (1990), leading to an important debate on the impact of competition on financial stability (see Freixas and Ma 2013). Second, competition policy defines the access of other institutions, whether foreign banks or non-banks, to the markets where macroprudential policy has imposed some restrictions. Third, competition policy on mergers and acquisitions has a direct effect on the market consolidation of financial institutions and on the creation of SIFIs, which affect systemic risk.

Finally, as mentioned earlier, consumer protection limits the error each financial institution makes in its risk assessment by requiring adequate clauses in the contracts of financial products (ranging from information disclosure to outright prevention) that may end up being considered abusive to consumers and lead to huge losses (either market losses or the costs of legal settlements).

Institutional Design   To limit political interference, it is important to design independent institutions with clearly defined objectives and measurable intermediate objectives that are responsible for their decisions and accountable to society's representatives. The creation of new macroprudential institutions has been one of the first steps toward the implementation of a macroprudential policy.

The designated institution will be in charge of deciding whether to implement regulation that will reduce systemic risk at the cost of reducing growth and distorting the market allocation of funds. As mentioned, such a decision implies weighing type I errors associated with missing the buildup of a crisis, and type II errors of putting the brake on economic growth when it was not required. The political pressure on the institution will be enormous, as the reduction on the rate of growth implies a high visible cost while the preservation of financial stability is not directly observable and, in the best case, will never be observed because the crisis has been averted.

Table 11.1 summarizes some of the recent institutional changes to deal with systemic risk and establish macroprudential authorities in the European Union, United Kingdom, and United States. The different approaches taken in the creation of an institution responsible for macroprudential policy illustrate the difficulties these bodies face.

The ESRB, as a newly created institution will have to establish its reputation of independence and prove its members are not colluding,

Table 11.1

Institutional changes in prudential regulation and macroprudential policy

EU	Following the 2009 De Larosiere report recommendations, elements of an EU supervisory structure were established in January 2011 with the creation of three new European Supervisory Authorities—the European Banking Authority (EBA), the European Securities and Markets Authority, and the European Insurance and Occupational Pensions Authority—and the creation of European Systemic Risk Board (ESRB) responsible for macroprudential oversight. These new agencies have limited powers (including because of fiscal safeguards) and resources, with ultimate decisions remaining at the national level. The EBA is a cooperative body for EU bank supervisors. It is tasked with issuing technical standards in regulatory and supervisory areas (subject to fiscal safeguards). It can organize and conduct peer reviews of competent authorities, including issuing recommendations and identifying best practices, to strengthen consistency in supervisory outcomes, promote supervisory convergence, address breaches of EU law, limit scope for regulatory arbitrage, foster a level playing field, and support consumer protection. It coordinates and ensures consistency of EU-wide stress tests. The ESRB's role includes establishing macroprudential frameworks and ensuring effective coordination and internalization of cross-border spillovers. Its main instrument is the issuance of nonbinding risk warnings and recommendations through a "comply or explain" mechanism. The establishment of a Single Supervisory Mechanism (SSM) was agreed upon at an EU Council meeting on December 13–14, 2012. According to this agreement, broad investigatory and supervisory powers were conferred to the ECB, which became responsible for the effective and consistent functioning of the SSM. The SSM covers all credit institutions established in participating countries (being mandatory to all eurozone countries), although most tasks related to the supervision of those institutions considered not "systemically important" will normally be carried out by the national authorities. The criteria under which banks will be under the direct supervision of the ECB include size, importance for the economy of the EU or of a member state, and significance of cross-border activities. The ECB retains the power to bring any bank under its direct supervision, if it deems this necessary. The SSM became fully operational in November 2014. The EU has also agreed upon the establishment of a Single Resolution
	Mechanism (SRM), backed by a Single Resolution Fund (SRF), which applies to all banks covered by the SSM. It has also adopted the Bank Recovery and Resolution Directive (BRRD) and the deposit insurance harmonization directive, which harmonizes deposit insurance coverage limits across EU member states. However, a common fiscal backstop to support the SSM and SRM and common deposit insurance are still missing from what would be a full-fledged banking union.

Table 11.1 (continued)

UK	Under the Financial Services Act (2012) coming into force on April 1, 2013, three new bodies have been established: (1) the Prudential Regulation Authority (PRA), a subsidiary of the Bank of England (BoE), responsible for the regulation and supervision of most systemic institutions, including banks, building societies, credit unions, insurers, and major investment firms (while disbanding the former independent Financial Services Authority); (2) the Financial Conduct Authority (FCA), a separate institution not overseen by the BoE, to supervise and regulate other financial firms (e.g., nonbank asset managers), and responsible for ensuring that relevant markets function well and for the conduct regulation of all financial firms; and (3) the Financial Policy Committee (FPC), established under the purview of the BoE, with responsibility for macroprudential policy. The head of the PRA is a deputy governor of the BoE and member of the FPC. The PRA is under a statutory obligation to consult the FPC on any rules that would have material implications for financial stability.
US	The 2010 Dodd–Frank Wall Street Reform and Consumer Protection Act (Dodd–Frank Act) established a new Financial Stability Oversight Council (FSOC) chaired by the US Treasury and assembling each of the federal supervisory agencies and securities regulators, including the Federal Deposit Insurance Corporation (FDIC) and the newly created Bureau of Consumer Financial Protection. The FSOC can issue recommendations to constituent agencies, and plays a coordinating role, while direct regulatory and supervisory authority continues to lie with constituent agencies. The Dodd–Frank Act empowers FSOC to designate nonbank financial companies as systemically important, subjecting such companies to supervision and regulation by the Federal Reserve. The Act also requires the Federal Reserve to establish enhanced prudential standards for such institutions and establishes mechanisms to resolve these institutions. On July 8, 2013, the FSOC designated two nonbank financial institutions as systemically important, followed by Prudential Financial on September 19, 2013. A new Office for Financial Research (OFR) was also established within the US Treasury, which is empowered to collect information and whose role it is to conduct analysis and research for FSOC.

Source: IMF (2011) and IMF staff reports

in the sense of country X being lenient with country Y today in the hope that country Y will return the favor to country X by being lenient in the future to country X whenever required. The "act or explain" approach allows for exceptions to the rules, which may improve the efficiency of the policy by reducing type II errors, that is, implementing unnecessary measures when there is no danger of a systemic crisis, if the country facing systemic risk has more information than the others. However, it may have a negative impact and lead to more type I errors if the country's central bank is under political pressure not to act.

Political pressures are likely to be minimized for the UK Financial Policy Committee (FPC), which consists largely of Bank of England officials and external financial experts that are not pursuing a political career. Also, because of their purely technical responsibility, FPC members may largely be protected from political pressures.

The Financial Stability Oversight Council (FSOC) being directly connected to the Fed may benefit from the Fed's reputation. Nevertheless, the collegial character of the institution may lead to political pressure for its members. Regardless, the inclusion of the Bureau of Consumer Financial Protection may constitute an excellent addition that is not present in the FPC or in the ESRB.

The independence of the systemic risk board is limited by one key aspect that has to be clearly designed when the institution is created. Indeed, independence is required at the prevention stage but is nonexistent in the crisis management stage.

A systemic risk board has to cope with both the time dimension and the cross-sectional dimension of systemic risk, and they require different approaches. The time dimension concerns the buildup of macroeconomic imbalances, excessive credit risk, and bubbles. As a consequence it has a clear link with monetary policy and even with fiscal policy. The cross-sectional dimension requires a completely different approach, and concerns herding arising from common exposures and interlinkages between financial institutions, as well as too big to fail issues. As a consequence the cross-sectional wing of the systemic risk board has to liaise with microprudential authorities. As mentioned, the two dimensions are related, as the risk of contagion depends on the overall macrofragility, which is time dependent, in that it is linked to the business and financial cycles. The existence of these two dimensions will make the internal structure of the institution especially complex.

Despite the complexity of systemic risk, there are several basic rules that the creation of a macroprudential authority should take into account. First, the existence of clear-cut, well-defined resolution policies facilitates the macroprudential task and therefore limits the political interference as the mechanisms of resolution are nonnegotiable (e.g., for bail-in policies). Second, intense interface with microprudential policy is essential in limiting the scope of macroprudential policy and reducing possible political pressures and the financial industry's lobbying. Third, access to timely precise information is essential and justifies a close link with the central bank. Consequently, even though we recognize that the macroprudential authorities will have to resist political interferences and lobbying, by providing its members with a set of rules that limit their power, the magnitude of the problem, although not solved, can be reduced.

11.3.2   Countercyclical Capital Buffers: The Political Economy Dimension

The lessons of the 2008 crisis have led to the design of a number of countercyclical mechanisms. Countercyclical capital requirements— raising bank capital requirements significantly in good times, while allowing them to fall somewhat in bad times—have been proposed by many as a form of "cycle-proof" regulation, and such a form of macroprudential regulation has become part of the new Basel III regulation.

The Basel III capital preservation buffer imposes a capital level of 10.5 percent in good times that may be reduced to 8 percent in bad times. This buffer gives banks the right incentives to manage their capital because the payouts both in dividends and in bonuses will be suppressed when the capital falls below 10.5 percent. On the other hand, the countercyclical buffer imposes an additional layer of capital when credit growth is excessive. The countercyclical credit buffer is based on positive deviations of the credit to GDP ratios from their trend, which, as previous empirical research (e.g., Borio and Drehman 2009; Alessi and Dekten 2009) has shown, allows for identification of the buildup of financial imbalances. The countercyclical buffer is an aggregate instrument, ill-fitted to solve problems emerging only in a given segment of the credit market, and as mentioned by Repullo and Saurina (2012), because the correlation between the gaps with respect to trend and GDP growth is negative in the majority of countries, countercyclical buffers would have to be enforced when the economy is in a downturn.

No matter the type of countercyclical mechanism that is imposed, two issues have to be considered. First, the effectiveness of countercyclical capital requirements is not without doubts. Forcing banks to hold more capital during booms than the market demands will shift activity to unregulated intermediaries. Similarly, forcing banks to hold less capital than the market demands during crisis times is bound to fail "as the will of the market will naturally prevail" (Rajan 2009). Such unintended consequences need to be taken into account when crafting new regulations.

Second, countercyclical regulations may not be immune to the cycle because of possible ex post renegotiations, and will thus likely suffer from a strong bias toward inaction. At the height of a crisis, a popular call for tougher regulations will frontally oppose the desire to implement countercyclical regulations. And, once memories of a recent crisis abate, the political pressure to relax regulations or their enforcement will increase. A tightening of macroprudential policy (e.g., a decrease in LTVs) during upswings will face stiff political resistance because it is politically challenging to "take away the punch bowl just as the party gets going," in particular with tougher lending standards. It will be difficult to impose a buffer during a downturn or when the system looks particularly strong, which is when it is most vulnerable (Borio 2010). A bias toward inaction would imply excessive risk-taking during upswings and excessive costs for the real economy on the downturn. We should not reform under the assumption that the regulatory environment will not adjust over the cycle. Tougher regulation in one country may constitute a great opportunity for foreign banks that do not have to face the same restrictions. While this is perfect in terms of risk diversification, the political pressure on regulators will be particularly strong, as domestic banking lobbies will argue that the country is sold to foreigners.

11.3.3 Data, Models, and Calibration of Macroprudential Policy

Effective macroprudential oversight requires the collection and analysis of supervisory data and financial transactions, including on counterparty risk and derivative positions. The institution responsible for macroprudential oversight needs access to complete supervisory data to discern, for instance, whether compositional changes in financial institutions' assets denote endogenous changes in systemic risk. Considering the advances in statistics and computing power, it should be relatively easy to collect and work with extensive datasets on financial transactions.

One challenge is that existing legislation in many countries prevents supervisory authorities from sharing supervisory information with other bodies. Such legislation would have to be amended to allow the institution responsible for macroprudential regulation to access such data. Access to data should apply to all the relevant parts of the financial system (not just the banking systems) such that regulatory arbitrage can be detected. If combined with better theoretical models, such datasets should help in measuring the time and cross-sectional dimensions of systemic risk and in calibrating macroprudential instruments, such as countercyclical capital requirements or systemic capital surcharges.

Another challenge is to build better models of systemic risk. As explained in chapter 3, better theoretical models should be based on corporate finance principles, and be incorporated in dynamic general equilibrium models and include such critical mechanisms as nonlinear relationships, feedback loops, and tipping points, and leave out less important macro real frictions. The incorporation of tail risks or Knightian uncertainty, and not only agency incentives, can make models more realistic and a more accurate depiction of systemic risk.

The development of improved theoretical models is obviously not enough. These models need to be calibrated and complemented with empirical evidence on the effectiveness of alternative macroprudential instruments. Indeed, to fine-tune macroprudential instruments, we need to analyze the impact of existing policies and to gain experience from new policies through an expansion of the macroprudential toolkit.

11.3.4   Macroprudential Communication Policy

An issue that has not been addressed so far is the communication policy of the institution in charge of macroprudential regulation. This poses a challenge because of the difficulties in identifying the counterfactuals to financial stability. Clearly, in a world characterized by uncertainty, type II errors are inevitable. The problem is that even if the macroprudential policy is successful, no evidence is available to certify that in the absence of the macroprudential policy a systemic crisis would have been likely to happen.

The design of a communication policy for the macroprudential institution depends on its transparency and accountability. It also depends on its institutional setup, which determines its independence. The complexity of setting up a communication policy is increased because the systemic risk board is in charge of both the time dimension and the cross-sectional dimension. Consequently its communication policy should cover both aspects.

Regarding the time dimension, transparency would lead to emphasis on the disclosure of the likelihood of a systemic crisis. This would allow for greater accountability to the public in general. Unfortunately, such a policy has two major drawbacks. First, when a systemic risk alert is issued it may trigger a systemic crisis as people update their beliefs and coordinate their actions (i.e., the alarm may turn into a self-fulfilling prophecy). Second, to justify its existence the systemic risk board may be overactive and send too many systemic risk alerts, thus creating a reputation of being alarmist and a "crying wolf" effect.

Consequently it may be more realistic for the systemic risk board to be responsible for recommending the implementation of a macroprudential instrument. Then the communication policy would be directed only to the institutions in charge of the implementation, not to the public. In addition the systemic risk board should interact with the microprudential regulatory authorities in order to identify bubbles and any kind of risks that internal risk models of banks working in isolation cannot adequately measure, and have the power to directly implement and enforce certain measures, such as countercyclical buffers or maximum LTV ratios (IMF 2013c). In both cases the communication and coordination would be with the microprudential regulatory authorities, and so could unavoidably create a conflict with the lobbies of the banking industry. It is important that the institution has sufficient independence to be protected from such pressures. In turn the independence of the systemic risk board has to be based on its credibility, as otherwise its opinions and recommendations could easily be discredited.

11.4 The International Challenges

11.4.1 Multinational Banks and Financial Integration
The provision of cross-border services by foreign banks implies that domestic banks and foreign banks may be submitted to different regulatory regimes. In particular, when a macroprudential measure is taken to reduce systemic risk, this may only directly affect domestic banks, especially where macroprudential policy-setting is a national affair.

The fact that foreign banks do not have to abide by the same rules could be seen as unfair competition by domestic banks, but this need not be the case. Indeed the portfolios of, say, French banks might have a much larger fraction of their investment in French real estate than foreign banks operating in France. As a consequence a higher capital requirement for French banks would simply reflect their risk, as measured by the covariance of real estate related loans to their portfolio, and not lead to unfair competition.

Likewise the issue of the increase of foreign banks' investment in a country may or may not be efficient. It would be efficient if it allows households and firms to obtain funding while systemic risk is reduced. It would be inefficient if it circumvents the macroprudential regulation, so that the regulation is not effective and the likelihood of a systemic crisis remains the same. The latter would be illustrated by the buildup of a real estate bubble: replacing domestic funding by foreign funding would not reduce the risk of the bubble.

11.4.2 Regulatory Competition and Cooperation

Countries Provide Implicit and Explicit Support to Their Financial Intermediaries The mandate of each country's regulator is to preserve stability in the domestic financial market. As a consequence it has to care about the expansion of the financial sector and the loss to foreign competitors. This leads to a regulatory race to the bottom in order to make domestic banks competitive in international markets. As explained in chapter 8, this type of competition will generate the underprovision of international banking regulation (see Dell'Ariccia and Marquez 2006b; Hardy and Nieto 2011). To improve efficiency, coordination among regulators is required.

Cross-country Cooperation Challenges The supervision and resolution of cross-border financial institutions continues to pose significant challenges. The resolution of multinational banks constitutes an issue because bankruptcy regimes may be based on territoriality in some countries while based on universality in others. In addition the bailout of multinational banks implies that a bank headquartered in country A but active in country B may in part be bailed out by taxpayers in country B, which may face strong political opposition. As a consequence, it is quite likely that (affiliates of) multinational banks that could be bailed out are liquidated in order to avoid the risk of cross-country transfers of taxpayers' money.

The responsibility of bank supervision should also move to the country that is to suffer the most should a bank fail. This is a very different setup from the home-host model of supervision that is currently in force in Europe, where branches of a foreign bank are supervised by the home regulator, even though the home country could stand to lose the most from failure of such a bank.

The Case for a European Banking Union In the euro area the monetary union with a single financial market poses challenges for intervention and resolution as well. Although supervision and resolution have been centralized under the single supervisory mechanism (SSM) and the single resolution mechanism (SRM), resolution and deposit insurance—and thus the provision of a financial safety net—remain largely a national affair because of the absence of a common fiscal backstop (although authorities have indicated their intention to eventually centralize these components of the safety net as well). Moreover monetary policy and lender of last resort policy focus on euro area financial conditions and need not respond optimally to national financial stability concerns in euro area member states. Sovereign stresses have put pressure on financial risks, intensifying sovereign-banking links. To create a sound financial safety net for the euro area as a whole and its individual member states, a full-fledged banking union—a single supervisory-regulatory framework, resolution mechanism, and safety net—with a credible backstop is needed. This would involve burden sharing across member states, through a combination of private sector contributions and fiscal financing arrangements (see Goodhart and Schoenmaker 2009; IMF 2013a).

The case for a banking union for the euro area is both immediate and longer term. Moving responsibility for potential financial support and bank supervision to a shared level can reduce fragmentation of financial markets, stem deposit flight, and weaken the vicious loop of rising sovereign and bank borrowing costs. In steady state a single framework should bring a uniformly high standard of confidence and oversight, reduce national distortions, and mitigate the buildup of concentrated risk that compromises systemic stability (IMF 2013a).

Without common safety nets and credible backstops, the SSM and SRM alone may be insufficient to sever vicious sovereign bank links. Common safety nets and credible backstops are also needed to limit conflicts of interest between national authorities, the SRM, and the SSM. A single resolution authority, with clear ex ante burden sharing mechanisms, must have strong powers to close or restructure banks and be required to intervene well ahead of insolvency, and be supported by a sufficiently large financing backstop. A common resolution/ insurance fund, with sufficient prefunding to resolve small- to medium-size bank failures, and with access to common backstops for systemic situations, is needed to add credibility to the safety net underpinning the EU financial system.

11.4.3 Macroprudential Policy and Capital Flows

Financial globalization has increased over the last thirty years. Both emerging and advanced economies have increasingly opened their financial markets to international financial flows. Financial globalization implies substantial gains by allowing specialization in comparative advantages, international risk-sharing and diversification, and the financing of investments (Kalemni-Ozcan et al. 2013). Still, financial globalization can transmit shocks internationally—financial contagion—and international liquidity can evaporate fast and give rise to fire sale prices, including credit crunches, with substantial negative real effects. Contributing to most crises are international financial flows, particularly short-term flows in foreign currency. For example, in 1931 during the Great Depression, the failure of the Austrian Bank Creditanstalt caused major global financial contagion. Such financial contagion typically results in the global spread of what initially are viewed mostly as regional shocks, as in, for example, the 1982 Latin American crisis, the 1997 to 1998 Asian crisis, the 2008 global financial crisis, the 2010 euro area crisis, and more recently, the turbulence in emerging markets in 2014.

Concerns about the adequacy of reserves or the sustainability of macroeconomic policies can quickly translate to exchange rate collapses and rapid capital outflows, known as sudden stops. These shocks in individual countries can rapidly spread to other countries as market sentiment turns against countries with similarly weak fundamentals, and in the process such financial contagion can lead to a generalized panic or market overreaction affecting also countries with otherwise strong fundamentals. Such shocks may be detrimental to global financial stability and may backfire to originating countries, for instance, by negatively affecting confidence in the financial system or depressing global growth prospects.

Credit cycles, notably credit to riskier borrowers, and more generally the prices of risky assets have a strong common component, both locally and internationally. Credit flows are particularly procyclical. Strong credit flows are normally financed with international flows, and as international flows can be volatile, credit flows are also volatile. Excessive credit growth is the best predictor of financial crisis as shown by Schularick and Taylor (2012); however, as Gourinchas and Obstfeld (2012) have shown, credit and international flows have *both* grown substantially since the 1970s. Global financial cycles are associated with surges and retrenchments in capital flows, as well as booms and busts in asset prices and crises. As Rey (2013) explains, the emerging picture is that of a world with powerful global financial cycles characterized by large common movements in asset prices, gross flows, and leverage.

As credit and liquidity cycles are affected by monetary policy, at the global level there are interrelations between the monetary conditions of the major advanced economies—the so-called center countries (i.e., the United States and Europe), international capital flows, and the leverage of the financial sector in many parts of the international financial system (Rey 2013; Shin 2012; Bruno and Shin 2013a). The global financial cycle can be related to monetary conditions in the center country and to changes in risk aversion and uncertainty (Bekaert et al. 2012; Miranda-Agrippino and Rey 2012; Bruno and Shin 2013b). Moreover the US Federal Reserve's "tapering talk" starting in 2013 has been blamed for outflows of capital from emerging markets.

Forbes and Warnock (2012) try to explain sharp movements of capital flows into and out of countries. They find that changes in global risk and uncertainty (measured by the VIX index of stock market volatility) are the most important variable determining large shifts in capital flows by foreign and domestic investors. They also find that global growth plays a role in determining swings in foreign capital flows, and increases in US interest rates can play a role in explaining 'sudden stops' of foreign flows. But changes in US interest rates and liquidity appear to play a less important role than other variables. However, as Rey (2013) shows, reductions in US interest rates tend to lower measures of risk and uncertainty. Eichengreen and Gupta (2013) analyze which countries were hit the most by the June 2013 US Fed's taper-talk shock. Those hit hardest had relatively large and liquid financial markets, and had allowed large rises in their currency values and their trade deficits. Good macro fundamentals did not provide much insulation, nor did capital controls.

Clearly, international flows are crucial for financial stability. Monetary policy by affecting the exchange rate may be a powerful tool to control international capital flows but may also have detrimental effects on financial stability. Moreover monetary policy may have little room for maneuver given the objective of price stability. Macroprudential policy then becomes a useful tool. For example, Eichengreen and Gupta (2013) argue that the best insulation from the taper-talk shock came from macroprudential policies that limited exchange rate appreciation and trade deficit widening in response to foreign capital inflows. In general, a common feature of most recent crises is excessive borrowing abroad in foreign currency and using short-term debt rather than more stable, long-term investments such as FDIs. Moreover macroprudential policy is not only important to better manage capital flows in emerging markets but also to strengthen the domestic financial systems in these countries because it would attract domestic investors that can be a buffer in case international liquidity evaporates and because it helps manage domestic credit and asset price bubbles (see Ostry et al. 2011).

We believe that macroprudential policy should therefore consider this international dimension of financial stability, both in terms of cooperation among different local regulators and supervisors and in terms of coordination of policies among macroprudential bodies. At an international or regional level it is desirable to have a centralized organization that coordinates macroprudential policies and takes into account the externalities of such policies for other countries. Consideration should be given to policies that stem the inflow of short-term capital flows and are prone to sharp reversals, such as short-term foreign wholesale positions through the imposition of liquidity requirements. Moreover macroprudential policy should coordinate with monetary policy, and vice versa, because monetary policy in advanced economies (e.g., the United States and Europe) affects global capital flows, including to emerging markets, which may in turn impact financial and economic conditions in advanced economies. When monetary policy rates in the advanced economies are low and liquidity is abundant, there is a risk of search for yield in emerging or peripheral countries, which could feed into real estate and other asset price bubbles, and the risk of a collapse in asset prices and the reversal of capital flows when monetary policy is being tightened. As a result the exit from the very low levels of monetary policy rates such as those seen today in advanced economies can impact not only the advanced economies but, by increasing interest rates globally, can spillover onto emerging market economies, with potentially negative repercussions for global growth.

11.5 Concluding Remarks

The future success of banking regulation will largely depend on the changes made to the current regulatory framework for banks. The new regulations that curtail bank activities or increase capital requirements will force banks to become smaller and less leveraged, and therefore less risky. At the same time there is a risk that bank activity would shift to less regulated parts of the financial system, including to nonbanks and financial markets. While there are benefits to having a more diverse financial system, without additional regulation, risk could become concentrated in unregulated entities and take systemic proportions. As a result systemic risk could increase even though banks become less risky.

Based on our analysis in this book, the new bank regulatory framework should have the following elements:

• Be more macroprudential with greater attention to systemic risks, including those emerging from outside the regulated sector

• Counter the buildup of financial imbalances and excessive leverage, including through increased capital requirements especially in good times

• Pay more attention to cross-border spillovers, including from cross-border financial flows

• Improve bank resolution frameworks and reduce the too big to fail problem

• Strengthen supervision including at the macroprudential level and be more resistant to political pressures and to regulatory loopholes

• Strengthen market discipline and sound corporate governance, including through bail-in policies

• Recognize that monetary and prudential policy cannot be entirely independent

• Avoid excessive costs on the regulated

But we are left with many unanswered questions regarding how best to build and implement such a regulatory framework in support of financial stability and economic prosperity. The analysis in this book points to the following key lessons from the crisis and the resulting metamorphosis of the banking regulatory framework that should serve as a guide in the pursuit of these objectives:

First, systemic risk needs to be managed preemptively, including through monitoring (and curtailing) rapid credit growth, asset bubbles, and other forms of leverage. Systemic risk generally builds up slowly but well in advance of an eventual crisis. Dealing with the buildup of systemic risk ex ante, for example, by curtailing credit growth and building up capital buffers, not only can help prevent a crisis but also help in dealing with the management of a crisis. For example, the buildup of capital buffers will help banks absorb the shocks from a crisis especially when markets for new capital are closed.

Second, systemic risk is an endogenous concept, complicating policy. Banks will respond to new regulations by altering their risk profile in ways that can result in unintended consequences. For example, by limiting risk in one part of the financial system, risk may be pushed elsewhere. There is a risk that new regulations, by focusing on one type of risk, could be crafted without consideration of such second-round effects. Additionally regulations may conflict, so macroprudential policies should be coordinated.

Third, the introduction of macroprudential policies alone will be insufficient to limit systemic risk. The macroprudential policies need to be strictly enforced, which requires that administrators be empowered to act without interference from vested interests. And they need to be supported by sound macroeconomic policies to manage the economic cycle. Additionally corporate governance reform is needed to limit systemic risk at the source, by requiring bank managers to act in the interests not only of bank shareholders but the bank's stakeholders at large. An important step in this direction is that capital requirements be substantially higher in good times when excessive risk is taken, as bank managers should not define the bank's strategy in the interest of only 4 percent of the liability holders. Incentives are crucial, and corporate governance and market disciplining are essential, including through capital requirements, compensation structures, and bail-in and resolution procedures.

Fourth, given the globalization of the financial and banking system, and the potential international spillovers, macroprudential policy needs to safeguard not only domestic financial systems but also address cross-border externalities. These effects are a consequence of the financial liberalization that started in the 1970s, and as evidenced by the major financial crises in recent decades, each domestic crisis had an important international dimension.

Given these challenges and limits, one has to be realistic about how much macroprudential regulation can accomplish in terms of managing financial imbalances and ensuring financial stability. Much depends on the strength and independence of the macroprudential authority and the risk attitude of the public at large toward boom-bust cycles. Moreover political economy constraints will continue to plague the resolution of what are deemed to be TBTF institutions during a systemic financial crisis. Our advice is to focus on the prevention of financial crises through higher capital requirements, which reduce risk-shifting incentives, combined with macroprudential measures that tame the buildup of leverage and credit booms, such as loan-to-value ratios. Where there is a will, there is a way. Financial crises are too costly for taxpayers. We cannot afford imprudence and negligence.

Appendix Data

Table A1
Macroprudential instruments, 2010
Panel A

Country	Size, complexity, and interconnectedness			
	Limits on interbank exposure	Capital surcharges for systemically important institutions	Size-dependent leverage limits	Size-dependent asset risk weights
Argentina	0	0	0	0
Australia	0	0	0	0
Austria	0	0	0	0
Belgium	0	0	0	0
Brazil	0	0	0	0
Bulgaria	0	0	0	0
Canada	0	0	0	0
Chile	0	1	0	0
China	0	0	0	0
Colombia	1	0	0	0
Croatia	0	0	0	0
Czech Republic	0	0	0	0
Finland	0	0	0	0
France	0	0	0	0
Germany	0	0	0	0
Greece	0	0	0	0
Hong Kong SAR	0	0	0	0
Hungary	0	0	0	0
India	0	0	0	0
Indonesia	0	0	0	0
Ireland	0	0	0	0
Italy	0	0	0	0
Japan	0	0	0	0
Jordan	0	0	0	0
Korea	0	0	0	0
Lebanon	0	0	0	0
Malaysia	0	0	0	0
Mexico	1	0	0	0
Mongolia	0	0	0	0
Netherlands	0	0	0	0
New Zealand	0	0	0	0
Nigeria	0	0	0	0
Norway	0	0	0	0
Paraguay	1	1	0	0

Procyclicality			

Countercyclical/ dynamic provisioning	Restrictions on profit distribution	Countercyclical/ time-varying capital requirements	Countercyclical/ time-varying liquidity ratios
0	1	0	0
0	0	0	0
0	0	0	0
0	0	0	0
1	0	1	0
1	1	1	0
0	0	0	0
0	0	0	0
0	0	0	0
1	1	0	0
1	0	0	0
0	0	0	0
0	0	0	0
0	0	0	0
0	0	0	0
1	0	1	0
0	0	0	0
0	0	0	0
1	0	1	0
0	0	0	0
0	0	0	0
0	0	0	0
0	0	0	0
0	0	0	0
0	0	0	0
1	0	1	0
0	0	0	0
0	0	1	0
1	0	0	0
0	0	0	0
0	0	0	0
0	0	0	0
0	0	0	0
0	1	1	0

Table A1 (continued)

Country	Size, complexity, and interconnectedness			
	Limits on interbank exposure	Capital surcharges for systemically important institutions	Size-dependent leverage limits	Size-dependent asset risk weights
Peru	1	0	0	0
Philippines	0	0	0	0
Poland	0	0	0	0
Portugal	0	0	0	0
Romania	1	0	0	0
Russian Federation	0	0	0	0
Serbia	0	0	0	0
Singapore	0	0	0	0
Slovakia	0	0	0	0
South Africa	0	1	0	0
Spain	0	0	0	0
Sweden	0	0	0	0
Switzerland	1	1	1	0
Thailand	0	0	0	0
Turkey	0	0	0	0
United Kingdom	0	0	0	0
United States	0	0	0	0
Uruguay	1	1	0	0

Panel B

Country	Credit growth and asset prices					
	Caps on loan to value ratio	Caps on debt to income ratio	Sector-dependent asset risk weights	Limit on exposure concentration	Caps on loan to deposit ratio	Ceiling on credit growth
Argentina	0	0	1	1	0	0
Australia	0	0	0	0	0	0
Austria	0	0	0	0	0	0
Belgium	0	0	0	0	0	0

Procyclicality			
Countercyclical/ dynamic provisioning	Restrictions on profit distribution	Countercyclical/ time-varying capital requirements	Countercyclical/ time-varying liquidity ratios
1	0	0	0
0	0	0	0
0	1	0	0
0	0	0	0
0	1	0	0
1	0	0	0
0	1	1	0
0	0	0	0
0	1	0	0
0	0	0	0
1	0	0	0
0	0	0	0
0	0	0	0
0	0	0	0
0	1	0	0
0	0	0	0
0	0	0	0
1	0	0	0

	Leverage and maturity mismatch				
Sector-specific ceiling on credit growth (e.g., real estate)	Limits on maturity mismatch	Minimum haircuts/ margins on collateral	Core funding ratios	Limits on off balance sheet positions (e.g., derivatives)	Limits on exposure by instrument (e.g., CDS)
0	0	0	0	0	0
0	0	0	0	0	0
0	0	0	0	0	0
0	0	0	0	0	0

Table A1 (continued)

Country	Credit growth and asset prices					
	Caps on loan to value ratio	Caps on debt to income ratio	Sector-dependent asset risk weights	Limit on exposure concentration	Caps on loan to deposit ratio	Ceiling on credit growth
Brazil	0	0	1	0	0	0
Bulgaria	0	0	1	0	0	0
Canada	1	0	0	0	0	0
Chile	1	0	0	0	0	0
China	1	1	0	0	0	0
Colombia	1	1	0	1	0	0
Croatia	0	0	0	0	0	1
Czech Republic	0	0	0	0	0	0
Finland	0	0	0	0	0	0
France	0	1	0	1	0	0
Germany	0	0	0	0	0	0
Greece	1	1	0	0	1	1
Hong Kong SAR	1	1	0	0	1	0
Hungary	1	1	0	0	0	0
India	1	0	1	0	0	0
Indonesia	1	0	0	0	0	0
Ireland	0	0	0	0	0	0
Italy	1	0	0	1	0	0
Japan	0	0	0	0	0	0
Jordan	0	0	0	0	0	0
Korea	1	1	0	0	0	0
Lebanon	1	1	0	0	1	0
Malaysia	1	0	0	0	0	0
Mexico	0	0	0	1	0	0
Mongolia	0	0	0	1	0	0
Netherlands	0	0	0	0	0	0
New Zealand	0	0	0	0	0	0
Nigeria	0	0	0	0	1	1
Norway	1	1	0	0	0	0
Paraguay	1	0	0	0	1	0
Peru	0	1	0	0	0	0
Philippines	0	0	0	0	0	0
Poland	0	1	1	1	0	0

Sector-specific ceiling on credit growth (e.g., real estate)	Leverage and maturity mismatch				
	Limits on maturity mismatch	Minimum haircuts/margins on collateral	Core funding ratios	Limits on off balance sheet positions (e.g., derivatives)	Limits on exposure by instrument (e.g., CDS)
0	0	0	0	0	0
0	0	0	0	0	0
0	0	1	0	0	0
0	0	0	0	0	0
1	0	0	0	0	0
1	1	1	0	1	0
0	0	0	0	0	0
0	0	0	0	0	0
0	0	0	0	0	0
0	1	0	0	0	0
0	0	0	0	0	0
0	1	1	1	0	1
0	0	0	0	0	0
0	0	0	0	0	0
0	0	0	0	0	0
0	1	0	0	0	0
0	0	0	0	0	0
0	1	0	0	0	0
0	0	0	0	0	0
0	0	0	0	0	0
0	0	0	0	1	0
0	0	1	1	0	1
1	0	0	0	0	0
0	1	0	0	0	0
0	1	0	0	0	0
0	0	0	0	0	0
0	1	0	1	0	0
0	1	0	0	0	0
0	0	0	0	0	0
0	1	0	0	0	0
0	0	0	0	1	1
0	0	0	0	0	0
0	1	0	1	0	0

Table A1 (continued)

Country	Credit growth and asset prices					
	Caps on loan to value ratio	Caps on debt to income ratio	Sector-dependent asset risk weights	Limit on exposure concentration	Caps on loan to deposit ratio	Ceiling on credit growth
Portugal	0	0	0	0	0	0
Romania	1	1	0	0	0	0
Russian Federation	0	0	1	0	0	0
Serbia	0	1	0	0	0	1
Singapore	1	0	0	0	0	0
Slovakia	0	0	0	0	0	0
South Africa	0	0	0	0	0	0
Spain	0	0	1	0	0	0
Sweden	1	0	0	0	0	0
Switzerland	0	0	0	0	0	0
Thailand	1	1	0	0	0	0
Turkey	1	0	1	0	0	0
United Kingdom	0	0	0	0	0	0
United States	0	0	0	0	0	0
Uruguay	0	0	0	1	0	0

Panel C

Country	Currency risk			
	Limits on net open foreign currency positions	Caps on foreign currency lending	Limits on currency mismatch	Differentiated reserve requirements for foreign currency
Argentina	1	0	1	1
Australia	0	0	0	0
Austria	0	1	0	0
Belgium	0	0	0	0
Brazil	0	1	1	0

| Sector-specific ceiling on credit growth (e.g., real estate) | Leverage and maturity mismatch | | | | |
	Limits on maturity mismatch	Minimum haircuts/ margins on collateral	Core funding ratios	Limits on off balance sheet positions (e.g., derivatives)	Limits on exposure by instrument (e.g., CDS)
0	0	0	0	0	0
0	1	0	0	0	0
0	0	1	0	0	0
0	0	0	0	0	0
1	1	0	0	0	0
0	1	1	0	0	0
0	1	1	0	0	0
0	0	0	0	0	0
0	0	0	0	0	0
0	0	0	0	0	0
0	0	0	0	1	0
0	0	0	0	0	0
0	0	0	0	0	0
0	1	0	1	0	0

| Foreign exchange policy measures | Capital flows | | |
	Unremunerated reserve requirements for nonresidents	Taxation of capital flows	Minimum holding periods for capital inflows
1	1	0	0
0	0	0	0
0	0	0	0
0	0	0	0
0	0	1	0

Table A1 (continued)

| Country | Currency risk | | | |
	Limits on net open foreign currency positions	Caps on foreign currency lending	Limits on currency mismatch	Differentiated reserve requirements for foreign currency
Bulgaria	0	0	0	0
Canada	0	0	0	0
Chile	0	0	0	1
China	0	0	0	0
Colombia	1	1	0	0
Croatia	0	0	1	0
Czech Republic	0	0	0	0
Finland	0	0	0	0
France	0	0	0	0
Germany	0	0	0	0
Greece	0	0	0	0
Hong Kong SAR	0	0	0	0
Hungary	1	1	0	0
India	0	0	0	0
Indonesia	1	0	0	1
Ireland	0	0	0	0
Italy	0	0	0	0
Japan	0	0	0	0
Jordan	0	0	0	0
Korea	1	1	1	0
Lebanon	0	0	1	0
Malaysia	1	0	0	0
Mexico	0	0	0	0
Mongolia	1	0	0	0
Netherlands	0	0	0	0
New Zealand	0	0	0	0
Nigeria	1	0	0	0
Norway	0	0	0	0
Paraguay	1	0	1	0
Peru	1	0	1	1
Philippines	0	0	0	0
Poland	0	1	0	0
Portugal	0	0	0	0
Romania	1	1	0	0
Russian Federation	1	0	0	1
Serbia	1	1	0	1

| Foreign exchange policy measures | Capital flows | | |
	Unremunerated reserve requirements for nonresidents	Taxation of capital flows	Minimum holding periods for capital inflows
0	0	0	0
0	0	0	0
1	0	0	0
0	0	0	0
0	1	1	0
0	0	0	0
0	0	0	0
0	0	0	0
0	0	0	0
0	0	0	0
0	0	0	0
0	0	0	0
0	0	0	0
0	0	0	0
0	0	0	0
0	0	0	0
0	0	0	0
0	0	0	0
0	0	0	0
0	0	1	0
0	0	0	0
0	0	0	0
1	0	0	0
0	0	0	0
0	0	0	0
0	0	0	0
0	0	0	0
0	0	0	0
0	0	1	0
1	1	0	0
0	0	0	0
1	0	0	0
0	0	0	0
0	0	0	0
1	0	0	0
0	0	0	0

Table A1 (continued)

Country	Currency risk			
	Limits on net open foreign currency positions	Caps on foreign currency lending	Limits on currency mismatch	Differentiated reserve requirements for foreign currency
Singapore	0	0	0	0
Slovakia	0	0	0	0
South Africa	1	1	1	0
Spain	0	0	0	0
Sweden	0	0	0	0
Switzerland	0	0	0	0
Thailand	1	0	0	0
Turkey	1	1	1	1
United Kingdom	0	0	0	0
United States	0	0	0	0
Uruguay	1	1	1	1

Source: IMF Macroprudential Regulations Survey, December 2010.
Notes: 0 indicates "no"; 1 indicates "yes."

	Capital flows		
Foreign exchange policy measures	Unremunerated reserve requirements for nonresidents	Taxation of capital flows	Minimum holding periods for capital inflows
0	0	0	0
0	0	0	0
0	0	0	0
0	0	0	0
0	0	0	0
0	0	0	0
0	1	0	0
0	0	0	0
0	0	0	0
0	0	0	0
1	0	0	0

Table A2
Macroprudential instruments, 2013
Panel A

| Country | Size, complexity, and interconnectedness | | Procyclicality | |
	Limits on interbank exposure	Capital surcharges for systemically important institutions	Dynamic provisioning	Countercyclical capital buffer/ requirement
Argentina	1	0	0	0
Australia	1	0	0	0
Austria	0	0	0	0
Bahrain	0	0	0	0
Belgium	0	1	0	0
Brazil	0	0	0	0
Bulgaria	1	0	1	0
Canada	1	0	0	0
Chile	1	0	0	0
China	0	1	1	0
Colombia	1	0	1	0
Croatia	1	0	0	0
Czech Republic	0	0	0	0
Estonia	0	0	0	0
Finland	0	0	0	0
France	1	0	0	0
Germany	1	0	0	0
Ghana	0	0	0	0
Hong Kong	0	0	0	0
Hungary	0	0	0	0
Iceland	0	0	0	0
India	1	0	0	0
Indonesia	0	0	0	0
Ireland	0	0	0	0
Israel	1	1	0	0
Italy	1	0	0	0
Japan	0	0	0	0
Jordan	0	0	0	0
Kazakhstan	0	0	1	0
Kenya	0	0	0	0
Kuwait	0	0	0	0
Lebanon	1	0	0	0

Table A2 (continued)

| Country | Size, complexity, and interconnectedness | | Procyclicality | |
	Limits on interbank exposure	Capital surcharges for systemically important institutions	Dynamic provisioning	Countercyclical capital buffer/ requirement
Lithuania	0	0	0	0
Malaysia	0	0	0	0
Mauritius	0	0	0	0
Mexico	1	0	0	0
Morocco	1	0	0	0
Netherlands	0	0	0	0
New Zealand	0	0	0	0
Norway	0	0	0	1
Oman	0	0	0	0
Pakistan	1	0	0	1
Peru	1	1	1	0
Philippines	0	0	0	0
Poland	0	0	0	0
Portugal	1	0	0	0
Romania	1	1	0	0
Russian Federation	0	0	0	0
Saudi Arabia	0	0	0	0
Serbia	0	0	0	0
Singapore	0	1	0	0
Slovakia	0	0	0	0
Slovenia	0	0	0	0
South Africa	0	0	0	0
South Korea	0	0	0	0
Spain	0	0	1	1
Sri Lanka	0	0	0	0
Sweden	0	0	0	0
Switzerland	1	1	0	1
Thailand	0	0	1	0
Turkey	0	0	0	0
Ukraine	1	0	0	0
United Arab Emirates	1	0	0	0
United Kingdom	0	0	0	0
United States	1	0	0	0

Table A2 (continued)

Panel B

| Country | Credit growth and asset prices | | | |
	Caps on loan to value ratio	Caps on debt to income ratio	Sector-specific capital buffer/ requirement	Limit on exposure concentration
Argentina	1	0	0	1
Australia	0	0	0	0
Austria	0	0	0	0
Bahrain	0	1	0	1
Belgium	0	0	0	1
Brazil	1	0	0	1
Bulgaria	1	1	1	1
Canada	1	1	0	1
Chile	1	1	0	1
China	1	1	0	1
Colombia	1	1	0	1
Croatia	0	0	0	1
Czech Republic	0	0	0	1
Estonia	0	0	0	0
Finland	1	0	0	0
France	0	0	0	1
Germany	0	0	0	0
Ghana	0	0	0	1
Hong Kong	1	1	1	1
Hungary	1	1	0	0
Iceland	0	0	0	1
India	1	0	0	1
Indonesia	1	0	0	1
Ireland	0	0	1	0
Israel	1	1	1	1
Italy	1	0	0	1
Japan	0	0	0	1
Jordan	1	0	0	1
Kazakhstan	0	0	0	0
Kenya	0	0	0	0
Kuwait	0	1	1	1
Lebanon	1	0	0	1
Lithuania	1	1	0	0
Malaysia	1	0	0	0

			Leverage and maturity mismatch	
Caps on loan to deposit ratio	Limits on leverage ratio	Caps on domestic currency lending	Minimum haircuts/ margins on collateral	Liquidity requirement/ buffers
0	0	1	1	0
0	0	0	0	1
0	0	0	0	1
1	1	0	0	1
0	0	0	0	1
0	0	0	0	0
0	0	0	0	1
0	1	0	0	1
0	1	0	0	1
1	1	0	0	1
0	0	0	1	1
0	0	0	1	1
0	0	0	0	0
0	0	0	0	0
0	0	0	0	0
0	0	0	0	1
0	0	0	1	0
0	0	1	0	0
1	0	0	0	1
0	0	0	0	1
0	0	0	0	1
0	0	0	1	1
1	0	0	0	0
1	0	0	0	0
0	0	0	0	1
0	0	0	1	0
0	0	0	0	0
0	1	0	0	1
0	0	0	0	1
0	1	0	0	1
0	0	1	0	1
0	0	0	1	1
0	0	0	0	0
0	0	1	0	0

Table A2 (continued)

Country	Credit growth and asset prices			
	Caps on loan to value ratio	Caps on debt to income ratio	Sector-specific capital buffer/ requirement	Limit on exposure concentration
Mauritius	0	0	0	1
Mexico	1	0	0	1
Morocco	0	0	0	1
Netherlands	1	1	0	0
New Zealand	1	0	0	0
Norway	1	1	0	1
Oman	1	0	0	0
Pakistan	1	1	0	1
Peru	0	0	1	1
Philippines	0	0	0	1
Poland	1	1	0	1
Portugal	0	0	0	0
Romania	1	1	0	1
Russian Federation	0	0	1	1
Saudi Arabia	0	1	0	0
Serbia	1	0	0	0
Singapore	1	1	0	1
Slovakia	1	0	0	0
Slovenia	0	0	0	0
South Africa	0	0	0	0
South Korea	1	1	0	0
Spain	1	0	0	1
Sri Lanka	0	0	0	1
Sweden	1	0	1	0
Switzerland	0	0	1	1
Thailand	1	0	0	0
Turkey	1	1	1	1
Ukraine	1	1	1	1
United Arab Emirates	0	1	0	1
United Kingdom	0	0	0	0
United States	1	0	0	1

			Leverage and maturity mismatch	
Caps on loan to deposit ratio	Limits on leverage ratio	Caps on domestic currency lending	Minimum haircuts/ margins on collateral	Liquidity requirement/ buffers
0	0	0	0	0
0	0	0	0	0
0	0	0	0	1
0	0	0	1	1
0	0	0	0	0
0	0	0	0	0
0	0	0	0	0
1	0	1	0	1
0	0	0	0	1
0	0	0	0	0
0	0	0	0	1
1	0	0	0	0
0	1	0	1	1
0	0	0	0	1
1	1	0	0	1
0	0	0	0	0
0	1	0	0	1
1	0	0	0	1
0	0	0	0	1
0	1	0	0	1
1	0	0	0	1
0	0	0	0	0
0	0	0	0	1
0	0	0	0	1
0	1	0	0	1
0	0	0	0	0
0	0	0	0	1
1	1	0	0	1
1	0	0	0	0
0	0	0	0	1
1	1	0	1	1

Table A2 (continued)

Panel C

| Country | Currency risk | |
	Limits on net open foreign currency positions or currency mismatches	Caps on foreign currency lending
Argentina	1	1
Australia	0	0
Austria	0	1
Bahrain	0	0
Belgium	0	0
Brazil	1	0
Bulgaria	0	0
Canada	0	0
Chile	1	0
China	0	1
Colombia	1	1
Croatia	1	0
Czech Republic	0	0
Estonia	0	0
Finland	0	0
France	0	0
Germany	0	0
Ghana	1	0
Hong Kong	1	0
Hungary	0	1
Iceland	1	1
India	0	0
Indonesia	1	0
Ireland	0	0
Israel	0	0
Italy	0	0
Japan	0	0
Jordan	1	1
Kazakhstan	1	0
Kenya	0	0
Kuwait	0	0
Lebanon	1	0
Lithuania	1	0
Malaysia	1	0
Mauritius	1	0
Mexico	1	0

Differentiated reserve requirements for foreign currency	Capital flows	
	Countercylical reserve requirements	Levy/tax on financial institutions
1	0	0
0	0	0
0	0	1
0	0	0
0	0	1
0	1	0
0	0	0
0	0	0
0	0	1
0	0	1
0	0	1
0	0	0
0	0	0
0	0	0
0	0	1
0	0	1
0	0	1
0	0	1
0	0	0
0	0	1
0	0	0
0	0	0
0	0	0
0	0	0
0	0	0
0	0	0
0	0	0
0	0	0
1	0	0
0	0	0
0	0	0
0	1	0
0	0	0
0	0	0
0	0	0
0	0	0

Table A2 (continued)

Country	Currency risk	
	Limits on net open foreign currency positions or currency mismatches	Caps on foreign currency lending
Morocco	1	1
Netherlands	0	0
New Zealand	0	0
Norway	1	0
Oman	0	1
Pakistan	1	1
Peru	1	0
Philippines	1	0
Poland	0	0
Portugal	0	0
Romania	1	1
Russian Federation	1	0
Saudi Arabia	0	0
Serbia	1	1
Singapore	0	0
Slovakia	0	0
Slovenia	0	0
South Africa	1	0
South Korea	1	1
Spain	0	0
Sri Lanka	1	0
Sweden	0	0
Switzerland	0	0
Thailand	0	0
Turkey	1	1
Ukraine	1	1
United Arab Emirates	0	0
United Kingdom	0	0
United States	0	0

Source: IMF Macroprudential Regulations Survey, December 2013.
Notes: 0 indicates "no"; 1 indicates "yes." Missing data correspond to nonresponses.

	Capital flows	
Differentiated reserve requirements for foreign currency	Countercylical reserve requirements	Levy/tax on financial institutions
0	0	0
0	0	1
0	0	0
0	0	0
0	0	0
0	0	1
1	1	0
0	0	1
0	0	0
0	0	1
0	0	0
0	0	0
0	0	0
1	0	0
0	0	0
0	0	1
0	0	0
0	0	0
0	0	1
0	0	0
0	0	0
0	0	0
0	0	0
0	0	0
1	0	0
1	0	1
0	0	0
0	0	0
0	0	0

Table A3
Systemic banking crises: dates and costs

Country	Start	End	Output loss (% of GDP)[a]	Fiscal costs (gross, % of GDP)[b]	Recapitalization costs (gross, % of GDP)[c]
Albania	1994	1994	...	...	...
Algeria	1990	1994	41.4	...	...
Argentina	1980	1982	58.2	55.1	...
Argentina	1989	1991	12.6	6	...
Argentina[d]	1995	1995	0	2	0.3
Argentina	2001	2003	70.9	9.6	9.6
Armenia	1994	1994	...	...	...
Austria	2008	...	13.8	4.9	2.9
Azerbaijan	1995	1995	...	...	...
Bangladesh	1987	1987	0	...	...
Belarus	1995	1995	...	...	...
Belgium	2008	...	19.1	6	5.8
Benin	1988	1992	14.9	17	...
Bolivia	1986	1986	49.2	...	...
Bolivia	1994	1994	0	6	1
Bosnia and Herzegovina	1992	1996	...	...	...
Brazil[d]	1990	1994	62.3	0	0
Brazil	1994	1998	0	13.2	5
Bulgaria	1996	1997	63.1	14	2.3
Burkina Faso	1990	1994	...	...	...
Burundi	1994	1998	121.2	...	...
Cameroon	1987	1991	105.5	...	...
Cameroon	1995	1997	8.1	...	...
Cape Verde	1993	1993	0	...	...
Central African Rep	1976	1976	0	...	...
Central African Rep	1995	1996	1.6	...	...
Chad	1983	1983	0	...	...
Chad	1992	1996	0	...	...
Chile	1976	1976	19.9	...	...
Chile	1981	1985	8.6	42.9	34.3
China, Mainland	1998	1998	19.5	18	...
Colombia	1982	1982	47	5	1.9
Colombia	1998	2000	43.9	6.3	4.3
Congo, Dem Rep	1983	1983	1.4	...	...
Congo, Dem Rep	1991	1994	129.5	...	...
Congo, Dem Rep	1994	1998	79	...	...
Congo, Rep	1992	1994	47.4	...	...
Costa Rica	1987	1991	0	...	...

Table A3 (continued)

Country	Start	End	Output loss (% of GDP)[a]	Fiscal costs (gross, % of GDP)[b]	Recapitalization costs (gross, % of GDP)[c]
Costa Rica	1994	1995	0	...	...
Cote d'Ivoire	1988	1992	44.8	25	small
Croatia	1998	1999	...	6.9	3.2
Czech Republic[d]	1996	2000	...	6.8	1
Denmark	2008	...	36.3	3.1	2.8
Djibouti	1991	1995	0	...	...
Dominican Rep	2003	2004	...	22	...
Ecuador	1982	1986	98.2	...	...
Ecuador	1998	2002	23.3	21.7	1.9
Egypt	1980	1980	0.9	...	...
El Salvador	1989	1990	0	...	...
Equatorial Guinea	1983	1983	0	...	...
Eritrea	1993	1993	...	...	...
Estonia	1992	1994	...	1.9	1.3
Finland	1991	1995	67.3	12.8	8.6
France[d]	2008	...	23.6	1	1
Georgia	1991	1995	...	...	...
Germany	2008	...	12.1	1.8	1.8
Ghana	1982	1983	14.1	6	6
Greece	2008	...	43.1	27.3	25.4
Guinea	1985	1985	0	3	...
Guinea	1993	1993	0	...	...
Guinea-Bissau	1995	1998	15.7	...	...
Guyana	1993	1993	0	...	...
Haiti	1994	1998	37.5	...	...
Hungary	1991	1995	...	10	...
Hungary[d]	2008	...	39.9	2.7	0.1
Iceland	2008	...	41.9	44.2	24.3
India	1993	1993	0	...	...
Indonesia	1997	2001	69	56.8	37.3
Ireland	2008	...	105.3	40.7	40.7
Israel	1977	1977	76	30	...
Italy	2008	...	33.2	0.3	0.3
Jamaica	1996	1998	32.2	43.9	13.9
Japan	1997	2001	45	14	6.6
Jordan	1989	1991	106.4	10	...
Kazakhstan[d]	2008	...	0	3.7	2.4
Kenya	1985	1985	23.7	...	...
Kenya	1992	1994	50.3	...	...
Korea	1997	1998	56.1	31.2	19.3

Table A3 (continued)

Country	Start	End	Output loss (% of GDP)[a]	Fiscal costs (gross, % of GDP)[b]	Recapitalization costs (gross, % of GDP)[c]
Kuwait	1982	1985	143.4	...	...
Kyrgyz Rep	1995	1999	...	...	...
Latvia	1995	1996	...	3	...
Latvia	2008	...	106.2	5.6	3.1
Lebanon	1990	1993	102.2	...	...
Liberia	1991	1995	...	...	...
Lithuania	1995	1996	...	3.1	1.7
Luxembourg	2008	...	36.4	7.7	7.7
Macedonia, FYR	1993	1995	...	32	...
Madagascar	1988	1988	0	...	...
Malaysia	1997	1999	31.4	16.4	16.4
Mali	1987	1991	0	...	...
Mauritania	1984	1984	7.5	15	...
Mexico	1981	1985	26.6	...	...
Mexico	1994	1996	10.2	19.3	3.8
Mongolia	2008	...	0	4.2	4.2
Morocco	1980	1984	21.9	...	...
Mozambique	1987	1991	0	...	...
Nepal	1988	1988	0	...	...
Netherlands	2008	...	23	12.7	6.6
Nicaragua	1990	1993	11.4	...	...
Nicaragua	2000	2001	0	13.6	...
Niger	1983	1985	97.2	...	...
Nigeria	1991	1995	0	...	...
Nigeria	2009	...	0	11.8	11.8
Norway	1991	1993	5.1	2.7	2.6
Panama	1988	1989	85	12.9	...
Paraguay	1995	1995	15.3	12.9	1.2
Peru	1983	1983	55.2	...	...
Philippines	1983	1986	91.7	3	...
Philippines[d]	1997	2001	0	13.2	0.2
Poland	1992	1994	...	3.5	...
Portugal[d]	2008	...	36.8	0	0
Romania	1990	1992	...	0.6	...
Russia	1998	1998	...	0.1	...
Russia[d]	2008	...	0	2.3	2.3
São Tomé & Príncipe	1992	1992	1.9	...	...
Senegal	1988	1991	5.6	17	...
Sierra Leone	1990	1994	34.5	...	...

Table A3 (continued)

Country	Start	End	Output loss (% of GDP)[a]	Fiscal costs (gross, % of GDP)[b]	Recapitalization costs (gross, % of GDP)[c]
Slovak Rep	1998	2002	44.2	...	...
Slovenia	1992	1992	...	14.6	...
Slovenia[d]	2008	...	38	3.6	0.8
Spain	1977	1981	58.5	5.6	...
Spain	2008	...	38.7	3.8	2
Sri Lanka	1989	1991	19.6	5	3.6
Swaziland	1995	1999	45.7	...	...
Sweden	1991	1995	31.6	3.6	1.9
Sweden[d]	2008	...	25.5	0.7	0.2
Switzerland[d]	2008	...	0	1.1	1.1
Tanzania	1987	1988	0	10	...
Thailand	1983	1983	24.8	0.7	...
Thailand	1997	2000	109.3	43.8	18.8
Togo	1993	1994	38.5	...	...
Tunisia	1991	1991	1.3	3	...
Turkey	1982	1984	35	2.5	...
Turkey	2000	2001	37	32	24.5
Uganda	1994	1994	0	...	...
Ukraine	1998	1999	0	0	0
Ukraine	2008	...	0	4.5	4.5
United Kingdom	2007	...	25.6	8.8	5
United States[d]	1988	1988	0	3.7	...
United States	2007	...	30.6	4.5	3.6
Uruguay	1981	1985	38.1	31.2	...
Uruguay	2002	2005	66.1	20	6.2
Venezuela	1994	1998	1.2	15	5.6
Vietnam	1997	1997	0	10	5
Yemen	1996	1996	12.2	...	...
Zambia	1995	1998	31.6	1.4	...
Zimbabwe	1995	1999	10.4	...	...

Source: Laeven and Valencia (2013).

a. Output losses are computed as the cumulative sum of the differences between actual and trend real GDP over the period $(T, T + 3)$, expressed as a percentage of trend real GDP, with T the starting year of the crisis.

b. Fiscal costs are defined as the component of gross fiscal outlays related to the restructuring of the financial sector. They include fiscal costs associated with bank recapitalizations but exclude asset purchases and direct liquidity assistance from the treasury.

c. Recapitalization costs are gross fiscal outlays associated with the recapitalization of financial institutions.

d. Refers to borderline banking crises.

Notes

Chapter 1

1. See Rajan (2009).

2. See Clement (2010), Laeven and Valencia (2010), and Reinhart and Rogoff (2009a).

3. See Goodhart and Perotti (2013), Adrian and Shin (2011), Allen and Gale (2007).

4. This holds at least in the Anglo-Saxon world. In continental Europe, banks typically have responsibilities also toward other stakeholders, including debt-holders. However, in Europe, leverage ratios in banks were substantially higher than US commercial banks.

5. See Raghuram Rajan in his speech as IMF Chief Economist at Jackson Hole in 2005 and Jeremy Stein in his speech as Governor of the Federal Reserve in March 2013. Moreover this herding behavior reinforced the tail risks stemming from the creation of "fake alpha."

6. Compensation via stock options, equity, and bonuses imply a convex payoff for managers, thereby leading to higher risk appetite (large positive payoffs imply high profits, but large negative payoffs do not imply high losses as there is not only limited liability but also the manager would not exercise the call option). Compensation in the form of bonds (as in the case of UBS in 2013) and with clawback options (as it has been proposed for new regulation) will decrease such excessive risk appetite.

7. See Johnson and Kwak (2010) and Acemoglu (2012) for the links between the political economy of the US banking sector and the US financial crisis in 2007 and 2008.

Chapter 2

1. This is similar to definitions proposed by the international regulatory community. For example, IMF-BIS-FSB (2009) defines systemic risk as "the risk that disruptions to financial services caused by an impairment of all or parts of the financial system can have serious negative consequences for the real economy." ECB (2009) defines systemic risk as "the risk that financial instability becomes so widespread that it impairs the functioning of a financial system to the point where economic growth and welfare suffer materially." Bernanke (2009) likewise defines systemic risk as "developments that threaten the stability of the financial system as a whole and consequently the broader economy, not just that of one or two institutions." We are not as comfortable with the BIS (2001) definition of systemic risk as "the risk that an event will trigger a loss of economic value or

confidence in, and attendant increases in uncertainty about, a substantial portion of the financial system that is serious enough to quite probably have significant adverse effects on the real economy" as it would encompass the dot-com crisis or the stock market crash of 1987, which we believe should not be considered systemic even if the effects were significant as there was no "impairment of the functioning of the financial system."

2. Iyer and Peydró (2011) take advantage of a quasi-natural experiment to isolate and quantify contagion of an idiosyncratic shock due to interbank exposures. They find that contagion is stronger when the banking fundamentals are weaker. Therefore contagion and weak overall banking fundamentals complement each other in increasing systemic risk.

3. There is an important piece of literature following Morris and Shin (1998) that nests fundamentals and panics in explaining financial fragility. See chapters 3 and 5 of this book for details.

4. Allen and Gale (2000a).

5. For a summary of such behavioral explanations, see http://www.economist.com/news/finance-and-economics/21594982-why-some-people-are-more-cautious-their-finances-others-risk.

6. For a history of financial crises over the last centuries, see Reinhart and Rogoff (2009a) and Kindleberger (1977).

7. For a comprehensive overview of the literature on the origins and causes of banking crises, we refer to Laeven (2011).

8. For financial crises over the last centuries, see chapter 4 and 6 of this book.

9. See, for example, Cecchetti, Mohanty, and Zampolli (2011), in particular their table A2.1.

10. In other cases, the setting up of a bad bank may forestall the drop in real estate prices from hitting bottom, which may delay the recovery. For example, in Spain the bad bank (called SAREB) in the recent crisis is basically internalizing the fire sales in real estate, which implies that it is slowly selling the assets in the market to reduce potential losses. This may lower the immediate fiscal and banking costs, but may delay the economic recovery and increase the ultimate fiscal costs.

11. For details on these proposals and the Liikanen report, see: http://ec.europa.eu/internal_market/bank/structural-reform/index_en.htm.

12. "Shadow banking" can broadly be defined as the production and sale of banking or financial products outside the traditional regulated sphere of banking, in particular through securitization and the market for credit default swaps. The "shadow banks" share similar risks as banks (e.g., maturity transformation and credit, liquidity, and market risks), but they were not regulated and did not receive deposit insurance nor central bank liquidity before the crisis. See Pozsar et al. (2010).

13. For a comparison of financial systems, bank versus market dominated, see Allen and Gale (2000b).

14. Of course, in a period of excessive risk-taking such as in the early 2000s, market-based measures of risk may be distorted. This should be taken into account when interpreting figure 2.4. See chapters 4 and 7.

Chapter 3

1. Of course, some of the measures used in this literature for financial development, such as credit or debt over GDP, one can also view as a proxy for financial imbalances to the extent that financial deepening was associated with rapid credit growth or an increase in leverage. In this sense it is interesting that countries with occasional financial crises (measured by the negative skewness of credit growth) tend to grow more than more financially stable countries, so as to suggest that some systemic risk is positive for long-run economic growth (Ranciere et al. 2008).

2. The next chapters explain in detail empirical findings related to financial frictions, fragility and systemic risk, and chapter 7 deals with measurement of systemic risk. Chapter 3, however, is mainly theory based.

3. One limitation of this type of model is that it does not offer insight into the optimal level of optimal bank capital requirements. Some macro models use this model to perform quantitative analysis of bank capital; hence one way for the synthetic third way of embedding realistic financial frictions into macro models is to extend micro-based models of incentives for financial intermediaries (e.g., see Holmstrom and Tirole 1997) into quantitative macro models.

4. Correlated risks can be taken by investing in a similar asset (a financial bubble) or by providing liquidity to each other in wholesale markets.

5. Knightian uncertainty is named after Frank Knight who distinguished risk and uncertainty (Knight 1921). For systemic risk and Knightian uncertainty, see Caballero (2010a, b).

6. See Kareken and Wallace (1978), Allen and Gale (2004b), and Mehran, Morrison, and Shapiro (2012).

7. See also Bryant (1980).

8. See Hirschman (1970) on voice versus exit.

9. DSGE models should also allow some beneficial endogenous risks arising from the financial sector. The correct functioning of financial markets and institutions under adequate regulation should lead to obtaining a constrained Pareto optimality in the allocation of capital, because the existence of financial market imperfections and information asymmetries prevent the market from reaching the first best. This implies that financial intermediaries compute a correct estimation of risks and expected returns that constitute the necessary information for the efficient allocation of funds. Thus some degree of risk, and in particular, some degree of systemic risk and financial crises, is to be accepted. Concomitant to this is the acknowledgment that a number of regulatory mechanisms have to be in place, to cope with risk and, in particular, with extreme events and systemic risk such that these extreme events do not generate a collapse of the banking system. See Allen and Gale (1998) model for optimality of financial crises, and the empirical evidence by Ranciere et al. (2004), where they find that countries that suffer financial crises enjoy subsequent higher economic growth. Therefore as we argue in this book, some systemic risk can be useful, and policy makers should pay attention to the costs of potentially excessive macroprudential regulation.

10. Adverse selection in credit markets can generate economic fluctuations even in the absence of exogenous shocks as in Suarez and Sussman (1997).

Chapter 4

1. See Laeven and Valencia (2008), Reinhart and Rogoff (2009a), and Schularick and Taylor (2012).

2. For explanations and models of excessive risk-taking by banks and its policy implications, see Rajan (2005, 2010), Calomiris (2009), Allen and Gale (2007), Pagano (2010), Acemoglu (2012), Stein (2013a), Perotti and Goodhart (2013), Brunnermeier (2009), and Shin (2009). For credit cycles, see the excellent books by Gorton (2012) and Mian and Sufi (2014b).

3. For excellent reviews of the main academic papers on the crisis, see Gorton and Metrick (2012) and Lo (2012). See Barro (2010) for the analysis and evidence on rare events. We follow closely Gorton and Metrick (2012) in this section.

4. They analyze the last six centuries in their excellent book. On the post-1945 period, they use data as identified by Kaminsky and Reinhart (1999) and Gerard Caprio et al. (2005). The banking crisis episodes include: The so-called Five Big Five Crises, which are systemic crises: Spain (1977), Norway (1987), Finland (1991), Sweden (1991), and Japan (1992), where the starting year is in parenthesis. Other banking and financial crises include those of Australia (1989), Canada (1983), Denmark (1987), France (1994), Germany (1977), Greece (1991), Iceland (1985), and Italy (1990), and New Zealand (1987), United Kingdom (1974, 1991, 1995), and United States (1984).

5. The dataset used in this paper covers fourteen advanced economies over the years 1870 to 2008 at annual frequency: United States, Canada, Australia, Denmark, France, Germany, Italy, Japan, Netherlands, Norway, Spain, Sweden, Switzerland, and United Kingdom.

6. Jorda, Schularick, and Taylor (2013) study how past credit accumulation impacts the behavior of not only output, but also of other key macroeconomic variables such as investment, lending, interest rates, and inflation. In addition to the unconditional analysis, they use local projection methods based on Jorda (2005) to condition on a broad set of macroeconomic controls and their lags.

7. There are some differences from their previous papers. First, Jorda, Schularick, and Taylor (2013) apply new statistical tools to describe the temporal and spatial patterns of crises and identify five episodes of global financial instability in the past 140 years. Second, they study the macroeconomic dynamics before crises and show that credit growth tends to be elevated and natural interest rates depressed in the run-up to global financial crises. Third, they show that recessions associated with crises lead to deeper recessions and stronger turnarounds in imbalances than during normal recessions. Finally, as mentioned, they check whether external imbalances help predict financial crises.

8. The analysis in Dell'Ariccia et al. (2012) focuses on bank credit, but obviously there are other sources of funds in the economy. However, with a few exceptions, notably US, bank credit accounts for the greatest share of total credit.

9. The methodologies differ in several respects, such as whether the trend and the thresholds identifying the booms should be country-specific, whether information unavailable at the time of the boom should be used for its identification, and whether the credit and GDP series should be filtered separately or directly as a ratio. For the IMF paper the set of booms identified using different methods is rather robust. See also Gourinchas, Valdes, and Landerretche (2001), Mendoza and Terrones (2008), Barajas,

Dell'Ariccia, and Levchenko (2008), Jordà, Schularick, and Taylor (2011), and Claessens, Kose, and Terrones (2012).

10. Other studies have also investigated whether initial conditions can explain the differential impact of the 2008 crisis across countries. For example, in two related papers, Rose and Spiegel (2009a, b) find that these initial conditions generally do poorly in explaining the economic performance of countries during a crisis period, and conclude that global factors have a more dominant role. Countries that experienced large run-ups in asset prices and countries with larger current account deficits are more likely to be hit hard. They also find some weak evidence that higher credit growth can be positively associated with the severity of the crisis. Giannone et al. (2011) make similar observations about the global crisis based on ex ante measures of vulnerabilities of the affected countries, and conclude that the liberalization of credit markets, while fostering financial deepening and economic growth, reduced the financial system's ability to insulate the economy from financial shocks.

11. Relevant surveys on behavioral finance are Dell'Avigna (2008), Barberis (2012) and Shleifer (2012). See also the books by Kahneman (2012) and Akerlof and Shiller (2008).

12. The field has mainly focused on three areas in the past: the pricing of financial assets; the portfolio choice and trading decisions of investors; and the behavior of firm managers. See Barberis (2012) for an excellent review of behavioral finance for financial crises and the research by Andrei Shleifer and co-authors on the exact channels by which psychology can affect excessive risk-taking in financial institutions and markets.

13. In Benabou's model, agents with anticipatory preferences, linked through an interaction structure, choose how to interpret and recall public signals about future prospects. In standard models of herding and cascades (Banerjee 1992; Bikhchandani et al. 1992; Caplin and Leahy 1994; Chamley and Gale 1994), by contrast, investors are rational information processors who follow others only when warranted by optimal inference.

14. Berger and Udell hypothesize that "institutional memory" problems may drive a pattern of business lending that is associated with a deterioration in the ability of a bank to recognize potential loan problems and an easing of credit standards over its own loan cycle.

15. See also Aghion, Bolton, and Fries (2000), Mitchell (2000), and Caballero, Hoshi, and Kashyap (2008).

16. See Boyd and De Nicolo (2005), Allen and Gale (2000b), and Stiglitz and Weiss (1981). See also the theoretical research by Matutes and Vives (1996, 2000) on the positive relationship between bank competition and excessive bank risk-taking.

17. Claessens and Laeven (2004) have criticized using concentration ratios as measures of bank competition, showing that concentration ratios are poor correlates of competition based on measures of competitive conduct derived from reduced-form models.

18. Demirguc-Kunt and Detragiache (1998) analyze the relationship between banking crises and financial liberalization using a panel of data for 53 countries for 1980 to 1995. They find that banking crises are more likely to occur in liberalized financial systems. But financial liberalization's impact on a fragile banking sector is weaker where the institutional environment is strong—especially where there is respect for the rule of law, a low level of corruption, and good contract enforcement. They examine evidence on the behavior of bank franchise values after liberalization. They also examine evidence on the relationship between financial liberalization, banking crises, financial development, and

growth. The results support the view that, even in the presence of macroeconomic stability, financial liberalization should be approached cautiously in countries where institutions to ensure legal behavior, contract enforcement, and effective prudential regulation and supervision are not fully developed.

19. Short-term wholesale debt is the cheapest way of finance for banks (after insured retail depositors), and even more so if liquidity is provided by foreigners (see Diamond and Rajan 2001, 2002).

20. See chapter 9 on why limits on deposit rates could be a good macroprudential tool during a crisis.

21. Part of this section is based on the excellent review by Mehran, Morrison, and Shapiro (2012). See Myers and Rajan (1997) on how bank liquid assets can be easily transformed, and therefore bank risk can be changed fast and easily. See Morgan (2002) on banks' opacity.

22. For the reasons why the composition of external finance affects the cost of finance in banking, see Morrison and White (2005), Adrian and Shin (2010), Shleifer and Vishny (2010b), Tirole (2011), Adrian and Boyarchenko (2012), Jeanne and Korinek (2012), and Malherbe (2014). Tax benefits of debt finance and asymmetric information about banks' conditions and prospects imply that raising external equity finance may be more costly for banks than debt finance (Tirole 2006; Freixas and Rochet 2008; Aiyar, Calomiris, and Wieladek 2014; Hanson, Kashyap, and Stein 2011). An increase in capital requirements will therefore raise the cost of bank finance. Admati et al. (2013) and Admati and Hellwig (2013) question whether equity capital costs for banks are substantial.

23. See the extensive summary in Mehran, Morrison, and Shapiro (2012) and chapter 8 of this book.

24. However, Flannery, Kwan, and Nimalendran (2004) show that the trading properties of banks and the accuracy of analysts' earnings forecasts for banks are similar to those of nonfinancial firms. Later Flannery, Kwan, and Nimalendran (2010) find that such similarity ended around the start of the financial crisis in mid-2007.

25. Credit cycles consist of periods during which the economy is performing well and credit growth is robust (on average 7 percent) and periods when the economy is in recession or crisis and credit contracts (on average, –2 percent) (Schularick and Taylor 2012). Credit cycles stem from either (1) banks' agency frictions (e.g., see Rajan 1994; Holmstrom and Tirole 1997; Diamond and Rajan 2006; Allen and Gale 2007; Shleifer and Vishny 2010a; Adrian and Shin 2011; Gersbach and Rochet 2012) or (2) firms' agency frictions (e.g., see Bernanke and Gertler 1989; Kiyotaki and Moore 1997; Lorenzoni 2008; Jeanne and Korinek 2010.

26. See Conlon (2004) and Doblas-Madrid (2012) for more robust versions of this kind of model.

27. This part is based on the excellent summary of behavioral finance for asset bubbles by Barberis (2012).

28. Hau et al. (2013) show that rating agencies give better ratings to banks with which they have closer business links, suggesting that conflicts of interest were an important factor behind the rating inflation prior to the crisis.

Chapter 5

1. Unlike the definition used in the analysis of contagion across countries, where if the residuals from explaining the stock market index are "correlated across countries, this residual correlation might be interpretable as contagion because it is comovement that is unexplained after controlling for fundamentals" (Pritsker 2001).

2. See chapters 6 and 7 of this book on how bank problems specifically affect the macroeconomy.

3. The Libor-OIS spread started to massively widen on the day of Lehman's failure, and it kept on widening until it peaked on October 10. On October 10, the finance ministers and central bank governors of the G7 meeting in Washington declared that they would "take decisive action and use all available tools to support systemically important financial institutions and *prevent their failure.*"

4. Twenty years ago it was the payment system that created counterparty risk as it operates through the end of day clearing that required banks implicitly to extend intraday credit to one another. This is nowadays a minor issue in well-developed financial systems where the bulk of the payment systems goes through real time gross settlements.

5. See also Brusco and Castiglionesi (2005).

6. As we will see later, repo markets have problems, primarily because the quality of the collateral can drop significantly in times of liquidity problems.

7. Thus, in 1991, in the aftermath of the closure of the Bank of Credit and Commerce International by the Bank of England, a closure that was caused by its fraudulent operations, and so was obviously not contagious, other UK ethnic banks had to close down because they lost a huge proportion of their core deposits to the main UK banks and could not obtain interbank loans from them.

8. Given the costs of a meltdown, there is a possible role for government intervention, but unfortunately, liquidity and solvency problems interact, making it hard to determine the source of a crisis. They propose a robust sequence of intervention (see Diamond and Rajan 2005).

9. See http://www.sec.gov/news/press/2010/2010-59.htm.

10. There is no jump in other homeowner attributes such as credit scores, income, or education levels.

11. Market illiquidity occurs when asset sales that are normally traded with little price impact can only be transacted at a substantial discount, if at all. The concept is asset specific. Funding illiquidity occurs when solvent counterparties have difficulty in borrowing to meet liabilities falling due. This concept is institution specific. Asset-specific illiquidity is marketwide (although it may materialize more in some assets), whereas institution-specific illiquidity is limited to certain institutions (though a number could be affected simultaneously). See "Market and Funding Illiquidity: When Private Risk Becomes Public" (IMF, Global Financial Stability Report, April 2008, ch. 3) for the definitions and for how risk management in banks can alleviate these problems in the future.

12. As we said earlier, most of these channels apply to other financial intermediaries.

13. Another solution is to reduce liquid assets. However, during periods of financial instability, banks prefer to increase liquidity (hoarding of liquidity) as wholesale markets may not work properly, as explained earlier.

14. Ivashina and Scharfstein (2010) note that after the failure of Lehman Brothers in September 2008 there was a run by short-term bank creditors, making it difficult for banks to roll over their short-term debt. They document a simultaneous run by borrowers who drew down their credit lines, leading to a spike in commercial and industrial loans reported on bank balance sheets. They then analyze whether these two stresses on bank liquidity led them to cut lending. In particular, they find that banks cut their lending less if they had better access to deposit financing and thus they were not as reliant on short-term debt. The authors also show that banks that were more vulnerable to credit line drawdowns were those that co-syndicated more of their credit lines with Lehman Brothers, which reduced their lending to a greater extent.

15. In Jiménez et al. (2013), banks had a reduction in capital requirements during the crisis in Spain. Yet their results suggest that some banks did not increase their credit supply because of binding capital requirements from the market, and such banks are the riskiest.

16. See Jiménez et al. (2012) for a summary of the main empirical papers analyzing the financial accelerator and for causal evidence on the impact of business cycles on credit cycles.

17. See chapter 3 for some of these new contributions.

18. The SPV in this way could get the triple A from a rating agency. Commercial paper is a short-term credit instrument traditionally used by financial and nonfinancial corporations. Since the early 1990s, banks and other financial institutions have structured ABCP programs or conduits to finance the purchase of pools of assets by issuing and rolling over commercial paper that is collateralized by the assets. To obtain high short-term credit ratings, the bank or financial institution that sponsors or structures the ABCP program typically commits to provide liquidity or credit support that covers all the liabilities of the conduit. See Duygan-Bump et al. (2013).

19. According to Duygan-Bump et al. (2013) as of September 10, 2008, the assets under management in the different types of US MMMFs totaled $3.5 trillion.

20. Duygan-Bump et al. (2013) analyze two unique micro datasets that allow them to exploit both time series and cross-sectional variation to evaluate the Asset-Backed Commercial Paper Money Market Mutual Fund Liquidity Facility (AMLF). The AMLF extended collateralized loans to depository institutions that purchased asset-backed commercial paper (ABCP) from money market funds, helping these funds meet the heavy redemptions that followed Lehman's bankruptcy. The program, which lent $150 billion in its first 10 days of operation, was wound down with no credit losses to the Federal Reserve. Their findings indicate that the facility was effective as measured against its dual objectives: it helped stabilize asset outflows from money market mutual funds, and it improved liquidity in the ABCP market. Using a differences-in-differences approach, the authors show that after the facility was implemented, money market fund outflows decreased more for those funds that held more eligible collateral. Similarly they show that yields on AMLF eligible ABCP decreased significantly relative to those on otherwise comparable AMLF ineligible commercial paper.

21. In the United States, the Securities and Exchange Commission (SEC) on July 23, 2014, adopted amendments to the rules that govern money market mutual funds. The new SEC rules require a floating net asset value (NAV) for institutional prime money market funds, which allows the daily share prices of these funds to fluctuate along with changes in the market-based value of fund assets and provide nongovernment money market fund boards new tools—liquidity fees and redemption gates—to address runs. Money

market funds focused on government debt and retail funds, meanwhile, can hold on to their constant $1-a-share valuation. The SEC rules come after commissioners rejected an earlier plan by former Chairman Mary Schapiro that included capital buffers.

On September 4, 2013, the European Commission (EC) proposed a European framework designed for money market funds. The EC proposal stipulates that all Europe-based funds either value their assets daily or build up capital buffers worth at least 3 percent of the assets they manage to absorb as potential losses. The EC proposal also sets minimum requirements for liquid assets, with 10 percent maturing daily and an extra 20 percent within a week, and limits the kind of investments that funds can make. These new rules should prevent banks and other institutions that sponsor money market funds from supporting their share prices, which the EC hopes would prevent contagion of funds' troubles to other parts of the financial sector. However, the EC proposal falls short of recommendations by the European Systemic Risk Board, an agency it set up after the financial crisis to monitor market risks. According to the ESRB, money market funds that profess to maintain a constant net asset value pose "systemic risks" to the financial system and should gradually move to a floating share price.

22. Allen and Carletti (2008) analyze fair value (mark to market) accounting and contagion. When liquidity plays an important role as in times of financial crisis, asset prices in some markets may reflect the amount of liquidity available in the market rather than the future earning power of the asset. Therefore mark to market accounting may not be a desirable way to assess the solvency of a financial institution in such circumstances. The authors show that a shock in the insurance sector can cause the current value of banks' assets to be less than the current value of their liabilities so the banks are insolvent. In contrast, if historic cost accounting is used, banks are allowed to continue and can meet all their future liabilities. The authors show that mark to market accounting can thus lead to contagion where none would occur with historic cost accounting.

23. The recent example is Hungary (and other Eastern European countries) where banks have heavily lent in Swiss francs at a lower interest rate, but the appreciation of the Swiss franc has led to an increase of risk in all the Swiss denominated loans.

24. If a negative collateral shock hits one region (because productivity falls for example), then both local and out of state banks move away from the affected region, delivering the same asymmetry result for regional business cycles.

25. Sometimes such information was not available, so researchers have had to use aggregate information on banks' aggregate gross position on the interbank market and make assumptions on how the aggregate counterparty risk was allocated to individual banks, which decreased the reliability of the whole simulation. Mistrulli (2005) shows this approximation to have introduced substantial biases.

26. Moreover important financial institutions had failed before Lehman, real estate prices were dropping in 2007, and liquidity problems in wholesale markets emerged in 2007 (e.g., as of August 9, 2007, in the European interbank market).

Chapter 6

1. Laeven and Valencia (2013) compute output losses as deviations of actual GDP from its trend, and the increase in public debt as the change in the public debt-to-GDP ratio over the four-year period beginning with the crisis year.

2. See chapter 4 for a description of the dataset used in Jorda, Schularick, and Taylor.

3. This result holds up even when the Great Depression is excluded from the prewar event analysis.

4. In post–World War II crises, five years after a crisis year the level of broad money was 14 percent below trend, and bank loans 24 percent below trend. In the postwar period, however, the declines were a mere 6 percent for broad money and 15 percent for bank loans. However, the effect on the securities side of banks' balance sheets in response to a financial crisis is even stronger, with bank assets falling 24 percent below trend in the postwar period, versus 11 percent prewar. This clearly confirms the modern findings by Adrian and Shin (2008a) who argue that the behavior of nonloan items on the balance sheets of financial institutions is particularly procyclical.

5. Note that as we explained in chapter 4, Schularick and Taylor (2012) also find that financial crises occur after periods of strong credit growth, and thus periods of excessive risk-taking in the financial system.

6. For a definition of the dataset, see Reinhart and Rogoff (2009a) and chapter 4 of this book.

7. Some empirical papers use natural experiments to analyze credit availability. Slovin, Sushka, and Polonchek (1993) study the share price response of borrowers of Continental Illinois Bank around its failure and rescue in 1984. Subsequent papers have used variation in lending stemming from the bursting of the Japanese real estate bubble (Peek and Rosengren 1997, 2000; Gan 2007; Amiti and Weinstein 2011), the response to the 1998 Pakistani nuclear tests (Khwaja and Mian 2008), the 1998 Russian crisis (Chava and Purnanandam 2011), Argentinian public policy shocks (Paravisini 2008), and the 2002 WorldCom bankruptcy (Lin and Paravisini 2013).

8. Aggregate credit data does not allow separating demand and supply of credit. In fact, in Schularick and Taylor's (2012) data, before World War II, crises were associated with slightly negative average loan growth in the year after the crisis began. However, this result is influenced by the Great Depression. In general, it is the second derivative of loan growth that changes sign during a crisis, not the first. Therefore positive credit growth is consistent with a credit crunch as credit demand may be high in a crisis when cash flows and other sources of finance are weak.

9. See also Garicano and Steinwender (2013), Ivashina and Scharfstein (2010), and Greenstone, Mas, and Nguyen (2014), and Giannetti and Laeven (2012b).

10. Consistent with this evidence, Stulz et al. (2012) find that there was no credit crunch for large US firms.

11. See, for example, "Easy Money a Lifeline for 'Zombie Banks'" in: *International Herald Tribune*, February 12, 2012, and Veron and Wolff (2013).

12. See also Akerlof and Romer (1993). Hellman, Murdock, and Stiglitz (2000) argue that banks have higher gambling incentives if they are poorly capitalized.

13. Gennaioli, Martin, and Rossi (2013) use data from Bankscope to analyze the holdings of public bonds by over 18,000 banks located in 185 countries and the role of these bonds in eighteen sovereign debt crises over the period 1998 to 2012. They find that (1) banks hold a sizable share of their assets in government bonds (about 9 percent on average), particularly in less financially developed countries; (2) during sovereign crises, banks on average increase their bond holdings by 1 percent of their assets, but this increase is concentrated among larger and more profitable banks; and (3) the correlation between a bank's holdings of public bonds and its future loans is positive in normal times but turns

negative during defaults. A 10 percent increase in bank bond holdings during default is associated with a 3.2 percent reduction in future loans, and bonds bought in normal times account for 75 percent of this effect.

14. Aguiar et al. (2009) and Aguiar and Amador (2011) show that high levels of public debt can reduce private investment and growth by increasing governments' incentives to default and expropriate private capital.

15. Not only does the value of collateral matter for crises, but the value of financial assets in general. By the so-called wealth effect, there is a relationship between a change in the value of financial assets and the level of consumer spending, which implies that a decrease in wealth (in financial assets) will cause a decrease in aggregate consumption. See Carroll and Zhou (2010).

16. Note, however, that the skewness of credit growth that the authors associate with financial crises do not necessarily capture the systemic financial crises that we write about this book.

Chapter 7

1. This chapter has benefited from numerous comments and suggestions by Christian Brownlees.

2. There are some problems, of course, such as whether to include volatile elements such as energy prices, or real estate and financial asset prices. However, it is clear that inflation is easily measured as compared to systemic risk.

3. See Blanchard, Dell'Ariccia, and Mauro (2013).

4. For example, recently Target II data are available to measure systemic risk in the short-term interbank market across the euro area. However, there is no complete data in the euro area for interbank transactions with longer maturity or for secure wholesale links among financial institutions' pairs, or for many derivatives positions.

5. After systemic financial crises, data limitations often become less stringent as supervisors and regulators will call for new data collection. For example, following the 2007 to 2008 crisis, with the passing of the Dodd–Frank law, US authorities were obtaining crucial financial data to measure systemic risk (as did the ECB in Europe); or, in previous crises, many credit registers started just after a financial crisis (e.g., the Spanish register in 1984 after the strong banking crisis at the beginning of 1980s in Spain). However, the risk is that with benefit of hindsight, detailed data is being collected to learn characteristics of the previous crisis rather than how to prevent future crises.

6. Existing reviews and similar classifications of systemic risk include Bisias et al. (2012), Hansen (2014), and Giglio, Kelly, and Qiao (2014), among others.

7. Amiti and Weinstein (2013) show that supply-side financial shocks have a large impact on firms' investment. They do this by developing a new methodology to separate firm credit shocks from loan supply shocks using a vast sample of matched bank–firm lending data. They decompose loan movements in Japan for the period 1990 to 2010 into bank, firm, industry, and common shocks. The high degree of financial institution concentration means that individual banks are large relative to the size of the economy, which creates a role for granular shocks. As a result idiosyncratic bank shocks (i.e., movements in bank loan supply net of borrower characteristics and general credit conditions) can have large impacts on aggregate loan supply and investment. They show that these

idiosyncratic bank shocks explain 40 percent of aggregate loan and investment fluctuations.

8. For example, if banks receiving a positive liquidity shock are more likely to lend to firms that simultaneously receive a positive credit demand boost, then the OLS estimator of would be biased upward.

9. Depending on data availability, it could include nonbank sources of credit as well.

10. Among others, these include Cetorelli and Goldberg (2012b) on international transmission of credit supply shocks during 2007 and 2008, Lin and Paravisini (2013) on the credit supply effect of bank reputation in the United States, Paravisini (2008) on credit supply effects in Argentina, and Schnabl (2012) on the international transmission of credit supply shocks in Peru.

11. See https://www.loanpricing.com/ and http://gib.dealogic.com.

12. Measurement of systemic risk should be analyzed both booms and busts. For example, Mian and Sufi (2014a) show that the recession was propagated by a dramatic decline in consumer demand, which was exacerbated by significant deleveraging at the household level and resulted in increased firm closures and unemployment. All their evidence is summarized in their excellent book on the House of Debt (Mian and Sufi 2014b).

13. An observable riskier borrower who is granted a loan application when monetary policy is restrictive must have some unobservable good characteristics, which will also make him get better loan conditions for the granted application (i.e., the correlation between the errors of the first- and second-stage regressions is positive).

14. The main question that banks have to answer is the following: "Over the past three months, how have your bank's credit standards as applied to the approval of loans or credit lines to enterprises changed?" (overall, to SMEs, to large enterprises, short term, long term; to households for house purchase; to households for consumer credit). The measure mainly used to quantify the answers is the net percentage of banks reporting a tightening of standards (which is equal to the difference between the banks reporting a tightening and the banks reporting a softening of lending standards). Finally, it is not clear that banks answer on the level or on the change in lending conditions, as they normally do not answer a softening. However, there are substantial differences between banks and over time.

15. House prices in United States increased twofold in nominal terms in 2000 to 2006, and mortgage rates fell substantially and were accompanied by a softening in lending standards, notably to subprime borrowers (Mian and Sufi 2009; Dell'Ariccia, Igan, and Laeven 2012). Some authors suggest that other (non-credit) factors could have been crucial for real estate prices (Glaeser, Gottlieb, and Gyourko 2013). See also Adelino, Schoar, and Severino (2012).

16. Fannie Mae and Freddie Mac are restricted by law from purchasing single-family mortgages with origination balances below a specific amount, known as the conforming loan limit. Loans above this limit are known as jumbo loans. See Adelino, Schoar, and Severino (2012).

17. See chapter 4 on financial stability and competition.

18. See ECB's recent advances in modeling systemic risk using network analysis (2010) on http://www.ecb.int/pub/pdf/other/modellingsystemicrisk012010en.pdf.

19. See Iyer and Peydró (2011) on the weakness of counterfactual simulations used in analyzing contagion in interbank markets, as they cannot capture the endogenous responses of depositors, which are crucial in crises.

20. Cont, Moussa, and Santos (2012) present a quantitative methodology for analyzing the risk of contagion and systemic risk in a network of interlinked financial intermediaries, using a metric for the systemic importance of institutions: the contagion index. They apply this methodology to a dataset of mutual exposures and capital levels of financial intermediaries in Brazil in 2007 to 2008. Their results highlight the contribution of heterogeneity in network structure and concentration of counterparty exposures to a given bank in explaining its systemic importance.

21. The model is formulated in terms of a stochastic default rate, which jumps at credit events, reflecting the increased likelihood of further defaults due to spillover effects.

22. This part is substantially based on Greenlaw, et al. (2012). Microprudential stress tests emphasize the traditional role of bank capital as a buffer against losses.

23. See also Wall and Petersen (1990) and Docking, Hirschey, and Jones (1997). De Nicolo and Kwast (2002) relate changes in correlations between bank stock prices over time to the process of banking consolidation in the United States. Other market-based measures used in the literature to assess bank contagion include bank debt risk premia (see Saunders 1986; Cooperman, Lee, and Wolfe 1992). We follow Hartmann, Straetmans, and de Vries (2007), who provide an excellent summary of all this literature.

24. Gropp and Moerman (2004) apply an ordered logit to estimate the impact of shocks in distances to default for some banks on other banks' distances to default.

25. Their empirical analysis covers both euro area countries and the United States to compare banking system stability internationally. They also apply the test of structural stability for tail indexes by Quintos, Fan, and Phillips (2001) to the multivariate case of extreme linkages and assess changes in banking system stability over time with it.

26. See the paper by Billio et al. (2012). Principal Components Analysis (PCA) is a technique in which the asset returns of a sample of increase institutions are decomposed into orthogonal factors of decreasing explanatory power. To investigate the dynamic propagation of shocks, it is also important to measure the directionality of such relationships, so they use Granger causality, a statistical notion of causality based on the relative forecast power of two time series. Time series j is said to "Granger-cause" time series i if past values of j contain information that helps predict above and beyond the information contained in past values of i alone. In an informationally efficient financial market, short-term asset price changes should not be related to other lagged variables; hence a Granger-causality test should not detect any causality. However, in the presence of frictions, they may find Granger causality among price changes of financial assets. Moreover this type of predictability may not easily be arbitraged away precisely because of the presence of such frictions. Therefore the degree of Granger causality in asset returns can be viewed as a proxy for return-spillover effects among market participants as suggested by Danielsson, Shin, and Zigrand (2011), Battiston et al. (2012b), and Buraschi, Porchia, and Trojani (2010). As this effect is amplified, the connections and integration among financial institutions get tighter, heightening the severity of systemic events as shown by Castiglionesi, Feriozzi, and Lorenzoni (2009) and Battiston et al. (2009).

27. Yet another possible interpretation, as the authors argue, is that because they are more highly regulated, banks and insurers are more sensitive to value at risk changes through their capital requirements; and hence their behavior may generate endogenous

feedback loops with perverse externalities and spillover effects to other financial institutions.

28. Counterparty risk stems mainly from the OTC nature of the market. Hence policy initiatives to limit systemic risk are on the creation of a centralized clearinghouse (see Giglio 2012; Duffie and Zhu 2011; and the next chapters of this book).

29. Important contributions on models for CDSs include Duffie, Pedersen, and Singleton (2003), Pan and Singleton (2008), and Arora et al. (2012).

30. The measurement approach is based on combining balance sheet data for the individual financial institution and to use reduced form time-series models to compute the impact of a market downturn on the market valued assets of the financial institution.

31. Giglio et al. (2014) propose two dimension reduction estimators to produce systemic risk indexes from the cross section of systemic risk measures. The first estimator is using principal components quantile regression (PCQR). They extract principal components from the panel of systemic risk measures and then use these factors in predictive quantile regressions. They prove that this approach consistently estimates conditional quantiles of macroeconomic shocks under mild conditions. Moreover they propose another estimator called partial quantile regression (PQR) and show consistent quantile forecasts with fewer factors than PCQR.

Chapter 8

1. In Europe, the Markets in Financial Instruments Directive (MiFID) and Unfair Commercial Practices (UCPD) Directives are part of the conduct of business regulation and introduce a client categorization that depends on the degree of knowledge of financial products and markets by the client.

2. Banks are to be run by "fit and proper" managers that are more unlikely to engage in fraudulent operations. Also takeovers in the banking industry could lead to banks that are managed by firms that run them in their own interest at the expense of minority shareholders and debtholders.

3. Although this view is the prevailing one (e.g., see Keeley, 1990), a dissenting view proposed by Boyd and De Nicolo (2005) goes in the opposite direction and states that in a more competitive banking industry, firms facing lower interest rates would choose to take less risk in their investment choices, making the banks' portfolios of loans safer.

4. The cooperation between the two institutions during the Northern Rock crisis led to harsh criticism of this structure. The FSA guaranteed the solvency of Northern Rock before and during the crisis, insisting that it was limited to a liquidity difficulty. After a while, it was clear that Northern Rock required additional capital and had to be nationalized. This implied losses to taxpayers of approximately 480m£ after the sale of the bank to Virgin Money. Nevertheless, while there might be an issue in the incentives structure, with one institution assessing the solvency and another institution injecting funds on the basis of the information provided by the former, it is not clear that a traditional supervisory structure with a specific banking regulator would have performed better.

5. This logic was underlying the Spanish statistical provisioning that is forward looking but was not adopted as an international rule because it contravened the international accounting standards.

6. An illustration of such a disparity is the definition of securitization that was more permissive in the United States and in the United Kingdom, where the originator could provide liquidity lines for the liabilities issued by the Special Purpose Vehicle, than in Spain where those assets would have remained in the originator's balance sheet.

7. Or at least in systems where deposit insurance is credible and honored, as demonstrated by the recent case in Cyprus where losses were imposed on uninsured but not insured depositors.

8. To be more precise, assets held for trading are assets for which market prices are available from orderly transactions (level 1 assets). This justifies the view that FVA is mark to market accounting. Yet, when level 1 inputs are not available, models have to use observable inputs (level 2), which include quoted prices for similar assets and other relevant market data. Finally, if observable inputs are not available, marking to model is to be used (level 3). According to the IMF Global Financial Stability report, on average, financial institutions value some 69 percent of their fair valued assets using the level 2 methodology. Nevertheless, level 1 methodology could be used for a high percentage of assets in investment banks that were at the forefront of the crisis in the United States. Additionally loans (including mortgages) and held to maturity securities are reported at amortized costs so that historical cost accounting applies. Finally, a bank can treat fair value losses of an available for sale debt security as temporary and avoid the effect of these losses on its income and regulatory capital if the bank does not sell the security.

9. Paradoxically, this is usually fostered ex ante, in a clear example of time inconsistency, by supervisory authorities that assert the banking system is perfectly safe and that there is no risk in any kind of banking investment or banking operation. As a consequence ex post, it is all the more difficult to make senior bond holders or uninsured depositors take their share of the bank's losses.

10. Hart and Zingales (2011) propose an interesting automatic version of this mechanism whereby, once the price for CDS reaches a critical threshold, it triggers the compulsory issuance of equity.

11. James (1987) computed the difference between book value and realized value and found that the bank failure resulted in a loss of 30 percent of assets and of 10 percent as direct associated expenses. In addition he showed that the average loss in all bank transactions, where a bank is sold as a going concern and all of a failed bank's assets are sold, was less than the losses in other transactions that imply a loss of charter value.

12. An interesting example of this complexity is in the US legislation that states universality for US banks and territoriality for foreign ones.

13. An interesting empirical analysis of these issues is considered by Ongena, Popov, and Udell (2012) who show that when a bank is more heavily regulated at home, it tends to take higher risks in its operation in foreign countries.

14. Estimating the size of shadow banking depends on the precise definition of the banking operations that non-bank institutions perform, such as whether or not money market mutual funds should be included. The Financial Stability Board (FSB) estimated the size of the global shadow banking system at around €46 trillion in 2010, representing 25 to 30 percent of the total financial system, and half the size of bank assets. As expected this size is larger in the United States where it reaches some 40 percent than in Europe (13 percent).

15. In addition the fact that the CDSs contracts were traded over the counter and not in an organized market led to imperfections in its pricing and to a higher risk of a default as margin calls are not made on a daily basis but only once some thresholds are met.

16. Because it was implemented as a reaction to the Enron scandal, the Sarbanes–Oxley Act of 2002 (SOX) mainly contributed to set the standards of behavior for firms and banks managers in their relationship with stakeholders, although the focus was rather defining individual responsibilities in certifying the accuracy of financial information. Nevertheless, SOX demanded more independence of the outside auditors in charge of corporate financial statements, and emphasized the oversight role of boards of directors.

17. The first resolution plans were submitted to the Federal Reserve and the FDIC in the third quarter of 2012.

18. The Volcker rule reverses elements of the Gramm–Leach–Bliley Act, which itself repealed the Glass–Steagall Act of 1933.

19. Based on the Liikanen Report. See http://ec.europa.eu/internal_market/bank /structural reform/index_en.htm for details.

Chapter 9

1. Central banks focused on the stable historical relationship between money aggregates and the price level that Friedman and Schwartz (1963) had found. This may have been fine for the pre-1970 period, but with rapid financial innovation and as financial intermediation shifted away from traditional banks, it worked less well. Realizing that the relationship between growth in monetary aggregates and inflation was too unstable to be useful in making monetary policy, central banks shifted attention to interest rates. As Gerald Bouey, governor of the Bank of Canada, put it in 1982: "We didn't abandon the monetary aggregates, they abandoned us." See Cecchetti (2013).

2. See next chapter and Svensson (2013) and Galí (2013) for a different view.

3. Houston, Lin, and Ma (2012) study whether cross-country differences in regulations have affected international bank flows. They find strong evidence that banks have transferred funds to markets with fewer regulations. This form of regulatory arbitrage suggests there may be a destructive "race to the bottom" in global regulations, which restricts domestic regulators' ability to limit bank risk-taking. However, they also find that the links between regulation differences and bank flows are significantly stronger if the recipient country is a developed country with strong property rights and creditor rights. This suggests that while differences in regulations have important influences, without a strong institutional environment, lax regulations are not enough to encourage massive capital flows.

4. The crisis has also shown that pure leverage ratios (on top of capital ratios) were also necessary for microprudential policy to reduce bank insolvency risk. However, in this chapter we concentrate on macroprudential policy.

5. Concentration limits on liabilities, such as limits that prevent banks to depend on mainly one provider of finance in the interbank market, should also be seen as part of this group of measures.

6. See micro-level evidence by Seru et al. (2012) on how some US laws induced (forced) higher bank credit supply to subprime borrowers.

7. However, higher capital and liquidity requirements may reduce the profits for share-holders, and banks may take higher risk to compensate the lower expected profits (Koehn and Santomero 1980; Kim and Santomero 1988).

8. During the period preceding the recent financial crisis, banks were free-riding on the liquidity provided by others. As Battacharya and Gale (1988) show, there are no incentives to provide liquidity in normal times since the returns are low. As Rajan (2005) argues, the easiest way to generate high returns with apparently no high risk (so-called fake alpha returns) is to invest in highly illiquid assets. The new Basel rules will make it more difficult to hold low levels of bank liquidity. However, as banks found ways to arbitrate (and evade) capital regulation, they will probably find ways to arbitrage the new liquidity rules. Therefore, not only is regulation crucial, but also strong oversight.

9. The Bank of England already developed a liquidity requirement during the crisis. See http://www.bankofengland.co.uk/pra/Pages/publications/liquiditymetricmonitor. aspx.

10. See http://blogs.ft.com/westminster/2013/06/a-one-minute-guide-to-the-banking-commission/.

11. On October 27, 2011, the Joint Progress Report to the *G20* by the *Financial Stability Board*, the *International Monetary Fund* and the *Bank for International Settlements* on "Macroprudential Policy Tools and Frameworks" featured dynamic provisions as a tool to address threats from excessive credit expansion in the system. On November 11, 2011, Yellen (2011b) discussed dynamic provisions in a speech on "Pursuing Financial Stability at the Federal Reserve." See also reports from the *Bank for International Settlements* (Drehmann and Gambacorta 2012), the *Eurosystem* (Burroni et al. 2009), the *Federal Reserve System* (Fillat and Montoriol-Garriga 2010), the *Financial Services Authority* (Osborne, Fuertes, and Milne 2012), discussions in, for example, *The Economist* (March 12, 2009), the *Federation of European Accountants* (March 2009), the *Financial Times* (February 17, 2010; June 15, 2012), *JP Morgan* (February 2010), the *UK Accounting Standards Board* (May 2009), and academic work by Shin (2011) and Tirole (2011). Laeven and Majnoni (2003) find evidence that banks around the world delay provisioning for bad loans until it is too late, when cyclical downturns have already set in, thereby magnifying the impact of the economic cycle on banks' income and capital. Dynamic provisioning increases provisioning in good times, so that the banks' need for new own funds (capital) in bad times is lower. See Fernández de Lis and Garcia-Herrero (2010) on the more recent experiences in Columbia and Peru.

12. See http://www.economist.com/blogs/freeexchange/2013/06/macroprudential-policy.

13. Put differently, one can see bank stocks as a call option written on bank assets with strike price equal to the face value of debt. Option pricing shows that an increase in volatility raises the payoffs for the call; hence higher risk benefits bank shareholders.

14. There was moreover little market disciplining in the most junior, subordinated, long-term debt (see Flannery et al. 1996).

15. See also Morgan (2002).

Chapter 10

1. See Blanchard, Dell'Ariccia, and Mauro (2013).

2. The origins of central banking can be traced to medieval public banks, such as Barcelona's Taula de Canvi (Municipal Bank of Deposit), which was established in 1401 for the safekeeping of city and private deposits.

3. See Allen and Gale (2007), Goodhart (1988), and Stein (2012).

4. For a summary of the overall monetary policy actions taken around different central banks, see chapter II of the 79th Annual Report of the BIS (June 2009); for the euro area, see Cour-Thimann and Winkler (2013) and http://www.ecb.europa.eu/mopo/implement/omo/html/communication.en.html; for the United States, see http://www.federalreserve.gov/monetarypolicy/bst.htm.

5. See Dell'Ariccia et al. (2012). Note, however, that large historical and cross-country studies only use an aggregate credit variable, thus for these studies it is impossible to detect excessive bank risk-taking on credit.

6. See, for example, Allen and Rogoff (2011), Rajan (2010), Taylor (2008, 2009), and Calomiris (2008) and numerous articles since summer 2007 in the *Financial Times*, *Wall Street Journal*, and *The Economist*. The soft lending standards and real estate bubble are the result of loose monetary policy and global imbalances that led to excessive credit availability (in addition to micro factors: e.g., financial innovation, weak supervision, and regulatory capital arbitrage).

7. Concerns about reaching for yield are old. Jones (1968) observed that life insurers tended to maximize yields within investment categories in 1968, and Cox (1967) raised the issue for banks. However, for a thirty-year period from the 1970s until around ten years ago, high yields in fixed-income markets made it relatively easy for institutions to get high yields. The environment changed with the low inflation period (the "great moderation") in conjunction with the low levels of monetary policy rates following the burst of the Internet bubble in the 2000s.

8. See the keynote speech by Governor Jeremy C. Stein at the ECB conference on "Banking, Liquidity and Monetary Policy," Frankfurt, Germany, September 26, 2013.

9. This section draws heavily on Blanchard et al. (2013). See also Besley et al. (2009), Svensson (2012, 2013), and Bernanke (2010).

10. One could consider the ECB two-pillar strategy a way to target credit aggregates to obtain financial stability, but the ECB's second pillar was more on monetary aggregates and on their medium term impact on price stability.

11. Galí (2014) analyzes asset price bubbles without credit, whereas the worst asset price bubbles in history tend to be associated with credit booms (see also Kindleberger 1978).

12. The bank lending channel is based on a failure of the MM proposition for banks. Consistent with this argument, monetary tightening has been shown to reduce lending by banks that are smaller (Kashyap and Stein 1995), unrelated to a large banking group (Campello 2002), hold less liquid assets (Kashyap and Stein 2000) or have higher leverage (Kishan and Opiela 2000; Gambacorta and Mistrulli 2004).

13. The definition of the bank capital- and liquidity-to-total-assets ratios they employ closely follows the theoretical literature that attributes a prominent role to net worth in

reducing the agency costs of borrowing (Holmstrom and Tirole 1997, 1998; Bernanke, Gertler, and Gilchrist 1999; Gertler and Kiyotaki 2011), which sharpens the interpretation of the coefficients on their interactions with monetary conditions.

14. A weak bank is in the 10th percentile in both bank capital and liquidity, whereas a strong bank is in the 90th percentile.

15. See Del Giovane, Eramo, and Nobili (2011) for an example of publicly available crosschecking of the bank lending survey data using detailed supervisory data on bank lending from Italy. They find robust evidence at the bank level that changes in lending standards from the survey are reflected in actual changes in lending conditions to firms (with a quarter lag). It should be noted also that the lending standards from the surveys are not only correlated with actual credit spreads and volume (see Maddaloni and Peydró 2011), but are also good predictors of credit and output growth (see Lown and Morgan 2006 for the US evidence; De Bondt et al. 2010 for the euro area).

16. Monetary policy is also expected to influence the amount of financial intermediation by nonbank financial intermediaries and markets (including shadow banking), though these nonbank channels of monetary policy have been less analyzed.

17. However, higher interest rates may increase the risk-taking incentives of borrowers due to moral hazard (Stiglitz and Weiss 1981), increase the opportunity costs for banks to hold cash, thus making risky alternatives more attractive (Smith 2002), or even reduce the banks' net worth or charter value enough to make a "gambling for resurrection" strategy attractive (Keeley 1990). These countervailing effects make the impact of the short-term interest rate on credit risk-taking ultimately a critical empirical question.

18. Galí (2014) examines the impact of alternative monetary policy rules on a rational asset price bubble without credit, through the lens of an overlapping generations model with nominal rigidities. A systematic increase in interest rates in response to a growing bubble is shown to enhance the bubble, thus calling into question the theoretical foundations of the case for "leaning against the wind" monetary policies.

19. Other factors that may explain the setting off of real estate bubbles but are left out of these models are the available of credit, that would support the continuation of a bubble, and the positive serial correlation of real estate returns (as established by Case and Shiller 1989; Englund, Quigley, and Redfearn 1998; Glaeser and Gyourko 2007). This empirical observation is important as it shows that if real estate prices are currently rising, then it is likely this will continue. For example, Glaeser and Gyourko (2007) find that a $1 increase in one year will on average be followed by a $0.71 increase the following year. Thus, once a real estate bubble has started, it is likely that it will persist for some time.

20. As in other similar models in banking, bank fragility is due to uncertainty about future household liquidity needs and the mismatch between the long gestation period for the investment projects and the demandable nature of deposits.

21. It is a bailout as the private banking sector is insolvent at rates that would prevail absent intervention, and it is the central bank's ability to lower overall market rates through its lending that allows it to "bail out" the banking system.

22. Another possibility is that the central bank will intervene to lower rates only if sufficient banks pick deposit levels that would render them insolvent if interest rates are not reduced (a "too many to fail," or strategic complementarity response). In that case multiple equilibria are possible for promised deposit payments, one of which is the too

important to fail level. This possibility is also emphasized by Acharya and Yorulmazer (2007) and Farhi and Tirole (2012a).

23. See also Borio and Lowe (2002, 2004).

24. For the main period analyzed in the paper, short-term interest rates in Spain were decided in Frankfurt, not in Madrid, assuaging concerns of reverse causality (e.g., future higher risk may imply current monetary expansion) and omitted variables (variables correlated with the stance of monetary policy that can also influence risk-taking). Further mitigating these concerns, time × firm and time × bank fixed effects absorb any observed and unobserved time-varying heterogeneity in firms and banks.

25. Total bank assets in Spain cover most of the banks' businesses. Banks did not develop conduits or structured investment vehicles (SIVs) because the prevailing accounting and regulatory rules made banks consolidate these items and set aside sufficient capital (see also Acharya and Schnabl 2009).

26. Related papers that obtain qualitatively similar results include papers using data from the United States (e.g., Altunbas, Gambacorta, and Marquez-Ibañez 2014; Buch, Eickmeier, and Prieto 2014a; Buch, Eickmeier, and Prieto 2014b; Delis, Hasan, and Mylonidis 2011; Paligorova and Santos 2012), Austria (Gaggl and Valderrama 2010), Colombia (López, Tenjo and Zárate 2010a; López, Tenjo and Zárate 2010b), the Czech Republic (Geršl, et al. 2012), Bolivia (Ioannidou, Ongena, and Peydró 2013), and Sweden (Apel and Claussen 2012).

27. For similar findings, see Rigobon and Sack (2004).

28. As Stein (2013b) argues, their findings can be illustrated with the events of January 25, 2012. On that date the FOMC changed its forward guidance, indicating that it expected to hold the federal funds rate near zero "through late 2014," whereas it had previously only stated that it expected to do so "through mid-2013." In response to this announcement, the expected path of short-term nominal rates fell significantly from two to five years out, with the two-year nominal yield dropping 5 basis points and the five-year nominal yield falling 14 basis points. More strikingly, ten-year and twenty-year real forward rates declined by 5 basis points and 9 basis points, respectively.

29. Pension funds and mutual funds hold a much larger fraction of their bond portfolios relative to insurance companies. Mutual and pension funds may therefore also reach for yield, but to a much smaller extent than insurance firms.

30. Their findings show how the institutional arrangements and regulation of financial intermediaries (insurance firms) may influence credit cycles. Specifically, reaching for yield has implications for the credit supply. When investors reach for yield, issuers that happen to belong to favored "buckets" (e.g., high-risk firms with A ratings on senior debt) become able to borrow at better terms than they should otherwise, given their risk and liquidity position.

31. For a similar argument in bank credit markets, see Dell'Ariccia and Marquez (2006a).

32. See, for example, Schoar et al. (2012) and Krishnamurthy, Nagel, and Orlov (2014). Schmidt, Timmermann, and Wermers (2013) study daily investor flows to and from each money market mutual fund during the period surrounding and including the money fund crisis of September 2008. They document outflows during the crisis period. Institutional investors focused their run-like behavior on large funds that were part of a complex having large amounts of institutional money funds (as a fraction of all money funds). Such investors were more likely to run from funds with higher yields, lower

expense ratios, and higher prior flow volatility, indicating that "hot money" chased yields, but selectively ran from higher-yield funds that were more vulnerable.

33. Since the start of the European Banking Union in late 2014, the ECB has access to supervisory information on all banks with more than 30 billion of assets.

34. Mian, Sufi, and Trebbi (2014b) argue that countries become more politically polarized and fractionalized following financial crises, reducing the likelihood of major financial reforms precisely when they might have especially large benefits. Their evidence from a large sample of countries provides strong support for the hypotheses that following a financial crisis, voters become more ideologically extreme and that, independently of whether they were initially in power, ruling coalitions become weaker. The evidence is less clear-cut that increased polarization and weaker governments reduce the chances of financial reform and that financial crises lead to legislative gridlock and anemic reform.

35. In chapter 4 we also saw that time-varying preferences can play a role in credit and asset booms and busts. Even in these cases, macroprudential policy could reduce the systemic risks, for example, through pro-cyclical capital requirements (Shleifer et al. 2012).

36. See International Monetary Fund (2011) for detailed country-specific information on limits on LTV ratios.

37. This is in fact one of the main purposes of the book, to systematize the current knowledge of macroprudential policy and systemic risk.

38. The next paragraph draws heavily on Blanchard et al. (2013).

Chapter 11

1. For the text of the EC proposal on structural reforms in the EU banking system, see http://eur-lex.europa.eu/LexUriServ/LexUriServ.do?uri=COM:2014:0043:FIN:EN:PDF.

References

Abbassi, Puriya, Falk Brauning, Falko Fecht, and José-Luis Peydró. 2015. Cross-border liquidity, relationships: Euro area interbank crisis. CEPR Discussion Paper 10479.

Abreu, Dilip, and Markus K. Brunnermeier. 2003. Bubbles and crashes. *Econometrica* 71 (1): 173–204.

Acemoglu, Daron. 2011. Thoughts on inequality in financial crisis. Presentation at the American Economics Association Meetings, January 2011.

Acemoglu, Daron, Asuman Ozdaglar, and Alireza Tahbaz-Zalehi. 2010. Cascades in networks and aggregate volatility. NBER Working Paper 16516.

Acharya, Sankarshan, and Jean-Francois Dreyfus. 1988. Optimal bank reorganization policies and the pricing of federal deposit insurance. *Journal of Finance* 44 (5): 1313–34.

Acharya, Viral V., and Nada Mora. 2015. A crisis of banks as liquidity providers. *Journal of Finance* 70 (1): 1–43.

Acharya, Viral V., and Hassan Naqvi. 2012. The seeds of a crisis: A theory of bank liquidity and risk taking over the business cycle. *Journal of Financial Economics* 106: 349–66.

Acharya, Viral V., Lasse H. Pedersen, Thomas Philippon, and Matthew Richardson. 2009. Measuring systemic risk. Mimeo. New York University.

Acharya, Viral V., and Matthew Richardson. 2009. *Restoring Financial Stability: How to Repair a Failed System*. Hoboken, NJ: Wiley.

Acharya, Viral V., and Philipp Schnabl. 2009. How banks played the leverage "game." In V. Acharya and M. Richardson, eds., *Restoring Financial Stability: How to Repair a Failed System*. New York: Wiley, 83–100.

Acharya, Viral V., and Sascha Steffen. 2015. The "greatest" carry trade ever? Understanding eurozone bank risks. *Journal of Financial Economics* 115: 215–36.

Acharya, Viral V., and Tanju Yorulmazer. 2007. Too many to fail: An analysis of time-inconsistency in bank closure policies. *Journal of Financial Intermediation* 16 (1): 1–31.

Acharya, Viral V., and Tanju Yorulmazer. 2008a. Cash-in-the-market pricing and optimal resolution of bank failures. *Review of Financial Studies* 21 (6): 2705–42.

Acharya, Viral V., and Tanju Yorulmazer. 2008b. Information contagion and bank herding. *Journal of Money, Credit and Banking* 40 (1): 215–31.

Adams, Renee, and Hamid Mehran. 2012. Bank board structure and performance: Evidence for large bank holding companies. *Journal of Financial Intermediation* 21 (2): 243–67.

Adelino, Manuel, Antoinette Schoar, and Felipe Severino. 2012. Credit supply and house prices: Evidence from mortgage market segmentation. NBER Working Paper 17832.

Admati, Anat R., and Martin F. Hellwig. 2013. *The Bankers' New Clothes: What's Wrong with Banking and What to Do about It*. Princeton: Princeton University Press.

Admati, Anat R., Peter M. DeMarzo, Martin F. Hellwig, and Paul Pleiderer. 2013. Fallacies, irrelevant facts, and myths in the discussion of capital regulation: Why bank equity is not socially expensive. Stanford GBS Working Paper 2065.

Adrian, Tobias, and Nina Boyarchenko. 2012. Intermediary leverage cycles and financial stability. Working Paper.

Adrian, Tobias, and Markus Brunnermeier. 2009. CoVar. Federal Reserve Bank of New York Staff Report 348.

Adrian, Tobias, Paolo Colla, and Hyun Song Shin. 2012. Which financial frictions? Parsing the evidence from the financial crisis of 2007–09. In Daron Acemoglu, Jonathan Parker, and Michael Woodford, eds., *NBER Macroeconomics Annual*. Chicago: University of Chicago Press.

Adrian, Tobias, and Hyun Song Shin. 2008a. Financial intermediaries, financial stability, and monetary policy. Staff Report 346. Federal Reserve Bank of New York.

Adrian, Tobias, and Hyun Song Shin. 2008b. Liquidity and financial cycles. BIS Working Paper 256.

Adrian, Tobias, and Hyun Song Shin. 2009. Money, liquidity and monetary policy. *American Economic Review* 99 (2): 600–605.

Adrian, Tobias, and Hyun Song Shin. 2010. Liquidity and leverage. *Journal of Financial Intermediation* 19 (3): 418–37.

Adrian, Tobias, and Hyun Song Shin. 2011. Financial intermediaries and monetary economics. In B. M. Friedman and M. Woodford, eds., *Handbook of Monetary Economics*, vol. 3. New York: Elsevier, 601–50.

Afonso, Gara, Anna Kovner, and Antoinette Schoar. 2011. Stressed, not frozen: The federal funds market in the financial crisis. *Journal of Finance* 66 (4): 1109–39.

Agarwal, Sumit, and Itzhak Ben-David. 2014. Do loan officers' incentives lead to lax lending standards? NBER Working Paper 19945.

Agarwal, Sumit, Effi Benmelech, Nittai Bergman, and Amit Seru. 2012. Did the Community Reinvestment Act (CRA) lead to risky lending? NBER Working Paper 18609.

Agarwal, Sumit, David O. Lucca, Amit Seru, and Francesco Trebbi. 2014. Inconsistent regulators: Evidence from banking. *Quarterly Journal of Economics* 129: 889–938.

Agarwal, Sumit, and Faye H. Wang. 2009. Perverse incentives at the banks? Evidence from a natural experiment. Working Paper 09–08. Federal Reserve Bank of Chicago.

Aghion, Philippe, George-Marios Angeletos, Abhijit Banerjee, and Kalina Manova. 2010. Volatility and growth: Credit constraints and the composition of investment. *Journal of Monetary Economics* 57: 246–65.

Aghion, Philippe, Patrick Bolton, and Steven Fries. 1999. Optimal design of bank bailouts: The case of transition economies. *Journal of Institutional and Theoretical Economics* 155 (1): 51–70.

Aghion, Philippe, Oliver Hart, and John Moore. 1992. The economics of bankruptcy reform. *Journal of Law Economics and Organization* 8: 523–46.

Aguiar, Mark, and Manuel Amador. 2011. Growth in the shadow of expropriation. *Quarterly Journal of Economics* 126: 651–97.

Aguiar, Mark, Manuel Amador, and Gita Gopinath. 2009. Investment cycles and sovereign debt overhang. *Review of Economic Studies* 76: 1–31.

Agur, Itai, and Maria Demertzis. 2010. Monetary policy and excessive banks risk taking. DNB Working Paper 271.

Aharony, Joseph, and Itzhak Swary. 1983. Contagion effects of bank failures: Evidence from capital markets. *Journal of Business* 56 (3): 305–22.

Aiyar, Shekhar, Charles W. Calomiris, and Tomasz Wieladek. 2014. Does macro-pru leak? Evidence from a UK policy experiment. *Journal of Money, Credit and Banking* 46: 181–214.

Akerlof, George A., and Paul M. Romer. 1993. Looting: The economic underworld of bankruptcy for profit. *Brookings Papers on Economic Activity* 2: 1–73.

Akerlof, George A., and Robert J. Shiller. 2009. *Animal Spirits: How Human Psychology Drives the Economy, and Why It Matters for Global Capitalism.* Princeton: Princeton University Press.

Akin, Ozlem, Jose M. Marin, and Jose-Luis Peydró. 2013. Anticipation of the financial crisis: Evidence from insider trading in banks. Mimeo.

Albertazzi, Ugo, and Domenico J. Marchetti. 2011. Credit crunch, flight to quality and evergreening: An analysis of bank-firm relationships after Lehman. Mimeo. Banca d'Italia.

Alessandri, Piergiorgio, Prasanna Gai, Sujit Kapadia, Nada Mora, and Claus Puhr. 2009. Towards a framework for quantifying systemic stability. *International Journal of Central Banking* 5 (3): 47–81.

Allen, Franklin, and Ana Babus. 2009. Networks in finance. In Paul Kleindorfer and Yoram Wind, eds., *The Network Challenge: Strategy, Profit, and Risk in an Interlinked World.* Upper Saddle River, NJ: Pearson Education, 367–82.

Allen, Franklin, and Elena Carletti. 2008. Mark-to-market accounting and cash-in-the-market pricing. *Journal of Accounting and Economics* 45 (2–3): 358–78.

Allen, Franklin, Elena Carletti, and Douglas Gale. 2009. Interbank market liquidity and central bank intervention. *Journal of Monetary Economics* 56 (5): 639–52.

Allen, Franklin, Elena Carletti, and Robert Marquez. 2014. Deposits and bank capital structure. *Journal of Financial Economics*, forthcoming.

Allen, Franklin, Michael Chui, and Angela Maddaloni. 2004. Financial systems in Europe, the U.S.A. and Asia. *Oxford Review of Economic Policy* 20 (4): 490–508.

Allen, Franklin, and Douglas Gale. 1998. Optimal financial crises. *Journal of Finance* 53 (4): 1245–84.

Allen, Franklin, and Douglas Gale. 2000a. Financial contagion. *Journal of Political Economy* 108: 1–33.

Allen, Franklin, and Douglas Gale. 2000b. *Comparing Financial Systems*. Cambridge: MIT Press.

Allen, Franklin, and Douglas Gale. 2000c. Bubbles and crises. *Economic Journal* 110: 236–55.

Allen, Franklin, and Douglas Gale. 2003. Asset price bubble and stock market interlinkages. In W. C. Hunter, G. G. Kaufman, and M. Pomerleano, eds., *Asset Price Bubbles: The Implications for Monetary, Regulatory, and International Policies*. Cambridge: MIT Press.

Allen, Franklin, and Douglas Gale. 2004a. Financial intermediaries and markets. *Econometrica* 72: 1023–61.

Allen, Franklin, and Douglas Gale. 2004b. Competition and financial stability. *Journal of Money, Credit and Banking* 36 (3): 453–80.

Allen, Franklin, and Douglas Gale. 2004c. Asset price bubbles and monetary policy. In M. Desai and Y. Said, eds., *Global Governance and Financial Crises*. London: Routledge, 19–42.

Allen, Franklin, and Douglas Gale. 2007. *Understanding Financial Crises*. New York: Oxford University Press.

Allen, Franklin, and Gary Gorton. 1993. Churning bubbles. *Review of Economic Studies* 60: 813–36.

Allen, Franklin, Stephen Morris, and Andrew Postlewaite. 1993. Finite bubbles with short sale constraints and asymmetric information. *Journal of Economic Theory* 61: 206–29.

Allen, Franklin, and Kenneth Rogoff. 2011. Asset prices, financial stability and monetary policy. In P. Jansson and M. Persson, eds., *Riksbank's Inquiry into the Risks in the Swedish Housing Market*. Stockholm: Sveriges Riksbank, 189–218.

Allen, Linda, Turan Bali, and Yi Tang. 2012. Does systemic risk in the financial sector predict future economic downturns? *Review of Financial Studies* 25 (10): 3000–36.

Almeida, Heitor, Murillo Campello, Bruno Laranjeira, and Scott Weisbenner. 2012. Corporate debt maturity and the real effects of the 2007 credit crisis. *Critical Finance Review* 1 (1): 3–58.

Almunia, Miguel, Agustín S. Bénétrix, Barry Eichengreen, Kevin H. O'Rourke, and Gisela Rua. 2010. From Great Depression to Great Credit Crisis: Similarities, differences and lessons. *Economic Policy* (April): 219–65.

Altunbas, Y., L. Gambacorta, and D. Marquez-Ibanez. 2014. Does monetary policy affect bank risk? *International Journal of Central Banking* 10: 95–136.

Amiti, Mary, and David Weinstein. 2011. Exports and financial shocks. *Quarterly Journal of Economics* 126: 1841–77.

Amiti, Mary, and David Weinstein. 2013. How much do bank shocks affect investment? Evidence from matched bank-firm loan data. NBER Working Paper 18890.

Andersen, Henrik, Christian Castro, Marc Farag, and Julia Giese. 2010. Macroprudential policy rules for the UK. Mimeo. Bank of England.

Ang, Andrew and Francis A. Longstaff. 2013. Systemic sovereign credit risk: Lessons from the U.S. and Europe. *Journal of Monetary Economics* 60 (5): 493–510.

Angeloni, Ignazio, and Ester Faia. 2013. Capital regulation and monetary policy with fragile banks. *Journal of Monetary Economics* 60 (3): 311–24.

Angeloni, Ignazio, Anil Kashyap, and Benoit Mojon. 2003. *Monetary Policy Transmission in the Euro Area.* Cambridge: Cambridge University Press.

Apel, Mikael, and Carl Andreas Claussen. 2012. Monetary policy, interest rates and risk-taking. *Sveriges Riksbank Economic Review* 2: 68–83.

Arora, Navneet, Priyank Gandhi, and Francis A. Longstaff. 2012. Counterparty credit risk and the credit default swap market. *Journal of Financial Economics* 103: 280–93.

Ashcraft, Adam. 2005. Are banks really special? New evidence from the FDIC-induced failure of healthy banks. *American Economic Review* 95: 1712–30.

Ashcraft, Adam, Morten L. Bech, and W. Scott Frame. 2010. The Federal Home Loan Bank System: The lender of next-to-last resort? *Journal of Money, Credit and Banking* 42 (4): 551–83.

Atkinson, Tyler, David Luttrell, and Harvey Rosenblum. 2013. *How bad was it? The costs and consequences of the 2007–09 financial crisis.* Mimeo. Dallas Federal Reserve.

Bae, Kee-Hong, Jun-Koo Kang, and Chan-Woo Lim. 2002. The value of durable bank relationships: Evidence from Korean banking shocks. *Journal of Financial Economics* 64: 181–214.

Bagehot, Walter. 1873. *Lombard Street: A Description of the Money Market.* London: H.S. King.

Baldursson, Fridrik Mar, and Richard Portes. 2013. Gambling for resurrection in Iceland: the rise and fall of the banks. CEPR Discussion Paper 9664.

Banerjee, Abhijit V. 1992. A simple model of herd behavior. *Quarterly Journal of Economics* 107: 797–817.

Bank for International Settlements. 2012. The limits of monetary policy. *BIS Annual Report*, ch. 4.

Bank for International Settlements. 2014. *BIS 84th Annual Report.*

Bank of England. 2011. Instruments of macroprudential policy. BoE Discussion Paper.

Barberis, Nicholas. 2012. A model of casino gambling. *Management Science* 58: 35–51.

Barberis, Nicholas, and Ming Huang. 2008. Stocks as lotteries: The implications of probability weighting for security prices. *American Economic Review* 98: 2066–2100.

Barberis, Nicholas, Ming Huang, and Tano Santos. 2001. Prospect theory and asset prices. *Quarterly Journal of Economics* 116: 1–3.

Barberis, Nicholas, and Andrei Shleifer. 2003. Style investing. *Journal of Financial Economics* 68: 161–99.

Barberis, Nicholas, Andrei Shleifer, and Robert Vishny. 1998. A model of investor sentiment. *Journal of Financial Economics* 49: 307–43.

Barlevy, Gadi. 2014. A leverage-based model of speculative bubbles. *Journal of Economic Theory* 153: 459–505.

Barojas, Adolfo, Giovanni Dell'Ariccia, and Andrei Levchenko. 2007. Credit booms: The good, the bad, and the ugly. Mimeo.

Barro, Robert J. 2009. Rare disasters, asset prices, and welfare costs. *American Economic Review* 99 (1): 243–64.

Barth, James, Gerard Caprio, and Ross Levine. 2001. The regulation and supervision of banks around the world: A new database. World Bank Policy Research Working Paper 2588.

Barth, James, Gerard Caprio, and Ross Levine. 2006. *Rethinking Bank Regulation: Till Angels Govern*. New York: Cambridge University Press.

Basel Committee for Banking Supervision. 2011. Capitalisation of bank exposures to central counterparties. Second consultative document. November. http://www.bis.org /publ/bcbs206.pdf.

Battiston, Stefano, Michelangelo Puliga, Rahul Kaushik, Paola Tasca, and Guido Caldarelli. 2012a. DebtRank: Too central to fail? Financial networks, the Fed and systemic risk. Scientific Report 2. Nature Publishing Group.

Battiston, Stefano, Domenico Delli Gatti, Mauro Gallegati, Bruce Greenwald, and Joseph E. Stiglitz. 2012b. Liaisons dangereuses: Increasing connectivity, risk sharing, and systemic risk. *Journal of Economic Dynamics and Control* 36 (8): 1121–41.

Bech, Morten, and Todd Keister. 2012. The liquidity coverage ratio and monetary policy implementation. Mimeo.

Beck, Thorsten, Hans Degryse, and Christiane Kneer. 2014. Is more finance better? Disentangling intermediation and size effects of financial systems. *Journal of Financial Stability* 10: 50–64.

Beck, Thorsten, Asli Demirgüç-Kunt, and Ross Levine. 2003. Bank concentration and crises. NBER Working Paper 9921.

Beck, Thorsten, Ross Levine, and Norman Loayza. 2000. Finance and the sources of growth. *Journal of Financial Economics* 58: 261–300.

Becker, Bo, and Victoria Ivashina. 2014a. Cyclicality of credit supply: Firm level evidence. *Journal of Monetary Economics* 62: 76–93.

Becker, Bo, and Victoria Ivashina. 2014b. Reaching for yield in the bond market. *Journal of Finance*, forthcoming.

Begeneau, Juliane, Monika Piazzesi, and Martin Schneider. 2012. The allocation of interest rate risk in the financial sector. Working paper, Stanford University.

Bekaert, Geert, Maria Hoerova, and M. Lo Duca. 2013. Risk, uncertainty and monetary policy. *Journal of Monetary Economics* 60: 771–88.

Belloni, Alexandre, and Victor Chernozhukov. 2011. L1-penalized quantile regression in high-dimensional sparse models. *Annals of Statistics* 39 (1): 82–130.

Benabou, Roland. 2013. Groupthink: Collective delusions in organizations and markets. *Review of Economic Studies* 80: 429–62.

Berg, Tobias, Manju Puri, and Jorg Rocholl. 2013. Loan officer incentives and the limits of hard information. Working Paper 19051.

Berger, Allen, Sally Davies, and Mark Flannery. 2000. Comparing market and supervisory assessments of bank performance: Who knows what when? *Journal of Money, Credit and Banking* 32: 641–67.

Berger, Allen N., and Gregory F. Udell. 2004. The institutional memory hypothesis and the procyclicality of bank lending behavior. *Journal of Financial Intermediation* 13: 458–95.

Berlin, Mitchell, and Loretta Mester. 1999. Deposits and relationship lending. *Review of Financial Studies* 12 (3): 579–607.

Bernanke, Ben S. 1983. Nonmonetary effects of the financial crisis in the propagation of the Great Depression. *American Economic Review* 73: 257–76.

Bernanke, Ben S. 2005. The global saving glut and the US current account deficit. Homer Jones Lecture. St. Louis, Missouri, April 15.

Bernanke, Ben S. 2007a. *The Financial Accelerator and the Credit Channel.* Washington, DC: Board of Governors of the US Federal Reserve System.

Bernanke, Ben S. 2007b. Global imbalances: Recent developments and prospects. Bundesbank Lecture. Berlin, September 11.

Bernanke, Ben S. 2009. Letter to the US Senator Corker, October 30.

Bernanke, Ben S. 2010. Monetary policy and the housing bubble. Speech before Annual Meeting, American Economic Association.

Bernanke, Ben S., and Alan S. Blinder. 1988. Money, credit and aggregate demand. *American Economic Review* 82: 901–21.

Bernanke, Ben S., and Allen S. Blinder. 1992. The Federal Funds rate and the channels of monetary transmission. *American Economic Review* 82: 901–21.

Bernanke, Ben S., and Mark Gertler. 1987. Banking and macroeconomic equilibrium. In William Barnett and Ken Singleton, eds., *New Approaches to Monetary Economics.* Cambridge, UK: Cambridge University Press.

Bernanke, Ben S., and Mark Gertler. 1989. Agency costs, net worth and business fluctuations. *American Economic Review* 79: 14–31.

Bernanke, Ben S., and Mark Gertler. 1990. Financial fragility and economic performance. *Quarterly Journal of Economics* 105 (February): 87–114.

Bernanke, Ben S., and Mark Gertler. 1995. Inside the black box: The credit channel of monetary policy transmission. *Journal of Economic Perspectives* 9 (4): 27–48.

Bernanke, Ben S., and Mark L. Gertler. 2001. Should central banks respond to movements in asset prices? *American Economic Review* 91 (2): 253–57.

Bernanke, Ben S., Mark Gertler, and Simon Gilchrist. 1996. The financial accelerator and flight to quality. *Review of Economics and Statistics* 78: 1–15.

Bernanke, Ben S., Mark Gertler, and Simon Gilchrist. 1999. The financial accelerator in a quantitative business cycle framework. In J. Taylor and M. Woodford, eds., *Handbook of Macroeconomics*, vol. 1. Amsterdam: Elsevier, 1341–93.

Bernanke, Ben S., and Kenneth N. Kuttner. 2005. What explains the stock market's reaction to Federal Reserve policy? *Journal of Finance* 60: 1221–58.

Bernanke, Ben S., and Cara S. Lown. 1991. The credit crunch. *Brookings Papers on Economic Activity* 2: 205–39.

Bernanke, Ben S., and Ilan Mihov. 1998. Measuring monetary policy. *Quarterly Journal of Economics* 113 (3): 869–902.

Bernard, Victor, Robert C. Merton, and Krishna Palepu. 1995. Mark-to-market accounting for banks and thrifts: Lessons from the Danish experience. *Journal of Accounting Research* 33 (1): 1–32.

Berndt, Antje, Robert Jarrow, and ChoongOh Kang. 2007. Restructuring risk in credit default swaps: An empirical analysis. *Stochastic Processes and Their Applications* 117: 1724–49.

Bhattacharya, Sudipto, Arnoud Boot, and Anjan Thakor. 1998. The economics of bank regulation. *Journal of Money, Credit and Banking* 30: 745–70.

Bhattacharya, Sudipto, and Gabriela Chiesa. 1995. Proprietary Information, financial intermediation, and research incentives. *Journal of Financial Intermediation* 4: 328–57.

Bhattacharya, Sudipto, and Douglas Gale. 1987. Preference shocks, liquidity, and central bank policy. In W. Barnett and K. Singleton, eds., *New Approaches to Monetary Economics*. Cambridge, UK: Cambridge University Press, 69–88.

Bhattacharya, Sudipto, Charles A. E. Goodhart, Dimitrios P. Tsomocos, and Alexandros P. Vardoulakis. 2011. Minsky's financial instability hypothesis and the leverage cycle. Financial Markets Group Special Paper 202. London School of Economics.

Bikhchandani, Sushil, David Hirshleifer, and Ivo Welch. 1992. A theory of fads, fashion, custom, and cultural change in informational cascades. *Journal of Political Economy* 100: 992–1026.

Billio, Monica, Mila Getmansky, Andrew W. Lo, and Loriana Pelizzon. 2012. Econometric measures of connectedness and systemic risk in the finance and insurance sectors. *Journal of Financial Economics* 104 (3): 535–59.

BIS. 2001. Group of Ten: Consolidation of the Financial Sector. www.bis.org/publ/gten05.htm.

BIS. 2011. Macroprudential policy tools and frameworks. Update to G20 Finance Ministers and Central Bank Governors. www.bis.org/publ/othp13.pdf.

Bisias, Dimitrios, Mark Flood, Andrew W. Lo, and Stavros Valavanis. 2012. A survey of systemic risk analytics. *Annual Review of Financial Economics* 4: 255–96.

Blanchard, Olivier, Giovanni dell'Ariccia, and Paolo Mauro. 2010. Rethinking macroeconomic policy. *Journal of Money, Credit and Banking* 42: 199–215.

Blanchard, Olivier, Giovanni Dell'Ariccia, and Paolo Mauro. 2013. Rethinking macro policy II: Getting granular. IMF Staff Discussion Note 13/03.

Bliss, Robert, and Mark Flannery. 2000. Market discipline in the governance of US bank holding companies: monitoring vs influencing. Working Paper, 2000–3. Federal Reserve Bank of Chicago.

Bofondi, Marcello, Luisa Carpinelli, and Enrico Sette. 2013. Credit supply during a sovereign crisis. Mimeo. Banca d'Italia.

Boissay, Frederic, Fabrice Collard and Frank Smets. 2013. Booms and systemic banking crises. Mimeo. ECB.

Boivin, Jean, Michael Kiley, and Frederic Mishkin. 2011. How has the monetary transmission mechanism evolved over time? In B. Friedman and M. Woodford, eds., *Handbook of Macroeconomics*, vol. 3. Amsterdam: Elsevier, 369–422.

Bolton, Patrick, Xavier Freixas, Leonardo Gambacorta, and Paolo Emilio Mistrulli. 2013. *Relationship and Transaction Lending in a Crisis*. Rochester, NY: SSRN.

Boot, Arnoud. 2000. Relationship banking: What do we know? *Journal of Financial Intermediation* 9: 7–25.

Boot, Arnoud, and Anjan Thakor. 1993. Self-interested bank regulation. *American Economic Review* 83: 206–12.

Bordo, Michael D. 1986. Financial crises, banking crises, stock market crashes and the money supply: Some international evidence, 1887–1933. In F. Capie and G. E. Wood. eds., *Financial Crises and the World Banking System*. London: Macmillan, 190–248.

Bordo, Michael D. 1990. The lender of last resort: Alternative views and historical experience. *Federal Reserve Bank of Richmond Economic Review* 76 (1): 18–29.

Bordo, Michael D. 2008. A historical perspective on the crisis of 2007–08. NBER Working Paper 14569.

Bordo, Michael D., Barry Eichengreen, Daniela Klingebiel, and Maria Soledad Martinez-Peria. 2001. Is the crisis problem growing more severe? *Economic Policy* 16 (32): 51–82.

Bordo, Michael D., and Joseph G. Haubrich. 2010. Credit crises, money and contractions: An historical view. *Journal of Monetary Economics* 57: 1–18.

Borio, Claudio. 2003. Towards a macroprudential framework for financial supervision and regulation? *CESifo Economic Studies* 49: 181–216.

Borio, Claudio. 2008. The financial turmoil of 2007–? A preliminary assessment and some policy considerations. BIS Working Paper 251.

Borio, Claudio. 2009. The macroprudential approach to regulation and supervision. http://www.voxeu.org/index.php?q=node/3445

Borio, Claudio. 2013. Macroprudential policy and the financial cycle: Some stylised facts and policy suggestions. Mimeo. BIS.

Borio, Claudio, and Matthias Drehmann. 2009. Towards an operational framework for financial stability: Fuzzy measurement and its consequences. In R. Alfaro and D. Gray, eds., *Financial Stability, Monetary Policy, and Central Banking*, vol. 15. Central Bank of Chile Series on Central Banking, Analysis, and Economic Policies, 63–123.

Borio, Claudio, Craig Furfine, and Philip Lowe. 2001. Procyclicality of the financial system and financial stability: issues and policy options. BIS Papers 1.

Borio, Claudio, and Philip Lowe. 2002. Asset prices, financial and monetary stability: Exploring the nexus. BIS Working Paper 114.

Borio, Claudio, and Philip Lowe. 2004. Securing sustainable price stability: Should credit come back from the wilderness? BIS Working Paper 157.

Borio, Claudio, and William R. White. 2003. Whither monetary and financial stability: The implications of evolving policy regimes. *Proceedings*. Federal Reserve Bank of Kansas City, 131–211.

Borio, Claudio, and Haibin Zhu. 2012. Capital regulation, risk-taking and monetary policy: A missing link in the transmission mechanism. *Journal of Financial Stability* 8: 236–51.

Bovenzi, John F., and Maureen E. Muldoon. 1990. Failure-resolution methods and policy considerations. *FDIC Banking Review* 3 (1): 1–11.

Boyd, John H., and Gianni De Nicolo. 2005. The theory of bank risk taking and competition revisited. *Journal of Finance* 60: 1329–43.

Boyd, John, Sungkyu Kwak, and Bruce Smith. 2005. The real output losses associated with modern banking crises. *Journal of Money, Credit and Banking* 37: 977–99.

Brázdik, Frantisek, Michal Hlaváček, and Ales Maršál. 2012. Survey of research on financial sector modeling within DSGE models: What central banks can learn from it. *Czech Journal of Economics and Finance* 62 (3): 252–77.

Brierley, Peter. 2009. The UK Special Resolution Regime for failing banks in an international context. Financial Stability Paper 5. Bank of England.

Broner, Fernando, Aitor Erce, Alberto Martin, and Jaume Ventura. 2013. Sovereign debt markets in turbulent times: Creditor discrimination and crowding-out effects. *Journal of Monetary Economics* 61: 114–42.

Brownlees, Christian, and Robert Engle. 2015. SRISK: A conditional capital shortfall index for systemic risk measurement. Mimeo. New York University.

Brunnermeier, Markus K. 2009. Deciphering the 2007–08 liquidity and credit crunch. *Journal of Economic Perspectives* 23 (1): 77–100.

Brunnermeier, Markus. 2013. Financial stability and systemic risk. Presentation at International Monetary Fund. http://scholar.princeton.edu/markus/files/covar_slides.pdf

Brunnermeier, Markus, Andrew Crocket, Charles Goodhart, Avinash D. Persaud, and Hyun Shin. 2009. The fundamental principles of financial regulation. Geneva Report on the World Economy 11. ICMB/CEPR.

Brunnermeier, Markus, Thomas M. Eisenbach, and Yuliy Sannikov. 2013. Macroeconomics with financial frictions: A survey. In *Advances in Economics and Econometrics*. New York: Cambridge University Press.

Brunnermeier, Markus, Gary Gorton, and Arvind Krishnamurthy. 2012. Risk topography. *NBER Macroeconomics Annual*. 2011: 149–76.

Brunnermeier, Markus, and Lasse Pedersen. 2009. Market liquidity and funding liquidity. *Review of Financial Studies* 22 (6): 2201–38.

Brunnermeier, Markus, and Yuliy Sannikov. 2012. Redistributive monetary policy. In *The Changing Policy Landscape: Proceedings of the 2012 Jackson Hole Economic Policy Symposium*. Jackson Hole, WY, August 31–September 1, 2012. Federal Reserve Bank of Kansas City.

Brunnermeier, Markus, and Isabel Schnabel. 2014. *Bubbles and central banks: Historical Perspectives. Mimeo.* Princeton University.

Brusco, Sandro, and Fabio Castiglionesi. 2007. Liquidity coinsurance, moral hazard and financial contagion. *Journal of Finance* 62: 2275–2302

Bryant, John. 1980. A model of reserves, bank runs, and deposit insurance. *Journal of Banking and Finance* 4 (4): 335–44.

Buch, Claudia M., Sandra Eickmeier, and Esteban Prieto. 2014a. Macroeconomic factors and microlevel bank behavior. *Journal of Money, Credit and Banking* 46: 715–51.

Buch, Claudia. M., Sandra Eickmeier, and Esteban Prieto. 2014b. In search for yield? Survey-based evidence on bank risk taking. *Journal of Economic Dynamics and Control* 43: 12–30.

Buiter, Willem. 2009. The unfortunate uselessness of most "state of the art" academic monetary economics. *Financial Times*, March 3. ft.com/maverecon.

Buraschi, Andrea, Paolo Porchia, and Fabio Trojani. 2010. The cross-section of expected stock returns: Learning about distress and predictability in heterogeneous orchards. Working Paper.

Buser, Stephen, Andrew Chen, and Edward Kane. 1981. Federal deposit insurance, regulatory policy and optimal bank capital. *Journal of Finance* 36: 51–60.

Caballero, Ricardo J. 2010a. Crisis and reform: Managing systemic risk. Prepared for the Angelo Costa Lecture delivered in Rome, March 23.

Caballero, Ricardo J. 2010b. Macroeconomics after the crisis: Time to deal with the pretense-of-knowledge syndrome. *Journal of Economic Perspectives* 24 (4): 85–102.

Caballero, Ricardo J., Takeo Hoshi, and Anil K. Kashyap. 2008. Zombie lending and depressed restructuring in Japan. *American Economic Review* 98 (5): 1943–77.

Caballero, Ricardo, and Arvind Krishnamurthy. 2001. International and domestic collateral constraints in a model of emerging market crises. *Journal of Monetary Economics* 48: 513–48.

Caballero, Ricardo J., and Arvind Krishnamurthy. 2006. Bubbles and capital flow volatility: Causes and risk management. *Journal of Monetary Economics* 53: 35–53.

Caballero, Ricardo J., and Arvind Krishnamurthy. 2008a. Collective risk management in a flight to quality episode. *Journal of Finance* 63 (5): 2195–2229.

Caballero, Ricardo J., and Arvind Krishnamurthy. 2008b. Knightian uncertainty and its implications for the TARP. *Financial Times* Economists' Forum, November 24.

Caballero, Ricardo J., and Alp Simsek. 2009. Complexity and financial panics. NBER Working Paper 14997.

Caballero, Ricardo J., and Alp Simsek. 2013. Fire sales in a model of complexity. *Journal of Finance* 68 (6): 2549–87.

Calomiris, Charles W. 1993. Regulation, industrial structure, and instability in US banking: An historical perspective. In M. Klausner and L. White, eds., *Structural Change in Banking.*New York: New York University, 19–115.

Calomiris, Charles W. 1994. Is the discount window necessary? A Penn Central perspective. Federal Reserve Bank of St. Louis *Review*, May, 31–55.

Calomiris, Charles W. 2008. The subprime turmoil: What's old, what's new, and what's next. Mimeo. Columia Business School.

Calomiris, Charles W. 2009. The subprime turmoil: What's old, what's new, and what's next. *Journal of Structured Finance* 15 (1): 6–52.

Calomiris, Charles W., and Charles Kahn. 1991. The role of demandable debt in structuring optimal banking arrangements. *American Economic Review* 81 (3): 497–513.

Calomiris, Charles W., and Charles Kahn. 1996. The efficiency of self-regulated payment systems: Learning from the Suffolk system. *Journal of Money, Credit and Banking* 28 (4): 766–97.

Calomiris, Charles W., Daniela Klingebiel, and Luc Laeven. 2003. A taxonomy of financial crisis resolution mechanisms: Cross-country experience. In L. Laeven and P. Honohan, eds., *Systemic Financial Crises: Containment and Resolution*. Cambridge, UK: Cambridge University Press, 25–75.

Calomiris, Charles W., and Joseph Mason. 2003. Consequences of bank distress during the Great Depression. *American Economic Review* 93: 937–47.

Campbell, John Y., and John H. Cochrane. 1999. By force of habit: A consumption-based explanation of aggregate stock market behavior. *Journal of Political Economy* 107 (2): 205–51.

Campbell, John Y., Stefano Giglio, and Pareg Pathak. 2011. Forced sales and house prices. *American Economic Review* 101 (5): 2108–31.

Campello, Murillo. 2002. Internal capital markets in financial conglomerates: Evidence from small bank responses to monetary policy. *Journal of Finance* 57 (6): 2773–2805.

Caplin, Andrew, and John Leahy. 1994. Business as usual, market crashes, and wisdom after the fact. *American Economic Review* 84: 548–65.

Caprio, Gerard, and Daniela Klingebiel. 1999. Episodes of systemic and borderline financial crises. Mimeo. World Bank.

Caprio, Gerard, Daniela Klingebiel, Luc Laeven, and Guillermo Noguera. 2005. Banking crisis database. In P. Honohan and L. Laeven, eds. *Systemic Financial Crises*. Cambridge University Press, 307–40.

Caprio, Gerard, Luc Laeven, and Ross Levine. 2007. Governance and bank valuation. *Journal of Financial Intermediation* 16: 584–617.

Carvalho, Fabia, and Cyntia Azevedo. 2008. The incidence of reserve requirements in Brazil: do bank stockholders share the burden? *Journal of Applied Economics* 11: 61–90.

Case, Karl E., and Robert J. Shiller. 1989. The efficiency of the market for single-family houses. *American Economic Review* 79 (1): 125–37.

Castiglionesi, Fabio, Fabio Feriozzi, and Guido Lorenzoni. 2009. Financial integration, liquidity and the depth of systemic crises. Working Paper.

Cecchetti, Stephen G., Marion Kohler, and Christian Upper. 2009. Financial crises and economic activity. NBER Working Paper 15379.

Cecchetti, Stephen G., Madhusudan Mohanty, and Fabrizio Zampolli. 2011. The real effects of debt. BIS Working Paper 352.

Cetorelli, Nicola, and Linda S. Goldberg. 2011. Global banks and international shock transmission: Evidence from the crisis. *IMF Economic Review* 59 (1): 41–76.

Cetorelli, Nicola, and Linda S. Goldberg. 2012a. Banking globalization and monetary transmission. *Journal of Finance* 67 (5): 1811–43.

Cetorelli, Nicola, and Linda S. Goldberg. 2012b. Follow the money: Quantifying domestic effects of foreign bank shocks in the Great Recession. *American Economic Review* 102 (3): 213–18.

Cetorelli, Nicola, and Stavros Peristiani. 2012. The role of banks in asset securitization. *Federal Reserve Bank of New York Economic Policy Review* 18 (2): 47–63.

Chamley, Christoph, and Douglas Gale. 1994. Information revelation and strategic delay in a model of investment. *Econometrica* 62: 1065–85.

Chan-Lau, Jorge, Marco A. Espinosa, and Juan Sole. 2009. On the use of network analysis to assess systemic financial linkages. Mimeo. IMF.

Chari, V. V., and J. Lawrence Christiano, and Patrick J. Kehoe. 2008. Facts and myths about the financial crisis of 2008. Working Paper 666. Federal Reserve Bank of Minneapolis.

Chari, V. V., and Ravi Jagannathan. 1988. Banking panics, information and rational expectations equilibrium. *Journal of Finance* 43 (3): 749–61.

Chava, Sudheer, and Amiyatosh Purnanandam. 2011. The effect of banking crisis on bank-dependent Borrowers. *Journal of Financial Economics* 99: 116–35.

Chen, Long, Pierre Collin-Dufresne, and Robert S. Goldstein. 2009. On the relation between the credit spread puzzle and the equity premium puzzle. *Review of Financial Studies* 22 (9): 3367–3409.

Chen, Yehning. 1999. Banking panics: The role of the first-come, first-served rule and information externalities. *Journal of Political Economy* 107 (5): 946–68.

Cheng, Ing-Haw., Sahil Raina, and Wei Xiong. 2014. Wall Street and the housing bubble. *American Economic Review* 104 (9): 2797–2829.

Chernyshoff, Natalia, David S. Jacks, and Alan M. Taylor. 2009. Stuck on gold: Real exchange rate volatility and the rise and fall of the gold standard, 1875–1939. *Journal of International Economics* 77: 195–205.

Chevallier, Judith, and Glenn Ellison. 1997. Risk taking by mutual funds as a response to incentives. *Journal of Political Economy* 105: 1167–1200.

Chodorow-Reich, Gabriel. 2014a. The employment effects of credit market disruptions: Firm-level evidence from the 2008–09 financial crisis. *Quarterly Journal of Economics* 129 (1): 1–59.

Chodorow-Reich, Gabriel. 2014b. Effects of unconventional monetary policy on financial institutions. *Brookings Papers on Economic Activity* 48: 155–227.

Christiano, Lawrence J., Martin Eichenbaum, and Charles L. Evans. 1999. Monetary policy shocks: What have we learned and to what end? In J. Taylor and M. Woodford, eds., *Handbook of Macroeconomics*. Amsterdam: Elsevier.

Christiano, Lawrence J., Cosmin Ilut, Roberto Motto, and Massimo Rostagno. 2010. Monetary policy and stock market booms. Paper presented at the 2010 Economic Policy Symposium, Jackson Hole, WY.

Christiano, Lawrence J., Roberto Motto, and Massimo Rostagno. 2003. The Great Depression and the Friedman–Schwartz hypothesis. *Journal of Money, Credit and Banking* 35 (6): 1119–97.

Christiano, Lawrence J., Roberto Motto, and Massimo Rostagno. 2010. Financial factors in economic fluctuations. ECB Working Paper 1192.

Ciccarelli, Mateo, Angela Maddaloni, and José-Luis Peydró. 2013. Heterogeneous transmission mechanism: Monetary policy and financial fragility in the euro area. *Economic Policy* 28 (75): 459–512.

Ciccarelli, Matteo, Angela Maddaloni, and Jose-Luis Peydró. 2014. Trusting the bankers: a new look at the credit channel of monetary policy. *Review of Economic Dynamics*, forthcoming.

Cifuentes, Rodrigo, Hyun Song Shin, and Gianluigi Ferrucci. 2005. Liquidity risk and contagion. *Journal of the European Economic Association* 3 (2–3): 556–66.

Claessens, Stijn, Giovanni Dell'Ariccia, Deniz Igan, and Luc Laeven. 2010a. Lessons and policy implications from the global financial crisis. IMF Working Paper 10/44.

Claessens, Stijn, Giovanni Dell'Ariccia, Deniz Igan, and Luc Laeven. 2010b. Cross-country experiences and policy implications from the global financial crisis. *Economic Policy* 62: 267–93.

Claessens, Stijn, Erik Feijen, and Luc Laeven. 2008. Political connections and preferential access to finance: The role of campaign contributions. *Journal of Financial Economics* 88: 554–80.

Claessens, Stijn, M. Ayhan Kose, and Marco E. Terrones. 2012. How do business and financial cycles interact? *Journal of International Economics* 87: 178–90.

Claessens, Stijn, and Luc Laeven. 2004. What drives bank competition? Some international evidence. *Journal of Money, Credit and Banking* 36 (3): 563–83.

Claessens, Stijn, Ceyla Pazarbasioglu, Luc Laeven, Marc Dobler, Fabian Valencia, Oana Nedelescu, and Katharine Seal. 2011. Crisis management and resolution policies: Early lessons from the financial crisis. Staff Discussion Note 11/05. IMF.

Clement, Piet. 2010. The term "macroprudential": Origins and evolution. BIS. *Quarterly Review* 1: 59–67.

Cocco, João F., Francisco J. Gomes, and Nuno C. Martins. 2009. Lending relationships in the interbank market. *Journal of Financial Intermediation* 18 (1): 24–48.

Cole, Harold L., and Timothy J. Kehoe. 1996. A self-fulfilling model of Mexico's 1994–85 debt crisis. *Journal of International Economics* 41: 309–30.

Cole, Rebel A., Joseph A. McKenzie, and Lawrence J. White. 1995. Deregulation gone awry: Moral hazard in the savings and loan industry. In A. Cottrell; M. Lawlor and J. Woo, eds., *The Causes and Consequences of Depository Institutions Failures*. Boston: Kluwer Academic, 29–73.

Cole, Shawn, Martin Kanz, and Leora Klapper. 2015. Incentivizing calculated risk-taking: Evidence from an experiment with commercial bank loan officers. *Journal of Finance* 70: 537–75.

Colon, Dina. 2005. The foreign bank exemption to the Sarbanes–Oxley prohibition on loans to directors and officers. *Journal of International Business and Law* 4 (1): 123–51.

Committee on the Global Financial System. 2012. Operationalising the selection and application of macroprudential instruments. CGFS Paper 48. http://www.bis.org/publ/cgfs48.pdf.

Cont, Rama, Amal Moussa, and Edson Bastos e Santos. 2013. Network structure and systemic risk in banking systems. In J. P. Fouque and J. Langsam, eds., *Handbook of Systemic Risk*. Cambridge, UK: Cambridge University Press, 327–68.

Correa, Ricardo, Horacio Sapriza, and Andrei Zlate. 2012. Liquidity shocks, dollar funding costs, and the bank lending channel during the European sovereign crisis. International Finance Discussion Paper 1059. Board of Governors of the Federal Reserve System.

Cooperman, Elizabeth S., Winson B. Lee, and Glenn A. Wolfe. 1992. The 1985 Ohio thrift crisis, the FSLIC's solvency, and rate of contagion for retail CDs. *Journal of Finance* 47 (3): 919–41.

Coval, Joshua, Jakub W. Jurek, and Erik Stafford. 2009a. The economics of structured finance. *Journal of Economic Perspectives* 23: 3–25.

Coval, Joshua, Jakub W. Jurek, and Erik Stafford. 2009b. Economic catastrophe bonds. *American Economic Review* 99: 628–66.

Covitz, Daniel, Nellie Liang, and Gustavo Suarez. 2009. The anatomy of a financial crisis: The evolution of panic-driven runs in the asset-backed commercial paper market. *Proceedings Federal Reserve Bank of San Francisco* 1: 1–36.

Cour-Thimann, Philippine, and Bernhard Winkler. 2013. The ECB's non-standard monetary policy measures: The role of institutional factors and financial structure. ECB Working Paper 1528.

Cutler, David M., James M. Poterba, and Lawrence H. Summers. 1991. Speculative dynamics. *Review of Economic Studies* 58: 529–46.

Cziraki, Peter. 2013. Trading by bank insiders before and during the 2007–2008 financial crisis. Working Paper. University of Toronto.

Dang, Tri Vi, Gary Gorton, and Bengt Holmström. 2013. Ignorance, debt, and financial crises. Mimeo. SOM, Yale.

Daniel, Kent, David Hirshleifer, and Avanidhar Subrahmanyan. 1998. Investor psychology and security market under- and overreactions. *Journal of Finance* 53: 1839–85.

Danielsson, Jon, Kevin R. James, Marcela Valenzuela Ilknur Zer. 2011. Model risk of systemic risk models. Mimeo. London School of Economics.

Danielsson, Jon, Hyun Song Shin, and Jean-Pierre Zigrand. 2011. Balance sheet capacity and endogenous risk. Financial Markets Group Discussion Paper 665.

Dasgupta, A. 2004. Financial contagion through capital connections: A model of the origin and spread of bank panics. *Journal of the European Economic Association* 2 (6): 1049–84.

De Bandt, Olivier, and Philipp Hartmann. 2000. Systemic risk: A survey. ECB Working Paper 35.

De Bandt, Olivier, Philipp Hartmann, and José-Luis Peydró. 2000. Systemic risk in banking: An update. *Oxford Handbook of Banking*. Oxford: Oxford University Press, 633–72.

De Bandt, Olivier, Philipp Hartmann, and José-Luis Peydró. 2015. Systemic risk in banking: An update. *Oxford Handbook of Banking*, 2nd ed. Oxford: Oxford University Press.

De Bondt, Gabe, Angela Maddaloni, José-Luis Peydró, and Silvia Scopel. 2010. The Euro Area Bank Lending Survey matters: Empirical evidence for credit and output growth. ECB Working Paper 1160.

De Bondt, Werner F. M., and Richard H. Thaler. 1985. Does the stock market overreact? *Journal of Finance* 40 (3): 793–805.

De Haas, Ralph, and Neeltje Van Horen. 2012. International shock transmission after the Lehman Brothers collapse: Evidence from syndicated lending. *American Economic Review* 102 (3): 231–37.

De Haas, Ralph, and Iman Van Lelyveld. 2006. Foreign banks and credit stability in Central and Eastern Europe: Friends or foes? *Journal of Banking and Finance* 30 (7): 1927–52.

De Haas, Ralph, and Iman Van Lelyveld. 2010. Internal capital markets and lending by multinational bank subsidiaries. *Journal of Financial Intermediation* 19 (1): 1–25.

De Haas, Ralph, and Iman Van Lelyveld. 2014. Multinational banks and the global financial crisis: weathering the perfect storm? *Journal of Money, Credit and Banking* 46: 333–64.

De Nicolò, Gianni, Philip Bartholomew, Jahanara Zaman, Mary Zephirin. 2003. Bank consolidation, internationalization, and conglomeration: Trends and implications for financial risk. IMF Working Paper 03/158.

De Nicolò, Gianni, Giovanni Dell'Ariccia, Luc Laeven, and Fabian Valencia. 2010. Monetary policy and bank risk taking. IMF Staff Position Note 10/09.

De Nicolò, Gianni, Giovanni Favara, and Lev Ratnovski. 2012. Externalities and macroprudential policy. IMF Staff Discussion Note 12/05.

De Nicolò, Gianni, and Myron Kwast. 2002. Systemic risk and financial consolidation: Are they related? *Journal of Banking and Finance* 26 (5): 861–80.

DeAngelo, Harry, and Rene Stulz. 2013. Why high leverage is optimal for banks. NBER Working Paper 19139.

Del Giovane, Paolo, Ginette Eramo, and Andrea Nobili. 2011. Disentangling demand and supply in credit developments: A survey-based analysis for Italy. *Journal of Banking and Finance* 35: 2719–32.

Delis, Manthos D., Ifthekar Hasan, and Nikolaos Mylonidis. 2011. The risk-taking channel of monetary policy in the USA: Evidence from micro-level data. Mimeo. Cass Business School.

Dell'Ariccia, Giovanni, Enrica Detragiache, and Raghuram Rajan. 2008. The real effects of banking crises. *Journal of Financial Intermediation* 17: 89–112.

Dell'Ariccia, Giovanni, Deniz Igan, and Luc Laeven. 2012. Credit booms and lending standards: Evidence from the subprime mortgage market. *Journal of Money, Credit and Banking* 44 (2–3): 367–84.

Dell'Ariccia, Giovanni, Deniz Igan, Luc Laeven, and Hui Tong. 2012. Policies for macrofinancial stability: How to deal with credit booms. IMF Staff Discussion Note 12/06.

Dell'Ariccia, Giovanni, Luc Laeven, and Robert Marquez. 2014. Monetary policy, leverage, and bank risk taking. *Journal of Economic Theory* 149: 65–99.

Dell'Ariccia, Giovanni, Luc Laeven, and Gustavo A. Suarez. 2013. Bank leverage and monetary policy's risk-taking channel: Evidence from the United States. Mimeo. IMF.

Dell'Ariccia, Giovanni, and Robert Marquez. 2006a. Lending booms and lending standards. *Journal of Finance* 61 (5): 2511–46.

Dell'Ariccia, Giovanni, and Robert Marquez. 2006b. Competition among regulators and credit market integration. *Journal of Financial Economics* 79 (2): 401–30.

DellaVigna, Stefano. 2009. Psychology and economics: Evidence from the field. *Journal of Economic Literature* 47 (2): 315–72.

Demirguç-Kunt, Asli, and Enrica Detragiache. 1998. The determinants of banking crises in developing and developed countries. *IMF Staff Papers* 45: 81–109.

Demirguc-Kunt, Asli, Edward Kane, and Luc Laeven. 2008. *Deposit Insurance around the World: Issues of Design and Implementation.* Cambridge: MIT Press.

Den Haan, Wouter J., Steven Sumner, and Guy Yamashiro. 2007. Bank loan portfolios and the monetary transmission mechanism. *Journal of Monetary Economics* 54: 904–24.

Dewatripont, Mathias, and Xavier Freixas. 2012. Bank resolution: Lessons from the crisis. In:Dewatripont, M. and X. Freixas, eds., *The Crisis Aftermath: New Regulatory Paradigms*, 105–43. London: Center for Economic Policy Research.

Dewatripont, Mathias, and Jean Tirole. 1994. *The Prudential Regulation of Banks.* Cambridge: MIT Press.

Diamond, Douglas W., and Philip Dybvig. 1983. Bank runs, deposit insurance, and liquidity. *Journal of Political Economy* 91 (3): 401–419.

Diamond, Douglas W., and Raghuram G. Rajan. 2001. Liquidity risk, liquidity creation, and financial fragility: A theory of banking. *Journal of Political Economy* 109 (2): 287–327.

Diamond, Douglas W., and Raghuram G. Rajan. 2002. Bank bailouts and aggregate liquidity. *American Economic Review* 92: 38–41.

Diamond, Douglas W., and Raghuram G. Rajan. 2005. Liquidity shortage and banking crises. *Journal of Finance* 60 (2): 615–47.

Diamond, Douglas W., and Raghuram G. Rajan. 2006. Money in a theory of banking. *American Economic Review* 96 (1): 30–53.

Diamond, Douglas W., and Raghuram G. Rajan. 2009. The credit crisis: Conjectures about causes and remedies. *American Economic Review* 99 (2): 606–10.

Diamond, Douglas W., and Raghuram G. Rajan. 2011. Fear of fire sales, illiquidity seeking, and credit freezes. *Quarterly Journal of Economics* 126: 557–91.

Diamond, Douglas W., and Raghuram G. Rajan. 2012. Illiquid banks, financial stability, and interest rate policy. *Journal of Political Economy* 120: 552–91.

Diebold, Francis, and Kamil Yilmaz. 2014. On the network topology of variance decompositions: Measuring the connectedness of financial firms. *Journal of Econometrics* 182: 119–34.

Djankov, Simeon, Jan Jindra, and Leora Klapper. 2005. Corporate valuation and the resolution of bank insolvency in East Asia. *Journal of Banking & Finance* 29 (8–9): 2095–2118.

Doblas-Madrid, Antonio. 2012. A robust model of bubbles with multidimensionality uncertainty. *Econometrica* 80: 1845–93.

Docking, Diane Scott, Mark Hirschey, and Elaine Jones. 1997. Information and contagion effects of bank loan-loss reserve announcements. *Journal of Financial Economics* 43 (2): 219–39.

Drehmann, Mathias, Claudio Borio, and Kostas Tsatsaronis. 2011. Anchoring countercyclical capital buffers: The role of credit aggregates. *International Journal of Central Banking* 7: 189–240.

Draghi, Mario. 2012. Speech by Mario Draghi, President of the European Central Bank, at the Global Investment Conderence in London, July 26, 2012. http://www.ecb.europa.eu/press/key/date/2012/html/sp120726.en.html.

Duffie, Darell, Haoxiang Zhu. 2011. Does a Central Clearing Counterparty reduce counterparty risk? *Review of Asset Pricing Studies* 1 (1): 74–95.

Duffie, Darrell. 2014. Systemic risk exposures: A 10-by-10-by-10 approach. In M. Brunnermeier and A. Krishnamurthy, eds., *Risk Topography: Systemic Risk and Macro Modeling*. Chicago: University of Chicago Press, 47–56.

Duffie, Darrell, Lasse H. Pedersen, and Kenneth J. Singleton. 2003. Modeling sovereign yield spreads: A case study of Russian debt. *Journal of Finance* 58 (1): 119–59.

Duygan-Bump, Burcu, Patrick Parkinson, Eric Rosengren, Gustavo A. Suarez, and Paul Willen. 2013. How effective were the Federal Reserve emergency liquidity facilities? Evidence from the asset-backed commercial paper money market Mutual Fund Liquidity Facility. *Journal of Finance* 68 (2), 715–37.

European Central Bank. 2009. The concept of systemic risk. *Financial Stability Review* (December): 134–42.

Edwards, Franklin R., and Frederic S. Mishkin. 1995. The decline of traditional banking: Implications for financial stability and regulatory policy. NBER Working Paper 4993.

Eggertsson, Gauti B., and Paul Krugman. 2012. Debt, deleveraging, and the liquidity trap: A Fisher–Minsky–Koo approach. *Quarterly Journal of Economics* 127 (3): 1469–1513.

Eichengreen, Barry, and Poonam Gupta. 2013. Tapering talk: The impact of expectations of reduced Federal Reserve security purchases on emerging markets. Mimeo. University of California, Berkeley.

Eichengreen, Barry, and Peter Temin. 2000. The gold standard and the Great Depression. *Contemporary European History* 9 (2): 183–207.

Eisenberg, Larry, and Thomas Noe. 2001. Systemic risk in financial systems. *Management Science* 47 (2): 236–49.

Ellul, Andrew, and Vijay Yerramilli. 2013. Stronger risk controls, lower risk: Evidence from U.S. Bank holding companies. *Journal of Finance* 68 (5): 1757–1803.

Elsinger, Helmut, Alfred Lehar, and Martin Summer. 2006a. Risk assessment for banking systems. *Management Science* 52 (9): 1301–14.

Elsinger, Helmut, Alfred Lehar, and Martin Summer. 2006b. Using market information for banking systems risk assessment. *International Journal of Central Banking* 2 (1): 137–65.

Elsinger, Helmut, Alfred Lehar, and Martin Summer. 2012. Network models and systemic risk assessment. In Jean-Pierre Fouque and Joseph A. Langsam, ed., *Handbook on Systemic Risk*. Cambridge University Press, 287–305.

Englund, Peter, John M. Quigley, and Christian L. Redfearn. 1998. Improved price indexes for real estate: Measuring the course of Swedish house prices. *Journal of Urban Economics* 44 (2): 171–96.

Epstein, Larry G. 1999. A definition of uncertainty aversion. *Review of Economic Studies* 66 (3): 579–608.

Esty, Benjamin. 1998. The impact of contingent liability on commercial bank risk taking. *Journal of Financial Economics* 47 (2): 189–218.

European Central Bank. 2007. Corporate finance in the euro area. ECB Structural Issues Report.

European Central Bank. 2009. Recent developments in the balance sheets of the eurosystem, the Federal Reserve System and the Bank of Japan. *ECB Monthly Bulletin* (October): 81–94.

Evanoff, Douglas and Larry Wall. 2000. Subordinated debt and bank capital reform. Working Paper 2000–24. Federal Reserve Bank of Atlanta.

Fahlenbrach, Rüdiger, and René M. Stulz. 2011. Bank CEO incentives and the credit crisis. *Journal of Financial Economics* 99 (1): 11–26.

Fama, Eugene. 1965. The behavior of stock market prices. *Journal of Business* 38: 34–105.

Fama, Eugene. 1970. Efficient capital markets: A review of theory and empirical work. *Journal of Finance* 25 (2): 383–417.

Fama, Eugene. 1980. Banking in the theory of finance. *Journal of Monetary Economics* 6 (1): 39–57.

Farhi, Emmanuel, and Jean Tirole. 2012a. Collective moral hazard, maturity mismatch and systemic bailouts. *American Economic Review* 102 (1): 60–93.

Farhi, Emmanuel, and Jean Tirole. 2012b. Bubbly liquidity. *Review of Economic Studies* 79: 678–706.

Favara, Giovanni, and Jean Imbs. 2011. Credit supply and the price of housing. CEPR Discussion Paper 8129.

Favara, Giovanni, and Mariassunta Giannetti. 2015. Forced asset sales and the concentration of outstanding debt: Evidence from the mortgage market. CEPR Discussion Paper 10476.

Feldman, Ron, and Gary Stern. 1994. *Too Big to Fail: The Hazards of Bank Bailouts*. Washington, DC: Brookings Institution Press.

Fernández de Lis, Santiago, and Alicia Garcia-Herrero. 2010. Dynamic provisioning: Some lessons from existing experiences. Working Paper 218. Asian Development Bank Institute.

Fernandez-Villaverde, Jesus, Luis Garicano, and Tano Santos. 2013. Political credit cycles: The case of the euro zone. *Journal of Economic Perspectives* 27: 145–66.

Feroli, Michael, Anil Kashyap, Kermit Schoenholtz, and Hyun Song Shin. 2014. Market Tantrums and Monetary Policy. Report for the 2014 US Monetary Policy Forum.

Financial Stability Board. 2011. Policy measures to address systemically important financial institutions. November 4.

Financial Stability Board. 2013. Policy framework for addressing Shadow banking risks in securities lending and repos.

Fisher, Irving. 1933. The debt-deflation theory of great depressions. *Econometrica* 1 (4): 337–57.

Flannery, Mark J. 1998. Using market information in prudential bank supervision: A review of the U.S. empirical evidence. *Journal of Money, Credit and Banking* 30 (3): 273–305.

Flannery, Mark J., and Christopher M. James. 1984. The effect of interest rate changes on the common stock returns of financial institutions. *Journal of Finance* 39 (4): 1141–53.

Flannery, Mark J., Simon H. Kwan, and M. Nimalendran. 2004. Market evidence on the opaqueness of banking firms' assets. *Journal of Financial Economics* 71: 419–60.

Flannery, Mark J., Simon H. Kwan, and M. Nimalendran. 2013. The 2007–2009 financial crisis and bank opaqueness. *Journal of Financial Intermediation* 22: 55–84.

Flannery, Mark, and Sorin Sorescu. 1996. Evidence of bank market discipline in subordinated debenture yields: 1983–91. *Journal of Finance* 51: 1147–77.

Foote, Christopher, Kristopher Gerardi, and Paul S. Willen. 2012. Why did so many people make so many ex-post bad decisions? The causes of the foreclosure crisis. NBER Working Paper 18082.

Forbes, Kristin, and Frank Warnock. 2012. Capital flow waves: Surges, stops, flight and retrenchment. *Journal of International Economics* 88 (2): 235–51.

Fostel, Ana, and John Geanakoplos. 2008. Leverage cycles and the anxious economy. *American Economic Review* 98 (4): 1211–44.

Frazzini, Andrea, and Owen Lamont. 2008. Dumb money: Mutual fund flows and the cross-section of stock returns. *Journal of Financial Economics* 88: 299–322.

Freixas, Xavier. 2003. Crisis Management in Europe. In J. Kremers, D. Schoenmaker, and P. Wierts, eds., *Financial Supervision in Europe*. Cheltenham: Edward Elgar, 102–19.

Freixas, Xavier, Curzio Giannini, Glenn. Hoggarth, and Farouk Soussa. 2000. Lender of last resort: What have we learnt since Bagehot? *Journal of Financial Services Research* 18 (1): 63–87.

Freixas, Xavier, and Cornelia Holthausen. 2005. Interbank market integration under asymmetric information. *Review of Financial Studies* 18 (2): 459–90.

Freixas, Xavier, and Christian Laux. 2011. Disclosure, transparency, and market discipline. CFS Working Paper 2011/11.

Freixas, Xavier, and Kebin Ma. 2013. Bank competition and stability: The role of leverage. Mimeo. Tilburg University.

Freixas, Xavier, Antoine Martin, and David Skeie. 2011. Bank liquidity, interbank markets and monetary policy. *Review of Financial Studies* 24 (8): 2656–92.

Freixas, Xavier, Bruno Parigi, and Jean-Charles Rochet. 2000. Systemic risk, interbank relations and liquidity provision by the central bank. *Journal of Money, Credit and Banking* 32 (2): 611–38.

Freixas, Xavier, and Jean-Charles Rochet. 1997. *Microeconomics of Banking*. Cambridge: MIT Press.

Freixas, Xavier, and Jean-Charles Rochet. 2008. *Microeconomics of Banking*, 2nd ed. Cambridge: MIT Press.

Freixas, Xavier, and Anthony M. Santomero. 2004. Regulation of financial intermediaries: A discussion. In S. Bhattacharya, A. Boot, and A. Thakor, eds., *Credit, Intermediation, and the Macroeconomy*. Oxford: Oxford University Press, 424–45.

Friedman, Benjamin M., and Kenneth N. Kuttner. 1992. Money, income, prices, and interest rates. *American Economic Review* 82: 472–92.

Friedman, Benjamin M., and Kenneth N. Kuttner. 1993. Economic activity and the short term credit markets: An analysis of prices and quantities. *Brookings Papers on Economic Activity* 2: 193–284.

Friedman, Milton, and Anna J. Schwartz. 1963. *A Monetary History of the United States: 1867–1960*. Princeton: Princeton University Press.

Furfine, Craig. 2003. Interbank exposures: Quantifying the risk of contagion. *Journal of Money, Credit, and Banking* 35 (1): 111–28.

Furth, Douglas L. 2001. Anticipating the Next Wave of Bad Loans: Function like a Secondary Market Player. *The Secured Lender* (September/October) 31.

Gaggl, Paul, and Maria T. Valderrama. 2010. Does a low interest rate environment affect risk taking in Austria? *Monetary Policy and the Economy (Austrian Central Bank)* 4: 32–48.

Gale, Douglas, and Onur Özgür. 2005. Are bank capital ratios too high or too low? Incomplete markets and optimal capital structure. *Journal of the European Economic Association* 3 (2–3): 690–700.

Galí, Jordi. 2014. Monetary policy and rational asset price bubbles. *American Economic Review* 104 (3): 721–52

Gambacorta, Leonardo, and Paolo Emilio Mistrulli. 2004. Does bank capital affect lending behavior? *Journal of Financial Intermediation* 13 (4): 436–57.

Gan, Jie. 2007. The real effects of asset market bubbles: Loan- and firm-level evidence of a lending channel. *Review of Financial Studies* 20 (6): 1941–73.

Garicano, Luis, and Claudia Steinwender. 2013. Survive another day: Does uncertain financing affect the composition of investment? Discussion Paper 1188. Centre for Economic Performance.

Garleanu, Nicolae, and Lasse Heje Pedersen. 2011. Margin-based asset pricing and deviations from the law of one price. *Review of Financial Studies* 24 (6): 1980–2022.

Geanakoplos, John. 2010. The leverage cycle. In D. Acemoglu, K. Rogoff, and M. Woodford, eds., *NBER Macroeconomic Annual 2009*, vol. 24. University of Chicago Press, 1–65.

Geanakoplos, John, and Lasse Pedersen. 2014. Monitoring leverage. In M. Brunnermeier and A. Krishnamurthy, eds., *Risk Topography: Systemic Risk and Macro Modeling*, 113–27. Chicago: University of Chicago Press.

Gelos, R. Gaston. 2009. Banking spreads in Latin America. *Economic Enquiry* 47: 796–814.

Gennaioli, Nicola, Alberto Martin, and Stefano Rossi. 2013. Banks, government bonds, and default: What do the data say? Mimeo. Pompeu Fabra.

Gennaioli, Nicola, Alberto Martin, and Stefano Rossi. 2014. Sovereign default, domestic banks, and financial institutions. *Journal of Finance* 69 (2): 819–66.

Gennaioli, Nicola, Andrei Shleifer, and Robert Vishny. 2013. A model of shadow banking. *Journal of Finance* 68 (4): 1331–63.

Gerardi, Kristopher, Andreas Lehnert, Shane M. Sherlund, and Paul S. Willen. 2008. Making sense of the subprime crisis. *Brookings Papers on Economic Activity* 2: 69–145.

Gerlach, Stefan. 2009. Defining and measuring systemic risk. Note. European Parliament.

Gersbach, Hans, and Jean-Charles Rochet. 2012. Capital regulation and credit fluctuations. CEPR Discussion Paper 9077.

Gersl, Adam, Petr Jakubik, Dorota Kowalczyk, Steven Ongena, and Jose-Luis Peydro. 2012. Monetary conditions and banks' behaviour in the Czech Republic. Working Paper. Czech National Bank.

Gertler, Mark. 1988. Financial structure and aggregate economic activity: An overview. *Journal of Money, Credit and Banking* 20 (3): 559–88.

Gertler, Mark, and Simon Gilchrist. 1994. Monetary policy, business cycles, and the behavior of small manufacturing firms. *Quarterly Journal of Economics* 109: 309–40.

Gertler, Mark, and Peter Karadi. 2011. A model of unconventional monetary policy. *Journal of Monetary Economics* 58 (1): 17–34.

Gertler, Mark, and Nobuhiro Kiyotaki. 2011. Financial intermediation and credit policy in business cycle analysis. In B. M. Friedman and M. Woodford, eds., *Handbook of Monetary Economics*, vol. 3a. Elsevier, North-Holland, 547–99.

Gertler, Mark, and Nobuhiro Kiyotaki. 2013. Banking, liquidity and bank runs in an infinite-horizon economy. NBER Working Paper 19129.

Gertler, Mark, Nobuhiro Kiyotaki, and Albert Queralto Olive. 2010. Financial crises, bank risk exposure and government financial policy. Mimeo. New York University.

Giannetti, Mariassunta, and Luc Laeven. 2012a. The flight home effect: Evidence from the syndicated loan market during financial crises. *Journal of Financial Economics* 104 (1): 23–43.

Giannetti, Mariassunta, and Luc Laeven. 2012b. Flight home, flight abroad, and international credit cycles. *American Economic Review* 102 (3): 219–24.

Giannone, Domenico, Michele Lenza, and Lucrezia Reichlin. 2010. Business cycles in the euro area, in Europe and the euro. In A. Alesina and F. Giavazzi, eds., *Europe and the Euro*. Chicago: University of Chicago Press, 141–67.

Giannone, Domenico, Michele Lenza, and Lucrezia Reichlin. 2011. Market freedom and the global recession. *IMF Economic Review* 59: 111–35.

Giavazzi, Francesco, and A. Giovannini. 2010. The low interest rate trap. VoxEU, July.

Giglio, Stefano. 2012. Credit default swap spreads and systemic financial risk. Mimeo. Booth School of Business, University of Chicago.

Giglio, Stefano, Bryan Kelly, and Xiao Qiao. 2014. Systemic risk and the macroeconomy: An empirical evaluation. Mimeo. Booth School of Business, University of Chicago.

Glaeser, Edward L., and Joseph Gyourko. 2007. Housing dynamics. Harvard Institute of Economic Research Discussion Paper 2137.

Glaeser, Edward L., Joshua Gottlieb, and Joseph Gyourko. 2013. Can cheap credit explain the housing boom. In Edward L. Glaeser and Todd Sinai, eds., *Housing and the Financial Crisis*. Cambridge, MA: NBER.

Goldsmith, Raymond W. 1969. *Financial Structure and Development*. New Haven: Yale University Press.

Goldstein, Itay, and A. Pauzner. 2005. Demand-deposit contracts and the probability of bank runs. *Journal of Finance* 60 (3): 1293–1327.

Goodfriend, Marvin, and Robert King. 1988. Financial deregulation, monetary policy and central banking. *Federal Reserve Bank Richmond Economic Review* 74: 3–22.

Goodfriend, Marvin, and Bennett T. McCallum. 2007. Banking and interest rates in monetary policy analysis: A quantitative exploration. *Journal of Monetary Economics* 54 (5): 1480–1507.

Goodhart, Charles A. E.. 1988. *The Evolution of Central Banks*. Cambridge: MIT Press.

Goodhart, Charles A. E. 2010. How should we regulate bank capital and financial products? What role for "living wills"?. In Adair Turner et al., eds., *The Future of Finance: The LSE Report*. London: London School of Economics and Political Science, 165–86.

Goodhart, Charles A. E., and Dirk Schoenmaker. 1995. Institutional separation between supervisory and monetary agencies. In Charles Goodhart, ed., *The Central Bank and the Financial System*. New York: Macmillan, 332–412.

Goodhart, Charles A. E., Anil K. Kashyap, Dimitrios P. Tsomocos, and Alexandros P. Vardoulakis. 2012. Financial regulation in general equilibrium. NBER Working Paper 17909.

Goodhart, Charles A. E., Anil K. Kashyap, Dimitrios P. Tsomocos, and Alexandros P. Vardoulakis. 2013. An integrated framework for analyzing multiple financial regulations. *International Journal of Central Banking* 9: 109–43.

Goodhart, Charles A. E., and Enrico Perotti. 2012. Preventive macroprudential policy. Column on VoxEU.org. http://www.voxeu.org/article/preventive-macroprudential-policy.

Goodhart, Charles A. E., and Dirk Schoenmaker. 2009. Fiscal burden sharing in cross-border banking crises. *International Journal of Central Banking* 5 (1): 141–65.

Gordy, Michael B. 2003. A risk-factor model foundation for ratings-based bank capital rules. *Journal of Financial Intermediation* 12 (3): 199–232.

Gorton, Gary. 1988. Banking panics and business cycles. *Oxford Economic Papers* 40: 751–81.

Gorton, Gary. 2008. The panic of 2007. NBER Working Paper 14358.

Gorton, Gary. 2009. Slapped in the face by the invisible hand: Banking and the panic of 2007. Paper prepared for the Federal Reserve Bank of Atlanta's 2009 Financial Markets Conference: Financial Innovation and Crisis, May 11–13.

Gorton, Gary. 2012. *Misunderstanding Financial Crises: Why We Don't See Them Coming.* New York: Oxford University Press.

Gorton, Gary, and Andrew Metrick. 2012. Securitized banking and the run on repo. *Journal of Financial Economics* 104 (3): 425–51.

Gorton, Gary, and George Pennacchi. 1990. Financial intermediaries and liquidity creation. *Journal of Finance* 45 (1): 49–71.

Gorton, Gary, and Andrew Winton. 2003. Financial intermediation. In G. Constantinides, M. Harris, and R. Stulz, eds., *Handbook of the Economics of Finance*, vol. 1. Amsterdam: North Holland, 431–552.

Gourinchas, Pierre-Olivier, and Maurice Obstfeld. 2012. Stories of the twentieth century for the twenty-first. *American Economic Journal: Macroeconomics* 4: 226–65.

Gourinchas, Pierre-Olivier, Rodrigo Valdes, and Oscar Landerretche. 2001. Lending booms: Latin America and the world. NBER Working Paper 8249.

Gray, Dale, and Andreas Jobst. 2011. Modeling systemic financial sector and sovereign risk: Sveriges Riksbank. *Economic Review* 2: 68–106.

Greenlaw, David, Anil Kashyap, Hyun Song Shin, and Kermit Schoenholtz. 2012. Stressed out: Macroprudential principles for stress testing. U.S. Monetary Policy Forum Report 5: Initiative on Global Markets. Booth School of Business, University of Chicago.

Greenspan, Alan. 2002. Opening remarks. Jackson Hole Symposium organized by the Kansas City Federal Reserve Bank, Jackson Hole, WY.

Greenstone, Michael, Alexandre Mas, and Hoai-Luu Nguyen. 2014. Do credit market shocks affect the real economy? Quasi-experimental evidence from the Great Recession and "normal" economic times. NBER Working Paper 20704.

Greenwood, Robin, and Samuel G. Hanson. 2013. Issuer quality and corporate bond returns. *Review of Financial Studies* 26 (6): 1483–1525.

Gropp, Reint, and Gerard Moerman. 2004. Measurement of contagion in banks' equity prices. *Journal of International Money and Finance* 23 (3): 405–59.

Guttentag, Jack, and Richard Herring. 1987. Emergency liquidity assistance for international banks. In R. Portes and A. Swoboda, eds., *Threats to International Financial Stability*. Cambridge, UK: Cambridge University Press, 150–86.

Haldane, Andrew. 2013. Self-regulation's last stand? Presentation at Federal Reserve Bank of Atlanta. http://www.frbatlanta.org/documents/news/conferences/13fmc_haldane_pres.pdf

Hancock, Diana, and James Wilcox. 1994. Bank capital and the credit crunch: The roles of risk-weighted and unweighted capital regulations. *Journal of the American Real Estate and Urban Economics Association* 22: 59–94.

Hansen, Lars Peter. 2014. Challenges in identifying and measuring systemic risk. In Markus K. Brunnermeier and Arvind Krishnamurthy, eds., *Risk Topography: Systemic Risk and Macro Modeling*. Chicago: University of Chicago Press.

Hanson, Samuel, Anil K. Kashyap, and Jeremy C. Stein. 2011. A macroprudential approach to financial regulation. *Journal of Economic Perspectives* 25 (1): 3–28.

Hanson, Samuel G., and Jeremy C. Stein. 2015. Monetary policy and long-term real rates. *Journal of Financial Economics* 115: 429–48.

Hardy, Daniel, and Maria J. Nieto. 2011. Cross-border coordination of prudential supervision and deposit guarantees. *Journal of Financial Stability* 7 (3): 155–64.

Harrison, J. Michael, and David M. Kreps. 1978. Speculative investor behavior in a stock market with heterogeneous expectations. *Quarterly Journal of Economics* 92: 323–36.

Hart, Oliver, and Luigi Zingales. 2011. A new capital regulation for large financial institutions. *American Law and Economics Review* 13: 453–90.

Hartmann, Philipp, Stefan Straermans, and Casper de Vries. 2004. Asset market linkages in crisis periods. *Review of Economics and Statistics* 86 (1): 313–26.

Hartmann, Philipp, Stefan Straetmans, and Casper de Vries. 2007. Banking system stability: A cross-Atlantic perspective. In *The Risks of Financial Institutions*. National Bureau of Economic Research, 133–92.

Hau, Harald, Sam Langfield, and David Marques Ibanez. 2013. Bank ratings: What determines their quality? *Economic Policy* 28 (74): 289–333.

Hautsch, Nikolaus, Julia Schaumburg, and Melanie Schienle. 2014a. Financial network systemic risk contributions. *Review of Finance*, forthcoming.

Hautsch, Nikolaus, Julia Schaumburg, and Melanie Schienle. 2014b. Forecasting systemic impact in financial networks. *International Journal of Forecasting* 30: 781–94.

Heinemann, Friedrich, and Martin Schüler. 2004. A Stiglerian view on banking supervision. *Public Choice* 121 (1): 99–130.

Hellmann, Thomas, Kevin Murdock, and Joseph Stiglitz. 2000. Liberalization, moral hazard in banking and prudential regulation: Are capital requirements enough? *American Economic Review* 90 (1): 147–65.

Hellwig, Martin. 2009. Systemic risk in the financial sector: An analysis of the subprime-mortgage financial crisis. *De Economist* 157: 129–207.

Hertzberg, Andrew, Jose Maria Liberti, and Daniel Paravisini. 2010. Information and incentives inside the firm: evidence from loan officer rotation. *Journal of Finance* 65: 795–828.

Hirschman, Albert. 1970. *Exit, Voice, and Loyalty: Responses to Decline in Firms, Organizations, and States.* Cambridge: Harvard University Press.

Hoggarth, Glenn, Ricardo Reis, and Victoria Saporta. 2002. Costs of banking system instability: Some empirical evidence. *Journal of Banking and Finance* 26: 825–55.

Holmström, Bengt. 2008. Discussion of "The Panic of 2007," by Gary Gorton. In *Maintaining Stability in a Changing Financial System, Proceedings of the 2008 Jackson Hole Conference.* Federal Reserve Bank of Kansas City.

Holmstrom, Bengt, and Jean Tirole. 1997. Financial intermediation, loanable funds, and the real sector. *Quarterly Journal of Economics* 112: 663–91.

Holmstrom, Bengt, and Jean Tirole. 1998. Private and public supply of liquidity. *Journal of Political Economy* 106 (1): 1–40.

Holmstrom, Bengt, and Jean Tirole. 2011. *Inside and Outside Liquidity.* Cambridge: MIT Press.

Holthausen, Cornelia, and Thomas Rönde. 2002. Regulating access to international large-value payment systems. *Review of Financial Studies* 15 (5): 1561–86.

Holthausen, Cornelia, and Thomas Ronde. 2004. Cooperation in international banking supervision. ECB Working Paper 316.

Hong, Harrison, and Jeremy C. Stein. 2007. Disagreement and the stock market. *Journal of Economic Perspectives* 21: 109–28.

Honohan, Patrick, and Luc Laeven, eds. 2005. *Systemic Financial Crises: Containment and Resolution.* Cambridge, UK: Cambridge University Press.

Hovakimian, Armen, Edward J. Kane, and Luc Laeven. 2012, Variation in systemic risk at US banks during 1974–2010. NBER Working Paper 18043.

Huang, Xin, Hao Zhou, and Haibin Zhu. 2009. A framework for assessing the systemic risk of major financial institutions. *Journal of Banking and Finance* 33 (11): 2036–49.

Huang, Xin, Hao Zhou, and Haibin Zhu. 2012. Systemic risk contributions. *Journal of Financial Services Research* 42: 55–83.

Huizinga, Harry, and Luc Laeven. 2012. Bank valuation and accounting discretion during a financial crisis. *Journal of Financial Economics* 106 (3): 614–34.

Humphrey, David B. 1986. Payment finality and risk of settlement failure. In A. Saunders and L. White, eds., *Technology, and the Regulation of Financial Markets: Securities, Futures, and Banking.* Lexington, MA: Lexington Books.

Igan, Deniz, and Heedon Kang. 2011. Do loan-to-value and debt-to-income limits work? Evidence from Korea. IMF Working Paper 11/297.

Inderst, Roman. 2013. Prudence as a competitive advantage: On the effects of competition on banks' risk taking incentives. *European Economic Review* 60: 127–43.

International Monetary Fund. 2009. *Global Financial Stability Report*. Washington, DC: IMF.

International Monetary Fund. 2011a. Macroprudential policy: An organizing framework. IMF Policy Paper. Available at www.imf.org/external/np/pp/eng/2011/031411.pdf

International Monetary Fund. 2011b. Macroprudential policy: An organizing framework: Background paper. Available at www.imf.org/external/np/pp/eng/2011/031411a.pdf

International Monetary Fund. 2011. Housing finance and financial stability: Back to basics? *Global Financial Stability Report*, ch. 3.

International Monetary Fund. 2013a. A banking union for the euro area. IMF Staff Discussion Note 13/01.

International Monetary Fund. 2013b. *The Interaction of Monetary and Macroprudential Policies*. Washington, DC: IMF.

International Monetary Fund. 2013c. *Key Aspects of Macroprudential Policy*. Washington, DC: IMF.

Ioannidou, Vasso P. 2005. Does monetary policy affect the central bank's role in bank supervision? *Journal of Financial Intermediation* 461: 58–85.

Ioannidou, Vasso P., Steven Ongena, and Jose-Luis Peydro. 2014. Monetary policy, risk-taking and pricing: Evidence from a quasi-natural experiment. *Review of Finance*, forthcoming.

Ivashina, Victoria, and David S. Scharfstein. 2010. Bank lending during the financial crisis of 2008. *Journal of Financial Economics* 97: 319–38.

Iyer, Rajkamal, and José-Luis Peydró. 2011. Interbank contagion at work: Evidence from a natural experiment. *Review of Financial Studies* 24: 1337–77.

Iyer, Rajkamal, Samuel Lopes, José-Luis Peydró, and Antoinette Schoar. 2014. The interbank liquidity crunch and the firm credit crunch: Evidence from the 2007–09 crisis. *Review of Financial Studies* 27 (1): 347–72.

James, Christopher. 1987. Some evidence on the uniqueness of bank loans. *Journal of Financial Economics*.

James, Christopher. 1991. The losses realized in bank failures. *Journal of Finance* 46 (4): 1223–42.

Jayaratne, Jith, and Philip E. Strahan. 1996. The finance-growth nexus: Evidence from bank branch deregulation. *Quarterly Journal of Economics* 111: 639–70.

Jeanne, Olivier and Anton Korinek. 2010. Managing credit booms and busts: A Pigouvian taxation approach. NBER Working Paper 16377.

Jeanne, Olivier, and Anton Korinek. 2013. Macroprudential regulation versus mopping up after the crash. NBER Working Paper 18675.

Jensen, Michael, and William R. Meckling. 1976. Theory of the firm, managerial behavior, agency costs and ownership structure. *Journal of Financial Economics* 3: 305–60.

Jermann, Urban, and Vincenzo Quadrini. 2012. Macroeconomic effects of financial shocks. *American Economic Review* 102 (1): 238–71.

Jiménez, Gabriel, Steven Ongena, José-Luis Peydró, and Jesús Saurina. 2012. Credit supply and monetary policy: Identifying the bank balance-sheet channel with loan applications. *American Economic Review* 102: 2301–26.

Jiménez, Gabriel, Steven Ongena, José-Luis Peydró, and Jesús Saurina. 2013. Macroprudential policy, countercyclical bank capital buffers and credit supply: Evidence from the Spanish dynamic provisioning experiments. Mimeo. UPF.

Jiménez, Gabriel, Steven Ongena, José-Luis Peydró, and Jesús Saurina. 2014a. Hazardous times for monetary policy: What do twenty-three million bank loans say about the effects of monetary policy on credit risk-taking? *Econometrica* 82 (2): 463–505.

Jiménez, Gabriel, Atif Mian, Jose-Luis Peydró, and Jesus Saurina. 2014b. The real effects of the bank lending channel. Mimeo. University of Pompeu Fabra.

Jiménez, Gabriel, and Jesus Saurina. 2006. Credit cycles, credit risk, and prudential regulation. *International Journal of Central Banking* 2: 65–98.

John, Kose, Teresa A. John, and Anthony Saunders. 1994. Universal banking and firm risk-taking. *Journal of Banking and Finance* 18(2): 307–23.

Johnson, Simon. 2009. The Quiet Coup. *The Atlantic* (May). http://www.theatlantic.com /doc/200905/imf-advice.

Johnson, Simon and Kwak. 2010. *13 Bankers: The Wall Street Takeover and the Next Financial Meltdown*. New York: Vintage.

Jorda, Oscar. 2005. Estimation and inference of impulse responses by local projections. *American Economic Review* 95 (1): 161–82.

Jorda, Oscar, Moritz Schularick, and Alan M. Taylor. 2011. Financial crises, credit booms and external imbalances: 140 years of lessons. *IMF Economic Review* 59: 340–78.

Jorda, Oscar, Moritz Schularick, and Alan M. Taylor. 2013. When credit bites back: Leverage, business cycles, and crises. *Journal of Money, Credit and Banking* 45 (s2): 3–28.

Jorda, Oscar, Moritz Schularick, and Alan M. Taylor. 2014. *Leveraged bubbles. Mimeo*. University of California at Davis.

Jordan, John S., Joe Peek, and Eric S. Rosengren. 2002. Credit risk modeling and the cyclicality of capital. Mimeo. Federal Reserve Bank of Boston.

Kahn, Charles, and Joao Santos. 2005. Allocating bank regulatory powers: Lender of last resort, deposit insurance and supervision. *European Economic Review* 49 (8): 2107–36.

Kahneman, Daniel. 2012. *Thinking, Fast and Slow*. New York: Farra, Strauss, Giroux.

Kahneman, Daniel, and Amos Tversky. 1974. Judgment under uncertainty: Heuristics and biases. *Science* 27: 1124–31.

Kahneman, Daniel, and Amos Tversky. 1979. Prospect theory: An analysis of decision under risk. *Econometrica* 47: 262–92.

Kahneman, Daniel, and Amos Tversky. 1982. Judgments of and by representativeness. In D. Kahneman, P. Slovic, and A. Tversky, eds., *Judgment under Uncertainty: Heuristics and Biases*. New York: Cambridge University Press, 84–98.

Kalemli-Ozcan, Sebnem, Elias Papaioannou, and Fabrizio Perri. 2013. Global banks and crisis transmission. *Journal of International Economics* 89 (2): 495–510.

Kalemli-Ozcan, Sebnem, Elias Papaioannou, and Jose-Luis Peydró. 2010. What lies beneath the euro's effect on financial integration? Currency risk, legal harmonization, or trade? *Journal of International Economics* 81: 75–88.

Kalemli-Ozcan, Sebnem, Elias Papaioannou, and Jose-Luis Peydró. 2013. Financial regulation, financial globalization, and the synchronization of economic activity. *Journal of Finance* 68: 1179–1228.

Kaminsky, Graciela L., and Carmen M. Reinhart. 1998. Financial crises in Asia and Latin America: Then and now. *American Economic Review* 88 (2): 444–48.

Kaminsky, Graciela L., and Carmen M. Reinhart. 1999. The twin crises: The causes of banking and balance-of-payments problems. *American Economic Review* 89 (3): 473–500.

Kaminsky, Graciela L., Carmen M. Reinhart, and Carlos A. Vegh. 2004. When it rains, it pours: Procyclical capital flows and policies. In Mark Gertler and Kenneth S. Rogoff, eds., *NBER Macroeconomics Annual 2004*. Cambridge: MIT Press, 11–53.

Kane, Edward J. 1977. Good intentions and unintended evil. *Journal of Money, Credit and Banking* 9: 55–69.

Kane, Edward J. 1989. *The S&L Insurance Crisis: How Did It Happen?* Washington, DC: Urban Institute Press.

Kareken, John H., and Neil Wallace. 1978. Deposit insurance and bank regulation: A partial-equilibrium exposition. *Journal of Business* 51 (July): 413–38. http://minneapolisfed.org/research/sr/ SR16.pdf.

Kashyap, Anil K., Raghuram Rajan, and Jeremy Stein. 2009. Rethinking capital regulation. Mimeo. University of Chicago.

Kashyap, Anil K., and Jeremy C. Stein. 1995. The impact of monetary policy on bank balance sheets. *Carnegie-Rochester Conference Series on Public Policy* 42: 151–95.

Kashyap, Anil K., and Jeremy C. Stein. 2000. What do a million observations on banks say about the transmission of monetary policy? *American Economic Review* 90: 407–28.

Kashyap, Anil K., Jeremy C. Stein, and David W. Wilcox. 1993. Monetary policy and credit conditions:Evidence from the composition of external finance. *American Economic Review* 83: 78–98.

Kashyap, Anil K., Jeremy C. Stein, and David W. Wilcox. 1996. Monetary policy and credit conditions: Evidence from the composition of external finance. Reply. *American Economic Review* 86 (1): 310–14.

Keeley, Michael C. 1990. Deposit insurance, risk, and market power in banking. *American Economic Review* 80 (5): 1183–1200.

Keys, Benjamin, Tanmoy Mukherjee, Amit Seru, and Vikrant Vig. 2010. Did securitization lead to lax screening? Evidence from subprime loans. *Quarterly Journal of Economics* 125: 307–62.

Khwaja, Asim I., and Atif Mian. 2008. Tracing the impact of bank liquidity shocks: Evidence from an emerging market. *American Economic Review* 98: 1413–42.

Kim, Daesik, and Anthony M. Santomero. 1988. Risk in banking and capital regulation. *Journal of Finance* 43: 1219–33.

Kindleberger, Charles P. 1978. *Manias, Panics, and Crashes: A History of Financial Crises.* New York: Basic Books.

Kindleberger, Charles P. 1993. *A Financial History of Western Europe,* 2nd ed. New York: Oxford University Press.

Kindleberger, Charles P., and Robert Z. Aliber. 2005. *Manias, Panics, and Crashes: A History of Financial Crises,* 6th ed. London: Palgrave Macmillan.

King, Robert, and Ross Levine. 1993. Finance and growth: Schumpeter might be right. *Quarterly Journal of Economics* 108: 713–37.

Kishan, Ruby P., and Timothy P. Opiela. 2000. Bank size, bank capital, and the bank lending channel. *Journal of Money, Credit and Banking* 32 (1): 121–41.

Kiyotaki, Nobuhiro, and John Moore. 1997. Credit cycles. *Journal of Political Economy* 105 (2): 211–48.

Klein, Michael W., Joe Peek, and Eric Rosengren. 2002. Troubled banks, impaired foreign direct investment: The role of relative access to credit. *American Economic Review* 92: 664–82.

Knight, Frank H. 1921. *Risk, Uncertainty, and Profit.* Boston: Hart, Schaffner and Marx.

Knüpfer, Samuli, Elias Rantapuska, and Matti Sarvimäki. 2013. Labor market experiences and portfolio choice: Evidence from the Finnish Great Depression. Working paper. Aalto University.

Kohn, Donald. 2009. Monetary policy research and the financial crisis: strengths and shortcomings. Speech before the Federal Reserve Conference on Key Developments in Monetary Policy, Washington, DC, October 9.

Koo, Richard C. 2009. *The Holy Grail of Macroeconomics. Lessons of Japan's Great Recession.* Hoboken, NJ: Wiley.

Kraft, Evan, and Tomislav Galac. 2011. Macroprudential regulation of credit booms and busts: The case of Croatia. Policy Research Working Paper 5772. World Bank.

Krishnamurthy, Arvind, Stephan Nagel, and Dmitry Orlov. 2014. Sizing up repo. *Journal of Finance* 69: 2381–2417.

Kritzman, Mark, Yuanzhen Li, Sebastien Page, and Roberto Rigobon. 2011. Principal components as a measure of systemic risk. Mimeo. *Journal of Portfolio Management* 37: 112–26.

Kroszner, Randall S. 1998. Is it better to forgive than to receive? Repudiation of the gold indexation clause in long-term debt during the Great Depression. Working Paper. University of Chicago.

Kroszner, Randall S. 2010. Implications of the financial crisis for the grand challenge questions for the NSF/SBE. http://www.nsf.gov/sbe/ sbe 2020/2020 pdfs/Kroszner Randall 304.pdf.

Kroszner, Randall S., Luc Laeven, and Daniela Klingebiel. 2007. Banking crises, financial dependence, and growth. *Journal of Financial Economics* 84: 187–228.

Kroszner, Randall S., and Raghuram Rajan. 1994. Is the Glass–Steagall Act justified? A study of the US experience with universal banking before 1933. *American Economic Review* 84 (4): 810–32.

Kroszner, Randall S., and Philip E. Strahan. 1999. What drives deregulation? Economics and politics of the relaxation of bank branching restrictions. *Quarterly Journal of Economics* 114 (4): 1437–67.

Kroszner, Randall S., and Phillip Strahan. 2001. Throwing good money after bad? Board connections and conflicts in bank lending. NBER Working Paper 8694.

Kroszner, Randall S., and Thomas Stratmann. 1998. Interest-group competition and the organization of Congress: Theory and evidence from financial services' political action committees. *American Economic Review* 88 (5): 1163–87.

Krugman, Paul, and Maurice Obstfeld. 2006. *International Economics: Theory and Applications*, 7th ed. Boston: Addison-Wesley.

Kruszka, Michal, and Michal Kowalczyk. 2011. Macro-prudential regulation of credit booms and busts: The case of Poland. Policy Research Working Paper Series 5832. World Bank.

Kumhof, Michael, Roman Ranciere, and Paolo Winant. 2015. Inequality, leverage, and crises. *American Economic Review*, forthcoming.

Kuritzkes, Andrew, and Til Schuermann. 2010. What we know, don't know, and can't know about bank risk: A view from the trenches. In F. X. Diebold, N. A. Doherty, and R. J. Herring, eds., *The Known, the Unknown and the Unknowable in Financial Risk Management*. Princeton: Princeton University Press, 103–44.

Laeven, Luc. 2011. Banking crises: A review. *Annual Review of Financial Economics* 3: 17–40.

Laeven, Luc. 2013. Corporate governance: What's special about banks? *Annual Review of Financial Economics* 5: 63–92

Laeven, Luc, and Ross Levine. 2007. Is there a diversification discount in financial conglomerates? *Journal of Financial Economics* 85: 331–67.

Laeven, Luc, and Ross Levine. 2009. Bank governance, regulation, and risk-taking. *Journal of Financial Economics* 93 (2): 259–75.

Laeven, Luc, Ross Levine, and Stelios Michalopoulos. 2015. Financial innovation and endogenous growth. *Journal of Financial Intermediation* 24: 1–24.

Laeven, Luc, and Giovanni Majnoni. 2003. Loan loss provisioning and economic slowdowns: Too much, too late? *Journal of Financial Intermediation* 12: 178–97.

Laeven, Luc, and Fabian Valencia. 2008. Systemic banking crises: A new database. IMF Working Paper 08/224.

Laeven, Luc, and Fabian Valencia. 2010. Resolution of banking crises: The good, the bad, and the ugly. IMF Working Paper 10/146.

Laeven, Luc, and Fabian Valencia. 2012. Systemic banking crises database: An update. IMF Working Paper 12/163.

Laeven, Luc, and Fabian Valencia. 2013. Systemic banking crises database. *IMF Economic Review* 61:225–270.

Lakonishok, Josef, Andrei Shleifer, and Robert W. Vishny. 1994. Contrarian investment, extrapolation, and risk. *Journal of Finance* 49: 1541–78.

Landier, Augustin, David Sraer, and David Thesmar. 2013. Banks' exposure to interest rate risk and the transmission of monetary policy. NBER Working Paper 18857.

Lane, Philip R., and Gian Maria Milesi-Ferretti. 2006. The external wealth of nations mark II: Revised and extended estimates of foreign assets and liabilities, 1970–2004. *Journal of International Economics* 73 (2): 223–50.

Lang, William W., and Leonard I. Nakamura. 1995. "Flight to quality" in banking and economic activity. *Journal of Monetary Economics* 36: 145–64.

Laux, Christian, and Christian Leuz. 2010. Did fair-value accounting contribute to the financial crisis? *Journal of Economic Perspectives* 24 (1): 93–118.

Lehar, Alfred. 2005. Measuring systemic risk: A risk management approach. *Journal of Banking and Finance* 29 (10): 2577–2603.

Lenza, Michele, Huw Pill, and Lucrezia Reichlin. 2010. Monetary policy in exceptional times. *Economic Policy* 62: 295–339.

Levine, Ross. 2004. The corporate governance of banks: a concise discussion of concepts and evidence. Policy Research Working Paper 3404. World Bank.

Levine, Ross. 2005. Finance and growth: Theory and evidence. In P. Aghion and S. Durlauf, eds., *Handbook of Economic Growth*, vol. 1. Amsterdam: Elsevier Science, 865–934.

Levine, Ross, and Sara Zervos. 1998. Stock markets, banks, and economic growth. *American Economic Review* 88: 537–58.

Liberti, Jose M., and Atif Mian. 2009. Estimating the effect of hierarchies on information use. *Review of Financial Studies* 22: 4057–90.

Lin, Huidan, and Daniel Paravisini. 2013. The effect of financing constraints on risk. *Review of Finance* 17: 229–59.

Lindgren, Carl-Johan, Gillian Garcia, and Matthew I. Saal. 1996. *Bank Soudness and Macroeconomic Policy*. Washington, DC: IMF.

Lo, Andrew. 2012. Reading about the financial crisis: A twenty-one book review. *Journal of Economic Literature* 50 (1): 151–78.

Lopez, Martha, Fernando Tenjo, and Hector Zarate. 2010a. The risk-taking channel and monetary transmission mechanism in Colombia. Working Paper. Banco de la Republica Colombia.

Lopez, Martha, Fernando Tenjo, and Hector Zarate. 2010b. The risk-taking channel in Colombia revisited. Working Paper. Banco de la Republica Colombia.

Lorenzoni, Guido. 2008. Inefficient credit booms. *Review of Economic Studies* 75: 809–33.

Loutskina, Elena, and Philip E. Strahan. 2009. Securitization and the declining impact of bank finance on loan supply: Evidence from mortgage originations. *Journal of Finance* 64: 861–89.

Lown, Cara S., and Donald P. Morgan. 2002. Credit effects in the monetary mechanism. *Federal Reserve Bank of New York Economic Policy Review* 8: 217–35.

Lown, Cara, and Donald P. Morgan. 2006. The credit cycle and the business cycle: New findings using the loan officer opinion survey. *Journal of Money, Credit and Banking* 38 (6): 1575–97.

Lown, Cara S., Donald P. Morgan, and Sonali Rohatgi. 2000. Listening to loan officers: The impact of commercial credit standards on lending and output. *Federal Reserve Bank of New York Economic Policy Review* 6: 1–16.

Lucas, Andre, Berndt Schwaab, and Xin Zhang. 2011. Conditional probabilities and contagion measures for euro area sovereign default risk. Discussion Paper 11-176/2/DSF29. Tinbergen Institute.

Lucas, Robert. 1976. Econometric policy evaluation: A critique. In K. Brunner and A. Meltzer, eds., *The Phillips Curve and Labor Markets*, vol. 1. New York: American Elsevier, 19–46.

Maddaloni, Angela, and Jose-Luis Peydró. 2011. Bank risk-taking, securitization, supervision, and low interest rates: Evidence from the euro area and the US lending standards. *Review of Financial Studies* 24: 2121–65.

Maddaloni, Angela, and José-Luis Peydró. 2013. Monetary policy, macroprudential policy and banking stability: Evidence from the euro area. *International Journal of Central Banking* 9: 121–69.

Malherbe, Frederic. 2014. Self-fulfilling liquidity dry-ups. *Journal of Finance* 69: 947–70.

Malmendier, Ulrike, and Stefan Nagel. 2011. Depression babies: Do macroeconomic experiences affect risk-taking? *Quarterly Journal of Economics* 126 (1): 373–416.

Manganelli, Simone, and Guido Wolswijk. 2009. What drives spreads in the euro area government bond market? *Economic Policy* 24 (58): 191–240.

Manganelli, Simone, Tae-Hwan Kim, and Halbert White. 2010. VAR for VaR: Measuring systemic risk using multivariate regression quantiles. Technical report.

Mankiw, N. Gregory. 2006. The macroeconomist as scientist and engineer. *Journal of Economic Perspectives* 20 (4): 29–46.

Marcus, Alan J. 1984. Deregulation and bank financial policy. *Journal of Banking and Finance* 8 (4): 557–65.

Martin, Antoine, and Bruno M. Parigi. 2013. Bank capital regulation and structured finance. *Journal of Money, Credit and Banking* 45 (1): 87–119.

Martin, Alberto, and Jaume Ventura. 2012. Economic growth with bubbles. *American Economic Review* 102 (6): 3033–58.

Merton, Robert C. 1973. Theory of rational option pricing. *Bell Journal of Economics and Management Science* 4 (1): 141–83.

Merton, Robert C. 1974. On the pricing of corporate debt: The risk structure of interest rates. *Journal of Finance* 29 (2): 449–70.

Mian, Atif. 2014. The case for credit registry. In Markus Brunnermeier and Arvind Krishnamurthy, eds., *Risk Topography: Systemic Risk and Macro Modeling*. Chicago: University of Chicago Press, ch. 11.

Mian, Atif, and Amir Sufi. 2009. The consequences of mortgage credit expansion: Evidence from the U.S. mortgage default crisis. *Quarterly Journal of Economics* 124 (4): 1449–96.

Mian, Atif, and Amir Sufi. 2010. Household leverage and the recession of 2007 to 2009. *IMF Economic Review* 58 (1): 74–117.

Mian, Atif, and Amir Sufi. 2011. House prices, home equity-based borrowing, and the U.S. household leverage crisis. *American Economic Review* 101 (5): 2132–56.

Mian, Atif, and Amir Sufi. 2014a. What explains the 2007–2009 drop in employment? *Econometrica* 82 (6): 2197–2223.

Mian, Atif, and Amir Sufi. 2014b. *House of Debt: How They (and You) Caused the Great Recession, and How We Can Prevent It from Happening Again.* Chicago: University of Chicago Press.

Mian, Atif, Amir Sufi, and Francesco Trebbi. 2014a. Foreclosures, house prices, and the real economy. *Journal of Finance*, forthcoming.

Mian, Atif, Amir Sufi, and Francesco Trebbi. 2014b. Resolving debt overhang: Political constraints in the aftermath of financial crises. *American Economic Journal: Macroeconomics* 6 (2): 1–28.

Mihov, Ilian. 2001. Monetary policy implementation and transmission in the European Monetary Union. *Economic Policy* 16 (33): 369–406.

Miller, Edward M. 1977. Risk, Uncertainty, and divergence of opinion. *Journal of Finance* 32 (4): 1151–68.

Minsky, Hyman P. 1977. The financial instability hypothesis: An interpretation of Keynes and alternative to standard theory. *Challenge* 20: 20–27.

Minsky, Hyman. 1986. *Stabilizing an Unstable Economy.* New Haven: Yale University Press.

Miron, Jeffrey A. 1986. Financial panics, the seasonality of the nominal interest rate, and the founding of the Fed. *American Economic Review* 76 (1): 125–40.

Mishkin, Frederic S. 1977. What depressed the consumer? The household balance sheet and the 1973–75 recession. *Brookings Papers on Economic Activity* 1: 123–64.

Mishkin, Frederic S. 1978. The household balance sheet and the Great Depression. *Journal of Economic History* 38: 918–37.

Mistrulli, Paolo. 2005. Interbank lending patterns and financial contagion. Mimeo. Banca d'Italia.

Mitchell, Janet. 2000. Bad debts and the cleaning, transferring of banks' balance sheets: An application to transition economies. *Journal of Financial Intermediation* 10 (1): 1–27.

Modigliani, Franco, and Merton Miller. 1958. The cost of capital, corporation finance and the theory of investment. *American Economic Review* 48 (3): 261–97.

Morgan, Donald P. 2002. Rating banks: Risk and uncertainty in an opaque industry. *American Economic Review* 92 (4): 874–88.

Morgan, Donald P., Bertrand Rime, and Philip Strahan. 2004. Bank integration and state business cycles. *Quarterly Journal of Economics* 119 (3): 1555–85.

Morris, Stephen, and Hyun Song Shin. 1998. Unique equilibrium in a model of self-fulfilling currency attacks. *American Economic Review* 88 (3): 587–97.

Morris, Stephen, and Hyun Song Shin. 2014. Risk-taking channel of monetary policy: A global game approach. Working Paper. Princeton University.

Morrison, Alan D., and Lucy White. 2005. Crises and capital requirements in banking. *American Economic Review* 95: 1548–72.

Morrison, Alan D., and Lucy White. 2009. Level playing fields in international financial regulation. *Journal of Finance* 64 (3): 1099–1142.

Morrison, Alan D., and Lucy White. 2013. Reputational contagion and optimal regulatory forbearance. *Journal of Financial Economics* 110 (3): 642–58.

Myers, Stewart. 1977. Determinants of corporate borrowing. *Journal of Financial Economics* 5 (2): 147–75.

Myers, Stewart, and Raghuram Rajan. 1998. The paradox of liquidity. *Quarterly Journal of Economics* 113: 733–71.

Myers, Stewart, and Nicholas S. Majluf. 1984. Corporate financing and investment decisions when firms have information that investors do not have. *Journal of Financial Economics* 13 (2): 187–221.

Nier, Erlend W., Jacek Osiński, Luis I. Jácome, and Pamela Madrid. 2011. Institutional models for macroprudential policy. IMF Staff Discussion Note 11/18 and Working Paper 11/250.

Nolan, Charles, and Christoph Thoenissen. 2009. Financial shocks and the U.S. business cycle. *Journal of Monetary Economics* 56 (4): 596–604.

O'Hara, Maureen, and Wayne Shaw. 1990. Deposit insurance and wealth effects: The value of being too big to fail. *Journal of Finance* 45: 1587–1600.

Obstfeld, Maurice, and Kenneth Rogoff. 2009. Global imbalances and the financial crisis: Products of common causes. Mimeo. Harvard University.

Oliner, Stephen D., and Glenn D. Rudebusch. 1996. Monetary policy and credit conditions: Evidence from the composition of external finance. A comment. *American Economic Review* 86 (1): 300–309.

Ongena, Steven, Alex Popov, and Gregory F. Udell. 2013. When the cat's away the mice will play: Does regulation at home affect bank risk-taking abroad. *Journal of Financial Economics* 108 (3): 727–50.

Ongena, Steven, José-Luis Peydró, and Neeltje van Horen. 2012. Shocks abroad, pain at home? Bank-firm level evidence on financial contagion during the 2007–2009 crisis. Mimeo. UPF.

Ostry, Jonathan D., Atish R. Gosh, Karl Habermeier, Luc Laeven, Marcos Chamon, Masvash S. Qureshi, and Annamaria Kokenyne. 2011. Managing capital inflows: What tools to use? IMF Staff Discussion Note 11/06.

Padoa-Schioppa, Tommaso. 2001. Bank competition: A changing paradigm. *European Finance Review* 5: 13–20.

Pagano, Marco. 2012. Finance: Economic lifeblood or toxin? CSEF Working Paper 326.

Paligorova, Teodora, and Joao A. C. Santos. 2012. Monetary policy and bank risk- taking: Evidence from the corporate loan market. Mimeo. Bank of Canada.

Pan, Jun, and Kenneth J. Singleton. 2008. Default and recovery implicit in the term structure of sovereign CDS spreads. *Journal of Finance* 63 (5): 2345–84.

Paravisini, Daniel. 2008. Local bank financial constraints and firm access to external finance. *Journal of Finance* 63: 2161–93.

Peek, Joe, and Eric S. Rosengren. 1995. The capital crunch: Neither a borrower nor a lender be. *Journal of Money, Credit and Banking* 27: 625–38.

Peek, Joe, and Eric S. Rosengren. 1997. The international transmission of financial shocks: The case of Japan. *American Economic Review* 87 (4): 495–505.

Peek, Joe, and Eric S. Rosengren. 2000. Collateral damage: Effects of the Japanese bank crisis on the United States. *American Economic Review* 90 (1): 30–45.

Peek, Joe, Eric S. Rosengren, and Geoffrey Tootell. 1999. Is bank supervision central to central banking? *Quarterly Journal of Economics* 114 (2): 629–53.

Peek, Joe, Eric S. Rosengren, and Geoffrey Tootell. 2003. Identifying the macroeconomic effect of loan supply shocks. *Journal of Money, Credit and Banking* 35: 931–46.

Peltzman, Sam. 1976. Toward a more general theory of regulation. *Journal of Law and Economics* 19 (August): 211–40.

Perotti, Enrico, and Javier Suarez. 2002. Last bank standing: What do I gain if you fail? *European Economic Review* 46: 1599–1622.

Philippon, Thomas, and Ariell Reshef. 2012. Wages and human capital in the U.S. financial industry: 1909–2006. *Quarterly Journal of Economics* 127: 1551–1609.

Philippon, Thomas. 2009. Financiers versus engineers: Should the financial sector be taxed or subsidized? *American Economic Journal: Macroeconomics* 2 (3): 158–82.

Plantin, Guillaume. 2015. Shadow banking and bank capital regulation. *Review of Financial Studies* 28: 146–75.

Poon, Ser-Huang, Michael Rockinger, and Jonathan Tawn. 2004. Extreme value dependence in financial markets: Diagnostics, models, and financial implications. *Review of Financial Studies* 17 (2): 581–610.

Pozen, Robert. 2009. Is it fair to blame fair value accounting for the financial crisis? *Harvard Business Review* 87 (11): 85–92.

Pozsar, Zoltan, Tobias Adrian, Adam Ashcraft, and Hayley Boesky. 2010. Shadow banking. Federal Reserve Bank of New York Staff Report 458.

Pritsker, Matt. 2001. The channels for financial contagion. In Stijn Claessens and Kristin J. Forbes, eds., *International Financial Contagion*. Boston: Kluwer Academic, 67–98.

Puri, Manju, Jorg Rocholl, and Sascha Steffen. 2011. Global retail lending in the aftermath of the US financial crisis: Distinguishing between supply and demand effects. *Journal of Financial Economics* 100: 556–78.

Qian, Jun, Philip E. Strahan, and Zhishu Yang. 2015. The impact of incentives and communication costs on information production: Evidence from bank lending. *Journal of Finance*, forthcoming.

Quadrini, Vincenzo. 2011. Financial frictions in macroeconomic fluctuations. *Economic Quarterly* 97 (3): 209–54.

Quintos, Carmela, Zhenhong Fan, and Peter C. B. Phillips. 2001. Structural change test in tail behaviour and the Asian crisis. *Review of Economic Studies* 68 (3): 633–63.

Raddatz, Claudio. 2006. Liquidity needs and vulnerability to financial underdevelopment. *Journal of Financial Economics* 80: 677–722.

Rajan, Raghuram G. 1992. Insiders and outsiders: The choice between Informed and arm's-length debt. *Journal of Finance* 47 (4): 1367–1400.

Rajan, Raghuram G. 1994. Why bank credit policies fluctuate: A theory and some evidence. *Quarterly Journal of Economics* 109 (2): 399–441.

Rajan, Raghuram G. 2005. Has financial development made the world riskier? NBER Working Paper 11728.

Rajan, Raghuram. G. 2006. Has finance made the world riskier? *European Financial Management* 12: 499–533.

Rajan, Raghuram G. 2009. The credit crisis and cycle-proof regulation. *Federal Reserve Bank of St. Louis Review* 91 (September): 397–402.

Rajan, Raghuram G. 2010. *Fault Lines*. Princeton: Princeton University Press.

Rajan, Raghuram G., and Luigi Zingales. 1998. Financial dependence and growth. *American Economic Review* 88: 393–410.

Ramey, Valerie A. 1993. How important is the credit channel in the transmission of monetary policy. *Carnegie-Rochester Conference Series on Public Policy* 39 (1): 1–45.

Ranciere, Romain, Aaron Tornell, and Frank Westermann. 2008. Systemic crises and growth. *Quarterly Journal of Economics* 123 (1): 359–406.

Reinhart, Carmen M., and Kenneth S. Rogoff. 2008. Is the 2007 US sub-prime financial crisis so different? An international historical comparison. *American Economic Review* 98 (2): 339–44.

Reinhart, Carmen, and Kenneth S. Rogoff. 2009a. *This Time Is Different: Eight Centuries of Financial Folly*. Princeton: Princeton University Press.

Reinhart, Carmen, and Kenneth S. Rogoff. 2009b. The aftermath of financial crises. *American Economic Review* 99 (2): 466–72.

Repullo, Rafael. 2000. Who should act as a lender of last resort? An incomplete contracts model. *Journal of Money Credit and Banking* 32 (2): 580–605.

Repullo, Rafael. 2005. Liquidity, risk-taking, and the lender of last resort. *International Journal of Central Banking* 1: 47–80.

Repullo, Rafael, and Jesus Saurina. 2011. The countercyclical capital buffer of Basel III: A critical assessment. CEPR Discussion Paper 8304.

Rey, Hélène. 2013. Dilemma not trilemma: The global financial cycle and monetary policy independence. Presented at the Jackson Hole Symposium hosted by the Federal Reserve Bank of Kansas City, August.

Rigobon, Roberto, and Brian Sack. 2004. The impact of monetary policy on asset prices. *Journal of Monetary Economics* 51: 1553–75.

Rochet, Jean-Charles. 1992. Capital requirements and the behavior of commercial banks. *European Economic Review* 36: 1137–78.

Rochet, Jean-Charles. 2004. Rebalancing the 3 pillars of Basel 2. *Economic Policy Review* (Federal Reserve Bank of New York) 10 (2): 7–25.

Rochet, Jean-Charles. 2004, Market discipline in banking: Where do we stand? In Claudio Borio, William Curt Hunter, George Kaufman, and Kostas Tsatsaronis, eds., *Market Discipline across Countries and Industries*. Cambridge: MIT Press, 55–68.

Rochet, Jean-Charles, ed. 2008. *Why Are There So Many Banking Crises? The Politics and Policy of Bank Regulation*. Princeton: Princeton University Press.

Rochet, Jean-Charles, and J. Tirole. 1996. Interbank lending and systemic risk. *Journal of Money, Credit and Banking* 28 (4): 733–62.

Rochet, Jean-Charles, and J. Tirole. 1996. Controlling risk in payment systems. *Journal of Money, Credit and Banking* 28 (4): 832–62.

Rochet, Jean-Charles, and Xavier Vives. 2004. Coordination failures and the lender of last resort: Was Bagehot right after all? *Journal of the European Economic Association* 2 (6): 1116–47.

Romer, Christina, and David Romer. 1990. New evidence on the monetary transmission mechanism. *Brookings Papers on Economic Activity* 1:149–98.

Rose, Andrew K., and Mark M. Spiegel. 2009a. Cross-country causes and consequences of the 2008 crisis: Early warning. Working Paper 2009–17. Federal Reserve Bank of San Francisco.

Rose, Andrew K., and Mark M. Spiegel. 2009b. Cross-country causes and consequences of the 2008 crisis: International Linkages and American Exposure. Mimeo. Haas School of Business, University of California, Berkeley, and Federal Reserve Bank of San Francisco.

Ruckes, Martin. 2004. Bank competition and credit standards. *Review of Financial Studies* 17: 1073–1102.

Samuelson, Paul A. 1958. An exact consumption-loan model of interest with or without the social contrivance of money. *Journal of Political Economy* 66 (6): 467–82.

Santos, Joao. 2009. Do markets discipline all banks equally. *Journal of Financial Economic Policy* 1: 107–23.

Santos, Manuel S., and Michael Woodford. 1997. Rational asset pricing bubbles. *Econometrica* 65: 19–58.

Sapienza, Laura. 2004. The effects of government ownership on bank lending. *Journal of Financial Economics* 72 (2): 357–384.

Saunders, Anthony. 1986. An examination of the contagion effect in the international loan market. *Studies in Banking and Finance* 3: 219–47.

Scheinkman, Jose A., and Wei Xiong. 2003. Overconfidence and speculative bubbles. *Journal of Political Economy* 111:1183–1219.

Schmidt, Lawrence D. W., Allan G. Timmermann, and Russ R. Wermers. 2013. Runs on Money Market Mutual Funds. January 2. http://ssrn.com/abstract=1784445.

Schoenmaker, Dirk. 1998. Contagion risk in banking. Manuscript. Ministry of Finance, Amsterdam.

Schnabl, Philipp. 2012. The international transmission of bank liquidity shocks: Evidence from an emerging market. *Journal of Finance* 67 (3): 897–932.

Schoenmaker, Dirk. 2011. The financial trilemma. *Economics Letters* 111: 57–59.

Schularick, Moritz, and Alan M. Taylor. 2012. Credit booms gone bust: Monetary policy, leverage cycles, and financial crises, 1870–2008. *American Economic Review* 102 (2): 1029–61.

Schwaab, Bernd, Siem Jan Koopman, and Andre Lucas. 2011. Systemic risk diagnostics, coincident indicators and early warning signals. ECB Working Paper 1327.

Shaffer, Sherrill. 1998. The winner's curse in banking. *Journal of Financial Intermediation* 7 (4): 359–92.

Sharpe, Steven A. 1990. Asymmetric information, bank lending, and implicit contracts: A stylized model of customer relationships. *Journal of Finance* 45 (4): 1069–87.

Shin, Hyun Song. 2009. Securitisation and financial stability. *Economic Journal* 119: 309–32.

Shin, Hyun Song. 2010. *Risk and Liquidity.* Oxford: Oxford University Press.

Shin, Hyun Song. 2011. Macroprudential policies beyond Basel III. Presentation on International Centre for Financial Regulation, September 7.

Shin, Hyun Song. 2012. Global banking glut and loan risk premium. *Economic Review* 60: 155–92.

Shleifer, Andrei. 2000. *Clarendon Lectures: Inefficient Markets.* Oxford: Oxford University Press.

Shleifer, Andrei. 2012. Psychologists at the gate: A review of Daniel Kahneman's *Thinking, Fast and Slow. Journal of Economic Literature* 50: 1080–91.

Shleifer, Andrei, and Robert W. Vishny. 2010a. Asset fire sales and credit easing. *American Economic Review* 100: 46–50.

Shleifer, Andrei, and Robert W. Vishny. 2010b. Unstable banking. *Journal of Financial Economics* 97: 306–18.

Sims, Christopher. 2007. Comment on Del Negro, Schorfheide, Smets, and Wouters. *Journal of Business and Economics Statistics* 25: 152–54.

Skinner, Douglas J. 2008. The rise of deferred tax assets in Japan: The role of deferred tax accounting in the Japanese banking crisis. *Journal of Accounting and Economics* 46 (2–3): 218–39.

Slovin, Myron, Marie Sushka, and John Polonchek. 1993. The value of bank durability: borrowers as bank stakeholders. *Journal of Finance* 48 (1): 247–66.

Smith, Bruce D. 2002. Monetary policy, banking crises, and the Friedman rule. *American Economic Review* 92: 128–34.

Sprague, Oliver. 1910. *History of Crises under the National Banking System.* New York: Kelley.

Stein, Jeremy C. 1998. An adverse-selection model of bank asset and liability management with implications for the transmission of monetary policy. *Rand Journal of Economics* 29: 466–86.

Stein, Jeremy C. 2012. Monetary policy as financial-stability regulation. *Quarterly Journal of Economics* 127 (1): 57–95.

Stein, Jeremy. 2013a. Overheating in the credit markets: Origins, measurement, and policy responses. Speech at the "Restoring Household Financial Stability after the Great Recession: Why Household Balance Sheets Matter" research symposium, Federal Reserve Bank of St. Louis, Missouri.

Stein, Jeremy. 2013b. Yield-oriented investors and the monetary transmission mechanism. Remarks at the "Banking, Liquidity and Monetary Policy" Symposium, Center for Financial Studies, Frankfurt.

Stein, Jeremy C. 2014. Incorporating financial stability considerations into a monetary policy framework. Remarks at the International Research Forum on Monetary Policy.

Stern, Gary H., and Ron J. Feldman. 2004. *Too Big to Fail: The Hazards of Bank Bailouts.* Washington, DC: Brookings Institution Press.

Stigler, George. 1971. The theory of economic regulation. *Bell Journal of Economics and Management Science* 2 (1): 3–21.

Stiglitz, Joseph E., and Bruce Greenwald. 2003. *Towards a New Paradigm in Monetary Economics.* Cambridge, UK: Cambridge University Press.

Stiglitz, Joseph E., and Andrew Weiss. 1981. Credit rationing in markets with imperfect information. *American Economic Review* 71: 393–410.

Straetmans, Stefan, Willem Veerschoor, and Christian Wolff. 2008. Extreme US stock market fluctuations in the wake of 9/11. *Journal of Applied Econometrics* 23 (1): 17–42.

Stratmann, Thomas. 2002. Can special interests buy congressional votes? Evidence from financial services legislation. *Journal of Law and Economics* 45: 345–73.

Sundaresan, Suresh, and Zhenyu Wang. 2015. On the design of contingent capital with market trigger. *Journal of Finance* 70: 881–920.

Svensson, Lars E. O. 2013. Some lessons from six years of practical inflation targeting. CEPR Discussion Paper 9756.

Swary, Itzhak. 1986. Stock market reaction to regulatory action in the Continental Illinois crisis. *Journal of Business* 59 (3): 451–73.

Taylor, John B. 2007. Housing and monetary policy. NBER Working Paper 13682.

Taylor, John B. 2009. *Getting Off Track: How Government Actions and Interventions Caused, Prolonged, and Worsened the Financial Crisis.* Stanford University: Hoover Press.

Thaler, Richard H., and Eric J. Johnson. 1990. Gambling with the house money and trying to break even: The effects of prior outcomes on risky choice. *Management Science* 36: 643–60.

Tirole, Jean. 1982. On the possibility of speculation under rational expectations. *Econometrica* 50: 1163–81.

Tirole, Jean. 1985. Asset bubbles and overlapping generations. *Econometrica* 53: 1499–1528.

Tirole, Jean. 2006. *The Theory of Corporate Finance*. Princeton: Princeton University Press.

Tirole, Jean. 2011. Systemic risk regulation. 20th Barcelona GSE lecture. Graduate School of Economics, April 1.

Tobin, James. 1989. Review of *Stabilizing an Unstable Economy* by Hyman P. Minsky. *Journal of Economic Literature* 27 (1): 105–108.

Trichet, Jean Claude 2009. The ECB's enhanced credit support. Keynote address at the University of Munich, July 13.

Turner, Adair. 2009. The financial crisis and the future of financial regulation. Speech at the Economists Inaugural City Lecture, January 21. http://www.fsa.gov.uk/library /communication/speeches/2009/ 0121 at.shtml.

Turner, Adair. 2010. What do banks do, what should they do, and what public policies are needed to ensure best results for the real economy? Speech at Cass Business School, March 17. http://www. fsa.gov.uk/library/communication/speeches/2010/0317 at. shtml.

Tversky, Amos, and Daniel Kahneman. 1981. The framing of decisions and the psychology of choice. *Science* 211 (4481): 453–58.

Valencia, Fabian. 2008. Banks' precautionary capital and credit crunches. IMF Working Paper 08/248.

Valencia, Fabian. 2014. Monetary policy, bank leverage, and financial stability. *Journal of Economic Dynamics and Control* 47: 20–38.

Van den End, Jan Willem and Mark Kruidhof. 2012. Modelling the liquidity ratio as macroprudential instrument. DNB Working Paper 342.

Véron, Nicolas, and Guntram B. Wolff. 2013. From supervision to resolution: Next steps on the road to European Banking Union. Policy Brief PB 13–5. Peterson Institute for International Economics.

Viñals, José, Ceyla Pazarbasioglu, Jay Surti, Aditya Narain, Michaela Erbenova, and Julian Chow. 2013. Creating a safer financial system: Will the Volcker, Vickers, and Liikanen structural measures help? IMF Staff Discussion Note 13/04.

Vissing-Jorgensen, Annette. 2004. Perspectives on behavioral finance: Does "irrationality" disappear with wealth? Evidence from expectations and actions. In Mark Gertler and Kenneth Rogoff, eds., *NBER Macroeconomics Annual 2003*. Cambridge: MIT Press, 139–94.

Von Hagen, Jurgen, and Tai-Kuang Ho. 2007. Money market pressure and the determinants of banking crises. *Journal of Money, Credit and Banking* 39: 1037–66.

Wachter, Jessica A. 2006. A consumption-based model of the term structure of interest rates. *Journal of Financial Economics* 79: 365–99.

Wall, Larry D., and David R. Peterson. The effect of Continental Illinois' failure on the financial performance of other banks. *Journal of Monetary Economics* 26 (1): 77–99.

White, William R. 1996. International agreements in the area of banking and finance: Accomplishments and outstanding issues. BIS Working Paper 38.

White, William R. 2006. Is price stability enough? BIS Working Paper 205.

Wojnilower, Albert. 1980. The central role of credit crunches in recent financial history. *Brookings Papers on Economic Activity* 2: 277–339.

Wong, Eric, Tom Fong, Li Ka-fai, and Henry Choi. 2011. Loan-to-value ratio as a macroprudential tool: Hong Kong's experience and cross-country evidence. Working Paper 01/2011. Hong Kong Monetary Authority.

Xiong, Wei and Jialin Yu. 2011. Chinese warrants bubble. *American Economic Review* 101 (6): 2723–53.

Yagan, Danny. 2014. Riding the bubble? Chasing returns into illiquid assets. NBER Working Paper 20360.

Yellen, Janet L. 2011. Macroprudential supervision and monetary policy in the post-crisis world. *Business Economics* 46: 3–12.

Yellen, Janet L. 2014. Monetary policy and financial stability. Michael Camdessus Central Banking Lecture.

Index

Printed in the United States
by Baker & Taylor Publisher Services